HATE CRIME AND RESTORATIVE JUSTICE

CLARENDON STUDIES IN CRIMINOLOGY

Published under the auspices of the Institute of Criminology, University of Cambridge; the Mannheim Centre, London School of Economics; and the Centre for Criminology, University of Oxford.

General Editor: Robert Reiner
(London School of Economics)

Editors: Manuel Eisner, Alison Liebling, and Per-Olof Wikström
(University of Cambridge)

Jill Peay and Tim Newburn
(London School of Economics)

Ian Loader, Julian Roberts, and Lucia Zedner
(University of Oxford)

RECENT TITLES IN THIS SERIES:

Policing the Waterfront: Networks, Partnerships, and the Governance of Port Security
Brewer

Traces of Terror: Counter-Terrorism Law, Policing, and Race
Sentas

Reorganizing Crime: Mafia and Anti-Mafia in Post-Soviet Georgia
Slade

Just Emotions: Rituals of Restorative Justice
Rossner

Beyond the Banality of Evil: Criminology and Genocide
Brannigan

Hate Crime and Restorative Justice

Exploring Causes, Repairing Harms

MARK AUSTIN WALTERS

OXFORD
UNIVERSITY PRESS

Great Clarendon Street, Oxford, OX2 6DP
United Kingdom

Oxford University Press is a department of the University of Oxford.
It furthers the University's objective of excellence in research, scholarship,
and education by publishing worldwide. Oxford is a registered trade mark of
Oxford University Press in the UK and in certain other countries

© Mark Walters 2014

The moral rights of the author have been asserted

First Edition published in 2014

Impression: 1

All rights reserved. No part of this publication may be reproduced, stored in
a retrieval system, or transmitted, in any form or by any means, without the
prior permission in writing of Oxford University Press, or as expressly permitted
by law, by licence or under terms agreed with the appropriate reprographics
rights organization. Enquiries concerning reproduction outside the scope of the
above should be sent to the Rights Department, Oxford University Press, at the
address above

You must not circulate this work in any other form
and you must impose this same condition on any acquirer

Crown copyright material is reproduced under Class Licence
Number C01P0000148 with the permission of OPSI
and the Queen's Printer for Scotland

British Library Cataloguing in Publication Data

Data available

Library of Congress Control Number: 2013956208

ISBN 978-0-19-968449-6

Printed in Great Britain by
CPI Group (UK) Ltd, Croydon, CR0 4YY

Links to third party websites are provided by Oxford in good faith and
for information only. Oxford disclaims any responsibility for the materials
contained in any third party website referenced in this work.

To my parents Jean and Allan for their constant love and encouragement, and to my husband Daniel whose devotion and support is enduring.

General Editor's Introduction

Clarendon Studies in Criminology aims to provide a forum for outstanding empirical and theoretical work in all aspects of criminology and criminal justice, broadly understood. The Editors welcome submissions from established scholars, as well as excellent PhD work. The Series was inaugurated in 1994, with Roger Hood as its first General Editor, following discussions between Oxford University Press and three criminology centres. It is edited under the auspices of these three centres: the Cambridge Institute of Criminology, the Mannheim Centre for Criminology at the London School of Economics, and the Centre for Criminology at the University of Oxford. Each supplies members of the Editorial Board and, in turn, the Series Editor.

Hate Crime and Restorative Justice: Exploring Causes, Repairing Harms by Dr Mark Walters is a noteworthy contribution to two burgeoning areas of debate and research in criminology and criminal justice: hate crimes and restorative justice (RJ). As Walters states, it is not the case that 'hate crime is a modern phenomenon, indeed countries such as Britain and the United States (US) have a long history of persecuting certain minority groups (so-called "Others")'. But 'it is only in recent years that crimes motivated by "hate" or "prejudice" have been identified as a serious "social problem"'. In the last thirty years 'governments have been keen to enact new laws that specifically proscribe hate-motivated offences', so that 'in recent years we have witnessed a vast expansion of hate crime legislation within dozens of countries' and 'various types of "hate crime" and "hate speech" are criminalized within multiple jurisdictions across the world, covering a range of different "victim groups"'. Typically these laws are predicated on a retributive justification, and involve 'the enhancement of punishment for any offender who "demonstrates", or who is (partly) motivated by, hostility towards a victim based on the victim's actual or presumed identity traits', for example s 28 of the UK Crime and Disorder Act 1998.

The emergence of this legislation is in some ways paradoxical, for as Eli Aharonson argues in a forthcoming book *From Slave*

Abuse to Hate Crime: The Criminalization of Racial Violence in American History (Cambridge University Press, 2014), the groups that hate crime laws are purportedly in the interests of have historically often been discriminated against by being disproportionately criminalized. This reflects broader shifts in political economy and culture that have halted or reversed grander projects of socioeconomic egalitarianism, and rendered the demand for criminalization of attacks against them a prime vehicle whereby relatively disadvantaged and powerless groups seek inclusion.

Walters begins with a clear analysis of legal and criminological arguments about hate crime, including the difficulties in defining the concept itself. Debates have flourished about what precisely are the 'harms' done by hate crime, how to conceptualize the 'hate' or prejudice elements, how the perceptual dimensions of hate or prejudice may be related to the causation of the crimes, and so on. Walters settles on an operational definition derived from a formulation of good practice guidelines by the Association of Chief Police Officers (ACPO) in 2005, which states that a hate crime is 'any hate incident, which constitutes a criminal offence, perceived by the victim or any other person, as being motivated by prejudice or hate'. This is chosen not because it settles the conceptual conundrums but because it is the definition that underlies the cases and practices studied in Walters' empirical research.

Walters' book also offers at the outset a clear and incisive analysis of the emergence of RJ as an increasingly influential perspective and set of practices in a growing number of contemporary jurisdictions. The growth of RJ is based on an account of conventional criminal justice as failing to meet the needs of victims, offenders, and the broader communities they come from. Formal criminal justice with its retributive and punitive sanctions stigmatizes and further excludes offenders, exacerbating the likelihood of future crime. Instead the aim is to achieve what John Braithwaite famously labelled as 'reintegrative shaming', repairing the harms done by crime to victims and the broader community as well as the harms done to offenders by the pains of punishment. 'Central to RJ practice is the reparation of harm caused by criminal or otherwise wrongful acts', argues Walters, and 'rather than punishing and stigmatizing perpetrators of crime, RJ is primarily concerned with the *engagement* of those affected by wrongdoing in a dialogic process which aims to achieve *reparation*—be it emotional, material or to relationships'.

Walters' powerful thesis is that hate crime victims are especially ill-served by conventional criminal justice, which fails to rectify the specific harms done or to go any way towards rehabilitating the offenders. This is because the 'enhanced emotional traumas caused by hate crime are intrinsically connected to the fact that targeted victimization goes to the very core of the victim's "self", ie incidents tear at the very essence of who a victim is'. Restorative justice offers a better prospect because of its targeting of the emotional and inter-personal violations that are the special harm of hate crime. 'The promise of RJ is that inclusive dialogue may be better suited to reducing the harms caused by hate, while simultaneously challenging the underlying causes which give rise to hate-motivated behaviour.'

The major part of the book is the discussion of three case studies that confirm the potential of RJ in handling hate crimes. These were: a 'Hate Crime Project' at Southwark Mediation Centre in South London; a 'Restorative Disposal' system used by Devon and Cornwall Police; and the Oxford Youth Offending Service. In total, Walters conducted thirty-eight qualitative interviews with victims who had been involved in these restorative practices and twenty-three in-depth interviews with RJ practitioners, and observed eighteen direct and indirect restorative meetings across the research sites.

The rich empirical data on the whole supports the hypotheses about the potential benefits of RJ in dealing with hate crime. The differences between more and less successful interventions allow Walters to draw important analytical and practical conclusions about how best to accomplish RJ interventions in hate crime cases, identifying such vital elements as the extent of preparation before meetings and the quality of practitioner selection and training. Walters' book is a significant contribution to understanding and practice in two key areas of current criminological debate, hate crime and restorative justice, and should make a considerable impact on these fields. It is a welcome addition to the *Clarendon Studies in Criminology* Series.

Robert Reiner
London School of Economics
December 2013

Acknowledgements

First and foremost I would like to acknowledge the many victims of hate crime whose experiences of victimization have not been forgotten. Without giving up their time to speak with me, this book would not have been possible. I hope that the book's findings help to mitigate the suffering of future victims. To all the restorative practitioners who went out of their way to help me with this project and who never tired of me following them around, I thank you. In particular, I would like to note the help and assistance of Elena Noel who allowed me to shadow her work at Southwark Mediation Centre for over a year. I learnt many things during my time in Southwark, but it was Elena's enduring belief that all human beings, regardless of their background, are capable of living peacefully together, that was truly inspirational. I also thank Pete Wallis at Oxford Youth Offending Service and Phil Skedgell of Devon and Cornwall Police for their help in accessing interviewees. It would be remiss of me not to mention two very cost effective transcribers (my parents) who spent many hours each evening helping me transcribe interview recordings. Finally, I would like to thank Dr Neil Chakraborti for his helpful comments on earlier drafts of this book, Nevada-Anne Mcevoy-Cooke for her diligent proofreading, and my PhD supervisor Professor Carolyn Hoyle for her encouragement and interest in my research. To all of you I owe a great debt of gratitude.

Contents

List of Abbreviations   xvii
Introduction: Readdressing Hate Crime   xix

1. Conceptualizing Hate Crime for Restorative Justice   1
    Introduction   1
    What is 'Hate Crime'?   2
    Defining 'Hate' in 'Hate Crime'   6
    Linking 'Hate' with 'Crime'   8
    Transposing 'Hate' into Law   12
    Understanding Hate Crime as a Process of Victimization   17
    The Process of Hate   18
    Victim–Offender Relationships   21
    Including 'Hate Incidents' Within Hate Crime Policy   23
    The Limitations of a Retributive Approach to Tackling Repeated 'Hate Incidents'   25
    Conclusion   30

2. Conceptualizing Restorative Justice for Hate Crime   32
    Introduction   32
    Part I: What is Restorative Justice?   33
    Part II: Repairing Harms? Normative Assumptions and Empirical Findings   45
    Part III: The Limits of Restorative Justice: Methodological Issues   53
    Part IV: Some Preliminary Thoughts on the Challenges and Opportunities of Restorative Justice for Hate Crime   56
    Conclusion   60

3. The Harms of Hate Crime: From Structural Disadvantage to Individual Identity   62
    Introduction   62
    Part I: Structural Inequality: The Beginnings of Hate Harm   63

Part II: The Direct Impacts of Hate Crime Victimization	71
Conclusion	89

4. Repairing the Harms of Everyday Hate Crime: Exploring Community Mediation and the Views of Restorative Practitioners — 91

Introduction	91
Part I: Community Mediation and the Hate Crimes Project	92
Part II: Repairing the Harms of Hate Crime	97
Part III: The Experiences of Restorative Practitioners	115
Conclusion: Understanding Hate Incidents and Repairing the Harms They Cause	119

5. Restorative Policing and Hate Crime — 123

Introduction	123
Part I: Restorative Policing	124
Part II: Could the Restorative Disposal Help Repair the Harms of Hate Crime?	129
Conclusion	146

6. Secondary Victimization, State Participation, and the Importance of Multi-Agency Partnerships — 148

Introduction	148
Part I: State Responses to Hate Crime: Exploring the Harms Caused by Housing and Police Officers	150
Part II: Reducing Harm Through Multi-Agency Partnerships	159
Conclusion	181

7. The Perils of 'Community': From Theory to Practice — 184

Introduction	184
Part I: The Perils of 'Community'	186
Part II: Avoiding Domination and Re-victimization	193
Conclusion	204

8. Humanizing 'Difference' and Challenging Prejudice Through Restorative Dialogue — 207

Introduction	207
Part I: Negotiating Cultural and Identity Difference: Overcoming Empathic Divides?	208

Part II: Humanizing 'Difference': the Importance of
   'Storytelling' 219
Conclusion 234

9. Conclusion: Uncovering Hidden Truths 236
The Need for a Restorative Approach to Hate Crime 236
What Did Restorative Justice Tell Us About the Nature
   of Hate Crime? 244
What Did Hate Crime Tell Us About the Practice of
   Restorative Justice? 252

Appendix A: Interview Schedule: Victims and
   Complainant Victims 261
Appendix B: Interview Schedule: Restorative Justice
   Practitioners 277
References 279
Index 299

List of Abbreviations

ACPO	Association of Chief Police Officers
AOPM	Association of Panel Members
ASBU	Anti-Social Behaviour Unit
BCS	British Crime Survey
BME	black and minority ethnic
CBT	cognitive behavioural therapy
CPS	Crown Prosecution Service
CRR	community and race relations
CSEW	Crime Survey for England and Wales
CSU	Community Safety Unit
FGC	Family Group Conference
HCP	Hate Crime Project
HCHAC	House of Commons Home Affairs Committee
JCAR	Joint Committee Against Racialism
LGBT	lesbian, gay, bisexual, transgender
NIBRS	National Incident Based Reporting System
ODHIR	Office for Democratic Institutions and Human Rights
RD	Restorative Disposal
RISE	Reintegrative Shaming Experiments
RJ	restorative justice
RJC	Restorative Justice Council
SAJJ	South Australia Juvenile Justice Research project
SMC	Southwark Mediation Centre
VOM	victim–offender mediation
YOP	Youth Offender Panel
YOS	Youth Offending Service
YOT	Youth Offending Team

Introduction: Readdressing Hate Crime

The emergence of an anti-hate crime movement in the United States (US) during the 1980s (Maroney 1998), and later in the 1990s and 2000s in parts of Europe (Witte 1996; Bowling 1998; Garland & Chakraborti 2012) thrust the 'social problem' of prejudice-motivated violence onto the agendas of governments across the globe (Jenness & Grattet 2001; ODIHR 2013). The political attention now given to the phenomenon we now commonly refer to as 'hate crime' has resulted in a new public policy domain that is focused on tackling both its causes and consequences (Jenness & Grattet 2001).[1] In particular, governments have been keen to enact new laws that specifically proscribe hate-motivated offences (Hare 1997; Jacobs & Potter 1998; Lawrence 1999; Malik 1999; Jenness & Grattet 2001). In fact, in recent years we have witnessed a vast expansion of hate crime legislation within dozens of countries (ODHIR 2012). This now means that various types of 'hate crime' and 'hate speech' are criminalized within multiple jurisdictions across the world, covering a range of different 'victim groups' (Garland & Chakraborti 2012).

Central to the vast majority of hate crime laws is the enhancement of punishment for any offender who 'demonstrates', or who is (partly) motivated by, hostility towards a victim based on the victim's actual or presumed identity traits.[2] The legislative response to hate crime has propagated a lively academic debate focusing, in the main, on retribution theory and arguments relating to the levels of *harm* and the *offence seriousness* of hate crimes (see eg Jacobs & Potter 1998; Iganski 1999, 2001, 2002, 2008; Lawrence 1999;

---

[1] Within the US context 'hate crime' is also often referred to as 'bias crime' (Lawrence 1999) while others have used phrases such as 'targeted violence' (Stanko 2001), and ethno-violence (Ehrlich 2009). However, it remains the case that the term 'hate crime' has gained most currency within academic literature, political discourse, and amongst state agencies (Hall 2013).

[2] See eg s 28 of the Crime and Disorder Act 1998 (UK). The various models of legislation are discussed in Chapter 1.

Stanton-Ife 2013). In many respects the criminal justice debate on hate crime has been polemic; the tendency being to focus on arguments in favour of introducing new laws that enhance punishment (Iganski 1999; Lawrence 1999) as against those which favour the retention of traditional criminal offences (Morsch 1991; Jacobs & Potter 1998). This book does not aim to critique the effectiveness of hate crime legislation, indeed the arguments for and against such laws are now well rehearsed within the extant literature (see, Jacobs & Potter 1998; Lawrence 1999; for an overview see, Stanton-Ife 2013). It is, however, important to the aims and objectives of this book to begin with a critique of both the pros and cons of criminalizing 'hate'.[3]

When justifying the enhanced punishment of hate crime offenders, advocates of hate crime legislation often refer to the retributive principle of proportionality (Lawrence 1999). In essence, legal scholars have asserted that the increased punishment contained within legislation acknowledges the enhanced culpability of 'hate-motivation', ie that a hate offender's intention/purpose carries a higher degree of moral blameworthiness, while simultaneously recognizing the enhanced level of harm that such crimes cause to victims, minority communities, and society more broadly (Lawrence 1999; see also Stanton-Ife 2013). Baroness Hale, delivering a unanimous decision in the House of Lords, sums up this rationale in the case of *R v Rogers* (2007):[4]

> The mischiefs attacked by the aggravated versions of these offences are racism and xenophobia. Their essence is the denial of equal respect and dignity to people who are seen as somehow other. This is more deeply hurtful, damaging and disrespectful to the victims than the simple version of these offences. It is also more damaging to the community as a whole, by denying acceptance to members of certain groups not for their own sake but for the sake of something they can do nothing about.

The assertion that hate crimes cause greater levels of harm is now well supported by empirical research which has documented the heightened levels of psychological trauma experienced by hate crime victims (see eg Iganski 2008; Home Office et al 2013). For instance, a number of quantitative studies have shown that victims of hate crime are more likely to experience emotional harms including

---

[3] Some further elaboration on the criminalization of hate will be found in Chapter 1.
[4] *R v Rogers* [2007] UKHL 8, [12]–[13].

anxiety, fear, shock, and depression, which are frequently endured for longer periods of time, compared with victims of similar but non-hate-motivated offences (see eg Herek et al 1997, 1999; McDevitt et al 2001; Iganski 2008; Smith et al 2012; Home Office et al 2013). Incidents have also been shown to cause immense fear amongst members of the victim's group, as these individuals fear that they too will be targeted (Perry & Alvi 2012; Noelle 2002). Indeed, whether one supports a retributive response to hate crime or not, it is certainly difficult to refute the assertion that 'hate crimes hurt more' (Iganski 2001).

However, hate crime legislation is not just about recognizing the harm caused to victims and minority communities. The process of criminalization also conveys important symbolic messages which become particularly important to the combating of pervasive forms of bigotry (Iganski 1999, 2001).[5] In particular, those who have expounded upon the utility of the law to tackle hate crime have highlighted the role of criminal censure (Iganski 2008: Ch 4; Walters 2013a). This is where the state expresses denunciation for an offender's actions and, in so doing, provides a public declaration as to the moral wrongfulness of a particular conduct (see Simester & von Hirsch 2011). The public message of denunciation contained within hate crime legislation is fundamental to the state's symbolic condemnation of identity-based prejudices, and, as such, to the future eradication of hate-motivated offences (Iganski 1999, 2008; Lawrence 1999). I have argued elsewhere that while the expressed denunciation contained in hate crime legislation is unlikely to have any direct individual deterrent effect, such laws will ultimately play an important longer-term role in shaping society's evolving attitudes towards racism, homophobia, and other pernicious prejudices (Walters 2013a; see also Stanton-Ife 2013). In other words, hate crime laws (like other laws) help to create a social climate that rejects public displays of identity prejudice which, over time, potentially brings about a reduction in hate-motivated incidents (Iganski 2008).

Linked to the denunciatory process of censuring hate offenders is a secondary declaratory message of support that is offered to those minority groups that have suffered from historic processes of victimization. By proscribing certain hate-motivated offences,

---

[5] As Baroness Hale hinted in her speech in *Rogers* (n 4).

the state communicates that it will no longer tolerate such abuse—including those incidents which have been committed by the state itself (Iganski 2008: Ch 4). The law therefore contains, simultaneously, both a warning to those contemplating public displays of prejudice, and a message that the state will actively protect minority groups from targeted victimization. In truth, without specific legislation there is little reason to believe that the police and other state agencies would focus as much time and resources in combating hate crime as they now currently do (Iganski 1999, 2001).

Yet while there remain cogent reasons for the retention, and possible expansion, of hate crime statutes (Stanton-Ife 2013), there are two fundamental criticisms of the current legislative approach that can be proffered, and which have formed the impetus for this book:

1. The enhancement of punishment and additional criminalization of hate-motivated perpetrators does little to *repair the harms* caused by incidents of hate (Hudson 1998; Whitlock 2001: Dixon & Gadd 2006).
2. Enhancing the penalties of offenders is unlikely to effectively challenge the underlying causes of prejudice, at least at an individual level (Jacobs & Potter 1998; Moran et al 2004a).

These criticisms stand in stark contrast to the UK government's assertion, made in their Home Office report *Improving Opportunity, Strengthening Society*, that by ensuring racially motivated crimes are 'vigorously prosecuted' the underlying causes of hate crime can be effectively addressed (Home Office 2005a: 50). This commitment was contained within the same chapter on 'helping young people from different communities grow up with a sense of belonging' (Home Office 2005a: 43), suggesting that hate crime laws could improve the social wellbeing of minority groups, ultimately helping to create 'cohesive communities' (Dixon and Gadd 2006).

On the contrary, opponents of hate crime laws have argued that legislation does little to change the vulnerability of hate crime victims and minority communities, at least in the short term. Les Moran et al, for example, have argued that punishment enhancements act only to uphold victims' emotional attachments to 'hate, anger, malice and revenge' (2004a: 42), none of which are conducive to the reducing of emotional or physical traumas. Of even greater concern is that researchers have found that some hate crime laws have been used disproportionately to prosecute minority individuals (Burney & Rose 2002; Dixon & Gadd 2006). Thus rather than protecting minority community members from victimization and improving 'community cohesion', hate crime laws may in fact add to the criminalization of those from disadvantaged backgrounds (Burney & Rose 2002; Dixon & Gadd 2006).

The retributive ideology which has informed the promotion of hate crime law has led some to argue that current legislation punishes offenders based on a form of institutionalized vengeance (Moran et al 2004a: 32); a practice which is akin to 'institutionalised cruelty' (Moran et al 2004a: 32; see also Hudson 1998; Whitlock 2001). This, in part, is fuelled by the demand for vengeance by those interest groups who have demanded greater protection by the state against hate crime (populist punitiveness) (Bottoms 1995; Jacobs & Potter 1998; Moran et al 2004a). Governments, realizing that the criminal justice system can do little to prevent hate crime or protect minority communities from it, use punitive measures to send symbolic messages of support to minority communities (Moran et al 2004a; Dixon & Gadd 2006). James Jacobs and Kimberly Potter (1998) have gone so far as to suggest that hate crime laws serve only to encourage minority identity groups to feel a sense of victimization, thereby promoting feelings of injustice that can contribute to the balkanization of society. Inevitably, this leads to minority groups competing to obtain 'legislative protection' (Jacobs & Potter 1998). Under this interpretation of the utility of hate crime legislation, it is difficult to see how the criminal justice system adequately supports the needs of victims *and/or* helps to increase tolerance of social and cultural 'difference'.

Repairing the Harms of Hate?

Whether one agrees with the use of hate crime legislation or not, it is doubtful that the current offender-based response to the problem does much to support *directly* the needs of victims. Victim support is of particular importance when we consider how damaging hate-motivated abuse is to those who are targeted. The enhanced emotional traumas caused by hate crime are intrinsically connected to the fact that targeted victimization goes to the very core of the victim's 'self', ie incidents tear at the very essence of who a victim is (Herek & Berrill 1992). As a result, victims can become anxious about leaving their homes and often avoid certain locations where they fear repeat victimization (Moran et al 2004b; Iganski 2008: 78–79). Some studies have even shown that victims will often change their appearance, or the way they act, in order to 'fit in' with society (Attorney General's Department 2003; Moran et al 2004b; Dick 2008).

We need only consider such empirical findings to appreciate that a new or additional approach to tackling hate crime is required if the state is to better aid the recovery of victims (Whitlock 2001: Perry 2003: 44). In this regard, a small but growing group of academics have begun to ask normative questions about the potential of restorative justice (henceforth RJ) as a response to hate crime (see Shenk 2001; Gavrielides 2007; Walters & Hoyle 2010). This is part of a wider body of literature that is developing on the use of RJ for so-called 'difficult' cases, including sexual offences (Daly 2006; McGlynn et al 2012) and domestic violence (Strang & Braithwaite 2002; Stubbs 2007; Hayden 2013). Advocates of RJ have argued that the criminal justice system should be reorientated away from state-led and offender-focused interventions towards more inclusive community-based processes that focus on the needs of the victim (Christie 1977; Braithwaite 1989; Zehr 1990). Central to RJ practice is the reparation of harms (Zehr 1990). This is best achieved by bringing the 'stakeholders'[6] of an offence together via a dialogic process that enables the parties to explore what has happened, why it has happened, and how it can be repaired (Braithwaite 1989; Zehr 1990).

In relation to hate-motivated offences, Alyssa Shenk asserts that 'victim–offender mediation fills many of the gaps in hate crime legislation. By placing emphasis on the victim's needs, victim-offender mediation will likely encourage victims to report future incidents of hate crime' (2001: 215). A number of case studies have since been highlighted where RJ has been used as a response to various forms of hate crime (Umbreit et al 2002; Gavrielides 2007, 2012; Walters & Hoyle 2010). These case examples have identified the potential benefits of the restorative approach in repairing the harms of hate. They have also suggested that differing identity traits and opposing cultural norms amongst victims and offenders may be overcome and in some cases even broken down via the dialogic processes typical of RJ interventions (Umbreit et al 2002; Gavrielides 2007; Walters & Hoyle 2010). The promise

---

[6] Typically the victim, offender, their supporters, and other affected community members.

of RJ is that inclusive dialogue may be better suited to reducing the harms caused by hate, while simultaneously challenging the underlying causes which give rise to hate-motivated behaviour (Walters & Hoyle 2010).

Methodology

While the small amount of research into the use of RJ for hate crime is to be welcomed, there has yet to be any extensive empirical or theoretical exploration of its use as a way of responding to such offences. This book seeks to address this lacuna through an empirical examination of whether RJ practices, used by criminal justice agencies and third sector organizations, can:

1. *help* to repair the emotional traumas caused by hate crimes;
2. effectively address issues relating to identity and/or cultural differences between participants; those which are causal to the offence/incident;
3. prevent the recurrence of hate incidents between the stakeholders of inter-personal conflicts.

The empirical study was conducted over a two-year period. The research was focused on the impacts of RJ on victims' emotional wellbeing. However, offenders were also observed at RJ meetings and analysis of case outcomes frequently considered the role that they played during restorative interventions. A total of four sites were identified as sources of data after extensive searches were made for restorative practices that were used in cases involving hate incidents. These included: Sussex Police, Brighton and Hove Division; Devon and Cornwall Police Service; Oxford Youth Offending Service; and Southwark Mediation Centre, South London. However, due to a paucity of cases in two of these locations, the study focused, in the main, on two restorative interventions: the Hate Crime Project (HCP) at Southwark Mediation Centre, South London, and the Restorative Disposal used by Devon and Cornwall Police Service. Several other cases were researched at Oxford Youth Offending Service, where three indirect restorative meetings were observed and one victim interview was carried out. In total, thirty-eight interviews were conducted with victims who had participated in a restorative intervention, while an additional eighteen observations of direct and indirect restorative meetings were carried out.

In order to enrich the study further, a nation-wide search was carried out for restorative practitioners who had direct experience facilitating hate crime cases. The study was advertised via several RJ networks, including the Association of Panel Members' (AOPM)[7] monthly bulletin, while practitioners were also recruited at conferences throughout the country. This resulted in twenty-three in-depth practitioner interviews, which took place either face to face or over the telephone.

Recordings of all interviews and notes taken during observations were fully transcribed. Thematic analysis was then employed when coding the data. Common themes between victims' accounts were identified allowing me to determine common factors that affected victims' experiences of victimization and emotional convalescence. During this process I constantly remained open to new themes emerging from the transcripts (Noakes & Wincup 2004: 131). Data gained from closed questions and likert-type responses (using both ordinal and interval scales) were used to determine levels of emotional harm (indicators) before and directly after an RJ process (see Appendix A). Descriptive statistics could then be linked to the qualitative information that each interviewee provided about their cases and linked back again to the observations that I made of individual case meetings. The mixed method approach allowed me to connect process variables (such as an apology) with process outcomes (such as reduced levels of anxiety) (see similarly Hoyle et al 2002; Wilcox et al 2005). For example, using the concept of harm (the central theoretical theme of the book), I was able to examine how many victims experienced emotional trauma (using qualitative and quantitative data gathered from open and closed questions) and then how many victims felt that the restorative process (the variable) helped them to recover from their experience of hate crime (for each type of practice examined). See Figure I.1 for details of mixed research methods.

Within the empirical study, a broad definition of hate crime was used that included 'hate incidents'. Hate incidents are described by the Association of Chief Police Officers as '... any incident, which may or may not constitute a criminal offence, which is perceived by the victim or any other person, as being motivated by prejudice or hate' (ACPO 2005: 2.2.1).[8] The hate

---

[7] Panel members sit on Youth Offending Panels, see Chapter 1.
[8] This definition was used by both the HCP and Devon and Cornwall Police Service. Oxford YOS identified hate crime cases as defined by law, see Chapter 1.

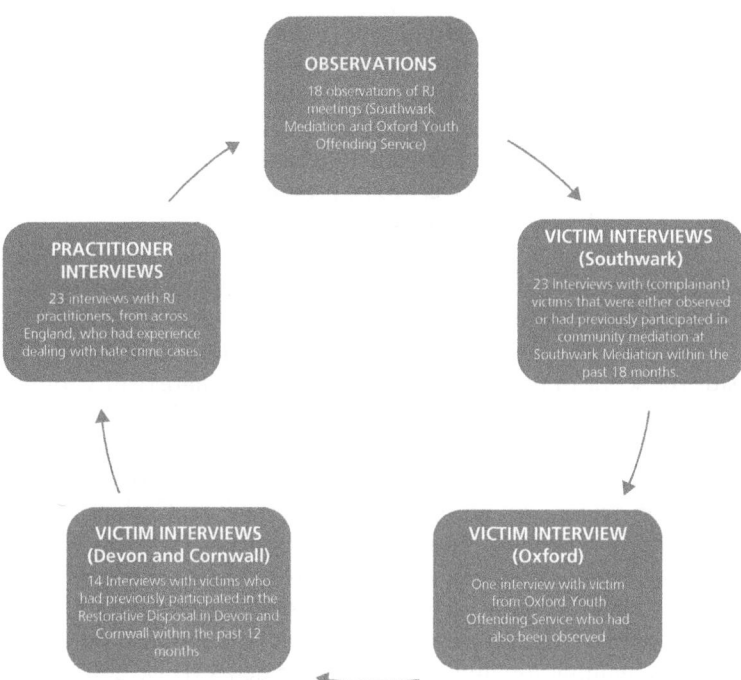

Figure I.1 Mixed methods approach to the study

incidents examined in this book therefore included both crimes and other wrongdoing, such as anti-social behaviour, which had led to the 'victim' making a complaint to a local state agency.[9] Incidents included serious forms of physical violence, verbal threats, verbal abuse, spitting, acts of intimidation such as 'menacing looks', or purposely causing noise or disturbance. The broadening out of hate crime conceptualization to include 'low-level' hate incidents was important to the endeavours undertaken for this book. From an early stage in the study it became apparent that cases involving non-criminal or 'low-level' hate incidents were extremely difficult to deal with retributively—most complaints being viewed by police officers as falling outside the purview of traditional policing. Not only did police officers feel powerless to resolve such cases, but, as

[9] Most commonly police services and housing associations. The potential implications of using such a liberal victim-centric definition of hate crime are discussed further in Chapter 1.

we will see in Chapter 1 and beyond, it was the regular commission of so-called 'low-level' hate incidents that frequently caused the most profound levels of emotional and physical distress amongst victims. This meant that an additional or alternative approach to dealing with persistent 'everyday' incidents of hate abuse was necessary if future incidents were to be prevented, and victims were to move beyond their experiences of victimization.

The book explores four categories of hate, including incidents that were perceived to be motivated by the victim's (actual or presumed) race, religious beliefs, sexual orientation, and/or disability. Other forms of hate crime (such as transphobic) incidents fell outside the scope of the study. This was an unfortunate reality for the type of research that was undertaken for this book; even more so considering the fact that transphobic hate crime remains an under-researched area of hate victimization which is in need of greater attention from criminologists (Chakraborti & Garland 2009: Ch 5). However, reported incidents of transphobic crime remain relatively low in comparison to other types of hate crime; especially when compared with racist and homophobic incidents (Home Office 2013). This may partly be due to victims of transphobic hate crime remaining unwilling to report incidents (Dick 2008). It is also likely to be due to the fact that there are many more *visible* black and minority ethnic, and gay and lesbian individuals in society and therefore hate incidents against these groups are inevitably more prolific. The result of both under-reporting and a lower number of transgendered individuals being victimized means that transphobic incidents are less likely to come to the attention of RJ practitioners;[10] at least in a number great enough to draw credible assertions about how restorative practices may or may not help to repair the harms caused. Furthermore, at the time the empirical research was conducted the victim groups included under hate crime legislation in England and Wales did not include 'transgender', meaning that these 'types' of victim were less likely to be identified specifically as 'hate crime' victims by practitioners working in either the criminal justice system or the third sector.[11]

---

[10] Of course other forms of prejudice may well be highlighted during an RJ meeting but at this point it will be too late for me to research the process.

[11] Ie community-based organizations, such as charities, which are often part funded by the state but remain independent from its authority.

Structure of the Book

Chapter 1 of the book begins by looking at both legal and criminological definitions of hate crime. Understanding these different conceptualizations of the phenomenon is intrinsic to the application of RJ. As cases filter through from conventional criminal justice measures, the types of cases that RJ practitioners will respond to will largely be determined by legal definitions of hate-motivated offences. Criminological conceptualizations of hate crime then become important to how RJ might effectively tackle both the *causes* and *consequences* of hate-motivated incidents (dealt with later in Chapters 4, 5, 6, 7, and 8).

Chapter 2 introduces the reader to the theory and practice of RJ. Drawing on a largely reparative conception of restorative practice, the chapter explores how dialogical and participatory responses to crime can help to repair the harms it causes. Both normative assumptions and empirical findings about RJ's repairing benefits are examined, while the limitations of existing research methods are outlined. The chapter concludes by summarizing the *potential* benefits and pitfalls of using RJ for hate crime. In particular, the chapter highlights how the restorative process attempts to reduce levels of fear, anxiety, and anger by breaking down identity and cultural differences. The challenges of bringing vulnerable and marginalized victims together with dominant aggressive offenders are also highlighted.

Chapter 3 provides a comprehensive analysis of the harms caused by hate crime/incidents drawing upon both the existing body of research as well as findings from the current study. It is argued that hate incidents make up part of a continuum of prejudice which is rooted to socio-structural inequality. The chapter examines how those who display identity difference become subjugated through a process of what Barbara Perry terms 'dominance over difference', resulting in the 'othering' of certain minority individuals (Perry 2001). Such individuals experience various forms of structural and institutional discrimination, which affects almost all aspects of their lives. The targeting of individuals because of their identity characteristics therefore acts to compound pre-existing experiences of structural disadvantage. Moreover, the targeting of victims because of their identity damages individuals' ontological security within society and thus compounds even further their feelings of fear, anger, and anxiety. This chapter provides theoretical and empirical grounding for the findings reported in Chapters 4, 5, and 6.

Chapter 4 presents the findings from the first empirical study conducted at the HCP in South London. It provides a detailed analysis of the differing 'types' of hate incidents that proliferate in multicultural communities and illuminates the situational foregrounds which often trigger hate-based conflicts. Pivotally, the chapter additionally examines whether community mediation meetings *helped* to repair the harms of hate crime. Both qualitative themes are drawn from interviews as well as some tentative quantitative data on levels of emotional harm that victims experienced directly before and after this restorative process. The chapter highlights the significance of active participation and the obtaining of assurances of desistance from offenders, as well as ongoing support offered by mediators, as being particularly helpful to the healing process.

Chapter 5 explores the second main source of data, gained from interviews with victims who had participated in restorative disposals in Devon and Cornwall. The same format as Chapter 4 is used in examining both the types of hate incident which occurred in this part of the UK and whether this restorative practice helped individuals to recover from their experiences of victimization. The findings are compared with those documented for community mediation—in many cases unfavourably. The chapter highlights the problems associated with using poorly trained facilitators of RJ and more broadly provides a critique of the use of police constables in the administration of RJ.

Chapter 6 examines the use of multi-agency partnerships within RJ practice—partnerships often ignored by other studies. Using data gained from victim interviews, the chapter first illuminates the secondary harms that were often caused by local state authorities who had initially responded to reports of hate crime. The chapter then provides a detailed analysis of the notion of 'community' and conceptualizes the role that local agencies—as part of the stakeholders' 'community of care'—can play within the restorative framework. This part of the chapter argues that a more nuanced picture of 'community' is required in order for RJ to fully appreciate both the harming and harm-repairing qualities of different aspects of 'community'. Case studies are used to show how community mediators often incorporated various agencies into the dialogic fold, some providing emotional and social support for victims, while others helped to repair the secondary harms that their organization had previously caused to the victim. The chapter highlights that certain restorative practices can help to repair not only the traumas of hate victimization, but also the institutional harms caused by state agencies, as examined in Chapter 3.

Chapter 7, finally, moves away from harm reparation to an analysis of the impacts that cultural and identity difference had on the restorative process. This chapter focuses again on the notion of community within restorative theory and practice. It is at this stage of the book that I examine, in detail, the risks posed by communities that support and nurture identity-based prejudices. The main concern of 'community' is that, rather than providing appropriate social condemnation of hate-motivated behaviour, its members may trivialize victims' experiences and expose them to re-victimization. The chapter therefore analyses the empirical data, which assessed whether, in practice, victims experienced domination and/or re-victimization during meetings. The findings suggest that restorative encounters rarely result in re-victimization due to the fact that dialogue is based on the values of respect, equality, and non-domination. Key to avoiding domination and re-victimization is the *preparation* of all participants as well as the setting of ground rules for discussion at the beginning of each meeting.

Chapter 8 uses both observational data and qualitative information gained from interviews with both victims and RJ practitioners in order to examine whether cultural and identity differences (including language skills and accents) inhibited the dialogic process, and whether facilitators could effectively challenge prejudice and enhance mutual understanding between the stakeholders. The chapter asserts that restorative dialogue can help to break down cultural divides and effectively challenge offenders' prejudice-motivated behaviours, especially where programmes that enhance 'moral learning' are incorporated into reparation agreements. Furthermore, the data suggest that restorative encounters reduce the likelihood for repeat victimization for most types of hate crime. However, a more cautious approach must be adopted where offenders' levels of hatred are deeply ingrained, with indirect approaches to dialogue being preferred by most practitioners interviewed.

The Conclusion reflects back on the study, looking again at why there is a need to use an alternative or additional approach to addressing the social problem of hate crime. The book draws together the themes found from the empirical study, summarizing both the benefits and limitations of RJ for hate crime. This final part of the book reflects on what the exploration of RJ told us about the nature of hate crime and what the nature of hate crime told us about the theory and practice of RJ. This should help us to better understand and respond to this invidious type of offending.

1
Conceptualizing Hate Crime for Restorative Justice

Introduction

Understanding the nature of 'hate crime' and examining how prejudice-motivated offences have been defined by legislatures and other state agencies is intrinsic to the exploration of whether restorative justice (RJ) can *help* to repair the harms it causes. The complex nature of 'hate' and the difficulties which arise in investigating its causal relationship to crime have been thoroughly examined within legal scholarship (see for example, Jacobs & Potter 1998; Lawrence 1999). For the purpose of this book it is important that the complexities faced when conceptualizing hate crime are re-examined in order to appreciate the types of cases that will be dealt with restoratively, and which were therefore researched as part of the empirical study undertaken for this book. These conceptual complexities, however, mark only the beginning of our consideration of both the risks and opportunities of using RJ for hate crime. An understanding of both the theoretical foundations of RJ and how restorative values are put into practice will become central to examining whether restorative practices are equipped to tackle this highly damaging type of offending (Chapter 2). Moreover, before we can examine whether RJ can aid victims' recoveries from hate crime victimization, we need first to explore the extent to which incidents impact victims, minority communities, and wider society (Chapter 3).

This chapter begins by examining what is meant by the term 'hate crime'. This entails an analysis of how it has been conceptualized within legal frameworks and more broadly within the field of criminology. The chapter describes how both legal and criminological conceptualizations of hate crime are important to the practical application of RJ processes for this type of crime. In particular, the chapter explores some of the difficulties encountered when defining 'hate', including the problems posed when attaching hate-motivation to the *mens rea* element of criminal law offences. The potential repercussions that hate crime laws have on offenders, victims, and wider communities, including concerns relating to labelling and stigmatization, are also detailed. The analysis presented in this first chapter helps to inform the broader practice of RJ by providing theoretical grounding on the complex nature of hate crime. Subsequent chapters illuminate further some of the social and cultural factors that must be addressed if restorative processes are to successfully repair the harms caused by hate crime victimization.

What is 'Hate Crime'?

Academics and government agencies have spent considerable resources conducting crime surveys in general and researching various aspects of victimization in particular over the past thirty to forty years (Hoyle 2012). Yet it has only really been in the past twenty to twenty-five years that victimization studies have focused on more specific, previously invisible areas, such as 'hate crime' offending (eg Home Office 1981; Sibbitt 1997). This is by no means to suggest that hate crime is a modern phenomenon, indeed countries such as Britain and the United States (US) have a long history of persecuting certain minority groups (so-called 'Others') (Levin & McDevitt 1993; Bowling 1998; Perry 2001; Iganski 2008). Rather, it is only in recent years that crimes motivated by 'hate' or 'prejudice' have been identified as a serious 'social problem' (Bowling 1998; Jenness & Grattet 2001). The desecration of Jewish cemeteries and synagogues (Iganski 1999, 2008), violence against people because of their race or ethnicity (Home Office 1981; Sibbitt 1997; Witte 1996; Bowling 1998) and 'gay bashing' (Moran et al 2004b; Dick 2008) are but a few types of hate crime that have caught the attention of governments in the United Kingdom (UK) and elsewhere across the globe (see Levin & McDevitt 1993, 2002 and Perry 2001 for US context).

The emergence of the term 'hate crime' and its proliferation in both public and academic discourse is rooted in the anti-hate crime movements in the US and later in the UK and Europe (Witte 1996 and Bowling 1998; Jenness & Grattet 2001; Garland & Chakraborti 2012). In the US, various social movements converged during the 1970s, including the black civil rights movement, the women's movement, the gay and lesbian movement, and the victims' movement, collectively forming the modern 'anti-hate crime movement' (Jenness 2002: 19). The term 'hate crime' was favoured amongst anti-hate crime campaigners as it could be used as an umbrella term which incorporated different types of prejudice-motivated crimes. The rapid growth of the movement during the 1980s and 1990s carried with it immense political influence (Jenness 2002; Jacobs & Potter 1998). The main aim of its activists was to compel legislatures to establish new laws which protected vulnerable minority communities from violence (Maroney 1998; Jenness & Grattet 2001). The combined efforts of various lobby groups resulted in legislatures throughout the US enacting new hate crime statutes which specifically enhanced the punishment of hate-motivated offenders (for a full analysis of the different state laws see Lawrence 1999). In fact, by the end of the 1990s the majority of US states had enacted some form of hate crime law onto their statute books, covering a multitude of different victim groups.[1]

The rapid expansion of such laws, propelled by the efforts of lobbyists, has led some to question whether hate crime is simply a new word for an old crime. For instance, James Jacobs and Kimberly Potter in their influential book *Hate Crimes* argued that the new hate crime policy domain ultimately created the 'social construction of a hate crime epidemic' (1998: 45), giving rise to the belief, rather than the actuality, that hate crime was a significant 'social problem'.

As with many criminal justice policies it was not long before the term 'hate crime' and the introduction of new laws proscribing hate-motivated offences found their way into UK public policy. The move towards criminalizing hate in England and Wales primarily centred on the issue of racial violence (Bowling 1998). Throughout the 1970s, high-profile racist attacks began to penetrate the public consciousness, a result of the prolific actions of the National Front and so called 'skinheads' (Witte 1996; Bowling 1998). Benjamin

---

[1] As of June 2013 forty-five states and the District of Columbia have statues criminalizing hate crimes. Note the Civil Rights Act of 1968 enacted 18 U.S.C. § 245(b)(2), which created the first Federal race-based hate offences relating to activities such as applying for employment or acting as a juror in a state court or voting. More recently, the Matthew Shepard and James Byrd, Jr Hate Crimes Prevention Act 2009 expanded these laws to include the victims who are targeted 'because of' their actual or perceived gender, sexual orientation, gender identity, or disability. The prerequisite that the victim must be engaged in a federally protected activity has also been dropped.

Bowling (1998) points out that it was during this period that a 'moral panic' about racist violence occurred and public opinion slowly began to move in favour of an anti-hate crime policy.[2] In response, the government set up the 1981 Joint Committee Against Racialism (JCAR) to investigate the problem. Directly after the Committee's report, the government commissioned its first study into racial violence and harassment (Home Office 1981). The report highlighted the widespread occurrence of racial attacks, focusing in particular on the disproportionate level of violence experienced by black and minority ethnic (BME) citizens (Home Office 1981). It finally gave validity to the concern, consistently vocalized by lobby groups, that racial violence was a 'social problem' in the UK (Bowling 1993). The government responded by implementing new policies directly aimed at tackling racist crime and the floodgates were opened for an array of reports into racist violence and later, statutory proscription (see Bowling 1993: footnote 6).

Nevertheless, it would be almost two decades later before the UK introduced hate crime laws that specifically proscribed racist violence—some twenty years after the first US state hate crime law (Lawrence 1999). The murder of Stephen Lawrence in South London in 1993 proved to be a seminal moment, bringing prolonged national media attention to the problem of racially motivated violence.[3] The ensuing public inquiry into the police investigation of Lawrence's murder and finally the publication of Sir William Macpherson's highly critical report (Macpherson 1999) created the impetus for government and police services to make sweeping changes to their policies and practices on tackling hate-motivated crime (Chakraborti & Garland 2009: Ch 2). In 1997 the 'New' Labour Government, then led by Tony Blair, responded to the growing social unease about racist violence by legislating to specifically criminalize and enhance the punishment of those who demonstrated racial 'hostility' during the commission of an offence (ss 28–32 Crime and Disorder Act 1998). During the second reading speech of the Crime and Disorder Bill, Lord Williams of Mostyn set out

---

[2] It should be noted that the government had already introduced the offence of incitement of racial hatred under the Race Relations Act 1965 (now transposed into the Public Order Act 1986).

[3] Similarly, the London nail bomber, David Copeland, who carried out attacks in Brixton, Brick Lane and the Admiral Duncan gay bar on Old Compton Street, Soho, London in 1999 attracted widespread public attention.

why the UK needed new racially aggravated offences stating: 'These [racist] crimes are particularly odious, damaging, as they do, not just the victim but the very fabric of the multi-racial society in which we live' (HL Deb 16 December 1997, col 534; see further analysis of these and other laws below). It had become clear that the state could no longer ignore the issue of racist violence, and as we will see, it could no longer close its eyes to the proliferation of other types of prejudice-motivated crime either.

Three years after its commencement, the Act was amended in order to include 'religiously' as well as 'racially' aggravated offences (amended by s 39 of the Anti-terrorism, Crime and Security Act 2001). It should also be noted at this point that UK legislation is yet to specifically proscribe offences where hostility is demonstrated towards a victim's sexual orientation, disability or transgender identity.[4] Instead, the Criminal Justice Act 2003 (UK) provides for sentencing provisions allowing judges to increase an offender's penalty where there is evidence that proves he or she demonstrated hostility towards the victim based on the victim's disability, sexual orientation, and/or transgender status (s 146).[5] It is unclear why these victim groups are protected under sentencing provisions only, leading one to question why racially and religiously aggravated offences are deserving of protection under the criminal law while other forms of hatred fall only under sentencing provisions.

Prior to the 1998 and 2003 statutes, the promotion of racial hatred was proscribed under the Race Relations Acts of 1965 and 1976 (often referred to as anti-vilification laws). This was later amended by the Public Order Act 1986, section 17 of which prohibits the use of words or behaviours that are 'threatening, abusive and insulting' and that are intended 'to stir up racial hatred' or where 'having regard to all the circumstances racial hatred is likely to be stirred up thereby'. In more recent years laws have been introduced which criminalize various other forms of incitement to hatred. After a prolonged period of lobbying by religious groups, the Racial and Religious Hatred Act 2006 was enacted, implementing 'stirring up of religious hatred' provisions into the Public Order Act 1986 (Idriss 2002; Hall 2005: 124). Following this, the Criminal Justice and Immigration Act 2008 amended the Public Order Act 1986 to

---

[4] The possible inclusion of sexual orientation, disability, and transgender is currently being considered by the Law Commission for England and Wales.

[5] These sections also provide for racial and religious aggravation.

include sexual orientation as a basis for stirring up of hatred; again after Stonewall (the UK's leading LGBT lobby group) argued for the implementation of incitement laws to protect gay, lesbian, and bisexual people from public vilification.[6]

Defining 'Hate' in 'Hate Crime'

The largely legislative response to hate-motivated crimes throughout the Western world has meant that to a great extent it has been defined within a legal framework. For example, Phyllis Gerstenfeld (2004: 9) defines hate crime as 'a criminal act which is motivated at least in part by the group affiliation of the victim'. While Kellina Craig (2002: 86) states that it is 'an illegal act involving intentional selection of a victim based on a perpetrator's bias or prejudice against the actual or perceived status of the victim'. The criminalization of hate crime during the 1980s and 1990s in both the US and UK meant that legal scholars began to critique the legal conceptualization of the phenomenon (Jacobs & Potter 1998; Lawrence 1999; Iganski 2008; Stanton-Ife 2013). In particular, the use of the word 'hate' has provoked considerable academic debate as to how this word could be transposed within the legal lexicon (Lawrence 1999), or indeed whether it should be at all (Morsch 1991; Hurd 2001).

What has become clear is that the word 'hate' is really a misnomer. An offender need not actually *hate* his victim in order to have committed a 'hate crime'; indeed he may feel no personal hatred towards that particular individual at all. Rather, it is the expression of *prejudice* or *bias* against the group that the victim is seen to be part of which is what the phrase 'hate crime' is really pertaining to (Lawrence 1999). Hence, the word 'hate' has been conceptualized by most to encompass, more broadly, conducts motivated by prejudice, bias, bigotry, animosity, ill-will, or hostility which is directed against an individual's identity traits (Lawrence 1999; Jacobs & Potter 1998). This has led Frederick Lawrence to re-term hate crime as 'bias crime', which he goes on to define as the 'criminal manifestation of prejudice' (Lawrence 2002: 37).

---

[6] Incitement to hatred laws remain absent within the US legal framework for hate crime. It is outside the scope of this book to examine why this is. I note here simply that First Amendment protections of freedom of speech mean that 'hate speech' laws are unlikely to find their way onto US statute books any time soon, see *R.A.V. v City of St. Paul*, 505 U.S. 377 (1992).

Conceptualizing hate to mean prejudice or bias has, however, created further confusion as to how it can be attached to various forms of offending. For Jacobs and Potter (1998), there are two important questions to be asked when defining 'hate crime'. First, how do we define prejudice in the criminal context and second, what prejudices are deserving of criminal attention? Defining prejudice can be extraordinarily difficult. Some prejudices may be viewed as positive, such as anti-fascist or anti-racist. Other prejudices are innocuous such as a dislike of the colour green (Jacobs & Potter 1998). Still, certain prejudices are deemed to be wholly unacceptable and socially damaging to the cohesiveness of society. These may include, amongst various other forms of prejudice, racism, homophobia, and anti-religious views (Jacobs & Potter 1998: 12). Whether it is possible to define each of these types of prejudice in law is less than clear. In fact, as we will see below, most hate crime laws do not define 'prejudice' or 'bias' (or other synonymous words) at all. Instead it is left to the jury (or judge) to determine whether prejudice has been expressed during the commission of an offence based on the ordinary dictionary meanings of words that are used in legislation such as 'ill-will' or 'hostility' (Walters 2013a). Ultimately, this means that the meaning given to hate crime offences may differ depending on how judges and juries decipher what is meant by the key words used by legislators (see further discussion on the law below).

Some judicial or legislative guidance in this regard may be of benefit to legal practitioners who must understand and then operationalize hate crime offences. Law makers may do well to refer to Gordon Allport's seminal *The Nature of Prejudice*, where he defines 'ethnic prejudice', for example, as 'an antipathy based upon a faulty and inflexible generalization. It may be felt or expressed. It may be directed towards a group as a whole, or towards an individual because he is a member of that group' (1954: 10). Clearly under this definition of prejudice, a person must feel or express animosity towards a whole group based on generalizations made about that group. Such generalizations are often the result of stereotyping. Negative stereotypes attached to certain identity groups are perpetuated through communication networks, most notably between family and friends (Byers et al 1999), but also via news and television media (see Green et al 2001).

Yet while helpful in determining what offences are prejudice-motivated crimes, Allport's definition of prejudice may also be restrictive in defining 'hate crime'. For example, Donald Green et al (2001) point out that hate crime can be influenced by economic competition and resentment between identity groups rather than a faulty generalization about a group of individuals. Though, as I have noted elsewhere, the experience of economic strain may well be intertwined with false generalizations about certain minority group individuals' worthiness as community members as well as their perceived economic prosperity—including the preferential access to state welfare that Others, such as immigrants, are *perceived* to receive (Walters 2011; see also, Ray & Smith 2002; Gadd et al 2005). Nonetheless, there may well be situations where an offender is hostile towards certain individuals without their prejudices arising from negative stereotypes. For example, an individual may view male to male anal sex as sinful or unnatural. The offender's beliefs about anal sex may well be deemed as repugnant by those who believe in sexual orientation equality, but the belief cannot necessarily be said to be based on a faulty generalization about gay men (though of course such prejudices will frequently be the result of faulty generalizations about the morality of gay people). The offender's views may instead be the result of his strict religious beliefs, which give rise to a strong sense of right and wrong, and perhaps to a fear of those who breach religiously prescribed sexual moral codes.

What this very short exploration of the meaning of prejudice tells us is that, although defining prejudice is certainly useful in explaining hate-motivated offences, it may not by itself provide a comprehensive definition of 'hate crime'. As we will see below, this may be why legislators have opted for more neutral terminology within legislation such as 'ill will' (Scotland) and 'hostility' (England and Wales), or why within some US states no hate element exists at all; instead offences can become hate crimes where they are committed 'because of' or 'by reason of' the victim's group affiliation (see the section 'Transposing "Hate" into Law' later in this chapter).

Linking 'Hate' with 'Crime'

Notwithstanding the definitional complexities of prejudice, there are also difficulties in linking it to the *mens rea* (ie the intention element) of a criminal act (Gadd 2009; Hall 2010: 153–154). Of greatest complexity is that prejudices can vary dramatically in degree. At one end of the spectrum, a prejudice against an identity group may involve a mild dislike or suspicion of members of that group, usually based on ignorance and/or general stereotypes about their worthiness as a people (Levin & McDevitt 1993). People who hold such prejudices may occasionally verbalize their negative feelings to other close friends and family members, who by and large unwittingly proliferate negative sentiments about those they know little about (Levin & McDevitt 1993; Sibbitt 1997). Such people are likely to deny that they are 'racist' or 'homophobic' by proclaiming that they 'know' someone who is 'black' or 'gay' (Burney & Rose 2002). We might label such prejudices as 'superficial'.

At the other end of the spectrum, feelings of prejudice may consume an individual's consciousness so as to produce a deep-seated hatred of all people who display certain identity characteristics. Such individuals may make it their 'mission' in life to eradicate all people who display such an identity (Levin & McDevitt 1993, 2002; see further, 'Challenging Prejudice', Chapter 8). Their deep-rooted bigotry may arise after years of learning to hate, having been subjected to macro- and micro-level messages about the immorality of certain identity groups (Levin & McDevitt 1993).

Once it is determined at what threshold prejudice should be criminalized, the courts will then need to set about proving that a 'causal relationship' existed between the offender's bigotry and the commission of the offence (Jacobs & Potter 1998: 23). If the threshold for prejudice is set very low and a relationship between prejudice and conduct can be shown (however slight), a substantial amount of crime will be classified as 'hate crime', leading potentially to what Stanley Cohen refers to as 'net-widening' (Cohen 1985). Jacob and Potter's (1998) famous table illustrates the vast differences which arise under this conceptualization between different levels of prejudice and their connection to an offence (see Figure 1.1).

The table in Figure 1.1 shows how different crimes may be constructed as 'hate crimes' depending on how narrowly or broadly the prejudice and causal relationship is defined. Low causation and low prejudice would cast a 'hate crime' net over a wide range of conduct, including incidents where a minor inter-personal dispute, unrelated to the identity of the victim, later culminates in one party sniping a racist or homophobic remark in the heat of the moment (see case examples in Chapters 4 and 5). In such examples, the 'crime' is not necessarily the *direct* result of prejudice, but rather includes an element of vocalized racism or homophobia that is primarily used as a means of venting frustration at the victim (see Gadd 2009).

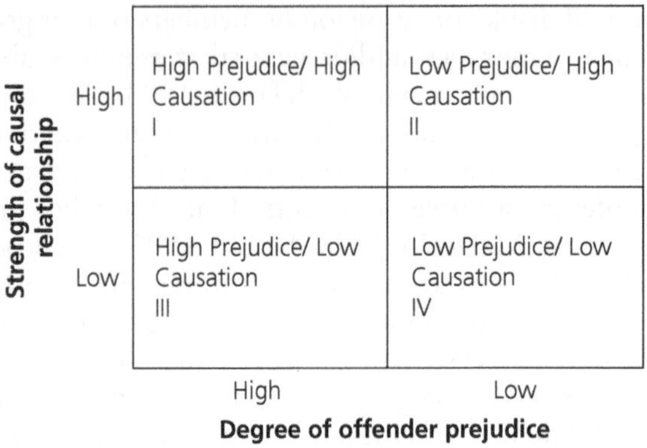

		High	Low
Strength of causal relationship	High	High Prejudice/ High Causation I	Low Prejudice/ High Causation II
	Low	High Prejudice/ Low Causation III	Low Prejudice/ Low Causation IV

Degree of offender prejudice

Figure 1.1 Labelling hate crime: the prejudice and causal components

Source: Jacobs & Potter 1998: 23.f

At the other end of the hate spectrum are crimes where prejudice is the sole or main reason for the commission of the offence (see examples in Chapter 4). These types of crime are most commonly recognized as 'hate crimes' by the media and often include extremist actions by what Jack Levin and Jack McDevitt (1993) classify as 'mission offenders'. Crimes of this nature would include, for example, the actions of David Copeland who unleashed several nail bomb attacks against various minority groups in London during 1999 (McLagan & Lowles 2000).

The proscription of prejudice-motivated crimes is further complicated by the fact that many offenders will have mixed motivations (Lawrence 1999). Their reasons for committing an offence may include elements of different types of prejudice as well as other motivating factors such as provocation or the acquisition of material goods (Chakraborti & Garland 2012). In such circumstances how does one determine whether the crime is a 'hate crime' or otherwise motivated? Lawrence (1999: 10) argues that we should ask whether the offence is a *sine qua non* of the offender's prejudice. In other words, *but for* the victim's (perceived) identity would the offence have been committed? Where it can be determined that the offence would not have occurred but for the victim's (perceived) identity (regardless of other motivating factors) the crime can truly be conceived as one of hate. This allows for the prosecution of an offence as a hate crime even where multiple motives and intersecting prejudices exist (see Walters 2013b).

Nevertheless, even this seemingly simple test may still lead to confusion over whether to prosecute an offence as a 'hate crime'. Take, for example, an ongoing conflict between two neighbours, which is initially triggered after Neighbour A plays his music too loudly, late at night. The constant noise frustrates Neighbour B until she has had enough and bangs on her neighbour's front door. This confrontation leads to an abusive altercation between the neighbours, who are both left feeling aggrieved. Over the following weeks the relationship between the neighbours deteriorates and frustration and anger starts to grow between the parties. Further noise pollution by Neighbour A leaves Neighbour B so upset that she rushes next door and again bashes on his front door. Knowing that Neighbour A is gay, she begins to make homophobic remarks while threatening him with physical violence if he does not turn the music off.

The conflict has morphed from one of inter-personal conflict about noise to that of a public order offence where the 'offender' has demonstrated hostility based on the 'victim's' sexual orientation (see legal definitions below). The hate incident arises primarily as a result of noise pollution, yet both parties are likely to be culpable for the ensuing acrimony which followed the first altercation. The homophobic abuse and threat of violence is the culmination of an ongoing conflict between neighbours who will need to live side by side for the foreseeable future. However, to some extent we are left unsure as to what role the victim's sexual orientation played in the overall conflict. For example, would Neighbour B have approached the victim differently had he not been gay? Was her homophobia to blame for threatening him with violence or would she have done the same regardless of his sexual orientation? Moreover, what role did Neighbour A's noise pollution and his responses to his neighbour's complaints play in his own victimization? These questions can become far too complex for an adversarial system that seeks to determine guilt of one party beyond reasonable doubt (Gadd 2009). As we will see in Chapters 4, 5, and 6, the commonality of conflicts that involve hate incidents such as these cannot always be effectively dealt with by retributive justice measures. In the vast majority of these cases the police will be unable to pursue the case beyond an initial warning to both of the parties (or recording it as a 'hate incident', see definition below) let alone lay charges or refer the case to the Crown Prosecution Service (CPS) for prosecution (Burney & Rose 2002; Gadd 2009).

Transposing 'Hate' into Law

Clearly then, determining how much hate crime there is and how we respond to it depends on how hate crime is conceptualized and defined (see Hall 2013: Ch 1). In constructing a definition of hate crime, Jacobs and Potter (1998) state that choices must be made regarding what 'hate' means in law and how it is then linked to an offender's motivation to commit an offence (Jacobs & Potter 1998: 27). In general, governments in the US and UK have implemented two models of hate crime legislation when proscribing prejudice-motivated offences (Lawrence 1999). The first type uses a 'hatred motivation' model (also commonly referred to as the racial animus model) to produce offences where the offender acts out of hatred or prejudice for his/her victim's group identity (Lawrence 1999). The second type of offence is based on a 'group selection' model (also referred to as the discriminatory selection model). Under these offences the offender need only 'select' his/her victim from a particular protected group. Proof of prejudice, bias, hostility, or hatred is not necessary. Under this interpretation of hate crime, definitions of prejudice such as those put forward by Allport (1954) become irrelevant (at least in law). Instead, the offender's intention to choose a victim *because of* their perceived association with a particular group is all that is required.

Legislatures have been far from consistent in their implementation of hate crime laws. It is therefore difficult to place jurisdictions into either the 'hatred motivation' or 'group selection' model without some ambiguity. In some US states the words 'intentionally selects' have been used (for example, Virginia). More commonly used phrases are 'because of' or 'by reason of'. Under these phrases, a penalty enhancement will be enforced where the offender has committed a parallel offence because of, or by reason of, the victim's group identity. For example, sentencing legislation in Maine reads as follows:

17-A MRSA §1151. The selection by the defendant of the person against whom the crime was committed or of the property that was damaged or otherwise affected by the crime because of the race, color, religion, sex, ancestry, national origin, physical or mental disability, sexual orientation or homelessness of that person or of the owner or occupant of that property.

Under this Act, the offender's sentence will be increased when he or she is convicted of an offence that has been committed 'because of' one of the specified characteristics of the victim. It is evident from the wording of this Act that 'hatred' (or prejudice or bias) for the victim is not a prerequisite of the offence.

The group selection model is both broader and narrower than statutes which incorporate a hatred model. Such an approach is broader in that provisions *may* encompass offences where no specific prejudice or bias is demonstrated by the offender. For example, an offender who robs a Jewish victim based on the erroneous belief that Jewish people carry more cash with them could fall within the ambit of this type of hate crime law. The offender may feel no ill-will towards Jewish people but simply think that it is more likely he will obtain a higher financial return by targeting those he perceives to be Jewish. Other 'because of' legislation in the US works similarly to this, but may include an intent element such as 'malice' or 'ill will' (see Lawrence 1999). This model of legislation makes the burden of proof more onerous as prosecutors must prove beyond reasonable doubt that the defendant demonstrated 'ill will' towards the victim based on the victim's identity.[7]

The UK was relatively late to legislate against hate crimes as compared to the US. As mentioned above, in 1998 new offences covering hate crimes were introduced under the Crime and Disorder Act 1998 (UK). Like most laws, the Act does not use the words 'hate crime', relying instead on more traditional criminal law language to create the specific offences of 'racially or religiously aggravated' assault, criminal damage, harassment, stalking, and several public order offences (ss 28–32). Section 28 of the Act states:

(1) An offence is racially or religiously aggravated for the purposes of sections 29 to 32 below if—

---

[7] Other legislatures have created new substantive laws which are not tied to existing criminal offences. These laws are less popular, not least because they involve the reformulating of entirely new offences (see, eg, California Cal. Penal Code s 422.6(a) and (b)).

(a) at the time of committing the offence, or immediately before or after doing so, the offender demonstrates towards the victim of the offence hostility based on the victim's membership (or presumed membership) of a racial or religious group; or
(b) the offence is motivated (wholly or partly) by hostility towards members of a racial or religious group based on their membership of that group.

The legislation is similar to many US statutes that include sentence enhancers. As a hatred model statute, the Crime and Disorder Act incorporates 'hostility' as part of the necessary *mens rea* of the offence. There are two parts to the section which work to cover different levels of prejudice and their causal relationship to the crime. Subsection (b) uses the terms 'motivated' or 'partly motivated' and covers situations where there is evidence that the offender committed an offence because of (or partly because of) a hostility for the victim's identity. The evidentiary threshold for this subsection will be relatively high as the prosecution will have to prove beyond reasonable doubt that the offender feels a genuine hostility towards the victim's group identity.

Subsection (a) incorporates a lower burden of proof. It states that the offender must have 'demonstrated' hostility during, before, or directly after the commission of an offence. This means that prosecutors do not need to prove that the offender was motivated by a prejudice against the victim's identity, but rather that he or she simply demonstrated hostility based on the victim's identity at the time of the offence. What 'demonstrates hostility' actually means in law is far from clear, it being up to the jury to determine in each case based on the ordinary dictionary meaning of the word. More often than not, demonstrations of hostility will translate in court as simply proving that the offender used prejudiced language during the commission of the offence (Burney & Rose 2002). This has caused some controversy both within the courts and amongst academics (for a full discussion of this see Walters 2013a). For example, research carried out by Burney and Rose (2002) found that many sentencers felt that 'the law came down rather hard on people who, in the course of "normal working class mayhem" as one person put it, uttered words which were part of their natural vocabulary' (Burney & Rose 2002: 20; see also, *DPP v Woods* [2002] EWHC Admin 85).

Other legal practitioners, however, have taken a more liberal approach to finding the racial element proved where, for example, any mention of the victims' racial or religious identity has been made (Burney & Rose 2002; see *Rogers* [2007] UKHL 8, where the House of Lords confirmed that the phrase 'bloody foreigners' amounted to a racial group and therefore if used towards the victim could amount to racial hostility).

Some commentators have suggested that 'demonstrations' as against motivations of hostility should not be conceived as 'hate crime' at all, but rather should be understood as expressions of anger and frustration, linked to other emotional factors, which are made in the 'heat of the moment' (Gadd 2009; see also Chakraborti & Garland 2012: 503). These incidents are typically reactions to a trigger situation, such as the one described above with neighbours A and B, and as such they might better be characterized as 'hate speech' rather than 'hate crime' (see also *Woods* [2002] EWHC Admin 85). In other words, as the offence itself is not one motivated by hate, the simple fact that hate speech has been used during its commission should not result in the incident in its entirety being conflated as a 'hate crime'.

I have attempted to counter these concerns based on two main arguments (Walters 2013a). The first asserts that expressions of bigotry, whether committed in the heat of the moment or not, are nonetheless still intended or recklessly expressed in order to subjugate the victim's identity (see Perry's (2001) definition of hate crime below). Despite this, offenders will frequently claim that they are not 'racist' or 'homophobic' following a hate incident (Gadd 2009) such as where they exclaim 'it was the drink talking not me' (see Burney & Rose 2002). Yet it is difficult to see how an offender could, during the commission of an offence, fail to be *aware* that his vocalization of prejudice would send a symbolic message to the victim and others like him or her. After all the vast majority of people become aware at an early age that public displays of prejudice are deemed offensive, even if an offender's family and friends remain resolute in their bigotry. As such, it is unlikely that an offender would be ignorant of both the moral reprehensibility and social harm that his expression of bigotry will contain. He may, of course, not care whether he causes harm, but this is a different matter. In terms of criminalization, it matters only that he intended or was aware that his actions would be perceived as an expression of prejudice and that his act causes harm to the victim. If the expression of prejudice is temporally connected with the commission of an offence it cannot be compartmentalized as being separate from it. The expression becomes an intrinsic component of the offence committed, and underlies part of the offender's desire to hurt the victim (Walters 2013a). Under such a construction it is difficult to comprehend a situation where prejudice is vocalized during the commission of an offence that would not give rise to a presumption that the offence amounts to a 'hate crime'. Perhaps only where the offender is unaware that the language he has used is deemed by others as referring to identity-based animus would this be the case.[8]

Appreciating the rationales underpinning the liberal approach to defining hate crime in English law is important to the endeavours of this book. In particular, it will be these types of hate offences, as defined by hate crime legislation, which will ultimately come to be dealt with by RJ practitioners working within and outside the criminal justice system.[9] It remains unclear whether RJ practitioners will be aware of hate-motivations in cases where homophobia and/or disability are highlighted only at sentencing.[10] This may also be especially the case where criminal justice measures have failed to uncover offenders' prejudices, even though their animosities may have been intrinsic to the causation of the offence. In some cases there may be a lack of evidence to prove beyond reasonable doubt that a hate-motivation existed and evidence of such may be lost by the time that the offender reaches any form of restorative process. In other cases, RJ will be used as an alternative to prosecution and therefore the identification of a hate-motivation may depend on communication between restorative practitioners and police officers, or more directly with the participants of the process themselves during preparatory meetings. Central to the analysis of this book is whether issues pertaining to prejudice and individual identity are raised and discussed during RJ processes. Data collated from interviews and observations (conducted as part of the empirical study) will therefore be used to explore how such issues are dealt with in restorative meetings (see Chapters 4, 5, 6, 7, and 8).

---

[8] Moreover, the failure to consider 'demonstrations' of prejudice as 'hate crimes' fails to acknowledge the heightened levels of harm which such expressions frequently cause (Iganski 1999; 2008; Levin 1999).
[9] In particular, those who work within the youth justice system: see Chapter 3.
[10] Explored further in Chapter 4.

Understanding Hate Crime as a Process of Victimization

Unlike legal scholarship, the emergence of criminological discourse on the causes of hate crimes has led to the development of a concept that takes into consideration both the sociological and cultural nature of prejudice-motivated offending. These explorations are more helpful to our understanding of both hate crime's aetiological determinants and the harms it causes to victims and minority communities (see Chapter 3). Important to this book is that criminological analyses have begun to illuminate the socio-cultural underpinnings of hate crime, thus providing important background information as to how restorative practices might impact upon those involved in hate crime cases (see Hall 2013: Ch 6).

In 1994 Lois Wolfe and Leslie Copeland defined hate crime as 'violence directed towards groups of people who generally are not valued by the majority of society, who suffer discrimination in other arenas, and who do not have full access to remedy social political and economic justice' (Wolfe & Copeland 1994: 201). This definition begins to include the social harms already experienced by certain members of the community who are vulnerable to prejudice-based violence and who, as a result, will be impacted more severely by it (see further, Chapter 3). Carole Sheffield (1995: 438) shares a similar view of hate crime stating that:

> Hate violence is motivated by social and political factors and is bolstered by belief systems which (attempt to) legitimate such violence...It reveals that the personal is political; that such violence is not a series of isolated incidents but rather the consequences of political culture which allocates rights, privileges and prestige according to biological and social factors.

Nathan Hall (2005; 2013) argues that such a definition provides context and understanding about cause and effect, which other legalistic definitions fail to provide. Barbara Perry (2001) in her influential book, *In the Name of Hate: Understanding Hate Crime* also argues that these broader definitions are more meaningful because they not only highlight the political and social context in which hate violence is incubated, but also refer us to the hierarchical nature of collective identity which underpins hate violence. However, Perry (2001) also states that while helpful, Sheffield's definition is also incomplete as it does not take into account the effects that hate crime has. Instead, Perry (2001) argues that hate crime should be defined by taking elements of Wolfe and Copeland's (1994) definition together with that of Sheffield's (1995). Perry (2001: 10) accordingly defines hate crime as:

...acts of violence and intimidation, usually directed towards already stigmatised and marginalised groups. As such, it is a mechanism of power and oppression, intended to reaffirm the precarious hierarchies that characterise a given social order. It attempts to re-create simultaneously the threatened (real or imagined) hegemony of the perpetrator's group and the 'appropriate' subordinate identity of the victim's group.

This definition includes both the social position of the victim and the oppressive power dynamics of society as expressed through violence. It helps us to understand that hate crimes are not just isolated acts committed by hate-filled individuals, but rather they are part of a process of what Perry termed 'doing difference'. The act of violence targeted against someone who is different is part of a wider picture of discrimination and marginalization experienced by such individuals. Perry (2001) goes on to argue that hate crime is better understood as the extreme form of discrimination which emanates from a culture of segregation, discrimination, and marginalization of individuals who are somehow 'different'.

I explore the structural and social harms of hate further in Chapter 3; it is, however, important to note here that hate crime is more than just an individualized expression of bigotry. It is beyond the scope of this chapter to analyse the various criminological theories explaining the causes of hate crime (see Perry 2001: Ch 2; Walters 2011; Hall 2013: C 6). However, it is important at this stage in the book to develop further our understanding of hate crime as a socio-cultural phenomenon that occurs not just as isolated incidents committed at the periphery of society, but as part of a broader everyday process of minority group marginalization (Iganski 2008).

The Process of Hate

Extreme forms of hate violence often capture the attention of media outlets. Coverage of particularly brutal cases helps to promote an image of hate crime as one-off acts of violence committed by hardened bigots (often labelled as 'stranger danger'; see Mason 2005). However, such an interpretation of hate crime fails to consider the pervasive and often ongoing nature of 'low-level' acts of harassment and verbal abuse. For example, recent data taken from the

Crime Survey for England and Wales (CSEW) showed higher rates of repeat victimization for hate crime compared with CSEW crime overall (Home Office et al 2013)[11] (see also, Smith et al 2012: 19–20).

Several criminologists have begun to examine how these frequent but discernibly minor acts of prejudice produce far-reaching social harms for victims (Sibbitt 1997; Bowling 1998; Chahal & Julienne 1999; Garland & Chakraborti 2006; Iganski 2008). 'Low-level' hate incidents may include verbal abuse, spitting, physical gestures of intimidation such as menacing looks, and the throwing of stones and eggs at property (Garland & Chakraborti 2006). Jon Garland and Neil Chakraborti (2006) found in their study of rural racism that 'low-level' forms of racist harassment, such as verbal abuse and throwing stones or eggs, were commonplace to many of the minority ethnic populations they researched in Suffolk, Northamptonshire, and Warwickshire. Some of these conducts will fall foul of criminal laws (most commonly as public order offences); however, viewed in isolation they are often deemed simply as acts of anti-social behaviour that need not be reported to the police, or if they are reported, the police will do little more than warn the accused party about their behaviour (Sibbitt 1997).

In his book *Hate and the City*, Paul Iganski (2008) argues that we must take seriously the 'everydayness' of hate crime if we are to better understand its effects. As such, an examination of the impact of hate crime must encompass 'the day-to-day reality of how bigotry is manifest in the lives of offenders and their victims' (Iganski 2008: 20). Hate incidents arise most frequently from opportunity and provocation, at least that which is perceived. Iganski (2008) explains that prejudices which simmer under the surface frequently boil over when people come face to face through their daily routine activities (Iganski 2008). The irritation of next door's music or the person who pushes past on the bus can instantly trigger a (partly) hate-motivated reaction.

Bowling's influential book *Violent Racism* (1998) similarly illustrates the repetitive nature of racist abuse. He refers to police records of racial incidents in North Plaistow, London documenting fifty-three incidents of racist abuse against families in two streets during 1987–88. In the vast majority of these cases, incidents

---

[11] 27 per cent of victims of personal hate crime were repeat victims, compared with 21 per cent of victims of personal crime overall.

involved verbal abuse and harassment, egg throwing, damage to property, and door-knocking (1998: Ch 7; see further, Bowling 1993, 1994). Bowling notes that many of these incidents were regarded by the police as 'minor' (Bowling 1998: 189). However, it is only when one considers the fact that 'minor' incidents are often repeated over an extended period of time that we begin to appreciate their devastating effects. Bowling also refers to the fact that other subtle behaviours, which amount to no more than an individual being aware that someone is annoyed or disgusted by their presence, all have the effect of compounding a victim's experience of victimization (1998: 230). Levels of abuse may build up over time with many cases escalating into more severe acts of violence (Bowling 1998: 189). Bowling argues that the experience of racist hate crime cannot, therefore, be 'reducible to an isolated incident, or even a collection of incidents' (1998: 230). Instead, racist hate crime (and by analogy other forms of hate crime) is better understood as a process of victimization which results in an accumulation of social harms (Bowling 1993, 1994, 1998; Netto & Abazie 2012). In other words, victims of targeted abuse will frequently experience victimization as just one part of a continuum of structural disadvantage that is made up of cultural processes which, collectively, support a general climate of antipathy towards certain minority groups (Sibbitt 1997; Garland & Chakraborti 2006).

As prejudice and acts of hatred become ingrained within many individuals' lives, their experiences of hate victimization can become normalized. This does not, however, equate to a dissipation of its harmful effects. Rather, normalization occurs only to the extent that hate incidents become an expected part of a person's life (Dick 2008). Over extended periods of time, the acceptance of hate as an unavoidable fact of life is not only demoralizing but extremely damaging to a victim's mental health (Herek & Berrill 1992). An example of persistent 'low-level' disablist abuse serves to illustrate the disastrous effects that persistent victimization can have. In 2007 the bodies of Fiona Pilkington, 38, and her daughter Francecca Hardwick, 18, were found in a Leicestershire lay-by. At the inquest into their deaths the jury heard that Ms Pilkington had apparently poured a 10-litre can of petrol over the back seat of the car, while both she and her daughter were in it, before setting it alight. It was revealed that the family had endured over ten years of abuse at the hands of neighbours' children who had repeatedly harassed them by throwing stones at their house and verbally abusing them and their relatives. On one occasion a group of teenagers marched Ms Pilkington's son into a shed at knife point before locking him in there. Over seven years the family made a total of thirty-three calls for help to Leicestershire Police. The inquest found that the council and police officers had 'contributed' to the deaths by failing to recognize the family's vulnerability and take action against those who made sustained efforts to victimize the family because of their disabilities ('Police errors in "bullying" deaths revealed at inquest', *The Guardian*, 18 September 2009; see also documentary *Tormented Lives*, BBC1, shown 20 October 2010; see further, case examples in Chapter 4).

The Pilkington case illustrates how repetitive hate abuse is compounded by the already disadvantageous socio-economic position that many minority individuals occupy, sometimes having disastrous consequences (see further Chapter 4). One might credibly posit that had Ms Pilkington been in a more privileged socio-economic position she may not have found herself in an environment where such anti-social behaviour occurred[12] or, if she had, she may have had the means and resources to cope better with her situation (see *Tormented Lives*, BBC1, 2010). Accepting that socio-economic disadvantage cannot be changed overnight, we must look to the state to provide greater protection for those who experience hate abuse such as that endured by the Pilkington family. Clearly, in that case, the local authorities failed Ms Pilkington and her children. Had the council and the police spent more time supporting those with severe disabilities, the victims may well have been moved, or at least provided with greater protection against the abuse they suffered. This, of course, is hypothetical, but one cannot help but hypothesize that such abuse would not have continued to the extent that it did had the victims been better supported and protected by local agencies (see Chapter 6 for how a multi-agency approach can help to prevent the recurrence of hate abuse).

Victim–Offender Relationships

Linked to the 'everydayness' of hate crime is the fact that many hate crime victims and offenders will be known to each other, often as neighbours, work colleagues, or through commercial transactions

---

[12] Though see Garland and Chakraborti (2006) who explored the experiences of racism by those who live in rural areas.

(Sibbitt 1997; Ray & Smith 2002; Mason 2005).[13] Previous conceptualizations of hate crime have suggested that offences are committed at random by those unknown to the victim (Perry 2001; Mason 2005). Levin and McDevitt's (1993) typology of hate offenders, for example, suggests that most perpetrators of hate crime will be 'thrill seeking' youths unfamiliar with their victims (see also Craig 2002). Some will even travel into communities at a distance from their own in order to seek out potential targets. Perry's (2001: 29) influential work also states that '[t]hese brutal acts of violence are commonly perpetrated on strangers—people with whom the perpetrator has had little or no personal contact'. There is certainly no shortage of examples of stranger danger cases; from the racist murder of Stephen Lawrence in 1993 to the brutal homophobic killing of Jody Dobrowski in 2005, there are undoubtedly many random acts of hate violence committed by those completely unknown to the victim (see further examples in Chakraborti & Garland 2009).

More recently though, there has been a shift away from conceptualizing hate crime as a form of 'stranger danger' (Mason 2005). The broadening out of hate crime research to include 'low-level' forms of harassment and abuse has begun to illuminate the types of personal relationships that exist between victims and offenders (Sibbitt 1997; Mason 2005). Gail Mason's (2005) study of homophobic harassment complaints recorded by the Metropolitan Police Service found that 90 per cent of incidents occurred at or near the victim's home. A vast majority of cases were committed by neighbours (82 per cent) while a further 7 per cent knew the perpetrator as being local to where they worked. Other studies have reported similar findings; Les Moran et al (2004b: 42–44), for example, found that two-thirds of homophobic hate victims knew their perpetrators and most of these were neighbours. While in Larry Ray et al's (2004) research, sixty out of sixty-four individuals who had committed a racist attack knew their victim. Most knew each other as a result of commercial transactions, for example in shops, restaurants, takeaways, or taxis (see further, Chakraborti & Garland 2009: 129–32). This book will further highlight the close relationships that often exist between offenders and victims (see Chapters 4, 5, and Conclusion). For now it is important to highlight the interpersonal

---

[13] Although it is unlikely that the relationship is intimate.

familiarity of those involved in hate crimes as underpinning the pervasive nature of the phenomenon (Iganski 2008).

Including 'Hate Incidents' Within Hate Crime Policy

Legislators' and governments' focus on 'hate crimes'—as differentiated from the more common 'low-level' incidents of hate—means that the ongoing forms of 'low-level' hate-motivated abuse and the devastating harms that these cause to communities remain largely ignored by the state and, to some extent, criminology (Bowling 1998; see, for example, the 'Pilkington case' explored above). Broadening out the scope of hate crime discourse and scholarly debate to include 'low-level' hate incidents therefore creates much-needed space within criminology to investigate the impacts that a wider variety of prejudice-motivated incidents has on individuals and society. With regard to this book, the expansion of hate crime scholarship to include 'hate incidents' has enabled me to explore in greater detail the restorative approaches that have been used to repair the harms caused by a broad array of prejudice-motivated conducts that occur throughout different communities in England.

In particular, the empirical endeavours undertaken for the book relied heavily on the definitions of both 'hate crime' and 'hate incidents' that were provided by the Association of Chief Police Officers (ACPO). In their 2005 *Good Practice and Guidance* report they define 'hate crimes' and 'hate incidents'. A hate incident is defined as '[a]ny incident, which may or may not constitute a criminal offence, which is perceived by the victim or any other person, as being motivated by prejudice or hate'. A hate crime is defined as '[a]ny hate incident, which constitutes a criminal offence, perceived by the victim or any other person, as being motivated by prejudice or hate'.[14]

---

[14] ACPO is yet to release an updated version of these guidelines. At the time of submission of this book the guidelines have been removed from ACPO's website with no new guidelines in their place. A new common definition of hate crime has, however, been agreed between ACPO and the CPS, which describes it as '[a]ny criminal offence which is perceived by the victim or any other person, to be motivated by a hostility or prejudice based on a person's race or perceived race; religion or perceived religion; sexual orientation or perceived sexual orientation; disability or perceived disability and any crime motivated by a hostility or prejudice against a person who is transgender or perceived to be' (Crown Prosecution Service 2012).

These definitions provide a liberal and victim-centred definition of hate crime/incidents. While they do not in themselves provide any further information as to the socio-cultural nature of hate crime or what is meant by the term 'prejudice', the definitions do allow for a broad array of prejudice-motivated incidents to be included within their scope. ACPO includes five separate victim groups within its definition of hate crime/incidents including prejudice based on the victim's race (including ethnicity and/or nationality), religious beliefs, sexual orientation, disability, and transgender identity.[15]

While ACPO's definition of hate crime/incidents may have several detrimental consequences if applied within a retributive framework (see discussion directly below), its broadness ensures that a vast array of prejudice-motivated action is captured by state agencies who must then respond to reported incidents. For instance, ACPO's (2005) guidelines note that 'making inappropriate reference to the colour of someone's skin, in a non-confrontational social setting, may well be perceived as a racist incident. However there may be insufficient evidence that it would constitute a racist crime' (Association of Police Chief Officers 2005). Still, in such cases the police should contact the complainant and record the incident as 'hate incident'.

It is worth my noting here that the two main sources of data used in the empirical study came from institutions that employed ACPO's definitions (see Chapters 4 and 5). It is for this reason that the definitions provided by ACPO are used in this book as a working definition of hate crime/incidents. However, I wish to note that the definitions are used for the purposes of exploring the hate crimes/incidents that were referred to the restorative practices that were observed for this book. Other criminological and legal definitions remain of immense importance to our understanding and appreciation of the nature of hate-motivated behaviours and ultimately to the way that RJ practitioners might facilitate the resolution of such cases.

It is only by appreciating that hate crime can occur in a variety of ways, motivated (or partly motivated) by intersecting prejudices, that we can investigate further the nuances between different *types*

[15] Though this book includes only four victim groups including, race, religious beliefs, sexual orientation, and disability due to limited accessibility of other types of cases. Please see further explanation of why transgender hate crimes are not included in the Introduction.

of prejudice (Garland et al 2006). As we will see from the empirical research carried out for this book, not only will hate crimes be marked by different *levels* of prejudice, but the prejudices which are demonstrated towards victims may be interconnected with various identity traits pertaining to such characteristics as race, ethnicity, nationality, sexual orientation and disability, as well as age and social class (see Chapter 4).

The Limitations of a Retributive Approach to Tackling Repeated 'Hate Incidents'

Although a broad definition of hate crime, which includes 'hate incidents', widens the scope of criminological investigation (including the use of RJ) and hate crime discourse more generally, it also means that considerable social activity is open to being labelled and/or recorded as motivated by 'hate', leading to what Stan Cohen has called 'net-widening' (Cohen 1985; see also Jacobs & Potter 1998). ACPO's wide interpretation of hate crime, for example, has meant that England and Wales records vastly higher amounts of racially and religiously aggravated offences/incidents when compared to other European countries (see ODIHR 2013 and the United States where more restrictive approaches to defining 'hate crime' have been implemented (Hall 2005: 10–14).

While some might view the high numbers of incidents being recorded as 'hate crime' a positive step towards combating such incidents, others will inevitably see it as an excessively aggressive response to conduct which is often only tangentially connected to identity-based animus (Jacobs & Potter 1998). For instance, Jacobs and Potter (1998) have argued that the classifying of offences that involve only a low level of prejudice (causal to the crime committed) as 'hate crimes' results in the state unfairly labelling and punishing swathes of offenders as 'hate offenders'. Ultimately, this allows the state to use its coercive powers to 'control' behaviours which infringe individuals' right to freedom of expression. We must therefore remain alive to the risks of automatically conflating victim perceptions of motivation with the 'actual' intention of the offender.[16] I have argued above and elsewhere why most 'demonstrations' of hatred should be pursued as hate crimes, even where

---

[16] A concern that the victim-centric definition of hate crime provided by ACPO may give rise to.

the criminalized conduct is not 'motivated' by prejudice (Walters 2013a). Essential to the classification of conduct as 'hate crime' is not whether the offender is motivated by hatred or bias, but whether he intends, or foresees that, his conduct will have the effect of subjugating the victim's identity. The enhanced culpability of the offender is based on his awareness that to vocalize hostility during the commission of an offence is wrongful and socially damaging, while the increased seriousness of the offence is additionally linked to the fact that such expressions are likely to cause immense harms both to the victim and to the community the victim identifies.

Such a broad interpretation of 'hate crime' does not mean, however, that any incident that is perceived by the victim or anyone else to be motivated by prejudice should be classified and punished as 'hate crime'. There will inevitably be cases where such a perception arises but where in actuality the offender was neither motivated by prejudice nor has he objectively demonstrated it. It seems unfair that the police label offenders as 'racist' or 'homophobic', for example, when in fact in some of these cases this may have been the result of a mistaken belief. If we pay regard to the stigma that labelling someone as racist or homophobic entails (see Burney & Rose 2002) such an approach to recording hate crimes/incidents may appear somewhat unjust. If hate crimes carry enhanced penalties it becomes essential that evidence of the offender's prejudice, or the demonstration of hostility towards the victim's identity, be proved beyond reasonable doubt before he or she is labelled and additionally punished as a 'hate offender' by the courts. In fact, a policy domain which favours overcriminalization may have unintended consequences, such as where vast numbers of offenders become stigmatized as 'haters'. For example, in relation to the stirring up of hatred offences, Kay Goodall reflects that '[society] will attach a tag of premeditated bigotry to convictions for something else. If the offenders are characterized as purveyors of extreme forms of racism, the message is lost. Those convicted should be stigmatized for their express acts of abuse, not for imagined acts of hatred' (2007: 102). With the potential negative effects that 'labelling' has on an offender's future behaviour (Becker 1963), it may be prudent of the courts to ensure that offenders are only labelled as such where there is unequivocal proof of racial, religious, homophobic, and/or disablist hostility.

Several academics have highlighted the potentially antagonistic effects that hate laws may have on offenders (and would-be offenders).

They argue that hate crime legislation may be perceived by some as simply amounting to another form of 'state protection' that provides minority groups with further preferential treatment over dominant members of society (Jacobs & Potter 1998: Whitlock 2001). The use of enhanced penalties for hate offenders acts only to reaffirm their sense of being victimized by a society that is increasingly pandering to the needs of the 'Other' (Hudson 1998; Whitlock 2001: 8). In turn, this gives rise to an even greater sense of grievance; one which emphasizes the ever expanding threat that minority groups pose to the social normativity of British or US society (see Perry 2001; Ray & Smith 2002).

While it is important for criminologists to remain watchful of the potentially invidious effects of over-policing of hate crime, the observed reality is that very few offenders accused of a hate offence are ever convicted or sentenced as 'hate offenders' (Burney & Rose 2002; Gadd 2009). For example, British Crime Survey (BCS) data published in 2012 estimated that there are 260,000 hate crimes committed each year covering the five recognized victim groups (race, religion, sexual orientation, disability, and transgender).[17] Data provided by ACPO in the same year showed that the police recorded a total of 44,519 hate offences. Out of this total, 15,561 cases were referred to the CPS resulting in 15,284 prosecutions. These prosecutions translated into 12,651 convictions; an 82.8 per cent successful conviction rate. However, when compared to the overall rate of hate crime as documented by the BCS, this conviction rate drops to 4.9 per cent.[18] For some victim groups the rate is even lower. For instance, out of the estimated 65,000 disablist hate

---

[17] Data include respondents from England and Wales only. Respondents were asked whether or not they perceived the incident to be motivated by their identity characteristic (Smith et al 2012). This is similar to the operational definition of hate crime but varies in that it does not ask whether victims perceived that the offence was motivated by 'hostility' or 'prejudice' towards their identity. This means that the data may be over-inclusive in the sense that someone may have believed that they had been selected because of their identity (eg disability) but not necessarily because of a hate motivation towards this characteristic. While potentially over-inclusive, the data may also be under-inclusive in that it only asks information about victims who are sixteen years and over, while the police record offences for all ages. As such, caution should be given to the comparison made here (see also Home Office et al 2013).

[18] Note the more narrow legal definition is used by the CPS when determining whether to pursue an offence in court as one aggravated by hostility. Hence, caution should again be given to the reliability of comparing these statistics.

crimes committed each year there were just 579 convictions for a disability-aggravated offence between 2011 and 2012. This equates to a 0.9 per cent conviction rate (see also, Gadd 2009: 757). In other words, fewer than one in a hundred offences aggravated by disability hostility result in a conviction (see further, Criminal Justice Joint Inspection 2013).[19]

The failure to prosecute and convict hate offenders is likely to be partially the result of, what in reality, is a highly complex task of proving prejudice-motivation, or a demonstration of hostility, beyond reasonable doubt (Hall 2010). This is especially the case where the offender is motivated by a multitude of factors (Burney & Rose 2002), or where the victim's perception of racism, for example, is in actuality erroneous. However, high attrition rates are also a product of the multifarious social contexts in which hate crimes frequently occur. As we will see in the chapters that follow, the common occurrence of 'low-level' incidents between individuals known to each other are often viewed as lacking in a level of seriousness that is required before the police will take any direct action against accused perpetrators. The earlier example involving Neighbour A and B illustrates the complex nature of many interpersonal conflicts which frequently give rise to accusations of hate crime/incidents. Such disputes are rarely resolved by the police charging one of the parties with a racially/religiously aggravated offence. This means that the majority of incidents involving racial/religious hostility, whether involving a high or low causal relationship to the offender's prejudice, fall outside the ambit of criminal punishment. The result is that despite the police's liberal victim-centred definition of 'hate crime/incidents', which has resulted in high levels of *recorded* incidents, prosecution/conviction rates remain comparatively low (Burney & Rose 2002; Gadd 2009).

While it is true that England and Wales record and prosecute more hate crime offenders than most other countries, it would seem that the concern that hate crime legislation will result in unfairly labelling and punishing swathes of offenders remains, to an extent, unfounded. Conversely, such a revelation gives rise to an even greater concern—that the vast majority of hate offenders are

---

[19] Other studies have provided similar evidence of the low attrition rates for hate crime. For example, Sam Dick's study into homophobic hate crimes reported that only 1 per cent of victims stated that a hate crime/incident resulted in conviction (2008: 25).

not being confronted, punished, or rehabilitated by the criminal justice system at all. In the comparatively small number of cases where an offender is convicted of a hate crime, he or she is unlikely to participate in any intervention, either in prison or via the probation service, which directly tackles the hate element of his or her offending behaviour (Gadd 2009). This means that the overwhelming majority of hate offenders' prejudice-motivated conduct and/or intentional displays of bigotry are never effectively challenged.

As a direct consequence, most victims of hate crime are left without a sense of having received 'justice'. In fact, the failure to offer victims a role in resolving their experiences of hate victimization may leave many feeling ignored and even sidelined by the authorities they first turned to (Dunn 2009). This in turn is likely to form yet another part of their process of victimization, and ultimately adds to their feeling of socio-cultural marginalization (see Chapters 4, 5, and 6). Without alternative or additional measures to tackle hate crime, hate offenders and their victims will continue to remain neglected by the state.

The conceptual complexities outlined in this chapter clearly give rise to a variety of issues that potentially impede the utility of the criminal law, and more broadly the criminal justice system, in tackling prejudice-motivated offending. That is not to underplay the importance of criminalizing hate. The arguments for legal proscription remain compelling for myriad reasons. In particular, the law remains an essential mechanism through which norms rejecting identity-based prejudices are supported and harmful behaviours are publicly challenged. The symbolic messages promoted by hate crime laws are further supported by the state resources that are allocated to tackling hate incidents, a direct result of the statutory provisions (see further the Introduction to this book). Nonetheless, while the law continues to play an important role in combating hate crime, it must not be relied upon as the state's sole response to addressing the problem. It has become clear within this chapter that, if the state is to effectively challenge the complex 'process of hate', additional and/or alternative interventions are required that directly target both the causes and consequences of hate crime.

Accordingly, the purpose of this book is to examine whether RJ practices, as both an alternative and addition to retributive justice, are equipped to take up the challenge of responding to hate crime. It is not within the scope of this chapter to explore the aims and objectives of restorative theory or practice—these will be introduced in the next chapter. It is, however, helpful at this point to summarize the conceptual and practical difficulties that restorative interventions *may* face:

1. How will legislative definitions of 'hate crime' impact upon the types of cases that will be dealt with restoratively? For instance, will restorative interventions be available for those cases where an offender has been convicted of a hate offence? Or can restorative practices be used as an alternative to prosecution?
2. Will a broad definition of 'hate crime', one which includes 'hate incidents', pose a similar threat of 'net-widening' and additional labelling within a restorative framework?
3. Are the concerns relating to unfairly enhancing the punishments of offenders, whose prejudice is only marginally causal to their offending behaviour, also relevant to reparation agreements signed during the restorative process?
4. Are restorative practices more amenable to responding to the different levels of prejudice and the varying causal relationships that prejudices have with the offending behaviour, compared with traditional policing methods and criminal prosecution?

The answers to these questions begin to become clearer in the next chapter where I examine in detail the theoretical aims of RJ and the empirical research that has evidenced its effects on victims' recovery from crime. The chapters that follow provide detailed analysis of: the types of harms offenders will be required to repair (Chapter 3); the types of hate crime/incidents that restorative practices currently deal with (Chapters 4 and 5); the role that victims and offenders play during restorative processes (Chapters 4 and 5); the undertakings that offenders agree to during restorative meetings (Chapters 4, 5, and 8); the healing qualities of RJ (Chapters 4, 5, and 6); the risks posed by RJ to victims (Chapter 7), and finally whether RJ can effectively challenge the varying degrees of prejudice which give rise to hate incidents (Chapter 8).

Conclusion

The conceptualization of hate crime is a perplexing task. The juxtaposition of legal and criminological definitions can at times muddy the waters of what, at first, appears to be a phenomenon that is easy to understand. The various types of prejudice that exist, combined with the levels of prejudice which can be demonstrated by perpetrators, means that finding a single definition that fits all is fraught with ambiguities. Proscribing offences as racially or religiously aggravated, for example, means that 'hostility' must be attached to the *mens rea* element of a criminal offence, something that the criminal law has previously resisted (Morsch 1991). Proving intention as well as hate-motivation (or a demonstration of hostility) beyond reasonable doubt can become a complex undertaking which many prosecutors will struggle to accomplish (Burney & Rose 2002).

Understanding the legal definitions given to hate crime provides us with an appreciation of the types of offences that restorative practitioners employed within and outside the criminal justice system, such as those working for youth offending panels or police services offering restorative interventions (see Chapters 4 and 5), are likely to encounter. The broader criminological conceptualization of hate crime is also important to the focus of this book. Understanding the difference between both 'serious' and 'low-level' hate incidents is vital to exploring whether restorative practices are equipped to tackle both the causes and consequences of different types of hate crime.

2
Conceptualizing Restorative Justice for Hate Crime

Introduction

The term restorative justice emerged in the latter part of the twentieth century as both a theory and practice of criminal justice (Barnett 1977; Christie 1977; Eglash 1977; Braithwaite 1989; Zehr 1990). Since then it has become one of the most debated areas of criminology within the Western world (Cunneen & Hoyle 2010). In general, advocates of RJ have argued that conventional methods of criminal justice fail to respond adequately to the needs of victims, offenders, and the communities they come from (Braithwaite 1989; Zehr 1990). Instead, the criminal justice system has tended to view crime as a violation against the state which, as representative of society, has punished offenders for wrongdoing. Victims and other affected community members remain on the periphery of justice, typically seen only as a source of evidence for criminal prosecution.

Restorative justice, on the other hand, proffers a more inclusive form of justice, seeing crime as interpersonal violations that are best resolved within the communities in which they occur (Christie 1977). Central to RJ practice is the reparation of harm caused by criminal or otherwise wrongful acts[1] (Zehr & Mika 1998: 52; Strang 2002). And, rather than punishing and stigmatizing perpetrators of crime, RJ is primarily concerned with the *engagement* of those affected by wrongdoing in a dialogic process which aims to achieve *reparation*—be it emotional, material, or to relationships.

It is outside the scope of this chapter to review the vast literature on RJ. Instead, in line with the book's central focus on repairing the

---

[1] Wrongful acts or 'wrongdoing' will be referred to as behaviour which causes harm but which will not always be criminalized. In Chapter 1 I referred to these as 'low-level' incidents which often involve anti-social behaviours which, when viewed in isolation, do not amount to a specific hate offence.

harms of hate crime, this chapter focuses on a reparative conception of RJ.[2] It begins by introducing the central tenets of RJ theory and outlining several modern justice practices that have incorporated its values. This part of the chapter reflects on the importance of victim participation in RJ as central to its reparative capabilities. Part II then explores the normative assumptions that are often made about the benefits of restorative processes and contrasts these with the empirical studies that have investigated the emotional healing effects of RJ. Part III moves on to an examination of some of the methodological limitations of the current body of research and to a discussion on what is meant by the RJ 'ideal'. It is here that I argue that the aims of RJ should not be confused with what restorative processes can realistically be expected to achieve within the complex societies we inhabit. Finally, in Part IV I summarize the key *theoretical* benefits and pitfalls of using RJ for hate crime.

Part I: What is Restorative Justice?

Restorative justice can take a variety of different forms (Braithwaite 1999).[3] This has led academics to conceptualize it in different ways. For some, it is simply a set of practices (the 'encounter conception', see Ashworth 2002: 578), while for others, RJ is conceived as an overarching theory of justice (Dzur 2003). A growing number of scholars have even considered RJ as a means of transforming the way that we live our lives; from criminal justice to social ordering (the 'transformative conception', see Sullivan & Tifft 2001). Divisions have also appeared within the extant literature as to: whether RJ is a type of process or an outcome (Marshall 1999; Daly 2002a); whether it incorporates retributive elements as well as restorative (Ashworth 2002; Daly 2002a); what practices should officially be labelled as 'RJ' (McCold 2000); whether RJ practices should focus on reducing reoffending or on repairing the harms of crime (Braithwaite 1989; Zehr 1990), and finally, whether RJ is a totally separate system of justice or a practice that can be incorporated into the current criminal justice system (Fattah 2004; Walgrave 2007). Such a broad range of views has meant that a single unifying

---

[2] Greater emphasis is given to RJ's reforming potential in Chapter 8.
[3] Victim–offender mediation, family group conferences, healing circles, restorative cautioning, amongst others.

definition of RJ remains elusive. Thus Theo Gavrielides (2007) reflects that the only consensus on the conception of RJ is that there exists no consensus as to its exact meaning.

To some extent, the failure of restorativists to form a common definition of RJ has meant that it has failed to gain political currency within most jurisdictions (Cunneen & Hoyle 2010). Nonetheless, while conceptual perplexities persist, several *values* of RJ are consistently articulated throughout the literature. Gerry Johnstone and Daniel Van Ness (2007a: 16), for example, state that regardless of whether RJ is deemed to be a practice, theory, or ideology, the same concepts of 'encounter', 'repair' and 'transformation' are embraced by most, if not all, restorativists. In this sense, it is perhaps best to view RJ not as a theory divided by opposing camps (Daly 2002a), but as a set of values, beliefs, processes, and outcomes, all of which continuously intersect.

The aims of restorative justice

Howard Zehr in his seminal book *Changing Lenses: A New Focus for Crime and Justice* argued that crime is a 'wound in human relationships' which requires convalescence (Zehr 1990: 181). Perpetrators of crime have 'obligations to restore and repair' the interpersonal harms that they cause. This is best achieved by bringing together the 'stakeholders' in the offence, typically the victim, offender, and other affected community members (Daly & Immarigeon 1998), who discuss the harms caused and the ways they might best be repaired (Zehr 1990; Considine 1995; Zehr & Mika 1998).

Vital to the restorative process is that all voices are heard with no stakeholder silenced by domination (Braithwaite 2003: 157). Ultimately, the objective is for the parties to find restoration through inclusive discussion followed by some form of restorative agreement (Zehr & Mika 1998). In most cases, this should entail the offender (or both 'parties' in community mediation meetings) putting right the wrongs committed. Restoration must not be imposed upon the stakeholders, but instead the parties must decide together how best the situation can be resolved (Marshall 1999). In most cases this will involve some form of active reparation such as making a verbal or written apology, rectifying damaged property, paying financial compensation, and/or giving assurances that the conduct will not be repeated.

This dialogic process typically begins by focusing on the offender's accountability for the crime or wrongdoing committed (Braithwaite 1989). He or she *should* have admitted to the offence before being asked to explain the motivations for offending.[4] John Braithwaite argues that part of the communication process within RJ is the shaming of the offender:

> Because shaming is a participatory form of social control, compared with formal sanctioning which is more professionalized than participatory, shaming builds consciences through citizens being instruments as well as targets of social control. Participation in expressions of abhorrence toward the criminal acts of others is part of what makes crime an abhorrent choice for us ourselves to make (1989: 80).

Social condemnation is conveyed, first and foremost, through active participation in a restorative intervention (Braithwaite & Braithwaite 2001). The very fact that the offender is asked to take part in a process that aims to repair harm means that he or she is more likely to appreciate the wrongfulness of his or her actions. Beyond this, the stakeholders of an offence, including the main parties' community supporters, help offenders to understand the hurt and suffering that has been endured by the victim. Gabrielle Maxwell and Allison Morris (2002) explain that such a process is likely to induce feelings of remorse which are the result of 'empathy or understanding the effects on victims' (Maxwell & Morris 2002: 280–1). Offenders who are confronted with the victim's pain will more often than not feel compassion for them (Harris et al 2004). They are like any other human being in that they will feel empathy for those who are suffering (see further Chapter 8). This provides greater scope for the offender to appreciate the immorality of his or her actions. In turn, offenders are likely to express contrition for the hurt they have caused and are therefore more willing to carry out some form of reparation for the victim (Harris et al 2004: 201).[5]

---

[4] Though as we will see in some restorative practices (such as community mediation) the offender may never fully admit to his or her crime, while in other cases both parties may be responsible for anti-social behaviour.

[5] The showing of remorse by the offender can often represent the turning point in offender–victim communication. In some cases this may be followed later by forgiveness by the victim and victim's family (Strang & Sherman 2003: 22; Harris et al 2004). Strang and Sherman (2003) argue that an apology can be central to the victim's healing and that for some victims to fully recover they will need to be able to forgive (Strang & Sherman 2003: 28).

The shaming process and/or empathic connections made during restorative meetings can additionally be a catalyst for attitudinal and behavioural transformation. The ultimate goal is for the offender to be reintegrated into the community where he or she is now less likely to reoffend (Braithwaite 1989). If this is possible, the benefit to the community as a whole is that the victim and offender are involved in reconciliation and a road to recovery is secured for all involved (Dzur & Olson 2004; see further analysis on empathy and attitudinal change in Chapter 8).

What practices are 'restorative'?

Johnstone and Van Ness (2007a: 7) state that for a justice process to be considered as credibly 'restorative' it must encompass a number of attributes. First, the process must be relatively *informal* and aim to involve the victim, offender(s), and others closely connected to them (or the crime) in a *discussion* about what happened, why it happened, what harms resulted from it, and what should be done to repair those harms. Second, emphasis must be given to *empowering* people who have been affected by the crime. Third, facilitators of any RJ practice must promote a response to the crime that focuses on *responsibility* and making *amends* rather than on labelling, punishing, and stigmatizing offenders. Fourth, decisions should be based on set values such as *equality*, *respect*, and *inclusion*, thereby resisting domination by any of the stakeholders. Fifth, there should be time devoted to *talking* about harms, the needs of victims, and what is required to help them recover from their experience of victimization. Finally, emphasis should be placed on strengthening *relationships* and resolving conflict (see also Zehr & Mika 1998 and Braithwaite 2003 for RJ 'signposts').

Legislators throughout the world have enacted new laws, both domestic and international, with the aim of integrating these values into various stages of the criminal justice process (see for example, EU Directive 2012/29/EU Establishing Minimum Standards on the Rights, Support and Protection of Victims of Crime, and UN Resolution 2002/12 on the Basic Principles on the Use of Restorative Justice Programmes in Criminal Matters). Some of the new interventions established within criminal justice systems have attempted to encompass *all* of the restorative principles outlined above, while others will incorporate just several of these values within their remit. Of some concern is that there are a growing number of justice practices that claim to be 'restorative' but which, in reality, fail to effectively incorporate RJ values—at least as they have been envisaged by restorative scholars (see, for example, Chapter 5). This chapter outlines some of the key practices that were researched as part of the empirical study for this book; there are, of course, many other restorative processes that have developed within various jurisdictions throughout the world (see McCold 2008 for an overview).

Victim–offender mediation

Perhaps the most commonly recognized restorative practice to have developed over the past forty years is victim–offender mediation (henceforth, VOM). Canada is often credited as the birthplace of VOMs (Raye & Roberts 2007: 212; McCold 2008: 26). The practice was first used in response to two teenage boys who had embarked on a spree of vandalism in Elmira, Ontario (Raye & Roberts 2007: 212). The probation officer in this case (Mark Yantzi), along with a volunteer and the judge, felt that the two offenders would benefit from meeting with their victims face to face in order to provide restitution (known as the 'Kitchener experiment') (McCold 2008: 26). This single case became a catalyst for the development of VOM programmes throughout Canada, with similar initiatives quickly spreading throughout the US and the UK (Liebmann 2000).[6]

Most VOMs are run using a single mediator who acts as an impartial facilitator of direct dialogue between the parties. However, some mediators run indirect meetings between the parties (known as shuttle mediation), whereby the facilitator meets with each of the parties separately before relaying information back and forth between them. The primary aim of VOM meetings is to provide an opportunity for offenders to take direct responsibility for their actions and to repair the harms they have caused directly to the victim. This interactive approach to conflict simultaneously allows victims and offenders to discuss the causes and consequences of an offence while also finding a solution to the conflict that is satisfactory to the parties.

Facilitators of VOM typically start by asking the perpetrator to explain his or her actions. All parties are then encouraged to talk

---

[6] The first UK-based VOM programme was established in Coventry and Leeds in 1985.

about how the incident/s has affected their lives. The aim of such meetings is for the wrongdoing to be discussed in a calm and empathic environment. Mediation meetings will often end with some form of agreement between the stakeholders, outlining how the offender will repair any hurt caused (known as a reparation agreement or mediation agreement; Johnstone & Van Ness 2007a). As VOM programmes have developed, other parties have been invited into meetings, including family members and other community representatives. Meetings are also sometimes run with more than one mediator (McCold 2008). This more inclusive approach to mediation has meant that some VOM programmes have become almost indistinguishable from their more recently developed cousins, the Family Group Conference (FGC).

Family Group Conferences

Arguably, the first practice to incorporate fully the key RJ principles outlined above was the FGC. The Children, Young Persons and Their Families Act 1989 (New Zealand) is heralded as the first statute in the English-speaking world to establish FGCs as an integrated part of the criminal justice system (Maxwell & Morris 1993, 2006). The aim of the Act was to respond more effectively to the needs of victims and to provide better support for families and their children (Maxwell & Morris 1993, 2006). Maxwell and Morris assert that FGCs were established as a way of integrating indigenous and Western approaches to justice. They note that Maori custom and law was based on the idea that responsibility for wrongdoing was collective. Redress was due not just to the victim, but to the victim's family as well (*tikanga o nga hara*). Responsibility was also collective, based on an individual's actions and the relationship that existed between his/her conduct and his/her social and family environment. The imbalance between the offender's and victim's family had to be restored and so meetings between families (*Whanau*) were held in order to put right the wrongs which had occurred (Maxwell & Morris 2006). The 1989 Act aimed to bring key components of *Whanau* meetings together with Western justice processes. In so doing, it required young offenders who were charged with an indictable offence to participate in a conference with their immediate and extended family whereby the parties collectively would explore ways in which the offender could repair the harms caused. The Act also created a new

Youth Justice Court where all serious offences committed by juveniles (except for homicide) were dealt with via FGCs (Maxwell and Morris 1993).

Since their inception in New Zealand, FGCs have become a commonly used practice within justice systems throughout the world, (both for young and adult offenders), being particularly popular in Australia, Canada, the US, and the UK (see Raye & Roberts 2007). Though models vary to some extent, conferences typically involve a face-to-face meeting between the victim, offender, and their family members in a safe environment to discuss the incident, the harms it has caused, and how these should be repaired (Zehr & Mika 1998). Some conferences will also engage state agency workers such as police officers, social workers, and/or housing officers. The purpose of this more inclusive approach to restorative dialogue is that the participants can decide *together* how to resolve the problems caused by the offence.[7]

Community Restorative Boards

Community Restorative Boards, also known as Community Justice Committees in Canada and Youth Offender Panels in the UK, comprise a mix of both community volunteers and professional justice practitioners who conduct meetings with offenders, victims, and their family supporters. Panels often run within the criminal justice system and make up part of an offender's sentence. For instance, within the UK, the Youth Justice and Criminal Evidence Act 1999 established the 'Referral Order', a mandatory sentence imposed on young offenders (ten to seventeen-year-olds) pleading guilty to an imprisonable offence.[8] Orders are administered by Youth Offender Panels (YOPs) and managed by Youth Offending Teams (YOTs). Panels consist of two trained volunteers who are advised by a YOT member. Victims are often invited to take part in panel discussions and may bring along parents or other family members for support; however the offender and his or her guardian must attend. The young offender is then asked to sign an agreement, a legally binding

---

[7] FGCs have been described as 'fully restorative' (as opposed to other 'partly restorative' processes) as they include all the recognized elements of RJ practice (described above) (McCold 2000).

[8] Unless the crime is serious enough to justify a custodial sentence or unless the court orders an absolute discharge.

document, which summarizes the outcome of the panel. There are two core elements that each contract should contain:

a. reparation to the victim and/or the wider community, and
b. a programme of interventions, delivered or organized by the YOT, which addresses the factors likely to be associated with any reoffending. (Ministry of Justice 2012).

Although referral orders are intended to be a type of 'restorative justice', there have been some concerns about whether the orders have fully utilized its principles in practice. For example, some academics have pointed out that victims rarely attend panel meetings, while those who do attend have often done so with little to no preparation (see, eg, Newburn et al 2002). However, as we will see in Chapter 8, Panels frequently set up additional RJ meetings (such as family group conferences), which are facilitated by a separate restorative practitioner, in order to ensure that victims are given a greater say in the justice process (see Case Study 2, Chapter 8).[9]

Restorative policing

The implementation of RJ within the criminal justice system has not just been through legislative means. The FGC model has also found its way into community-based policing initiatives within various countries. The first of such initiatives was developed in 1991 in Wagga Wagga, New South Wales, Australia, by Terry O'Connell (Hoyle 2007). Police conferencing was seen as an expedient way of dealing with low-level offending by extending the commonly used, but rarely effective, police caution. The Wagga Wagga model of conferencing was widely supported by the community and front-line police officers and soon gained international acclaim (Moore & O'Connell 1994). In fact, the success of the model was such that new restorative policing initiatives replicating

---

[9] For example, a letter of apology, manual work done for the victims, or compensation. The government has also introduced several other restorative measures under the Criminal Justice Act 2003. Section 22 of the Act introduces the conditional caution allowing police officers to impose conditions to a caution 'ensuring that...[the offender aged over 18] makes reparation for the offence' (s 22(3)(b)). Section 142 of the Act consolidates the use of RJ within the criminal justice system by introducing a new purpose of sentencing at subsection (e) which states 'the making of reparation by offenders to persons affected by their offences'.

it spread throughout North America and the UK during the 1990s (see McCold & Wachtel 1998).

Terry O'Connell brought police-led restorative conferencing to the UK in 1994 and after some 'ad hoc experimentation', the Thames Valley Police Service, under the leadership of Chief Constable Charles Pollard, established a restorative justice cautioning scheme based on the Wagga Wagga model in 1998 (Hoyle 2007: 293; see analysis of the scheme by Hoyle et al 2002). The model was based on structured dialogue that used a script with an 'ordered set of explanatory statements, questions and prompts' (Hoyle 2002: 101). Victims and offenders would directly discuss the ways in which the offender might help to put right the harm he or she had caused. Unlike agreements made at YOPs, restorative cautions did not provide means through which victims could get redress if acts of reparation were not carried out.

Nevertheless, the development of restorative cautions has proved popular and similar schemes have proliferated across the UK as police services find new ways of disposing of minor offences, often in cases where prosecution is not deemed viable (Hoyle 2002; CJJI 2012; see Chapter 5).[10] Research by ACPO in 2010 found that thirty-three out of the forty-three police forces in England now use some form of RJ (cited in CJJI 2012). Restorative interventions are now used at three levels by the police in the UK. Level One involves the use of street-level RJ, which entails police officers and police community support officers using RJ as a way of addressing 'low-level' crime and anti-social behaviour without resorting to more punitive measures. Level Two involves police officers facilitating RJ conferencing (such as the Thames Valley Scheme). Finally, Level Three is used post sentence and involves the offender meeting with the victim in addition to the sentence/penalty he or she has already received. It is outside the scope of this chapter to critically examine the suitability of police forces to administer and/or facilitate restorative interventions. Some of the implications that police-led RJ may have for the restorative goal of restoration are explored further in Chapter 5.

[10] During 2008–09 a Youth Restorative Disposal was piloted in eight police forces across the country as a means of disposing of minor 'low-level' offences and anti-social behaviour. The scheme proved popular but is yet to be rolled out nationwide. Other restorative work continues to be undertaken by probation services under the auspices of Victim Liaison Officers, though due to government cutbacks this work has recently been restricted.

Community mediation

Just twenty-five years have passed since RJ first found a legislative footing within criminal justice (fifteen years in the UK). Before then, restorative approaches had already developed within the 'third sector', most prominently through charity-based community mediation centres. Hundreds of mediation services opened their doors during the 1970s and 1980s in Australia, Canada, Europe, the US, and the UK in order to resolve interpersonal conflicts within local communities (for a short history of their development see McCold 2008: 24–5).[11] These bodies established restorative-based processes long before theoretical work on RJ had begun (Barnett 1977; Christie 1977). Mediation centres continue today, working alongside conventional justice processes either as an alternative to traditional methods of crime control or in addition to them (Gavrielides 2007).[12]

Community mediation, like VOM, uses both direct and indirect meetings between the stakeholders of a crime or those embroiled in anti-social behaviour in order to repair damaged relationships. At the heart of community mediation are the notions of 'encounter', 'repair' and 'transformation' (Johnstone & Van Ness 2007a). In conflicts where one party has been accused of a crime the aims will be: to explore what has happened and why; to consider how the alleged incidents have affected participants' lives; to enquire into issues around causation; and finally to find a resolution that is acceptable to all or most. Mediation meetings typically end with a written agreement outlining the undertakings that both parties have agreed to.[13] This may include an apology,[14] but in most cases it will include a promise to cease certain activities and to avoid combative communication if similarly provoked in the future.

---

[11] More recently, restorative approaches have been utilized in schools as a means of resolving cases of bullying and other student disputes (Morrison 2007).

[12] Such organizations became central to the empirical endeavour of this book, see Chapter 6.

[13] These agreements are not legally binding but can in some cases have implications for participants who break the agreement. For example, where housing officers are party to a mediation meeting, breach of the agreement may also result in breach of the participant's tenancy agreement (see Chapter 6).

[14] It should be noted that, while community mediation rarely results in direct apologies or material reparation, participants frequently make physical gestures, such as shaking hands and facial expressions, such as smiling, during meetings, which are indicative of apologetic gesturing (see Chapter 5).

While this type of mediation is largely based on restorative values, it lacks certain attributes which have prevented some restorativists from labelling it as 'fully restorative' (McCold 2000). Primarily, 'the parties' involved in community mediation do not participate with the pre-existing labels of 'offender' and 'victim'. Instead, participants will commonly be referred to mediation services by other organizations, such as the police and/or local housing authorities who have made previous attempts at resolving accusations and counterclaims of crime or anti-social behaviour (see Chapter 4). This means that stakeholders will remain as 'complainants' and 'accused perpetrators', rather than victims and convicted wrongdoers and, as such, perpetrators of harm may lack a willingness to take *direct* responsibility for their wrongdoing and/or provide reparation to the other party.

Nonetheless, as we will see in the chapters that follow, the non-stigmatizing process found in community mediation does not prevent the parties from taking responsibility and/or making reparations for their actions. In fact, in many cases it is the non-labelling of parties that gives mediation its greatest potency (see Chapter 4), allowing meetings to explore both context and culpability before finding resolution and reparation for the harms that have been inflicted by *both* sides (see Chapters 4, 5, and book Conclusion).

The importance of victim participation

This chapter has already begun to highlight how harm reparation is contingent on victims participating in RJ practices (Strang & Sherman 2003). Of some concern, then, is that several studies in the UK and elsewhere have found that victims are frequently absent from direct RJ meetings (Hoyle et al 2002; Newburn et al 2002; Crawford & Newburn 2003; Sherman & Strang 2007[15]). Victims' reluctance to participate has been attributed, at least in part, to feelings of anger and fear held towards the offender (Sherman & Strang 2007: 62). Concerns about confronting offenders and the potential for repeat victimization can also hold victims back (Hoyle 2002: 105; Green 2007: 180).

---

[15] For example, Hoyle et al (2002) found that only 14 per cent of victims were present at a restorative cautioning scheme. Crawford and Newburn found that only 13 per cent of victims attended referral panels.

Other studies, however, have found much higher rates of participation, for example Heather Strang et al's (2006: 288) study in Canberra (RISE)[16] reported victim attendance rates of up to 90 per cent; the authors suggesting that this may be due to Canberra being a 'well-bonded city' with a strong sense of 'civic duty' (Strang et al 2006: 288; see also Wundersitz and Hetzel 1996; Strang 2002). It is also likely to be a result of the way in which victims were asked to attend conferences. Instead of inviting victims to consider whether they wanted to participate, they were simply asked 'when' would be a good time to attend (Strang et al 2006), inferring that the meeting was not something they might wish to consider but rather something they *should* be present at.[17] More recently, Peter Merry, ACPO lead on Youth Restorative Justice in Norfolk, England, reported local victim attendance rates of 84 per cent in RJ conferences held by the police (Merry 2009). Merry asserted that such high attendance rates were the result of effective dissemination of information to victims about the purpose of RJ and expectations about what might be achieved. Two teams worked on providing RJ meetings. The first team prepared cases by contacting victims and providing them with information about the process, while the second team facilitated meetings. By working together in this way, Merry explained that participation rates could be dramatically increased.

There will continue to be limitations to harm reparation if victim participation remains low. This is inevitably connected to the dissemination of information about RJ which, in turn, is linked to organizational constraints, including limited resources (Maxwell & Morris 1993; Crawford & Newburn 2003: 187). James Dignan (2005) notes that RJ programmes that run outside or on the margins of the criminal justice system will continue to experience developmental problems, including difficulties attracting referrals and tensions between programme managers and mainstream criminal justice agencies. In the longer term, increasing public knowledge about RJ processes may help to improve victims' willingness to participate. The continued proliferation of RJ practices within criminal justice systems will also increase the acceptance of it as a legitimate form of justice by other professional agencies. Indeed, unless RJ practices become embedded within both youth and adult

---

[16] The Reintegrative Shaming Experiment in Canberra.
[17] This, of course, has implications for the notion of 'informed consent'.

criminal justice, the public will continue to focus their expectations of 'justice' on retributive penalties.[18]

Indirect participation

While the involvement of victims and offenders in face-to-face meetings can prove highly beneficial to both parties, the failure of victims to take part in such meetings should not equate to their not having participated in RJ. Rather, victim participation refers to active involvement at some point during the restorative process (Hoyle 2002). This approach to RJ will, of course, lack much of the emotional empathy gained from face-to-face communication, it being more difficult for offenders to appreciate the hurt they cause without observing, first-hand, the pain that the victim has suffered (Hoyle 2002). However, this does not mean that shuttle mediation will fail to provide restoration to victims (Hoyle 2002; Hoyle et al 2002; Shapland et al 2006: 64). As we will see in Chapter 4, victims can still gain many therapeutic benefits by engaging with restorative practices indirectly (see Part II). Separate meetings with mediators still provide victims with the opportunity to express how the crime affected them. This will allow victims to feel that they are taking an active role in the justice/conflict resolution process. Information about why the wrongdoing was committed and whether the perpetrator feels contrition can also be conveyed through letters or by facilitators (Hoyle 2002). Hence, a key component of the reparative conception of RJ is not necessarily face-to-face communication between offender and victim (though this can often enhance the process), but rather the engagement of victims in a process that provides them with a voice and an opportunity to obtain restitution.

Part II: Repairing Harms? Normative Assumptions and Empirical Findings

Conventional justice processes are often criticized for exacerbating victims' emotional turmoil, such as where the police, prosecutors, and defence lawyers interrogate victims and question their version

---

[18] The Ministry of Justice's Restorative Justice Action Plan for the Criminal Justice System (2012) sets out the government's commitment to rolling out RJ at all stages of the criminal justice system.

of events (a form of 'secondary victimization') (Zehr 1990; Strang & Sherman 2003; see Chapter 6). Advocates of RJ assert that restorative practices avoid this more formalistic process of justice, and instead attempt to aid victim healing in a variety of different ways (Considine 1995; Zehr & Mika 1998). Gwen Robinson and Joanna Shapland (2008) note, however, that many RJ advocates have been keen to distance themselves from notions of therapeutic treatment because of scepticism as to whether the criminal justice system should, or is capable of, providing such a service (Robinson & Shapland 2008: 339). Yet while studies into the crime reduction capabilities of RJ remain largely inconclusive, a growing body of research has begun to provide persuasive evidence as to its healing qualities. Many of these studies have used quasi-experimental methods, comparing the satisfaction outcomes among participants in RJ meetings with a sample of those who have attended court proceedings (see, for example, Strang 2002). Those studies which have examined conferences have, in particular, used rigorous long-term research methods of observations, interviews, and self-administered questionnaires (see, for example, Daly 2001). The statistical analysis of resulting data has enabled researchers to identify a number of process-related factors relevant to harm reparation.

Levels of satisfaction and procedural fairness?: the importance of having a voice

Lawrence Sherman and Heather Strang's review of the international body of RJ research states that studies 'almost always indicate a high level of satisfaction with the process' (2007: 62: see also Braithwaite 1999; Latimer et al 2005). These studies often highlight the dissemination of 'information' and the provision of inclusive 'participation' as two key components that are fundamental to victim contentment (Strang and Sherman 2003; see further Miers et al 2001: 33). By providing victims with authentic information about the offender(s) and his or her reasons for committing the offence, victims often gain a greater sense of satisfaction with the justice process. Importantly, research has shown that those who attend FGCs are provided with information about their case in good time at a much higher rate than those who attend court (see, for example, Strang 2002: 119). However, information must outline what the participants can expect from the *procedure* of RJ rather than what they will get as an *outcome*. Provided stakeholders are not given false expectations as to what they will gain from the process, participants may gain a sense of self-worth simply by taking part (Strang 2002; Van Camp & Wemmers 2013).

The inclusion of victims in the justice (or conflict resolution) process also acknowledges the impact that the incident has had on them. Research has found that the majority of victims are given the opportunity to express their feelings about how the crime affected them which, in turn, provides them with a sense of empowerment and control over the resolution of their case (see McCold & Wachtel 1998: 55; Miers et al 2001: 31; Triggs 2005: 5.7; Shapland et al 2007: 24).[19]

Both information and inclusivity are additionally linked to victims' perceptions of 'procedural fairness' within the justice process. Tinneke Van Camp and Jo-Anne Wemmers found that perceptions of procedural fairness are largely based on whether participants experience trust, respect, and neutrality and are given a voice (2012: 124). It is therefore essential that stakeholders within RJ programmes have an opportunity to engage in dialogue about their victimization, during which they can trust the facilitator to act objectively and impartially. The role of facilitators becomes pivotal in ensuring that victims and offenders feel safe in meetings and are provided with an opportunity to communicate with each other. Studies which have asked questions about the facilitator's role in RJ indicate that most participants feel that facilitators are in control of meetings (see for example, Shapland et al 2007: 26). Victims are more likely to go on to experience genuine healing where each component part of the restorative process is perceived to be fair (Van Camp & Wemmers 2013).

Overall, the consistently high levels of satisfaction reported in most RJ studies show that victims find restorative practices to be a largely positive experience. Victim satisfaction reflects the experience a victim has of RJ as a whole. If victims are satisfied with the RJ process, more often than not, this is *one* indication that the process is effective at responding to victims' needs. Nevertheless, satisfaction and procedural fairness cannot, themselves, be used as a benchmark for assessing the effectiveness of RJ (Braithwaite 1999; Green 2007). For instance, satisfaction levels do not tell us, conclusively, whether RJ actually repaired the harms of crime, or indeed

---

[19] Though it should be noted that Maxwell et al's (2004) study found that only about half of victims felt that they were involved in the decision-making process.

whether it reduced reoffending rates. Thus, there are several other processes within RJ which must be examined in order to more thoroughly assess its healing capabilities.

Material reparation

In cases of material loss, such as property damage or theft, reparation agreements made at the end of restorative meetings often include some form of material restitution (such as financial compensation and/or an order to return property) (Sharpe 2007). This type of reparation can also take the form of reparative work such as mending a damaged fence or painting over graffiti. Such acts help to restore those material possessions taken or damaged during an offence and, in this sense, can help to return victims to a position (at least materially) to that prior to the incident.

Material reparation can also help with emotional healing (Strang 2002). The fact that the offender is working to repair the damage in itself suggests that he or she is taking responsibility for his or her actions. This demonstration of responsibility indicates that the offender is accountable for his or her actions, which can potentially help to free victims from feelings of self-blame. The act of 'repairing' creates a new message to the community that the offender's actions were wrong and that the victim has suffered. In some cases, this can give victims a renewed sense of 'righteousness' (Strang 2002).

'Storytelling'

One of the most effective ways of aiding victim recovery is to give individuals a voice. Fundamental to all types of restorative dialogue is that victims have a platform from which they can articulate their experiences of victimization and, importantly, where others listen to them (Zehr 1990; Morris & Young 2000). Kay Pranis describes this process as 'storytelling', she notes:

> Storytelling is fundamental for healthy social relationships. To feel connected and respected we need to tell our own stories and have others listen. For others to feel respected and connected to us, they need to tell their stories and have us listen. Having others listen to your story is a function of power in our culture. The more power you have, the more people will listen respectfully to your story. Consequently, listening to someone's story is a way of empowering them, of validating their intrinsic worth as a human being (2001: 7).

By describing the impacts of the offence, victims are able to create their own personal narrative. Judith Kay believes that it is this aspect of the dialogical process that is the 'heart and soul of restorative justice' (2008: 231). Narratives help victims to create and recreate their own identity. It is through this process that victims can be rescued from the shadows of 'silence, isolation and despair' as they move forward into a place of greater security (Kay 2008: 231). Stories therefore help to reinvigorate victims, allowing them to form new connections with those who listen to them. In fact, most victims who vocalize their experience of pain, in a safe and secure environment, will gain a cathartic release from doing so. Simultaneously, victims will feel more supported by those who are interested in hearing their story (Kay 2008; see also 'The role of mediators in supporting parties', Chapter 4).

Lawrence Sherman et al (2005) have used research into cognitive behavioural therapy (CBT) to explain how victims' recovery can be aided by vocalizing their experiences of victimization. They state that victims who discuss their previous traumas in a secure and safe environment can undergo a process of what is called 'deconditioning'. This relates to 'conditioning theory', which explains the ways in which fear is acquired and later relinquished. It is argued that feelings of fear can be extinguished by deconditioning memories of the trauma through associating them with safe settings, such as an RJ conference. The process involves victims being exposed to 'prolonged periods of anxiety provoking stimuli' (Sherman et al 2005: 369) which in turn help to decondition their cognitive attachments to fear. This is best achieved where victims confront their fears and relive their experiences by meeting with the people involved in the traumatic events. The memories and feelings associated with the events begin to change as victims confront their trauma and challenge their fears. Restorative justice, as a means of 'deconditioning', therefore allows victims to take back the power they lose through victimization; a process less likely to occur through conventional practices where the state has traditionally denied victims an active role in the resolution of their case (Christie 1977; Zehr 1990).

Understanding why: the power of empathy

Restorative dialogue provides additional opportunities for victims to ask offenders why they committed the crime (Sherman et al 2005) and for the offender to recognize the consequences of their actions (Van Camp & Wemmers 2013). This time it is the offender's story that can help victims' emotional wellbeing. In some cases, victims will come to realize that they were not to blame for their own victimization, providing them with further means through which they can address issues of self-blame (Sherman et al 2005: 369; Van Camp & Wemmers 2013).[20] The offender's own story can, in some cases, act to bridge the emotional gap between the parties as the victim comes to appreciate the motives of the offender, as well as the socio-economic and personal background factors relevant to his or her offending behaviour (see Chapters 4 and 8).

Restorative justice meetings can also provide opportunities for victims to ask offenders questions without the fear of violent retaliation, a prospect that will be of particular importance to victims of hate crime—though facilitators cannot *guarantee* that victims will not be abused in some way by participants (see Chapters 3 and 7). Victims do, however, frequently obtain assurances that the offence will not happen again; ultimately reducing their fears of repeat victimization (Sherman et al 2005: 369: see Chapter 4). It is through such inclusive dialogue that both victim and offender can begin to empathize with each other, breaking down stereotypes and paving the way for the rebuilding of individual and community relationships (Zehr 1990; Maxwell & Morris 2002; Harris et al 2004).

Empirical research has shed positive light on the empathic aspect of RJ. Joanna Shapland et al's (2007: 37) study reported that conferencing provided 69 per cent of victims with an understanding of why the offence was committed against them. Similarly, Paul McCold and Ted Wachtel (1998) found that 62 per cent of victims agreed that they now had a better understanding of why the offence was committed. In line with these findings, Carolyn Hoyle et al (2002: 36) showed that victims often felt differently about their offenders post conference, suggesting that their experience of RJ had helped to overcome the stereotypes that had previously divided them (see further McCold and Wachtel 1998: 56; Miers et al 2001: 34; Umbreit et al 2001: 18; Shapland et al 2006: 63).

---

[20] As we will see, this aspect of RJ is complicated in hate crime cases where the victim will be aware that they have been targeted because of who they are (Chapter 3).

Receiving apologies

Research has shown that offenders often display remorse and contrition in direct response to victims' stories (Harris et al 2004). This is typically expressed via a verbal or written apology from the offender; though other physical gestures such as a handshake, smiling, and changes in body language can also display the offender's regret for wrongdoing (see Chapter 4). Physical gestures can be crucial to a victim's sense of the offender's genuineness. A positive change in body language may be indicative of the offender's contrition. A genuine apology suggests that the offender is truly sorry for what he or she has done (Strang 2002: 56; Sherman et al 2005: 388). This allows for the emergence of a new relationship based on acceptance. In turn, a sincerely expressed apology provides victims with an opportunity to relinquish their attachment to feelings of resentment and frustration, allowing them to move on with their lives more peacefully (Strang et al 2006). This is perhaps why many studies have shown that victims find 'closure'—an under-researched concept but generally taken as meaning that victims experience emotional healing—enabling them to put the incident behind them before moving on with their lives (Hoyle et al 2002; Maxwell et al 2004; Shapland et al 2007).

The offender's sincerity is of central importance to a victim's ability to move beyond their experience of crime (Strang et al 2006: 286). Apologies which are viewed as disingenuous are likely to adversely affect the victim's sense of being wronged (Daly 2001; Hoyle et al 2002: 35). In such cases, the victim will be angry that the offender has not taken seriously the wrongs committed or, worse, they may view the apology as a means through which the offender can manipulate the process in order to receive a lesser punishment (Daly 2001). If the process fails to elicit a genuine reaction of contrition it risks exacerbating, rather than repairing, interpersonal wounds (see Chapter 5).[21]

---

[21] The offering of a genuine apology may lead to victims offering forgiveness. Forgiveness is not a goal of RJ, however it can provide therapeutic benefits for victims (Strang et al 2006; see also Holter et al 2007). In particular, it has been shown that forgiveness can reduce feelings of anger and resentment and lead to later reductions in anxiety and depression as victims release negative thoughts associated with the crime (Holter et al 2007: 313; see further Enright & North 1998).

Reducing emotional traumas: fear, anger, and insecurity

In Chapter 3 I explore the deleterious effects that hate crimes have on victims. These incidents often cause immense emotional traumas, heightening victims' feelings of fear, anxiety, anger, and insecurity. Such traumas frequently prevent individuals from moving freely within their local community. Reducing emotional traumas is therefore a central part of restoring the harms of hate crime through RJ. While there are few studies which have looked at the harm-repairing capabilities of RJ for hate crime (see Part IV), there are numerous studies which have attempted to measure levels of fear amongst victims (in general) before and after RJ meetings. Strang et al's (2006) study, which covered four different locations comprising Canberra (RISE), London, Northumbria, and the Thames Valley, reported that in all four studies victims' levels of fear were substantially reduced after conferencing. In particular, within the London study—which included victims of violence—the level of fear experienced by victims dropped from 30 per cent before conference to 0 per cent after (Strang et al 2006: 293). Strang's (2002: 98) earlier study similarly found that, while 38 per cent of victims of violent offences were afraid of their offender before conference, this reduced to just 14 per cent after (20 per cent to 9 per cent respectively in property offence cases). Moreover, only 2 per cent of victims of violent offences anticipated that the offender would repeat the offence against them after the conference, compared to 18 per cent who went to court (reductions in feelings of fear after RJ are also reported by: Umbreit & Coates 1993: 574; Sherman et al 2000; Umbreit et al 2000: 224; Daly 2001: 78; Hoyle et al 2002). Such findings suggest that RJ practices consistently help to reduce levels of fear and therefore help to free victims from its oppressive effects. As we will see, this will be of particular importance to those who are targeted for being 'different' (see Chapters 3, 4, and 5).

Feelings of fear are often associated with those of anger as victims become frustrated and resentful towards their offender. Anger is a dangerous emotion and is a key factor in violent retaliations between identity groups (see Chapter 3). As with findings on fear, research has also suggested that reductions in anger can be achieved through RJ meetings. For example, Strang et al's (2006: 295) study reported that while 87 per cent of victims felt anger towards their young offenders before a conference, this dropped to just 17 per cent after.

Results from the RISE study also showed that conferencing led to a decrease in levels of anger from 63 per cent before to only 29 per cent after (Sherman et al 2000).

Compounding victims' feelings of fear and anger will be the heightened levels of insecurity that they feel about their personal safety within the community. If victims are to regain confidence in others they must feel safe when going about their daily routines. Research findings have shown that a substantial proportion of victims who lose their sense of security regain this after RJ, especially in cases involving violence (Sherman et al 2000; Hoyle 2002; Strang 2002). A lack of personal safety will be especially evident in cases involving hate, as victims live with the constant fear of being retargeted (Herek et al 1997). Thus increasing individuals' sense of security will be imperative to the healing process of victims of hate crime.

Of course, a *full* experience of the type of healing which RJ *might* offer is only obtainable if each stage of the RJ process is successfully completed. In many cases victims will only complete part of this cycle and in a small minority of instances victims will inevitably come away from RJ meetings feeling worse (Maxwell & Morris 1993: 120; Strang 2002: 56). Nonetheless, it is clear that the growing body of research now strongly suggests that RJ practices provide both material and emotional reparation to a greater percentage of victims when compared to those whose cases go to court.

Part III: The Limits of Restorative Justice: Methodological Issues

The vast majority of research studies reviewed for this chapter used rigorous research designs, incorporating a variety of quantitative and qualitative methods that compared RJ with conventional justice processes such as court. It is fair to surmise that the findings from these studies provide persuasive evidence that restorative practices frequently *help* to repair the harms of crime. Nevertheless, the extant research into the reparative effects of RJ, while cogent, is not yet conclusive. There are some limitations relating to methodology which must be noted. First, some studies (especially those examining VOMs) have not included control groups, the most reliable of which should involve random allocation of participants to either mediation or court (or other non RJ disposals).

Other VOM studies have made comparisons with participants who are assigned to mediation but fail to attend. The benefit of using a control group is that results from the study can be compared and contrasted, giving weight to differences in outcomes between the groups. Dignan (2005) notes that findings from studies that use mediation participants only may be skewed as they represent outcomes from RJ practices where the stakeholders are enthusiastic about participating compared with those who are not (see also Latimer et al 2005). Furthermore, studies which fail to make observations of RJ meetings and rely simply on interviews or questionnaires may miss 'process variables', such as whether the victim received a genuine apology, which relate to process outcomes (Dignan 2005). In this respect, researchers may miss important data that help to explain how RJ impacts participants.

Such methodological limitations, however, do not negate the value of interviews and questionnaires. Studies which use such qualitative techniques provide vital information about participants' perceptions of, and opinions about, RJ practices. This book adds to the growing body of qualitative research on the use of RJ by providing detailed analyses of hate victims' experiences of different types of restorative interventions. While my findings, and those of others, are not directly comparable to conventional justice processes, much insight can be gained into victims' experiences of the practices currently on offer. Such data show us *how* and *why* restorative processes work,[22] rather than merely showing that they do work. Moreover, it can also be asserted that exploring the value of a process does not necessarily require its direct comparison with an alternative process in order to evidence its utility or validity as an effective justice intervention (Wilcox et al 2005). Rather, what is of greatest importance is that empirical studies are rigorously administered by researchers who fully consider the limitations of the data (Wilcox et al 2005).

The restorative justice 'ideal'?

Despite various studies suggesting that RJ can aid victim recovery, Kathy Daly (2002a, 2002b) argues that we must remain cautious about the reparative benefits of its practices. She argues persuasively that there is a gap between the 'ideals' of RJ and that which

---

[22] And in some cases why they do not work.

can be achieved in practice. Referring to research findings from the South Australia Juvenile Justice Research project (SAJJ), Daly (2001, 2002b) notes that a significant proportion of participants do not obtain 'full reparation'. This is partly because victims experience crime differently; some are only mildly affected by feelings of insecurity and fear while others experience more severe emotional turmoil (Daly 2008). There are also varying degrees of distress relating to gender, type of offence, and relationship to offender (Daly 2008). Daly argues that those victims who are more distressed by the crime are less likely to embrace RJ values and more likely to remain angry and fearful of the offender (Daly 2008). For example, within her 2001 study, 43 per cent of high distress victims still had a negative attitude towards the offender after conference. She also notes that '*just* 38 per cent' (emphasis added) of victims said that the offender's story had an effect on them and '*just* 53 per cent' (emphasis added) said that they had a better understanding of why the offence was committed (Daly 2001: 77). Daly (2002a: 13) therefore expresses caution about RJ, explaining that 'a prudent interpretation of [victims']...responses would be that while conferences do assist victim recovery, victims also rely on personal resources and support from others'. The 'nirvana story' of RJ is an 'ideal' that simply assumes people are ready to empathize, apologize, and forgive and move amicably on with their lives (Daly 2002a). These are things that should happen 'most of the time' yet SAJJ research shows that this happens only 'some of the time' (Daly 2002a: 18).

Such expressions of concern encourage us to pause and reflect on the aims and objectives of RJ. This cautious approach is helpful in that it reminds restorativists that RJ will rarely be the panacea that some might have originally hoped for or advocated. Equally, however, Daly's note of caution must not be used to disparage the use of RJ. No criminal justice system, or social justice measure for that matter, will rehabilitate *all* offenders and repair *all* the harms caused. Thus we must not confuse the *aims* of RJ with our *expectations* about harm reparation. The attainment of justice requires an ongoing struggle to reach an ideal goal, whether that be complete retribution, deterrence, rehabilitation, or restoration (or an amalgamation of all these purposes). As Barbara Hudson asserts, justice is 'an aspiration, which is supremely important and worth striving for constantly and tirelessly' (2003: 192). However the ultimate goal of 'justice' must be differentiated from our expectation about whether it can ever be fully achieved. By this I mean that, while we must strive to achieve complete reparation (for example) for every crime committed, we cannot expect to achieve such a goal for everyone. Failure to reach the optimal goal of a justice measure is of little surprise. Sociological, cultural, individual, and statutory constraints will inevitably limit the effectiveness of any justice process. In this sense, RJ, as with any justice practice, must operate within society's socio-structural parameters, ultimately limiting its ability to provide 'full reparation'.

Hence, the fact that research has not shown that RJ repairs the harms of all crimes does not mean that it should not be utilized as a legitimate practice of criminal justice. Rather, what is fundamental to any assessment of the utility of RJ is to ascertain:

1. whether the restorative process aids the recovery of a substantial[23] number of victims—be that to their emotional wellbeing, material possessions, or interpersonal relationships;
2. whether the restorative process is more harmful than healing to a significant[24] number of participants.

As we have seen, a large body of empirical research now shows that RJ practices improve the emotional wellbeing of a substantial number of those who participate, while only a small minority of participants will experience further harm.

Part IV: Some Preliminary Thoughts on the Challenges and Opportunities of Restorative Justice for Hate Crime

In Chapter 3 I begin to present the empirical findings collated for this book, exploring how and why hate crime victims frequently experience heightened levels of emotional trauma, including feelings of fear, anxiety, and anger. We will see that victims often experience ongoing and regular abuse that is directed towards members

---

[23] What amounts to substantial is a question that requires further development. It may well depend on what form of reparation is under scrutiny. If the majority of victims obtain some form of reparation, be that emotional or material, we might say that a substantial number of victims have attained restoration. In reducing feelings of fear, we might say that a significant minority is 'substantial' where, for example, other conventional forms of justice provide even lower levels of reparation.

[24] What amounts to a significant number of people also requires further development. If only a small minority of victims find the restorative process harmful it could be asserted that this is not a significant enough number to prohibit the use of RJ.

of already marginalized identity groups (Perry 2001; Iganski 2008). Within this chapter we have explored how RJ attempts to reorientate victims of crime from a position of disempowerment to that of central players within the justice process. This is best achieved by encouraging victims to voice their experiences of crime and by offenders attempting to repair the damage they have caused.

The exploration of empirical research into RJ in this chapter suggests that, for a substantial number of victims, it helps to reduce the emotional traumas caused by crime, improving levels of fear and anger while simultaneously increasing individual security. It is this reparative component of RJ which yields the greatest potential for victims of hate crime (see McConnell & Swain 2000; Shenk 2001). Furthermore, the dialogic process may also promote an empathic response from offenders who, having witnessed first-hand the emotional traumas they have caused, frequently go on to offer reparation for their wrongdoing. Thus RJ not only helps to repair the harms of crime but may additionally engender a change in offenders' behaviours.

It is, however, overly simplistic to draw inferences about RJ's harm-repairing capabilities by referring to theoretical goals and empirical research that shows victims of non-hate-motivated crime frequently obtain emotional benefits. In particular, we must remain cautious about the impact that RJ may have on stakeholders from different identity and social backgrounds (Smith 2006). Issues pertaining to power imbalances, social inequalities, and cultural differences may yet create vulnerabilities which prove inhibitive to the restorative process. While some have begun to critique RJ in terms of social inequality and cultural difference (Hudson 1998; Busch 2002; Coker 2002; Daly 2002c; Strang & Braithwaite 2002; Stubbs 2007), few have carried out empirical research into these issues, including whether RJ can repair the harms caused by hate.

In his book, *Restorative Justice Theory and Practice: Addressing the Discrepancy*, Gavrielides (2007) documents various RJ case studies which illustrate the potential benefits of RJ for hate crime (see also Gavrielides 2012). In one case study an armed robbery was committed by two Arab men against a female Israeli who had perceived the attack to be racially motivated. Afterwards her relationship with Arab people became strained. Through an RJ programme of family group conferencing, the victim retold the events she had experienced. The perpetrators spoke of their involvement and of their sorrow, fully accepting responsibility. The process allowed the victim to vent her feelings and anger and was a successful part of her healing process, allowing her to again feel safe in the community. It allowed the perpetrators to seek forgiveness and reintegration back into the community by renewing trust in them. All parties expressed feelings of satisfaction and emotional relief after the process (Gavrielides 2007: 203; see also, Rice 2003 who explores her own journey of hate victimization and RJ).

From this example, and other similar case studies (see Umbreit et al 2002; Walters & Hoyle 2010; Coates et al 2013), we can begin to comprehend how RJ might diffuse conflict and expose ignorance and bigotry to critical scrutiny. If prejudices are explored in a safe environment there may be scope for effective challenge and subsequent modification of perspectives. Thus, it is hoped that RJ will help to reduce the levels of anxiety, anger, fear, and frustration experienced by hate victims, simply by allowing them to become a central part of the justice process. Ultimately, victims of hate crime may find some form of closure by receiving reparation, including assurances that the hate-motivated conduct will stop.

Yet isolated case studies that are taken from small-scale studies can only really hint at the potential of RJ for hate crime. As such, a much more rigorous, larger-scale and long-term study is required before more credible assertions can be made about the use of RJ in cases involving hate-motivated victimization. Before this book provides such an empirical analysis, it is helpful to summarize here the main *theoretical* opportunities and pitfalls of RJ, which the rest of this book will go on to investigate.

The theoretical promises of restorative justice for hate crime

- RJ will empower victims of hate crime by providing them with a platform to vocalize the pain that prejudice-motivated incidents have caused—including the heightened levels of fear, anxiety, and anger that many will experience. This will, in turn, help them to relinquish these negative emotions.
- The significance of 'storytelling' for hate victims is amplified by the very fact that such individuals will have previously been without a voice, it being lost at the margins of society where minority groups are oppressed by hegemonic norms and cultural values (see Chapter 3). Storytelling will therefore allow victims to regain the power they lose through hate crime victimization.

- Reparation provided by offenders will help to free victims (and other affected stakeholders) from feelings of self-blame, common amongst hate victims (Herek et al 1997).
- Promises made by the offender that the offence (or anti-social behaviour) will not be repeated will help to reduce the often enhanced levels of fear experienced by hate victims, allowing them to feel a greater sense of safety in their community (see Chapters 3 and 4).
- Hate victims will have the opportunity to question offenders about their motivations. The offender's own story will encourage empathic connections between victim and offender that will help to create renewed relations based on respect and feelings of mutuality. This will reduce the likelihood of reprisal attacks.
- Inclusive dialogue will evoke in hate offenders that which they have previously resisted—empathy. The vocalization of the emotional trauma caused by prejudice-motivated crimes may act to induce a natural response of contrition in offenders (see Chapter 8).
- The victim and his or her community supporters will help to demonstrate appropriate social condemnation of bigotry and prejudice (see Chapters 4 and 5), reducing the likelihood of offenders repeating their invidious behaviour.
- Offenders will gain insight into the effects that their actions have had, not just on the primary victim, but on others who hold similar identity traits, improving broader inter-group community relations.
- Offenders will gain moral learning by having a greater understanding of cultural and identity 'difference', which can act as a catalyst for broader attitudinal change within the offender and, in turn, in his or her community of care.

The theoretical pitfalls of restorative justice for hate crime

- The social distance between offender and victim may mean that neither party can identify with each other's cultural and/or identity backgrounds. This will mean that participants of cross-cultural dialogue will struggle to form the empathic connections central to the repairing of damaged relationships.
- In some communities, a culture of prejudice is cultivated and nurtured within families and friendship circles and by neighbours. Thus rather than inducing contrition, victims' revelations

may be viewed as provocative and elicit a hostile response from the offender and his or her supporters.
- Offenders emboldened by a sense of justification may manipulate the more informal restorative process to diminish their guilt, trivialize their prejudice, and potentially shift the blame onto the 'Other'.
- The vulnerability of most hate crime victims and their pre-existing unequal relationship with their abusers will undermine the RJ process, leaving victims open to re-victimization.
- Restorative processes led by facilitators from dominant group backgrounds will actively perpetuate the power imbalances inherent in most hate crime cases by imposing hegemonic cultural norms and values onto minority group individuals.
- If the restorative process fails to elicit social condemnation from community members for the offender's wrongful actions, victims are unlikely to obtain genuine forms of reparation, while offenders will be reintegrated back into a community that supports their hateful actions.

Conclusion

This chapter has introduced the reader to the main aims and objectives of RJ. Analysis of both theoretical and empirical research provides persuasive evidence of the harm-repairing qualities of restorative practice. The promise of RJ for hate crime is that it will aid the emotional recovery of victims by engaging and empowering those deemed as 'different'. The very fact that many hate victims experience heightened levels of emotional harm, disempowerment, and disenfranchisement means that, *theoretically*, RJ is most ideally suited to respond to this type of crime. Furthermore, the engagement of offenders in restorative dialogue may also have a reforming effect, far beyond that which can be provided by a retributive approach to tackling hate crime. The inclusivity of RJ combined with its focus on 'storytelling' promotes empathic connections between stakeholders that ultimately help to humanize the participants.

That said, the difficulties posed by cultural and identity difference, highlighted above and in Chapter 1, may yet deal an inhibitive blow to the restorative process. The challenge for RJ practice will therefore be to create safe environments where victims are able to communicate openly, free from the fear of re-victimization and

Conclusion 61

domination by other stakeholders (including the RJ practitioner). Whether RJ can help to repair the harms of hate crime and/or break down pernicious stereotypes is explored in depth in Chapters 4, 5, 6, 7, and 8. Before then, we turn to a detailed examination of the impact that hate-motivated offences have on victims and minority communities. Only then can we comprehend fully whether RJ is equipped to repair the harms caused by hate crime.

3

The Harms of Hate Crime: From Structural Disadvantage to Individual Identity

Introduction

Hate crimes have far-reaching consequences for both individual and community wellbeing. Those directly victimized are particularly susceptible to psychological, behavioural, financial, and physical harms (Garnets et al 1992). However, hate crimes also convey a symbolic message that communicates to entire groups of people that they are unwelcome and unworthy of social respect (Weinstein 1992; Ahn Lim 2009; Perry & Alvi 2012). The negative effects of such incidents therefore quickly 'ripple out', creating immense fear and distrust between identity groups (Noelle 2002). These invidious impacts ultimately tear at the social fabric of local communities, inevitably damaging the cohesiveness of our multicultural society (Noelle 2002).

This chapter reveals the harms of hate crime (henceforth 'hate harms') by examining both the current body of literature on this topic and the empirical findings collated for this book. Analysis of both theoretical and empirical research illustrates how hate victims are frequently exposed to feelings of immense fear and insecurity about their personal safety. Studies show that victims frequently experience heightened levels of anxiety and depression when compared to victims of non-hate-motivated incidents (Herek et al 1997, 1999, 2002, McDevitt et al 2001; Smith et al 2012; Home Office et al 2013). The emotional traumas endured by hate victims are deeply embedded in their identity (Herek et al 1997). As such, incidents go straight to the heart of an individual's 'self', thereby damaging the very essence of who they are as a person.

However, in order to fully comprehend the emotional traumas caused by hate incidents, we must also examine the socio-cultural and socio-economic contexts in which they occur (Perry 2001;

Ray et al 2004; see Chapter 1). To this end, the chapter begins by re-examining how processes of othering, explored already in Chapter 1, create socio-economic inequalities that inevitably compound an individual's experience of hate victimization (Perry 2001). By exploring the structural disadvantages that are experienced by many of those deemed to be 'different', we begin to more fully comprehend the totality of social harms that hate victims are likely to experience. This process-based analysis illustrates how acts of hatred form but one part of a continuum of prejudice and discrimination that is ingrained in almost all aspects of a victim's life.

Developing an understanding of 'hate crime' as a process of victimization allows for a more holistic picture of 'hate harm' to emerge (Chapter 1). This is a picture which further illuminates the cumulative consequences of hate crimes, both to individual victims and minority communities. It also highlights the need to focus attention on criminal justice measures (and other community-based initiatives) that are equipped to address both isolated incidents of prejudice as well as the more structural processes of hate. Such analysis is of central importance to the research carried out for this book. Hence, this chapter will provide important theoretical and empirical grounding upon which the exploration of whether RJ practices can *help* to repair the harms of hate crime will be based (see further, Chapters 4, 5, and 6).

Part I: Structural Inequality: The Beginnings of Hate Harm

Barbara Perry's seminal work on 'doing difference' has gained much currency within hate crime literature. The notion of 'difference' and the process of 'othering' are frequently used to explain why hate crimes occur (Chapter 1). This chapter draws upon Perry's theory, not to examine why hate crimes happen, but to explore the potential impacts of hate crimes on minority groups. A brief summary of 'doing difference' helps us to understand why hate crimes frequently 'hurt more' than other types of crimes (Iganski 2001). Perry argues that social hierarchies and the resulting distribution of wealth and resources can be constituted by what she refers to as 'dominance over difference' (Perry 2001: Ch 4). The oppression of minority groups finds its roots in expressions of *fear* (Walters 2011). People who display identity and cultural characteristics which differ from hegemonic norms are frequently perceived as posing a threat to dominant culture. Such a threat increases as certain identity groups become more visible within society (Perry 2001). Differences in cultural tradition, customs, and general ways of living can be seen by many dominant group citizens as being an affront to their civility. Threats to cultural norms and the potential loss of power and control over the way that society is structured destabilizes many individuals' sense of ontological security (Ray & Smith 2002). In response to this, dominant group members develop mechanisms to suppress the social mobility of 'Others', thereby ensuring that they do not encroach upon established sociocultural norms (Perry 2001; see also Spalek 2008).

As the threat of 'difference' increases so does dominant groups' use of various forms of violent and non-violent oppression—including hate violence (Levin & McDevitt 2002). More subtle, but equally damaging, are the negative labels which are attached to particular minority groups. Labels are applied to whole groups who display certain characteristics (a process of stereotyping) in an attempt to stigmatize the group (othering) (see Hall 2013: 85–86). In some cases, labels are extremely pernicious and lead to the demonizing of entire identity groups as immoral or abnormal. Labels can also give rise to beliefs about certain groups' worthiness as respectable citizens as well as their 'rights' to jobs and other state resources (Levin & McDevitt 2002). Other stereotypes may appear innocent or harmless. However, the odd black or gay joke stokes the flames of prejudice (Levin 2002). This can be more harmful than one might generally think. By stigmatizing certain groups in society, dominant groups actually begin to dehumanize minority individuals. Over time, prejudices become entrenched and are difficult to change (Craig 2002; Levin & McDevitt 2002).

Through the process of othering emerges a culture of prejudice which can permeate entire communities (Sibbitt 1997). Some members of the community perpetuate feelings of animosity towards 'Others' via channels of communication, be that interpersonal or through media networks (Craig 2002). Inevitably, those who are 'othered' become subordinated and marginalized within society (Perry 2001). Discriminatory practices—the behaviours of prejudice—within both private and public sector organizations become institutionalized (see, for example, Macpherson 1999). It is these practices that reinforce 'Others'' unequal position in society.[1]

---

[1] See more analysis of these processes in Chapter 1.

The social harms of being 'different': the examples of homophobia and anti-immigration

Perry's construction of hate crime as a form of 'dominance over difference' helps us to understand the structural aspects of hate harm which affect certain community members in a variety of insidious ways. The subordination of certain identity groups leads to various 'social harms', including economic, personal, or financial inequities (see generally, Hillyard et al 2004; in relation to sexual orientation see Bibbings 2004). For example, hegemonic norms, as constructed through dominant culture, produce indirect harms by enforcing upon a minority individual customs and behavioural norms that are an affront to that person's 'self' (essentialism) or to his or her cultural ways of living. Thus those individuals who fall outside of racial, ethnic, religious, or sexual norms can often be subjugated and quickly become ostracized from mainstream cultural activities (Perry 2001). For instance, those who fall outside of dominant sexual norms have often been labelled as deviant and a threat to heterosexual normality (Bibbings 2004). The social construction of heterosexual normality is not just about sexual activity and sexual orientation, but also about 'ways of being' (Bibbings 2004). The ontology of heterosexuality is dismorphic and hierarchical. There must be one masculine male and one feminine female. The male is dominant and is the basis from which the 'Other' is measured (hegemonic masculinity). The female comes second and is passive and accommodating. Sexualities which stray outside of this construct become an affront to the decency of heterosexual normality (known as heteronormativity) and are therefore resisted (Bibbings 2004). Resistance is born out of fear of the 'Other'; a fear that translates into prejudice and hatred. Prejudice is then demonstrated through acts of discrimination, by actively excluding homosexuals in public spaces, and, of course, through the commission of hate crimes (Perry 2001; see also Tomsen 2009).

In the UK, and many other countries, this has led in the past (and present) to the criminalization of homosexual activity. Criminalizing same-sex sexual encounters delegitimizes gay men as 'normal', and punishes them for acting outside of the heterosexual norm (see generally Tomsen 2009).[2] In turn, the pressure to

---

[2] In other countries, for example Iran, Saudi Arabia, Yemen, United Arab Emirates, Sudan, Nigeria, Mauritania, sexual intercourse between two men is still punishable by death.

conform which arises out of suppressing difference through heterosexual dominance has meant that many gay men and women have gone about changing the way they act, dress, and even speak in order to be perceived by others as 'heterosexual' (Moran et al 2004b; Dick 2008). Within various religious contexts, homosexuals have often been urged to remain celibate in order to maintain a moral lifestyle (Johnson et al 2007; see for example, 'Church to let gay clergy "marry" but they must stay celibate', *The Times*, 29 May 2005) thus restricting any sexual urges so as to purge themselves of what has been constructed as 'unnatural'. More troubling is the disproportionately high rate of suicide among young gay men associated 'with discriminatory practices of homophobia, transphobia and heterosexism that are embedded within institutions such as education, health, religion, media and the family...' (Johnson et al 2007: 57; see also Chakraborti & Garland 2009: Ch 4; Tomsen 2009).

It is not just gay people who experience social harms as a result of being 'different'. Similarly, immigrants and asylum seekers can face various forms of structural harm. The process of assimilation and acculturation, whereby immigrants attempt to integrate into society, can be fraught with difficulties that inevitably place them in a disadvantaged position. Yasmin Jiwani's (2005) research into young female migrants in Canada highlights the various difficulties faced when integrating into a new culture. She notes that immigrants will often face limitations when accessing schooling systems, with particular difficulties experienced by those who speak English as a second language. Immigrants will also find accessing housing and skilled employment difficult as they struggle to align their qualifications and work experience with those expected from the host country.

Pressures also exist for migrant individuals to fit into society and to conform to the various customs and norms that have been established. Jiwani states that 'the isolation and ostracism experienced by...immigrants and refugees living in rural communities are compounded by the fact that they do not have peers who share their cultural background' (2005: 866; see also Garland & Chakraborti 2006). Pressure to fit in can itself be harmful to an individual who denies him- or herself cultural and identity heritage in an attempt to assimilate. Jiwani (2005) asserts that the negation of 'self' through the process of being othered is the ultimate form of violence. Hence, whether someone is an immigrant, gay, black, or

Muslim, the fact that they are deemed by hegemonic norms to be 'different', means that they are likely to find themselves marginalized within society.

Legalizing harm: the example of Islamophobia

While dominant norms indirectly work to marginalize certain identity groups, prejudice and the social harms it causes have also frequently been woven into state-led practice and policy (McGhee 2008). In particular, legislation has been used to directly and indirectly affect particular groups in society. Take, for example, the response to terrorism post 9/11 and the raft of anti-terrorist legislation which has been proffered by right-wing movements across the globe. The laws are ostensibly aimed at preventing terrorism but are disproportionately used to target members of Islamic communities. The targeting of minority communities and the media coverage this attracts fuels the anti-Islamic sentiments which proliferated after 9/11 in the United States and 7/7 in the UK (Fekete 2009; Chakraborti & Zempi 2013).

Media coverage of terrorist activity, combined with right-wing propaganda and political discourse on Islam and immigration, help to spread fear and animosity towards those who display Islamic characteristics, which may include both their racial appearance and the wearing of religious garments, such as the burka and/or the turban. Those who display Islamic traits are perceived as a threat, not just to Western culture, but to the safety and security of the state (McGhee 2008). To many, Islam equates to fundamentalism and terrorism. Even sections of the feminist movement have been accused of oppressing faith-based custom by advocating the ban of the burka (Fekete 2009). They have argued that the treatment of women within the Islamic community is an affront to women's rights, a form of oppression amounting to gendered violence (Fekete 2009; Chakraborti & Zempi 2013). In fact, in some countries the wearing of niqabs or burkas has been banned altogether as part of a crusade to protect the rights of women. In France, for example, the wearing of any religious garment is expressly prohibited within public spaces and institutions such as schools or hospitals, disproportionately affecting Muslim women, many of whom wear, by custom, religious headscarves and other faith-specific garments. The growing animosity towards the wearing of Islamic clothing and the use of legislation in some jurisdictions to ban such clothing adds to the acceptance of public displays of social condemnation of Muslim customs and inevitably to incidents of anti-religious hate (Fekete 2009; McGhee 2008).[3]

Institutional discrimination: the example of racism

As we have so far seen, structural disadvantage and the social harms that it gives rise to will be played out through both private and state agencies that systematically discriminate against certain individuals via the practices and policies that they implement (see Macpherson 1999; Phillips & Bowling 2007). Within the criminal justice context, research has frequently evidenced the unfair or unequal treatment of certain minority ethnic groups by state agencies. For example, in his report on the failed police investigation into the murder of Stephen Lawrence by the Metropolitan Police Service, Sir William Macpherson identified the process of 'racial stereotyping' as a key indicator of the unfair treatment of BME groups (Macpherson 1999). He pointed to the fact that the police failed to treat Stephen Lawrence's parents with due care and respect. They were constantly 'patronised and fobbed off' during the investigation while the family consistently expressed their concern that the police treated them with distrust; especially after they were accused of being primed by their Asian lawyer to manipulate the police into looking racist (Macpherson 1999). Moreover, the report highlighted the disproportionate use of stop and search powers by the police against BME individuals as evidence of what was termed 'institutional racism' within the Metropolitan Police Service (Bridges 1999; Macpherson 1999).

There have been various other studies into the effect of direct and indirect racism on criminal justice processes including arrest rates, sentencing, and particularly the use of custody (Hood 1992; Kalunta-Crumpton 1998; Bowling & Philips 2002; Lyons et al 2013). Research has also shown that BME people are disproportionately strip-searched while in custody (Newburn et al 2004), while indirect discrimination has had a disproportionate effect on remand status and ensuing sentencing practices (Hood 1992; Spohn & Holleran,

---

[3] The criminalization of homosexuality throughout various parts of the world is also evidence of how laws can create immense social harm. Other laws which prevent gay and lesbian people from marrying, adopting, serving in the military, etc can also be seen as a source of marginalization and oppression.

2000; Bowling & Phillips 2002). For example, there is an increased likelihood that a BME suspect who has been placed on remand will be sentenced to custody if convicted (Bowling & Phillips 2002). One of the most common criteria for refusing bail is homelessness or 'no fixed address'. People with African-Caribbean or Black-African heritage are more likely to fall under this criterion due to socio-economic conditions which disadvantage BME communities (Home Office 2005a; 2005b).

Research therefore suggests that the unequal treatment of some minority communities is the result of an interaction that exists between unwitting prejudice, ignorance, and racial stereotyping *and* inequality in socio-economic conditions. This rather short and somewhat superficial examination of discrimination within the criminal justice system does not provide evidence that the entire criminal justice system is biased against minority groups, but illustrates the frequently discriminatory nature of many criminal justice processes. Moreover, the examination of discrimination within the criminal justice system does not suggest that *all* minority individuals will experience unequal treatment by state organizations. Indeed, many minority individuals are moving into the middle classes, a product of improvements in twenty-first-century meritocracy and equality laws, obtaining greater wealth and, with it, greater socio-economic power. However, such individuals continue to be exceptions rather than the rule and, for many, socio-structural factors ensure that they remain marginalized (O'Brien 2000; Home Office 2005b). In particular, unemployment levels continue to be much higher within BME communities than for their white counterparts, irrespective of qualification, age, gender, or geographical location (Home Office 2005a, 2005b; Ball 2012). Average income among BME groups tends to be lower, while they are more likely to live in deprived areas and in poor housing (O'Brien 2000; Home Office 2005a, 2005b; Kenway & Palmer 2007). Such groups are also disproportionately excluded from good quality schools and have limited access to other social goods (Bruce et al 1998; O'Brien 2000; Home Office 2005a, 2005b; Fuller & Davey 2010), inevitably pushing many minority community individuals to the outer limits of 'decent' society.[4] Tahir Abbas (2007: 10) states, for example, that

---

[4] See further discussion by Shedd & Hagan (2006) in the American context on racial minorities' perceptions of injustice in relation to criminal justice, education, employment, health care and housing.

Muslims often 'live in poverty, in overcrowded homes, segregated areas, declining inner city zones, face educational underachievement, high unemployment, low graduate employment, and experience poor health'. The Home Office's *Strength in Diversity* consultation strategy (2004: 5) similarly states that '[s]tructural inequalities and the legacy of discrimination have resulted in whole groups that are effectively left behind, with young people failing to share in the opportunities that should be available to all, which in turn fuels their disengagement from mainstream society...'.

The socio-economic and socio-structural disadvantages that many minority individuals encounter inevitably place them in a distinctly vulnerable social position. The lived experience of socio-economic disadvantage and various forms of discrimination that individuals face will inevitably compound any direct form of hate crime victimization. Access to state agencies such as the police, the courts, and in many cases housing associations, will be vital to the support of victims of crime (Victim Support 2006). Support from employers and other work colleagues can also be instrumental in helping victims to come to terms with what has happened to them. Yet despite the introduction of a raft of new criminal justice policies post Macpherson (1999) aimed at improving responses to hate incidents (see Hall 2013: Ch 2), many victims still believe that state agencies do little to prevent hate crime, or otherwise respond ineffectively to it (Victim Support 2006; Dunn 2009; see further Chapter 6). In some cases individuals may even fear that agencies will make matters worse (see, for example, Dick 2008; and further Chapter 6).

Of course the picture of discrimination and structural disadvantage painted here is not one which is static. Improvements made to equality law, evolving attitudes towards certain groups and general wealth creation among minority communities, all impact upon the ways in which such groups function in society. Nevertheless, the various processes of minority oppression discussed here illustrate how victims of hate are likely to endure social harms far beyond those experienced by those within more privileged socio-economic and socio-cultural sections of society. Intrinsic to the occurrence of hate incidents, therefore, is the broader understanding of the socio-structural contexts in which acts of hatred take place. It is important to consider this 'social harm' perspective when examining the harms caused by hate crime (see more broadly Hillyard et al 2004). We are better able to understand how hate incidents harm victims if we first consider how minority groups are affected by prejudice and institutional forms of direct and indirect discrimination. A social harm perspective also allows us to better comprehend the extent to which hate victims will be equipped to deal with their experiences of victimization. The next section builds upon this approach by examining the direct impacts of hate crime.

Part II: The Direct Impacts of Hate Crime Victimization

Victimization can impact individuals and other affected community members in myriad ways. Generally, victims may experience fear, anxiety, anger, insecurity, nightmares, loss of property, loss of wage-earning family members, and weakened social ties (Garnets et al 1992; Spalek 2006). Dennis Sullivan and Larry Tifft (2008b) describe these harms as 'socio-political experiences' that not only affect the lives of victims but also the victim's family and sometimes members of the affected community. The emotional traumas caused by crime/victimization occur for several reasons. The first is that it fractures a victim's sense of individual security. Sullivan and Tifft (2008b: 208) describe this as disruptions to the beliefs, values, and concepts of a person which make up the 'self'. Victims' perceptions of their place within the world can become destabilized. Within what is now perceived as a less stable environment, others suddenly appear more malevolent and less trustworthy (Garnets et al 1992; Kauffman 2008). Howard Zehr (1990: 24) explains that:

Crime is...a violation of the self; a desecration of who we are, of what we believe, of our private space. Crime is devastating because it upsets two fundamental assumptions on which we base our lives: our belief that the world is an orderly, meaningful place and our belief in personal autonomy. Both assumptions are essential for wholeness.

Crime and other targeted anti-social behaviours communicate a message to the victim that they do not count and are not worthy of respect (Harris et al 2004). As victims try to grapple with this violation they ask themselves, 'why did it happen to me?' (Garnets et al 1992). In many cases individuals experience self-blame, having 'allowed' themselves to be violated in such a way. In turn, self-blame can lead to feelings of shame and embarrassment (Garnets et al 1992).

The emotional harms of victimization can have short- or long-term impacts (Garnets et al 1992; Kauffman 2008). Morton Bard and Dawn Sangrey posit that there are three stages of emotional trauma which directly result from victimization (Bard & Sangrey 1979 cited in Garnets et al 1992). Stage one is the 'impact phase' and occurs when victims start to feel vulnerable and confused. In this early stage, victims can become dependent on others to help them with even small matters of decision making. They feel exposed and may be shocked by feelings of disbelief. Stage two is the 'recoil phase' and can swiftly follow stage one. It is characterized by changes in mood and feelings of fear, rage, frustration, denial, guilt, self-blame, shame, humiliation, grief, revengeful thoughts, and the projection of anger onto others (see further Sharpe 2007; Kauffman 2008: 217). The third stage is the 'reorganizing phase' where victims begin to process their experience and place it within a broader perspective. At this stage, victims begin to move on with their lives after regaining a renewed sense of security.

The majority of victims negotiate successfully through these stages, aided by time and the support of family and friends. Some may experience all of these emotions while others experience just a few. The phases may also come at different times and in a different order (Bard and Sangrey 1979 cited in Garnets et al 1992). Longer term, some victims can experience post-traumatic stress disorder or clinical depression as they relive the incident over and over in their minds (Kauffman 2008).

Victims' experiences of crime will differ depending on their personal characteristics including their age, gender, social class, life experience, and personality traits (Daly 2002a). The frequency with which a person experiences victimization may also colour their reaction to it. For example, individuals who experience victimization on a daily basis may have different reactions from those who experience it for the first time. Similarly, men may experience violent crime in different ways from women, while elderly people may find victimization more difficult to recover from than do younger generations. These differences cannot be ignored. They mean that there is no hard and fast rule to healing victims' emotional traumas. Nonetheless, appreciating that victims will usually respond to crime differently does not deny the commonalities that can be found amongst certain types of victims. In fact, establishing common themes in victimization will provide essential information from which we can then explore ways to mitigate different types of harm.

Commonalities in hate harm: attacking identity

Every hate crime is an attack on the victim's identity—whether it be a brutal racist assault by a gang of extremists or an off-the-cuff homophobic insult made by a neighbour. In each case the victim and others who display similar characteristics will know that they have been targeted because of the way they look, what they believe in, or whom they are sexually attracted to. That is not to deny that subtle differences exist between the effects of different types of hatred.[5] However, most incidents will create a similar set of unique challenges for victims due to the fact that that part of the victim's identity which has been targeted becomes central to their internal awareness of why they have been victimized (Garnets et al 1992). This general commonality amongst all hate crimes remains consistent regardless of the level of seriousness or type of victim group.

First and foremost is the fact that attacking a victim's identity will heighten his or her sense of vulnerability (Garnets et al 1992; Herek et al 1997). Vulnerability relates to two elements of victimization. The first is the *risk* of victimization posed to certain groups or individuals, while the second relates to the *level* of harm one is likely to suffer as a direct result of victimization (Green 2007). In the first sense, hate crime victims' vulnerability becomes heightened due to the personal danger which is associated with their belonging to a particular identity group (Herek & Berrill 1992; Herek et al 1997, 1999). This elevated sense of vulnerability is compounded by the high levels of hate crimes committed each year and by the repetitive nature of the phenomenon (see Smith et al 2012). As we saw in Chapter 1, not only are there disproportionately high levels of hate crime but victims are also often targeted persistently over long periods of time (see Bowling 1998; Garland & Chakraborti 2006; Smith et al 2012). This means that targeted groups not only have to contend with the heightened risk of being victimized, but they are also likely to have to cope with repeated abuse, sometimes on a daily basis (Smith et al 2012; Iganski 2008).

Victims who grapple with their experience of victimization will attempt to make sense of the world as a just and fair place (Garnets et al 1992). In trying to bring about a renewed sense of security, non-hate victims may attempt to rationalize the behaviour of the offender as having nothing to do with them; perhaps thinking that

---

[5] In particular, differences in the cause and effect of disablist abuse may give rise to a different analysis of hate harm, see Hunter et al (2007).

they were merely in the wrong place at the wrong time. However, in hate crime cases the victim cannot rationalize the crime in this way as the message attached to the incident clearly demonstrates that they have been specifically targeted because of who they are. Consequently, the impact of a hate incident is built upon a foundation of oppression and/or persecution that other types of victim do not necessarily experience.

In coming to terms with their experience of hate, some victims will feel that they are to blame for their own victimization and, consequently, that they deserve to be punished for being 'different'. Prejudice is often internalized, bringing about a sense of shame (Herek 2004; Noelle 2009). The victim will be aware that they have attracted their own victimization because of what their identity represents (Ahn Lim 2009). For instance, those who have to come to terms with their homosexuality in an environment hostile towards gay people and who have parents who disapprove of homosexual relationships will have had emotional burdens placed upon them to conform to a heterosexual lifestyle (Bibbings 2004; Noelle 2009). Such a situation can give rise to feelings of internalized homophobia, a sense that being gay equates to their being less decent, to being dirty and even immoral when compared to others (Noelle 2002, 2009). Being the victim of anti-gay abuse can therefore create 'characterological self-blame... in which one feels there is something they could do differently if faced with the situation again' (Noelle 2009: 86).

In Sam Dick's study into homophobic hate crime for Stonewall, one respondent sums up this process by stating 'I am the one who feels ashamed because the inference is that they abused me in this way because of my body language or the way in which I looked at them...' (2008: 31). Questioning one's own value as a human being like this will eventually destabilize a person's sense of 'self'. As a result of both internalized and externalized experiences of hate, victims will often attempt to adjust the way they portray themselves to the world in order to 'fit in' (see later in this chapter, 'The wider impact on minority communities').

The fear of victimization and internalized expressions of prejudice ultimately act to aggravate other feelings of isolation, anxiety, and depression arising from their victimization (Garnets et al 1992; Herek et al 1997, 2002; McDevitt et al 2001). Attacking someone's identity consequently leads to the second element of vulnerability (level of harm) becoming elevated as victims endeavour to come to terms with what has happened to them. It should be noted at this point that the concept of vulnerability is one which, in some contexts, has been considered as counterproductive (Quarmby 2008: 33ff). The main concern is that if certain individuals are perceived as being inherently 'vulnerable' they become viewed as incapable, or even childlike, leading to their being viewed as less able to fend for themselves. This can give rise to a form of prejudice in itself as these individuals are treated by others like helpless children (infantilization) (Roulstone et al 2011). Such perceptions of vulnerability may also give rise to the belief that some victims of hate abuse are partially to blame for their own victimization where they have acted recklessly, for example by venturing out into the community when they should 'know better' not to place themselves in danger.

Labelling certain individuals as 'vulnerable' can also blur the line between hate motive and the situational context in which they were victimized (Quarmby 2008). By this I mean it can be difficult, especially within a courtroom context, to determine whether an offender is motivated by a hostility (ie a prejudice) towards the victim or whether they are taking advantage of the victim's perceived vulnerability (Mason-Bish 2010: 70–1; Walters 2013b). This is particularly relevant to cases involving the victimization of disabled people. Questions arise as to whether a hate-based motive against the victim's disability is the same as a motive linked to a situational context that is intrinsically correlated with identity (ie the victim's perceived or actual vulnerability).

The term 'hostility' within the current body of UK legislation certainly leaves enough room for the courts to interpret the actions of offenders who abuse disabled individuals as proof of hate motivation. As where the offender's actions are caused by a direct prejudice against disabled people *or* where they see the victim's 'difference' as making them innately 'vulnerable' (itself disablist) (Chakraborti & Garland 2012). It seems that criminal justice agencies in the UK are slowly coming round to this way of thinking—the CPS, for instance, now provide guidance that makes it clear that vulnerability and hostility may be two sides of the same coin (CPS 2010). However, it appears that the police and other criminal justice practitioners are yet to fully appreciate the subtle differences (similarities) between vulnerability and hostility (Mason-Bish 2010: 70–1), while many are still failing to understand the difference between legal and policy definitions of hate crime (CJJI 2013; see Chapter 1).

While the complexities involved in determining the meaning of vulnerability in hate crime cases remain important, they do not mean that the concept is in itself counterproductive. Neil Chakraborti and Jon Garland argue that vulnerability 'encapsulates the way in which many hate crime perpetrators view their target: as weak, defenceless, powerless or with a limited capacity to resist' (2012: 9). The concept therefore remains central to explanations of the impact that hate crimes have on minority communities. As we have seen above, 'dominance over difference' not only acts to increase the likelihood of hate victimization, but also compounds victims' experience of it. The harms of hate crime are built upon a foundation of discrimination and socio-economic marginalization. Hence victims of hate crime are likely to experience a form of double victimization, first through their experience of direct victimization and second through their socio-structural marginalization. Consequently, hate victims will typically struggle to cope with their victimization as they grapple with coming to terms with how their 'difference' impacts upon their place in the world. Such differences provide a sense of the 'self', not viewed through a prism of unified empowerment, but through a socially constructed lens of vulnerability (Chakraborti & Garland 2012).

Empirical findings on the emotional harm of hate crime

A growing body of research has begun to provide empirical evidence supporting the theoretical assertions that victims of hate crime are likely to experience heightened levels of physical, psychological, and emotional harm[6] (Herek & Berrill 1992; Garofalo 1997; Herek et al 1997, 1999, 2002; Levin 1999; McDevitt et al 2001; Iganski 2008; Smith et al 2012; Home Office et al 2013). While various studies in the twentieth century highlighted the traumatic emotional impact that hate crimes can have (Barnes & Ephross 1994) it was not until comparison groups were used over the past ten to fifteen years that it has been possible to determine whether hate harms were significantly different to non-hate incidents (see eg Herek et al 1999, 2002 McDevitt et al 2001).

Paul Iganski (2008) has demonstrated the heightened levels of emotional harm via the presentation and analysis of data from three British Crime Surveys (BCS) dating from 2002 to 2005. He

---

[6] Compared to other similar (parallel) non-hate-motivated crimes.

found statistically significant higher levels of victims involved in racially motivated incidents (compared to non-hate -related incidents) had reported feelings of: shock, fear, depression, anxiety, panic attacks, feelings of loss of confidence, feeling vulnerable, difficulty sleeping, and crying (Iganski 2008: 12, 13, 82, and 83). Feelings of fear yielded the highest differential amongst emotional reactions (Iganski 2008: 81; elevated levels of fear for hate victims are also reported in Herek et al 1997, 1999, 2002; Bowling 1998; McDevitt et al 2001; Smith et al 2012; Home Office et al 2013). Iganski also found that a slightly higher proportion of victims of assault, burglary, theft,[7] and threats, where the victim believed that the offender was racially motivated, reported an 'emotional reaction' compared to victims of incidents not believed to be motivated by racism (2008: 12). For example, victims of assault[8] who had believed the attack was racially motivated had an emotional reaction in 92.4 per cent of cases. This is compared to those who did not believe the attack was racially motivated where the emotional reaction occurred in 86.8 per cent of cases. By itself this is not a significant difference, however Iganski documented higher levels of emotional reactions for victims who had believed their offender to be racially motivated in *all* types of crime (Iganski 2008: 12).[9] More recent CSEW data has shown that victims of hate crime are more likely to say they were emotionally affected by the incident, with 34 per cent of hate victims stating that they were 'very much' affected compared to 14 per cent of victims of CSEW crime overall (Home Office et al 2013: 46; see also Smith et al 2012: 22). The survey also found that:

> twice as many hate crime victims said they had suffered a loss of confidence or had felt vulnerable after the incident (39%), compared with CSEW crime overall (16%). Hate crime victims were also more than twice as likely to experience fear, difficulty sleeping and anxiety or panic attacks compared with victims of overall CSEW crime (Home Office et al 2013: 46).

Not only are hate victims more likely to experience psychological trauma but the trauma is also more likely to last for longer periods of time compared with that of non-hate-related victims. Gregory

---

[7] And attempted versions of these offences.
[8] Or attempted assault.
[9] Though it should be noted that only five out of the six types of offence researched showed a statistically significant result.

Herek et al (1997) found that victims of homophobic violence suffered from periods of depression, stress, and anger for as long as five years after their primary experience of a hate crime (see also Garofalo 1997; Herek et al 1999, 2002). In contrast, non-hate-related victims showed vast improvements within two years (Herek et al 1997). Supporting these findings, McDevitt et al (2001) also found that victims were three times more likely to report that overcoming the crime was very difficult compared to non-hate victims.

The prolonged periods of enhanced emotional trauma that hate victims endure are likely to be linked to a heightened perception of future victimization (Herek et al 1997, 1999; see also, Victim Support 2006). Iganski, for example, found that higher proportions of hate victims reported being 'worried' or 'very worried' about future victimization (2008: 83). Connected to the fear of victimization is the fact that many hate victims no longer feel safe in their own neighbourhood and therefore refuse to return to where the incident took place (McDevitt et al 2001: 710; Iganski 2008: 78–79).[10]

Results from Southwark, Devon, and Cornwall

Research conducted for this book concurred with the findings of other studies. While the number of participants in the study is relatively small (thirty-eight), there was a clear pattern amongst those interviewed concerning the psychological trauma they had endured. Each interviewee was asked to explain how the incident/s had impacted upon their emotional wellbeing.[11] Interviewees were then read a list of emotional harms and asked to agree or disagree whether they had experienced each as a direct result of the incident/s (see Table 3.1; see Appendix A, question 17 for list of emotional harms).[12] The vast majority of victims interviewed agreed that they had experienced feelings of anxiety (thirty-three) and a fear of being re-victimized (thirty-two) directly after the hate incident.[13] In particular, the fear of repeat attacks or abuse left victims anxious

---

[10] Using a national telephone survey of 2,078 respondents, Ehrlich et al (1994) found that hate victims experienced more symptoms of post-traumatic stress and behavioural changes than did non-hate victims (see also Herek et al 1999).

[11] All thirty-eight interviewees agreed that the incident had affected their emotional wellbeing.

[12] Those who agreed they had experienced certain harms were then asked to elaborate on how these had affected them.

[13] HCP and Devon and Cornwall victims aggregated.

Table 3.1 Number of victims (complainant victims) who experienced emotional harms—grouped by type of restorative intervention

Emotional harm suffered	HCP*	D&C**	Oxford***	Total
	N=23	N=14	N=1	N=38 (aggregated percentage)****
Feelings of anxiety	19	13	1	33 (87)
Fear of being attacked/victimized again	22	9	1	32 (84)
Anger	17	13	1	31 (82)
Depression or feeling depressed	17	10	1	28 (74)
Loss of self-esteem	14	8	1	23 (61)
Sleeplessness	11	8	1	20 (53)
Loss of confidence	10	9	1	20 (53)
Nightmares or bad dreams	5	4	0	9 (24)
Self-blame	3	0	0	3 (8)

* Hate Crimes Project, Southwark Mediation. Total number of interviewees 23.
** Devon and Cornwall Police, Restorative Disposal. Total number of interviewees 14.
*** Oxford restorative conferencing. Total number of interviewees 1.
**** Percentages are used for illustrative and comparative purposes only and are not intended to indicate generalizable data.

NB: Interviewees were asked: 'Did you experience any of the following emotional or psychological impact/s because of the incident/s?' See Appendix A, questions 16 and 17.

about their personal safety (see similarly Victim Support 2006; Iganski 2008). As one interviewee succinctly put it, 'I am always on my guard.' While another commented: 'Just to be frightened in the communal hallway. Yesterday he spat all over me while shouting. Today would he touch me, would he do something?'

Other emotional traumas were documented as damaging the wellbeing of victims. A high proportion of victims stated that they had: felt depressed (twenty-seven); lost self-esteem (twenty-two); and lost confidence (nineteen). These interlinking emotions all stress the damaging impact of targeting an individual's identity (Herek et al 1997, 1999; see also Garland & Chakraborti 2006). One interviewee commented, 'it makes me depressed sometimes', while another admitted that her ordeal left her feeling 'sad' and 'tearful'. Several victims stated that they had also been prescribed anti-depressants as a means of dealing with their victimization.

Spatial and behavioural implications

The constant fear of repeat victimization clearly had implications for the spatial mobility of those who were interviewed (see Table 3.2). Victims were asked whether, as a result of the incident, they avoided certain locations, were now more careful about what they said and did, and/or tried to change their appearance or the way they acted when out in the community (see Appendix A, questions 18 and 19). Twenty-seven out of the thirty-eight interviewees agreed that they now avoided certain locations as a direct result of their victimization. Many went on to explain that they would no longer visit certain areas of town, with some now refusing to walk by themselves late at night. This finding replicated those from other studies that have shown that victims of hate crime frequently avoid certain locations in order to evade harassment and/or violence (Gordon 1994; Garland & Chakraborti 2006; Iganski 2008). For instance, a victim of racist abuse commented: 'living with the fear all the time... I have this fear of walking in the night. I still feel now if I go out at night... I might be attacked [or]... abused'. Changes made by victims to their day-to-day behaviours could be directly linked to their feelings of anxiety about what had happened to them and to their fear that they would be targeted again (see similarly, Garland & Chakraborti 2006; Iganski 2008). For others, the frequency of incidents also served to compound their emotional turmoil, leading to self-imposed restrictions on where

Part II: The Direct Impacts of Hate Crime Victimization   81

Table 3.2 Number of victims (complainant victims) whose social behaviours were affected by a hate incident/s—grouped by type of restorative intervention

Behavioural impacts	HCP*	D&C**	Oxford***	Total
	N = 23	N = 14	N = 1	N = 38 (aggregated percentage)****
Avoid certain locations	17	9	1	27 (71)
More careful about what you say or do	13	8	0	21 (55)
Try to change your appearance or the way you act	5	6	1	12 (32)

* Hate Crimes Project, Southwark Mediation. Total number of interviewees 23.
** Devon and Cornwall Police, Restorative Disposal. Total number of interviewees 14.
*** Oxford restorative conferencing. Total number of interviewees 1.
**** Percentages are used for illustrative and comparative purposes only and are not intended to indicate generalizable data.
NB: See Appendix A, questions 18 and 19 for exact questions asked.

they were prepared to go and what they would now say to others within the local neighbourhood. One interviewee summed up the oppressive nature that incidents could have when he explained how he frequently sat indoors with all the lights off so as to avoid the attention of his neighbour. He also stated that he waited until the middle of the night before cautiously venturing out to purchase groceries (see Case Study 1, Chapter 4; see also Garland & Chakraborti 2006: 14).

Physical harm

Research has shown that hate-motivated physical attacks are often more brutal when compared to other non-hate-motivated assaults, leading to higher rates of hospitalization (Levin & McDevitt 1993: 11; see also Levin 1999; Messner et al 2004; Dunbar 2006). Using data from the National Incident Based Reporting System (NIBRS), Steven Messner et al (2004: 605) found that hate crime victims are almost three times more likely to be seriously injured by assault compared with assaults where no bias motive is present. Recent analysis of US FBI data by Wen Cheng et al similarly found that hate crimes targeted towards gay men were more likely to be committed against the person (as against property) and were additionally associated with more severe crimes such as aggravated assault (2013: 789; see also Dunbar 2006).

Interviewees at Southwark, Devon, and Cornwall were all asked whether they sustained 'any physical injury resulting from the incident/dispute'. If they answered yes they were then asked what their injury was and whether this required medical attention (see Appendix A, question 14). Seven interviewees indicated that they had suffered some form of physical violence. In two cases this entailed a common assault, including one victim being 'shoved' and another being slapped on the face. More serious forms of violence involved a brick being thrown at a young victim's head resulting in an injury that required several stitches, a victim of homophobic abuse being pushed to the floor causing a gash to his chin and his teeth to penetrate his upper lip, and a case involving racially aggravated grievous bodily harm wherein the young victim's wrist was broken.

Many other victims, whose victimization was characterized by long-term abuse, developed physical illnesses that they directly attributed to their victimization (Victim Support's 2006 report also found that hate victims experienced a deterioration of physical ailments). For example, in a case that had lasted over ten years the victim stated:

The hair just started dropping out...I've got high blood pressure from all of this...my record was completely clean from when I was born...but then BAM! 1998 and 1999, the whole affects just started coming up one after another. So, it's like you can see there is a pattern here and it is because of her...having all these things happen...to me...I don't like saying it ruined my life, but it took a big portion of my life.[14]

Other interviewees encountered symptoms of stress such as 'heart palpitations', 'high blood pressure', 'nightmares', 'sleeplessness', and 'headaches' (see also, Victim Support 2006).

Additional social harms

The emotional traumas caused by hate incidents can adversely affect other areas of a victim's life. For example, several studies have shown that a higher percentage of hate victims have reported that they lost their jobs (McDevitt et al 2001: 710), while some

---

[14] See further Case Study 1, Chapter 6.

Table 3.3 Number of victims (complainant victims) who experienced financial costs, and housing and employment difficulties—grouped by restorative intervention

Social harms	HCP*	D&C**	Oxford***	Total
	N=23	N=14	N=1	N=38 (aggregated percentage)****
Housing difficulties	15	2	0	17 (45)
Financial costs	6	2	0	8 (21)
Employment difficulties	3	3	0	6 (16)

* Hate Crimes Project, Southwark Mediation. Total number of interviewees 23.
** Devon and Cornwall Police, Restorative Disposal. Total number of interviewees 14.
*** Oxford restorative conferencing. Total number of interviewees 1.
**** Percentages are used for illustrative and comparative purposes only and are not intended to indicate generalizable data.
NB: See Appendix A, questions 15, 18, and 19 for exact questions asked.

have reported experiencing disruptions to their daily routines and breakdowns in relationships with spouses and friends (Chahal & Julienne 1999).[15] Interviewees in the current study were also asked whether they experienced any financial costs, housing difficulties, and/or employment difficulties as a direct result of the incident/s (see Table 3.3 and Appendix A, questions 15, 18, and 19). Six victims stated that they had experienced employment difficulties as a direct result of their victimization, with two of the six stating that they lost their job as a result of their ordeal.[16] Six victims had incurred financial costs associated with their victimization, while many victims (seventeen) also spoke of housing problems that the incident had caused. Most of these victims wished to move away from the location where they had been targeted, but were unable to obtain enough 'housing points' to be relocated by their local housing officer. Other victims spoke of persistent false complaints made by their neighbours to the housing association which they believed were racially or homophobically motivated. This led to some victims receiving letters and threats of eviction from the housing association. It should also be noted here that many interviewees also spoke of secondary victimization that resulted from reporting incidents

---

[15] The types of harm experienced by victims who went through a restorative process are reported in Chapter 5.

[16] A total of six interviewees stated that they experienced employment difficulties as a direct result of their victimization.

to local agencies. Due to the commonality amongst interviewees of such encounters, the subject of secondary victimization and harm reparation via multi-agency partnerships through mediation will be dealt with separately in Chapter 6.

The wider impact on minority communities

Beyond the direct impact on individual hate victims are the negative consequences that hate crimes have on minority communities more broadly. Hate incidents are symbolic messages to society about the worthiness of certain groups of people. This message rings loud and clear: certain identity groups are unequal, unwelcome, and undeserving of social respect (Byers et al 1999; Noelle 2002; Ahn Lim 2009; Perry & Alvi 2012). As such, hate crimes have a damaging effect, not just on individual victims, but on other 'in-group' members of an identity group (Weinstein 1992; Iganski 2001). The reporting of hate violence by local and national media helps to promote a message of *danger*, which in turn creates a climate of fear amongst minority communities (Herek & Berrill 1992: 3; Iganski 2001: 630–31; Herek et al 2002; McGhee 2005: 126). This means that a single act of targeted violence can result in an entire community (or communities) experiencing a heightened sense of vulnerability (Perry & Alvi 2012).

It was common for interviewees in the current study to explain how feelings of fear and anxiety spread to other affected community members. In many cases, entire families became the targets of abuse, or in cases involving young victims, parents became fearful that their children would be seriously hurt. One father of a young victim whose wrist had been broken in a racially motivated attack spoke of the effect the incident had on the entire family: 'the fear whenever he went to school or went out, that was a nightmare for us... The mother was screaming all the time thinking that something is going to happen to him, it was really affecting us emotionally'. The threat of hate has been characterized as a form of 'terror' as the fear of violence spreads to other like people within minority groups (Weinstein 1992; Lawrence 1999: 43–4; Iganski 2001: 629). The constant worry of potential victimization, often compounded by experiences of prejudice in the past, permeates the consciousness of many minority community members who may live with the fear of possible victimization at all times (see *inter alia* Dick 2008: 29ff; Smith et al 2012:

23–4). Other people in society may feel sympathetic and want to help but choose not to for fear that they may become targets (Lawrence 1999: 43–44).

Dick's study into homophobic crime is illustrative of how oppressive hate crimes can be to other members of the gay community (Dick 2008). He found that three-quarters of eighteen to twenty-four-year-old gay and lesbians feel that they are more at risk of being assaulted for being gay, while around 40 per cent of all lesbian, gay and bisexual (LGB) people said they are worried about being the victim of a crime (Dick 2008: 30). Recent CSEW data indicate that hate crimes may give rise to greater concerns of victimization amongst minority ethnic groups. The survey found that 16 per cent of adults from a BME background were 'very worried' about being attacked because of their skin colour/ethnic origin or religion compared with only 3 per cent of white adults (Home Office et al 2013: 47). Previous BCS data have also shown that a higher rate of BME adults feel that there is a problem in their areas with people being attacked or harassed because of their race, ethnicity, or religion compared with white adults (16 per cent compared with 5 per cent respectively, Smith et al 2012: 24; see also Bowling 1998: 195; Perry & Alvi 2012: 62).

Most respondents to hate victimization surveys have indicated that their behaviour in public is restricted through the fear of violence (Herek & Berrill 1992). Such fears mean that many minority group individuals feel it necessary to adjust their behaviour and/or appearance in order to assimilate into the dominant culture (Chahal & Julienne 1999; Dick 2008).[17] Dick (2008) found that a third of lesbian and gay people alter their behaviour so as not to appear lesbian or gay to prevent being a victim of crime. One respondent within that study stated that 'we censor our behaviour so much. If I behaved as I would like to—holding hands...in public etc, then things would be very different' (2008: 32; see also Gordon 1994: 48; Attorney General's Department 2003: 26).

We see here an interconnection between the direct impacts of hate crime and the broader disadvantages which emulate from 'difference'. The everydayness of hate as experienced through both interpersonal interactions and through institutional practices operates

---

[17] This is often referred to as 'code switching' and allows individuals to switch from one form of cultural behaviour to another depending on their environment (Shedd & Hagan 2006).

to antagonize entire groups' feelings of vulnerability about possible victimization. This is unsurprising given the often repetitive nature of hate incidents and the pervasiveness of cultures of prejudice (Chapter 1). The constant fear of hate victimization will inevitably penetrate minority group members' cognition at a much deeper level, such that many will actively attempt to deny their own individuality in order to 'fit in'.

Inter-group backlashes

A major concern that derives from the symbolic nature of hate incidents is that they give rise to the potential for minority groups to 'fight back' (Perry & Alvi 2012). Brian Levin (1999) notes that hate crimes can pose a potential risk to social order as identity groups seek to find redress via reprisal attacks (see also Levin & McDevitt's (2002) typology of offenders). Isolated incidents spark angry responses from members of the targeted group who seek to defend their 'in-group'. Left unresolved this may result in an escalation of violence as groups target and re-target each other.

Most victims interviewed for this book (thirty-one) spoke of the immense anger they felt about the incident/s. One interviewee tried to express this, stating: 'I wanted to explode, I don't know how to explain it...to put it into words'. In many cases, the toxic combination of hate and anger will inevitably lead to further acts of violence. A victim of racist abuse summed this up: 'Hatred is a bad thing, hatred leads to violence and violence leads to crime. You hate, you hate...You might do me things...and I might take it but after a while I might lash out because I can only take so much'. Ongoing conflicts that were left to escalate commonly led to greater levels of violence between community members (see Chapter 4). For example, one RJ practitioner interviewee spoke of a case involving a young white British student who had made a racist comment to his classmate who was of Pakistani heritage. Frightened to go back to school the victimized student asked his cousins to protect him. Retaliatory intimidation then resulted in the original perpetrator becoming afraid of going back to school. As the case escalated into what the school feared might result in a white against Asian gang fight, an RJ practitioner was brought in by the headmaster in order to bring the parties together to discuss what had happened. It was felt that in order to prevent such incidents from escalating into serious forms of violence, a new relationship built on trust needed to be established between victim and offender, allowing for the dissipation of previous tensions (see more on how RJ might challenge prejudice in Chapter 8).

A major concern for all communities is that individual incidents of hate crime can spark larger-scale rioting between identity groups as already tense community relations come to a head. There are many examples of hate incidents resulting in large-scale violence. In the UK, race riots erupted during the months of May, June, and July 2001 within the northern towns of Oldham, Burnley, and Bradford. In Oldham, 200 Asian youths rioted after an elderly white pensioner was mugged by an Asian male and a group of white men attacked a house in the predominantly Asian Glodwick area (McGhee 2005: Ch 2). Similar events occurred in Burnley after a clash between a group of Pakistani and white youths. Later on in Bradford, clashes between Pakistani and white youths occurred after the British National Party announced it would march through the town (McGhee 2005: Ch 2). More recently the English Defence League has held demonstrations against Muslim communities throughout England in response to the murder of a white soldier in Woolwich, London. This has led to several clashes with anti-fascist groups, while a number of mosques have been damaged (one being burnt to the ground) (Garland 2013; Milmo & Morris 2013).

Tensions within communities which culminate in hate incidents and, in turn, to retaliatory violence must be dealt with at a grassroots level. Such incidents disrupt 'expectations of harmony, community, and inclusion' (Perry & Alvi 2012: 63) and as such require initiatives which bring various members of the community together in order to re-establish these values. Inclusive dialogue on intergroup conflicts must be encouraged if we are to help prevent the escalation of isolated hate incidents turning into larger-scale riots. Left unchallenged, simmering prejudices within a community will inevitably spark violent clashes between identity groups. Key to this book is an emphasis on processes that encourage dialogue, empathy, and understanding between individuals of 'difference'. As tensions increase within local communities and hate incidents begin to occur more frequently, bringing community members together to discuss incidents of hatred may well enable communities to find resolutions to their fears and anxieties about each other (see more on this in Chapters 4, 5, and 6).

Does hate harm matter more?

Needless to say, minority groups' experiences of hate crime can have far-reaching consequences both in terms of individuals' emotional wellbeing and other minority community members' reactions to hate incidents. Even so, some academics have argued that hate victimization is no more harmful than any other form of crime. At the close of the twentieth century, James Jacobs and Kimberly Potter (1998) asserted that all crimes have impacts which go beyond that of the individual victim and therefore hate offences are no different to any other type of crime (Chapter 1; see also Sullivan 1999). They disputed the validity of contrasting research evidence, stating that '[t]hese assertions depend on empirical assumptions that seem dubious and have not been substantiated' (Jacobs & Potter 1998: 90). Some fifteen years later, a growing body of research, much of which is based on large random samples with statistically significant results (such as McDevitt et al 2001; Herek et al 2002; Iganski 2008), suggests they were wrong. That said, more attention should be given to the diversity of victims and their experiences of crime (Spalek 2006). With this in mind, it is important that the field of hate victimization continues to grow.

We must also be alive to the fact that not all victims of hate crime will be harmed more than other victims. Criminologists should resist assuming that a whole group will be disproportionately affected by a particular type of crime as inevitably there will be variability (Sullivan 1999). People experience crime differently according to a whole host of personal and social variables as mentioned above (Green 2007). Not only will victims from different identity groups experience crime differently but there will be variations within a group. One concern regarding differentiating hate harm from other types of harm is that we may unintentionally set up 'a contest of vulnerability in which one group vies with another to establish its particular variety of suffering, a contest that can have no dignified solution' (Sullivan 1999: 8). In this regard, Andrew Sullivan (1999) suggests that responding differently to hate victimization simply illuminates the social divisions that exist between identity groups.

It is worth highlighting the tensions that can be caused when differentiating between the harms experienced by different identity groups. By emphasizing one group as more deserving of support than another we may unintentionally create further tensions between groups of different people. For example, one causal mechanism of hate crime that is commonly highlighted by criminologists is the (mis)perception that certain minority groups obtain greater support with regards to social benefits and resources from the state when compared to dominant white groups (Ray & Smith 2002). In most cases, such perceptions are created by unsubstantiated rumours (Levin & McDevitt 2002). These perceptions lead to resentment and further frustration at certain groups if they are seen to be getting more than everyone else. In this sense we must be cautious not to over-accentuate the needs of minority groups in *direct* contrast to the needs of other groups in society for fear of pitching identity groups against each other. It is also important that we do not simply assume that all hate crime victims will experience incidents in the same way. To socially construct hate victims as always experiencing heightened levels of vulnerability—both in terms of risk and level of harm—may be to provide a false generalization of hate victimization (see generally, Green 2007).

Paying regard to these cautionary notes does not, however, mean that we must ignore empirically evidenced variations between victims of crime. When investigating the harms caused by hate crime, criminologists do not aim to set up a 'contest' between different types of victim. Rather, we attempt to identify commonalities in victims' experiences, brought about by the very nature of the offending behaviour. This must be done by acknowledging disparate experiences within identity groups and across different groups (Garland et al 2006). Nevertheless, if we are to provide the best possible measures for tackling different types of crime and supporting different types of victims, we must not ignore that 'difference' in both these respects is fundamental to the challenge. In other words, findings that hate crimes *typically* cause greater harms when compared to non-hate offences must not be disregarded as divisive but instead as important to the task of effectively responding to disparate forms of victimization.

Conclusion

The examination of hate victimization clearly shows that there is a need to find ways to help support victims of hate crime and to reduce the damaging effects it has on minority communities. The vulnerability of hate victims has been highlighted by research conducted for this book and by other studies which shows that minority group members frequently experience ongoing targeted forms of violence and harassment. The harms caused by incidents that are often weekly or even daily occurrences will inevitably accumulate over time—sometimes to disastrous effect (see the Pilkington case in Chapter 1). It is unsurprising that such crimes cause enhanced levels of emotional trauma, such as fear, panic, anxiety, and depression, or that these psychological harms often persist for longer periods of time compared with those suffered by non-hate victims. The fact that hate victims are targeted because of who they are inevitably impacts upon their emotional wellbeing at a much deeper emotional level. It has also been important to view experiences of victimization within the broader socio-structural contexts in which they take place. The chapter therefore began by briefly exploring some of the social harms experienced by marginalized identity groups. By viewing hate-motivated crime within its social context we can begin to see how, for many victims, hate incidents become just *one* part of a continuum of prejudice and victimization.

The heightened levels of harm commonly experienced by hate victims demonstrates a clear need for measures specifically aimed at reducing harm—rather than solely focusing on enhancing the punishment of offenders (see book Introduction). Restorative justice may be one measure through which the harms of hatred can be addressed. We must not, however, be too idealistic in our expectations as to how far restorative processes can aid this process (see Chapter 2). As this chapter has highlighted, hate victimization is symptomatic of a much broader socio-structural problem. In attempting to put right the wrongs of a crime, justice processes cannot be expected to repair the structural ills of society (Kelly 2002; though see Chapter 6).[18] Nevertheless, as we will see in the chapters that follow, restorative processes may well be equipped to *help* victims recover from their direct experiences of hate crime (Chapters 4 and 5), as well as secondary forms of victimization caused by state institutions (Chapter 6).

---

[18] Although some scholars have posited a vision of RJ as a way of ordering society (see Sullivan & Tifft 2001) most see it only as a means through which justice can be served (Braithwaite 1989; Zehr 1990).

4

Repairing the Harms of Everyday Hate Crime: Exploring Community Mediation and the Views of Restorative Practitioners

Introduction

This chapter evaluates the first set of empirical findings regarding the main aim of the research study: to explore whether RJ *helps* to repair the harms of hate crime. I begin by introducing the reader to the first restorative intervention that was examined for this book—The Hate Crimes Project (henceforth HCP) administered at Southwark Mediation Centre (henceforth SMC) in London. I evaluate how 'restorative' community mediation meetings were in practice in order to assess whether this particular intervention could be legitimately labelled as a 'restorative practice' (see Chapter 2). The chapter then highlights the different types of hate crime cases which were referred to the HCP.

The second part of the chapter provides an analysis of interviewees' levels of satisfaction with the mediation process, as well as their perceptions of procedural fairness. I then examine the qualitative (and some quantitative) data on the levels of emotional harm experienced by complainant victims directly before and after mediation. This part of the chapter also identifies the various parts and processes within community mediation that were emphasized by interviewees as being *helpful* to their emotional recovery.

In the final part of the chapter I briefly explore the data obtained from practitioner interviews, highlighting again the various aspects of the restorative process that were considered by restorative facilitators as aiding victims' emotional wellbeing. It is at this point that I illuminate the importance of victims and their family members exploring not only the harms caused by prejudice, but what their identity means to them. Finally, the chapter is drawn to a close by setting out the common processes within RJ—as found across the two datasets—that supported victims' recovery from hate crime. These included: 'storytelling', support offered by facilitators, physical gestures that indicate contrition, and promises made by offenders that incidents would not be repeated.

Part I: Community Mediation and the Hate Crimes Project

The HCP was set up over ten years ago at SMC (an independent charity-based organization) to specifically deal with conflict in local communities where an incident of hate or prejudice had been reported to them or another local agency. The HCP's caseload includes all types of hate crime/incidents as defined by the Association of Chief Police Officers (ACPO) (see Chapter 1) and uses both direct and indirect forms of community mediation, as explained in Chapter 2. Cases are referred to the HCP by various state agencies, most commonly the police, housing associations, and anti-social behaviour units. However, in some cases parties contacted the HCP themselves.

In the majority of cases where an incident had been reported to the police, officers had failed to take any direct action against the accused perpetrator (most frequently because there had been a lack of tangible evidence to pursue the allegations), or the complainant victim was told that the matter related to a domestic dispute that was better dealt with by the council (see Chapter 6; see also Bowling 1998). In cases where one or both parties had (also) reported the incident to a housing association, housing officers had typically responded to each of the parties by writing letters to them restating the terms of their tenancy agreements and warning them that breaches may lead to eviction. In several of the cases under research, housing officers had also notified the local Anti-Social Behaviour Unit (ASBU). Common among all of the cases researched was that the police, housing associations, and ASBUs had failed to resolve conflicts that involved hate crime/incidents. This meant that disputes had commonly escalated over a period of weeks, months, or even years. It was during such escalation that cases were referred to the HCP, in the hope that mediation could resolve conflict.

The main aims and objectives of HCP could be summarized in the following terms: to use inclusive dialogue to explore the effect that inter-personal conflicts had on the lives of those directly and indirectly involved; to enquire into issues around prejudice which may be at the heart of the conflict; and to find a resolution that is acceptable to all or most. The mediation process typically ended with a written agreement outlining the undertakings that both parties had agreed to. In some cases this involved an apology by one or more parties. More commonly, agreements included a written and signed promise to cease certain activities (including hate speech), and sometimes an agreement to avoid combative communication if similarly provoked in the future.

The mediation process always began with separate meetings with each of the stakeholders of the conflict at their home or at SMC. These initial meetings would often be followed up by telephone calls or a second home visit before any direct mediation took place. The importance of preparation is discussed in detail in Chapter 7; suffice to say here that part of this preparatory process was to ascertain the participants' experiences and aspirations, as well as their willingness to participate in a direct meeting or conference with the other stakeholders of the incident/conflict. It was the responsibility of the mediator to make clear the ground rules for engagement, emphasizing the goal of resolution, rather than adversarial debate. Mediators also frequently re-contacted, or referred clients to, other organizations, such as housing associations, ASBUs, schools, colleges, or the police, if a conflict could not be resolved by mediation alone (see Chapter 6).

How 'restorative' was the mediation process?

Leena Kurki (2000) explains that the goal of RJ is 'to rebuild ruptured relationships in a process that allows three parties (victims, offenders and the wider community) to participate'. If we were to accept such a definition, community mediation at the HCP would clearly be included under the label of RJ. The mediation process was about repairing relationships by allowing the parties, as well as other community members, to resolve conflict (including any hate incidents) that had harmed them. Typically, the mediator focused on the fact that all stakeholders wanted an end to the conflict. Although direct offerings of reparation, such as an apology or compensation, were atypical, other displays of contrition were displayed through physical gesticulation, such as shaking hands, and by the parties signing a mediation agreement that outlined the undertaking both parties had agreed to (see below).

Unlike most other restorative interventions, participants were not labelled as 'victims', 'offenders', and the 'wider community' (Kurki 2000). Instead, stakeholders were simply referred to as 'the parties' or as 'party one' and 'party two'. The neutrality of such labels was both community mediation's strength and weakness. The main criticism which can be made about community mediation, in relation to its restorative credentials, is that unlike victim–offender mediation or conferencing, the 'offender' will not necessarily have agreed to take responsibility for the alleged wrongdoing before any direct meeting takes place. Many RJ theorists argue that it is essential that offenders take responsibility for their actions *before* attending an RJ meeting, as this demonstrates a willingness to repair the harms that have been caused (Braithwaite 1989, 2002). In community mediation meetings therefore, not only were 'accused perpetrators' (party two) less likely to directly admit to wrongdoing, but they were also less likely to undertake direct measures of reparation to other stakeholders. After all, the process ran outside the criminal justice system and, as such, there lacked any 'official' coercion to participate. This also meant that mediation agreements lacked any legal enforcement.[1]

The fact that 'the parties' did not take the specific roles of 'victim' and 'offender' was, however, where community mediation gained its greatest potential in both resolving hate incidents and potentially repairing harm. Other RJ practices (particularly VOM) assume a binary classification of the parties, dividing those involved into 'victims' (those who have been wronged) and 'offenders' (those who have wronged) (Dignan 2005). These labels suggest dichotomous roles in the offence and therefore diametrically opposed responses by the criminal justice system (Christie 1986). However, as is made clear in this chapter, many 'hate conflicts' involve highly complex and multi-layered disputes between parties who have *both* taken part in various anti-social behaviours. It also becomes apparent that although responsibility is not always apportioned before mediation, the open discussion within meetings, and agreements later made between the parties that draw on common goals between participants, hint at both responsibility and reparation. Indeed, it is the exploration of the social contexts in which such crimes and

---

[1] Though as we will see in later chapters there is often pressure on those accused of wrongdoing to take part in the process from certain organizations (see Chapter 6).

anti-social behaviours occur combined with discussion on the cause and effect of the actions committed by *both* parties that provides for the best opportunity for resolution (see further below and book Conclusion).

In other words, in many of the conflicts which involved allegations of hate crime, labelling one party as 'wrongdoer' and the other as 'victim' would not necessarily have reflected the true nature of the complex social conflicts that parties were embroiled in, even though one party may well have committed an actual hate offence. The inclusive approach taken to resolving hate crimes at the HCP—combined with its emphasis on empowering participants in a dialogic process that aimed to find resolution to conflict—meant that while community mediation could not be classified as a 'fully restorative' practice (see McCold 2000) it drew significantly upon RJ principles (see Chapter 2).

Types of hate crime

A broad range of hate crimes/incidents were investigated during the eighteen months spent observing restorative meetings and interviewing victims at the HCP. In total, twenty-three complainant victims who had previously participated in mediation at the HCP were interviewed. At times it was difficult to classify which forms of prejudice were central to each victim's[2] experience of victimization because, as we will see, a combination of identity traits can affect both the causation of hate incidents and how victims react to them. Nevertheless, in the majority of cases, a clear 'type' of prejudice was identified by the victim and other stakeholders as causal to the incident.

Fifteen victims stated that they believed the incident was motivated by hostility against their race, ethnicity, or nationality.[3] In one case the victim identified the incident as being solely motivated by hostility towards his sexual orientation, while another was

---

[2] For reasons of simplicity, I will refer frequently to victims and complainant victims collectively as 'victims'. This is because all interviewees self-identified as having been victimized. The differentiation between 'victim' and 'complainant victim' made elsewhere in this chapter/book is recognition of the slightly different roles that are played by participants within the restorative practices researched and not a reflection of differing levels of the harm suffered by individuals (see further, book Conclusion).

[3] See Appendix A, question 11.

believed to be motivated by hostility against the victim's disability. However, various other cases were thought to be motivated by a combination of different prejudices. For example, in a conflict lasting over eighteen months, the victim was targeted not only because of his sexual orientation but because of his HIV status and other physical disabilities (see Case Study 1). Other victims believed that the offender had targeted them because of their race *and* disability, or race *and* sexual orientation, and in one case the victim expressed that the offender had abused her in terms of her race, disability, *and* sexual orientation.[4]

Hate crimes/incidents also varied in seriousness,[5] ranging from verbal abuse and intimidation to grievous bodily harm. The majority of cases researched involved an ongoing conflict that had escalated over an extended period of time. Complaints about noise between tenants in large local authority housing blocks often sparked tensions between neighbours which, when left to fester, developed into larger-scale disputes. It was common for such disputes to culminate in verbal outbursts, at which point comments about the race, sexual orientation, and/or disability of the complainant victim were made. This changed what was initially a neighbour dispute about noise or rubbish into a 'hate incident'.[6]

In a significant minority of other cases (seven), it was clear that the victim had been specifically targeted over a sustained period of time by someone who held animosity against his or her cultural and/or identity background (see similarly, Bowling 1993, 1998; Garland & Chakraborti 2006). Some of these cases were marked by extreme episodes of violence (see Case Study 1 and book Conclusion) and in several others, the victim had suffered damage to their property. In all other cases, conflict involved one or more incidents of verbal abuse or harassment (including persistent complaints made about an individual to the police and/or housing associations that were perceived by the victim to be racially motivated).

---

[4] The variety of different prejudice-motivated incidents researched enhances the validity of the study's exploration of RJ and hate crime. However, due to the relatively small sample of disablist and homophobic incidents there is little room to explore the nuances between different types of hate victimization or how RJ might respond differently to different types of hate crime.

[5] 'Seriousness' refers to the severity of an offence based on its classification under the criminal law and not necessarily on the level of harm that an incident causes.

[6] See further analysis of these types of conflict later in this chapter, 'Resolving multi-layered hate disputes'.

Part II: Repairing the Harms of Hate Crime

Before I analyse the emotional benefits that might be gained from participating in community mediation, it is instructive for us to begin by examining how satisfied participants were with the process, as well as whether they found it to be procedurally fair. Out of the twenty-three interviewees from Southwark Mediation, eleven had taken part in both direct *and* indirect mediation meetings with the other party, leaving twelve complainant victims who had participated in indirect (shuttle) mediation only. Twenty out of the twenty-three interviewees stated that they were either 'very satisfied' or 'satisfied' with the mediation process, with only two stating they were either 'dissatisfied' or 'very dissatisfied' (see Appendix A, Sections 3 and 5).[7] All but one interviewee agreed that the mediator explained to them how mediation worked and what it aimed to achieve, while twenty interviewees also stated that the mediator acted fairly throughout the process. As one interviewee remarked: 'I felt that she gave us both exactly the same amount of time to speak, to talk about what we were going through. So we both talked and it was there that she was able to see that these are the issues that we were both experiencing and this is where it started from.' In total, twenty-one complainant victims expressed that they found the mediation process to be either a 'positive' or 'very positive' experience. Based on these findings it was unsurprising that twenty-two out of the twenty-three participants went on to state that they would recommend mediation to other individuals who were involved in a similar incident/s.

In Chapter 2 we saw that, provided stakeholders are not given false expectations about what they could gain from RJ and are given the chance to describe how the crime has impacted upon them, participants should gain a sense of empowerment and emotional healing from participating in restorative dialogue (Zehr 1990; Strang 2002).[8] It was important, therefore, that the vast majority (twenty-one) of interviewees felt that the mediator provided them with an opportunity to explain how the incident had affected them.[9] One interviewee stated:

---

[7] One other interviewee stated that they were neither satisfied nor dissatisfied.

[8] See below how ineffective facilitation can lead to dissatisfaction and in some cases greater levels of anger and anxiety.

[9] With one stating 'no' and another stating they were 'unsure'. All eleven interviewees who participated in direct mediation stated that they had been given an opportunity to express how the incident had affected them.

She wanted to know in detail what happened and how do we feel now and how we were feeling before he [perpetrator] moved in. She asked us all different questions which I never thought she would ask. And she was interested in what we were going through... Just sitting down and talking it though with [her]. She has tried to comfort us, it was very helpful.

This finding was supported by observations of meetings where parties were clearly given several opportunities to express how they were feeling and to explain how the incident/s had affected their emotional wellbeing (see similarly Strang 2002).

Healing emotional harms: anxiety, fear, and anger

Research reviewed in Chapter 3 highlighted the fact that hate victims often endure heightened levels of fear and anxiety as they anticipate repeat attacks or abuse by the perpetrator (see Herek et al 1997; McDevitt et al 2001; Iganski 2008). It was therefore important that the study explored whether community mediation helped to improve these emotional traumas. I did this by asking both open and closed questions about complainant victims' experiences of the mediation process (see Appendix A).

To begin with, interviewees were simply asked whether the mediation process *directly* helped to improve their 'emotional wellbeing'. Seventeen agreed that it had, 1 stated they were unsure, leaving 5 who did not feel that it helped to improve their emotional wellbeing.[10] One positively affected interviewee explained: 'I'm more out there... I feel like I have gotten my confidence back. I am... looking for a job... There is peace... for me and my family so I'm back to being myself.' Using a 10-point scale, 1 being very low and 10 very high, interviewees were additionally asked to indicate a level of anger and a level of anxiety (that they felt towards the other party/about the incident) directly *before* and directly *after* the mediation process had concluded (see Appendix A, questions 37–40). The most common level of anxiety before mediation (mode), indicated by nine complainant victims, was ten. Two recorded an anxiety level of

---

[10] Though some of these five also indicated that the incident/s had only a limited impact on their emotional well-being to begin with. There was little variation between those who had participated in direct mediation compared to indirect mediation. Nine out of the eleven interviewees who took part in direct mediation stated that the process helped their emotional well-being, compared with eight out of the twelve who participated indirectly.

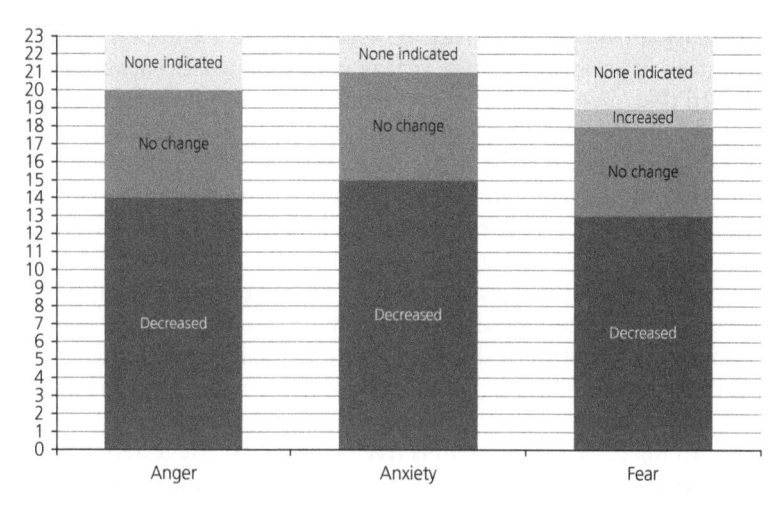

Figure 4.1 Impact of community mediation on complainant victims' feelings of anger, anxiety, and fear (Total N = 23)

NB: Measurement of fear was carried out on a 6-point ordinal scale. The measurement of anger and anxiety was based on a 10-point interval scale. See Appendix A, questions 33–40 for exact questions/scales.

3 or below (indicating a mild level of anxiety), with the remaining ten stating that their level was between 5 and 9 (with only two stating that the question was not applicable to them). For a majority of complainant victims (fifteen of the twenty-one), their levels of anxiety decreased, albeit not dramatically, directly after mediation. A Wilcoxon Signed-ranks test indicated that median levels of anxiety were higher directly before mediation (Mdn = 9) than they were directly after (Mdn = 5, Z = –3.313, p = .001). No interviewee indicated a higher level of anxiety after mediation. Similar results were recorded for levels of anger (see Figure 4.1).[11]

A slightly different method of data collection was used when measuring levels of fear by using likert-type questions (see Appendix A, questions 33–35), which asked interviewees whether they were fearful of the accused offender (or what he or she might do) before and after mediation.[12] Eighteen interviewees stated that they either 'agreed' or 'strongly agreed' that they were fearful before

[11] Mdn = 10 before, Mdn 7 after, Z = –3.317, p = .001.
[12] Based on a scale of strongly agree, agree, neither agree nor disagree, disagree and strongly disagree.

mediation (five were not fearful before or after mediation). Of the eighteen interviewees who were fearful before mediation, half (nine) stated that they 'disagreed' or 'strongly disagreed' that they were fearful of the other party directly after mediation. This indicated that the mediation process can reduce feelings of fear for a significant number of hate crime victims. A complainant victim who had been racially assaulted remarked: 'Before mediation I was scared to do anything as I thought they might come. So I didn't want to, like, do anything wrong to them or go near them basically. But after I was more confident to mix with other people.' Another complainant victim of disablist abuse similarly commented: 'I'm more happy, it [direct mediation] made me talk more, I'm more confident, back to my old self and I'm enjoying my working, enjoying talking to people ...'. Collectively, the results suggested that the mediation process had the effect of *partially* reducing some of the negative emotions caused by hate crime victimization. The findings are consistent with other studies which have shown that restorative processes can help to reduce feelings of anger and anxiety among victims (see for example, Daly 2001; Strang 2002; Strang et al 2006).

What helped to repair the harms?

It was clear from the interviews that the majority of participants found mediation to be a positive experience that aided their emotional recovery from hate crime (see similarly Strang 2002). However, this finding alone does not show how or why mediation was able to help repair emotional traumas. Hence, the research was also focused on exploring what aspects of the mediation process helped or hindered participants' emotional wellbeing. A list of different parts/processes (ie process variables) involved during mediation was read out to interviewees who were then asked to state 'yes' or 'no' as to whether each part/process had helped to improve their emotional wellbeing. The process variables identified by interviewees were: 'having the opportunity to take part in the process'; 'explaining (directly or indirectly) to the other party how they felt'; 'explaining how the incident had affected their life'; 'meeting the other party face to face'; 'witnessing the other party's comprehension of how the incident/conflict had affected them'; 'receiving an apology from the other party'; and 'obtaining assurances that the incident(s)/dispute would stop'.

Talking about harm

The two most common (and connected) variables that were elaborated upon by the majority of interviewees as having aided their recovery were: 'being able to explain how they felt to the other party (directly or indirectly)' and 'having an opportunity to express how the incident/s had affected their life'.[13] This finding was well supported by the observations of both direct and indirect meetings, where it became very clear that mediators gave many opportunities for both parties to explain how the incident had affected them and for the other party to respond to this.

Restorative justice scholars argue that victims who are given the opportunity to describe how a crime has impacted upon their life can gain a sense of empowerment (Braithwaite 2002). As one interviewee explained, 'that's the main thing, being able to talk to someone about it, because initially you don't think anyone is interested'. Judith Kay (2008) explains that this amounts to a process of 'storytelling' that enables victims to be rescued from the shadows of silence, isolation, and despair, bringing them to a place of greater security. Victims who vocalize emotional pain often gain therapeutic release and feel emotional support from those who listen (see Chapter 2). One interviewee explained: 'It helped me because I talked to them and they [the other party] listened to me. The way that she [the mediator] was talking, she know where I was coming from and she know that I was getting intimidated and bullied.'

Another interviewee who had experienced ongoing racial abuse expressed how important it was to her that she and her husband were able to take part in a process that gave them an active role in their own conflict resolution: 'It's like they opened the door to us. If we know of anyone else in trouble we can always advise them to go to the mediation and do something about it instead of sitting there suffering.' Mediation therefore created the space for many individuals to explain to the accused perpetrator, either directly or indirectly, how they had been affected by the incident/s. In fact, there was little qualitative difference between indirect and direct

---

[13] Twenty of the twenty-three interviewees stated that they were either 'very satisfied' or 'satisfied' with the mediation process; twenty-one had found the mediation process to be either a 'positive' or 'very positive' experience; and unsurprisingly twenty-two of the twenty-three participants also stated that they would recommend mediation to other individuals who were involved in similar incidents.

meetings with regard to complainant victims' ability to express how they had been affected by the incidents. For example, in one case where the complainant victim took part in indirect mediation he stated: 'they [the accused perpetrator] don't actually see the effect that it [prejudice] is having on you, so it's great to sit down and actually say this is what it is doing'.

Of course the communication of harm during indirect meetings will be dependent on how much trust is built between the mediator and complainant victim. Mediators must then relay these harms back to the accused perpetrator. During the observations that were made, the mediator made detailed notes of what had been said by both parties. She then asked participants for their permission to explain to the other party what they had said during the meeting. The relaying of information was in most occasions expressed articulately and accurately. In cases where a direct mediation meeting was arranged, the parties were encouraged to explain in their own words how the incident/s had affected them.

The mediator also asked complainant victims, before direct meetings took place, whether they felt comfortable with her raising the issue of identity-based prejudice if they did not feel comfortable mentioning this during the meeting themselves. I observed the mediator introduce the issue of prejudice in several direct meetings. In each case the topic was approached carefully without accusing participants of being bigoted. I recorded several statements made by the mediator, including, 'We need to be upfront about issues of identity.... you told X that "you're one sick individual", what did you mean by that?'. In another case the following question was asked: 'Can we talk about the issue of identity, about being "different"?'. This allowed the participants to open up a dialogue concerning identity-based prejudice, including how bias affects some of the stakeholders' everyday lives. It was common during such discussions for accused perpetrator/s to deny that they had committed a 'hate crime'; nonetheless the mere fact that the mediator was able to facilitate structured dialogue about minority identity and the effects of prejudice meant these issues were aired openly between the parties. This, in turn, often led to the development of mutual respect between the parties, helping to avoid future hostilities being directed towards any of the stakeholders (see Case Study 2 and further discussion in Chapter 8 on how participants develop mutual understanding).

Talking about harm in cases involving learning impairments

Mediators will frequently come across children and adults with learning difficulties, mental health issues, and language impairments (Talbot 2010: 7). Applying the 'normal' rules of communication to participants with such difficulties is unlikely to support inclusive dialogue. Restorative practitioners must therefore use the flexibility of restorative practice to find innovative ways for participants to express themselves during meetings. This will entail facilitators using different methods of communication that encourage participants to express themselves. Bonita Holland (2011) has highlighted several methods of improving communication between children with learning difficulties and language impairments. Some such methods include: rehearsing what might be said to others before saying it out loud; providing a mind map and highlighter pen for them to use to follow the restorative process; and using visual comic strips so participants can draw their stories.

Practitioners may also wish to explore the physical effects of a crime rather than simply asking victims to talk about their emotional problems. In several of the interviews carried out for this book, interviewees did not understand terms such as 'anxiety' or 'depression' and I often struggled to explain what these meant. Instead, adolescent interviewees were more often readily able to explain physical reactions to a crime such as that they had a 'sick feeling in their tummy' or that they 'felt shaky' or that they 'could not sleep at night'. Exploring such physical sensations may help to elicit the emotional sufferings that children find difficult to articulate verbally (see further Snow & Sanger 2011).[14]

Reparation: non-verbal expressions of contrition

It was unusual in community mediation meetings for verbal apologies to be offered, with only four interviewees stating that they had received a direct apology.[15] Instead, it was more common for participants to offer subtle forms of apologetic gestures, such as offering a hand-shake and/or placing a hand on the other party's arm. Changes in participants' physical demeanours were also indicative

---

[14] The fundamental importance of victims explaining the effects of prejudice and detailing their experiences of 'difference' is discussed below in Part III and further in Chapter 8.

[15] This finding was supported by observations.

of their willingness to rebuild their damaged relationship. For example, participants often began meetings with their arms folded; some even sat to the side of their chair facing away from the other party and refusing to make eye contact. However, throughout these meetings the mediator frequently (re)emphasized general points of agreement that were drawn out during discussions and, as the parties began to find points of mutual understanding, their body language then softened. In a case involving an elderly participant and her housing officer in a complex case involving disability hate crime and false accusations of racism, I noted in my fieldwork diary:

> Mrs A [complainant victim *and* accused perpetrator] was shaking and very tearful...She maintains most of her eye contact with me, the only other white person in the room...she is very defensive towards the other party and refuses to look her in the eye...As the meeting has progressed her body language has dramatically changed...Mrs A smiles and Mrs B [a housing officer who had accused Mrs A of racism] smiles back at her, she then touches Mrs B's hand, Mrs B smiles widely... By the end of the discussion both Mrs A and B are laughing and they again hold each other's hand.

Such observations were illustrative of the non-verbal means of communication that often helped to transform damaged relationships (see further Chapter 8). This meant that conflict resolution could be supported by those symbolic gestures that sent non-verbal messages of contrition and inter-personal mutuality; despite no verbal apology ever being made.

Assurances of desistance

It was clear that the mediation process brought about a variety of emotional benefits to the majority of complainant victims interviewed. However, for many, the road to emotional wellbeing remained partially blocked until the accused perpetrator provided an assurance that his or her prejudice-motivated actions would not be repeated. Many victims commented that although the process of mediation had helped to improve levels of fear, anxiety, and anger, such feelings could not be *significantly* reduced until they had tangible evidence that the perpetrator would not target them again. For instance, a victim of disablist harassment commented, 'They [the group of teenage offenders] said they would go a different way. At first I was not sure but they do that nowadays ...'.

Promises of desistance were ordinarily contained within mediation agreements, which outlined the undertakings each party had agreed to. In some cases this was spelt out specifically, for example, as a promise *not* to use racist language or *not* to direct animal sounds at the other party.[16] In other agreements, more subtle wording was used such as 'ceasing to use abusive language'. All agreements were written in neutral terms, ie undertakings were not party specific, though it was usually evident to whom certain undertakings were directed. Of particular significance was that in the majority of cases the accused perpetrator desisted from further abuse[17] having signed a mediation agreement to such effect (explored further in Chapter 8).[18]

It should be noted that signed agreements were not legally binding. Nonetheless, for many victims they were perceived to be valid. Furthermore, the breaching of agreements could have consequences for one or both parties. In cases where housing authorities had tried and failed to resolve hate conflicts, letters were frequently sent to one or both parties outlining their tenancy agreement and warning that anti-social behaviour and/or the commission of hate offences would breach the terms of this agreement. This meant that for some parties the mediation agreement was the last attempt at remedying their case. If incidents continued post mediation, the mediator could contact the parties' housing officer, at which point either the complainant victim/s could be relocated or the accused perpetrator would be found in breach of his or her tenancy agreement and the lease rescinded. Such recourse occurred in several cases (see Chapter 6).

---

[16] In several cases the making of monkey sounds, which were perceived as racially motivated, had caused distress to the complainant victim. Such sounds can amount to proof of racial aggravation, see *R v SH* [2010] EWCA Crim 1931.

[17] Hate incidents stopped in eleven out of the nineteen cases researched directly after mediation. In six cases the mediator used a multi-agency approach, bringing various other agencies into the mediation process to help resolve the conflict (see Chapter 6). In two cases the complainant victim stated that he or she continued to experience hate abuse post mediation.

[18] A further two interviewees were still fearful but less so than before mediation. In only one case did the interviewee indicate that he felt more fearful directly after the mediation process, though one week later the incidents ceased and he told me that he now feels much safer in his neighbourhood.

The role of mediators in supporting parties

One unanticipated finding, common amongst half of those interviewed, was the significance victims placed on the 'support' that was offered by the mediator. This support was intrinsically linked to the role practitioners played in engaging victims and their supporters in dialogue. In particular, interviewees spoke at length about how important it had been to them that the mediator had 'listened to their story' (see generally Sawin & Zehr 2007: 53–4). One complainant victim explained, 'I needed that support, I don't want to be shoved in a corner, it is something that should be followed up. I am glad that she [the mediator] does that.' Unsurprisingly, all interviewees agreed that the mediator had tried to help them to resolve the problems that the incident had caused. The role of the mediator was therefore seen by complainant victims as a vital part of their re-empowerment and ensuing restoration.

Later in this book I examine the negative impacts that were caused by local authorities and state agencies who became involved in hate crime cases (see Chapter 6). In many of these cases, complaints made to housing authorities led to further frustrations when housing officers failed to react to complaints of hate crime, or worse, their insensitive dealings with complainant victims served only to exacerbate their ordeal. Many interviewees also spoke of a lack of support from the police, who frequently redirected their complaints to the council as 'domestic disputes'. These experiences led to what is now commonly known as 'secondary victimization'. Such experiences compound victims' original trauma. Hence, when the mediator became involved in complainant victims' cases a great sense of relief was experienced by those who had felt 'let down' by other local agencies. The mediator often followed this up by re-contacting those agencies which had failed to offer the required support in the first instance. Mediation meetings were then set up between the complainant victim and an agency employee in order to ensure that the most vulnerable individuals were offered the support that these local authorities were statutorily obliged to provide (see Chapter 6).

Additional support offered by mediators post mediation was also seen as 'caring', and reassuring to individuals who felt that they mattered. This typically involved the mediator telephoning participants periodically to ensure that they were not experiencing any further problems (see Case Study 1). The extension of the restorative hand in this way was clearly an important source of comfort during a time when complainant victims felt at their most vulnerable. In this sense, the support offered by mediators to victims of hate crime must not be underestimated as an essential part of victims' recovery, especially for those individuals who feel marginalized within their own community.

The next case study demonstrates how the odious harms of ongoing hate abuse can be partly resolved using restorative dialogue.

Case Study 1 Mr V: Persistent homophobic and disablist violence
Mr V, a forty-two-year-old 'gay man' of 'mixed Afro-Caribbean-European'[19] heritage, lives in a small block of flats in South London. He is HIV positive and registered disabled. In 2007 a new neighbour (Mr X) moved into the flat directly above his. At first their relationship was cordial but after finding out that Mr V was gay Mr X became hostile towards him, calling him, among other offensive names, a 'queer cunt' and an 'AIDS spreader'. On one occasion, Mr V came home to find 'AIDS FUCKER' spray painted on his front door. After waiting several days for the council to clean it off, Mr V purchased his own solvents and erased it.

The homophobic abuse continued and escalated. Over a period of eighteen months Mr V had his car scratched with a key, rubbish and fluids poured onto his head from an upstairs balcony, and his and his partner's faces were spat on by Mr X. The harassment came to a head when, on one occasion, Mr V returned home from hospital on crutches (having broken his toe in an unrelated incident) and was met by a group including Mr X and his friends. After taunting him, one group member pushed Mr V to the ground whereby his two front teeth cut through his top lip and later needed replacing, while his chin required several stitches. Mr V described the impact of his ordeal in the following terms:

> I'd been a kick boxer up until my mid 30s... so to suddenly find yourself in a position where you are so ill that you have no strength and you can barely walk and somebody is attacking you and pushing you over and causing you injury... it's really hard to explain, it's almost soul destroying... it took away everything I had and am as a person.... I used to sit in here in the dark because I didn't want anyone to know I was in because I was frightened... that they would do something. I was terrified because I literally couldn't, I couldn't... *(At this point Mr V became distressed)*.

---

[19] Interviewees were asked to self-identify their identity characteristics.

The mediation process provided space for Mr V to express in detail his experiences of homophobic harassment. He stated that the dialogic aspect of mediation came as an immense relief to him and that simply by having someone listen to his story he felt that someone was finally taking his victimization seriously. The fact that Mr X was then asked to explain his behaviour, and to then think about the effects that it had, led Mr V to believe that mediation had improved Mr X's understanding of his identity as a gay man (see further, Chapter 8). As with many other complainant victims, he found the continuing support provided by the mediator post mediation of great comfort:

... it didn't just stop... even after the mediation [the mediator] rang me three or four times at regular intervals of a couple months to establish that everything was still OK, that I wasn't having anymore problems, that I was still feeling fine and that things were improving... it didn't you know, O.K. we're done, we've dealt with that, let's move on to the next case... It felt personal.

While the process of mediation clearly aided Mr V's recovery he, like various other interviewees, additionally spoke of the significance of observing that the offender kept to his promises of desistance:

After the mediation process I was initially still afraid of being attacked or, you know, spat on, but as each day went past you grow more in confidence that nothing is going to happen to you and I felt well supported at that time as the mediation process had taken place ...[20]

This case study is representative of several of the cases where the complainant victim had been targeted over a sustained period of time. It illustrates how community mediation can *help* to repair the harms of hate crime and, perhaps more importantly, prevent targeted abuse from recurring.

Resolving multi-layered hate disputes

Seven of the nineteen cases researched at Southwark Mediation were characterized by persistent targeted abuse that had been motivated (or partly motivated) by the accused perpetrators' prejudice towards the complainant victim. This left twelve other cases that

---

[20] Case Study also referred to in Walters & Hoyle (2012).

did not fit neatly into the conceptualizations of hate crime found within the broader literature (see Chapters 1 and 3). Deconstructing the characteristics of these highly complex conflicts was perhaps the most unanticipated component of the empirical study. In these cases, hate incidents often occurred within a broader context of inter-personal conflict between neighbours, the most frequent of which had primarily been sparked by complaints about noise. In these more intractable conflicts it was not uncommon for *both* parties to engage in various anti-social acts towards each other. This meant that in some cases both parties shared, at least to some extent, culpability for the broader conflict within which they had become involved.

Parties often lived in social housing blocks that were poorly insulated. Disputes commonly began with, or were further provoked by, frustrations and anger over loud music.[21] In other cases, screaming children or inconsiderate disposal of refuge lead to altercations which later resulted in a 'hate incident'. Some interviewees also felt that their ordeal had been exacerbated by the other party's drug and alcohol misuse. One interviewee noted: 'the neighbour next door was making this expression like a monkey noise... especially when he was drunk'. In other cases complainant victims also felt that the accused perpetrator's mental health had been partly to blame for his or her behaviour. For instance, one interviewee remarked: 'it could have been [racism] but I think part that and part that I later learned that he has got mental illness as well... his brother said at the mediation he has depression because he is sick. He might be sick but it doesn't mean you can carry on like that.' These multifaceted disputes typically escalated into protracted conflicts and eventually to accusations of racist, homophobic, or disablist abuse. Failure to explore and understand these precipitating social factors will compromise conventional criminal justice processes and even some RJ practices employed within the current justice system where focus is given to the pre-defined roles of 'victims' and 'offenders' (see further, book Conclusion). Responses that focus only on the cause and effect of an isolated crime or incident, without exploring its social context and the relationships that exist between the parties, are likely to be of limited success. Furthermore, it will be difficult to rebuild damaged relationships between

---

[21] Noise was a factor in the majority of cases.

community members unless justice interventions explore *all* the causal factors and consequences of inter-personal conflicts.

Assigning 100 per cent blame to one party and 100 per cent innocence to another will only act to aggravate the former's sense of injustice. This is not to deny that a hate crime/incident has occurred and that someone must be held responsible for this. In fact, it is intrinsic to the restorative process that social condemnation is conveyed towards such behaviour and in turn that the harms caused by hate-motivated conducts are repaired. However, both of these processes/outcomes are best achieved when performed within a broader discussion about wrongdoing, harm, and social disadvantage which have affected all stakeholders.

The following case study illustrates how the use of dichotomous labels and assumptions about 'victim' and 'offender' status would have served to deny the messy reality of some hate conflicts, and further explores the potential efficacy of mediation in such complex cases.

Case Study 2 Homophobic intimidation and racial and age-related stereotypes

Mr J, a young 'gay man' of 'mixed race', perceived himself to be the victim of homophobic harassment from his elderly neighbours, Mr and Mrs M (a 'black Caribbean' man and a 'white British' woman). They were accused of giving Mr J 'dirty looks', and pointing at him in the street. Frustrated by their behaviour, Mr J confronted Mr and Mrs M by knocking on their front door. Mr J stated that on doing this he had been met with 'a barrage of abuse', with Mr and Mrs M both repeatedly shouting *'people like you* are sick in the head' [my emphasis]. They also called him 'a thief, a drug addict and a psycho'. Mr J perceived these words to be homophobic. He responded by calling Mrs A an 'old witch'. Soon after this altercation other neighbours became involved in what became a complex conflict involving a multitude of disputants. At interview Mr J explained how many people had been involved in the conflict:

Well...for and against, so the people that was arguing for them there was them two and a man and his wife...after this happened they basically tried to force me out of here, getting my neighbours upstairs involved, the neighbours next door, the neighbours up the road, the neighbours next door to them...I would say by the end of it...like 15 people were involved.

Mr M was later approached by his housing officer about the conflict and he told the officer that he would hit Mr J with a bat if he came back. At interview Mr J told me that in response he 'told them both I'll knock you out cause I'll get my Nan down here and sort you out'.

Mr M's statement to the housing officer resulted in an intervention by the neighbourhood policing team and later a referral to the HCP. Both parties took part in indirect mediation meetings before participating in a face-to-face meeting. During indirect mediation Mr J explained that the incident had made him feel 'really worried' that he may be physically assaulted and that he wanted someone to 'make them understand' how he felt and for them to stop harassing him. The mediator raised the issue of identity, and Mr J said, 'people have misconceptions about gay people, especially elderly Caribbean people. There is a misconception that gay people are drug addicts and steal from people to feed their habit'. The mediator interjected, 'not all Caribbean people' feel like this and Mr J agreed. In a separate meeting Mr and Mrs M explained that Mr J had friends over all the time and that he had a 'chip on his shoulder' because he was young.

During direct mediation the issue of homophobia and the effects that this had had on Mr J were explored in detail. Mr and Mrs M responded by denying they were homophobic. However, they engaged in a discussion about how homophobia could affect people and later remarked that they had a gay nephew that they would 'never turn away'.

Mr J went on to apologize to Mr M for appearing rude when he knocked at their door, in response to which Mr M smiled and stood up to shake Mr J's hand. An agreement was then drawn up stating that the parties would not use prejudiced language towards each other and neither party should talk to other neighbours about the dispute. Finally, the parties agreed that the next time they saw each other on the street they should say hello. The parties shook hands again and thanked the mediator before leaving.[22]

The victim in this case felt that homophobia had been the main motivation underpinning his experience of harassment and threats of violence. However, he also recognized that his relative youth had

[22] This case study is also discussed in Walters and Hoyle (2012).

provided further provocation to the alleged perpetrators. During my observations of the mediator's preparatory meetings with Mr and Mrs A they had freely spoken about the problem with 'young people' whom they accused of frequently acting in an anti-social manner. In a similar manner, during my observations of a meeting between Mr J and the mediator he referred to the homophobic attitudes held by Caribbean people, often framing his criticism of his neighbours both in terms of their ethnic origin and their age.

As such, it would have been unfair to classify this case solely as a homophobic hate crime—as a police report may have concluded. The conflict involved various incidents perceived by Mr J to be motivated by homophobia, while his neighbours viewed the complainant victims' actions as both rude and ageist. While the apparent intimidation made Mr J fearful and anxious when leaving and returning to his home, the conflict only escalated once he confronted Mr and Mrs A at their home, during which he used ageist and gendered language towards one of the alleged perpetrators. This meant that the altercation involved verbal abuse from both sides that was marked by perceived bias. This single incident was to be a turning point in the dispute, allowing the conflict to turn from 'finger pointing' and 'dirty looks' into a serious threat, and counter-threat, of violence.

Although motivations were difficult to prove in this case, homophobia may well have been at the heart of the conflict. However, to an extent, age and race also influenced the perceptions and attitudes of the respective parties. Although Mr and Mrs A denied that their actions were homophobic, the mediation process provided a platform from which homophobia and the effect that it had on Mr J's life were discussed in detail. Mr J was able to explain why he felt their behaviour was homophobic and how this had made him feel. At the end of the direct mediation session Mr J said, 'we understand each other much better', to which Mrs A responded, 'each and every person in this world is an individual... He's found out how we feel and we've found out how he feels'.

This mediation process illustrated how dialogical processes, if managed sensitively and according to restorative principles, can diffuse conflict and expose ignorance and prejudices to critical scrutiny. An adversarial contest, played out in court, would not have been equipped with the tools to root out the many intersecting prejudices revealed by such a dispute, nor would the criminal process adequately consider the varied socio-economic factors that formed the social context within which hate-motivated conflict emerged. In these more complex cases, a variety of social factors need to be explored and addressed together if 'victims' are to obtain emotional restoration and all 'parties' are to find a peaceful resolution to their experiences of conflict.

Community mediation: a panacea?

The mediation process clearly promoted emotional benefits for the majority of complainant victims. However, it would be idealistic to assume that the process can provide complete emotional reparation for all those who participate. There will inevitably be a variety of other factors that are important to emotional healing. Interviewees were additionally asked what 'other factors have helped with your emotional wellbeing since the incident?' A list of other factors was read out including: the passing of time; support from a partner, friends and/or family; support from a housing officer; support from a non-government/charity organization; other (see Appendix A, questions 31 and 32). Several interviewees spoke of the importance of emotional support from family, friends, and other neighbours in helping them to feel secure again. In some cases, additional support from charitable organizations was also obtained. For example, one interviewee felt that his employer MENCAP (a charity that supports people with learning disabilities) was very supportive in helping him come to terms with his abuse, while Mr V (from Case Study 1) mentioned that contact from 'the Metropolitan Gay Policing Group... was reassuring'. Although these additional factors were commonly helpful in supporting emotional wellbeing, it was clear from the interviewees' other answers that the mediation process had remained a key component in their emotional recovery.

While mediation had aided the majority of victims' emotional recovery, there remained two cases where the complainant victim stated that the process had made matters worse. In one case the interviewee explained, 'it has made it worse... because I haven't been able to get where I want to get to, I wanted to be on band 1–3 but I am still on band 4 [referring to housing bands in order to move]'. In this case the victim was clearly angry that the mediator had not changed her housing band. It was evident during interview that she did not appreciate that the mediation service was not in a position to change individuals' housing bands, or that this was something mediators should aim to influence.[23]

It should also be noted that for a minority of victims (five) mediation was simply unable to aid their emotional wellbeing. In one case, lasting over ten years, direct mediation between the complainant victim and the accused perpetrator could do little to heal the trauma that the victim had endured. Rather, it was only once she was moved away from the offender that she could start to rebuild her life. She explained: 'I don't think any service can improve you emotionally. Emotionally, that is something you have to do yourself. So I wouldn't say they improved me I would just say that they are there to help.' Long-term abuse that persisted over a period of years often left victims with emotional scars that could not be 'fixed' by community mediation. This was reflected in the findings on closure. All victims were asked if they could now put the whole incident behind them. Only eight agreed that they could. Seven interviewees stated that they 'neither agreed nor disagreed' while some victims stated that they were somewhere in the 'middle' with regards to moving on from the incident. This left eight interviewees who stated that they disagreed that they could put the whole incident behind them. Such a finding was not surprising given the persistent and long-term nature of many hate conflicts. Moreover, in most cases the complainant victims still lived next door, or close by, to the perpetrator, and this acted as a constant reminder of their previous victimization.

The fact that mediation could not heal *all* victims of hate crime could also be linked to the socio-structural disadvantages that are endured by minority identity groups—as explored in Chapter 3. The 'process' of prejudice and discrimination that many minority communities experience inevitably leaves many hate victims feeling vulnerable to future hate abuse—whether that be to the possibility of further victimization from their neighbour or attacks by other members of the local community (Ahn Lim 2009). It will not always be possible for criminal justice measures to offer victims a clear pathway to emotional recovery due to the pervasive nature of hate abuse. Even those victims who stated that their levels of fear, anxiety, and anger had been reduced post mediation, did not feel they were completely free of these negative emotions. Hence, we

---

[23] Though, as we will see in the next chapter, mediators sometimes work with housing officers in order to relocate victims.

might best view RJ as only ever really *helping* to repair the harms of hate crime, as against providing full reparation for victims. This is because hate victims' experience of harm will remain attached to a continuum of social, structural, and cultural disadvantage.

Such a conclusion does not mean that RJ fails in its aims to repair harm, far from it. Indeed, we have seen how restorative dialogue can play a pivotal role in aiding the recovery of a substantial number of hate victims. We will also see in Chapter 6 how community mediators often implement multi-agency approaches to the mediation process that help to repair some of the institutional harms caused by local state authorities, while in Chapter 8, we will explore how restorative dialogue often prevents targeted victimization from recurring.

Part III: The Experiences of Restorative Practitioners

A total of eighteen months was spent at the HCP conducting observations and interviewing complainant victims. However, in order to make more general observations about the use of RJ for hate crime it was necessary to broaden the research out to cover other restorative practices. In the next chapter I explore the use of a restorative disposal implemented in Devon and Cornwall for minor hate incidents. However, before then, this chapter concludes by analysing data from interviews carried out with RJ practitioners from across England who had direct experience facilitating hate crime cases. Due to the similarities in the practice used by these practitioners and the processes used at SMC, these data are evaluated as part of this chapter.[24]

A total of twenty-three interviews were completed with restorative practitioners. Collectively, they described in detail a total of twenty-eight separate cases of hate crime that had been resolved using RJ. Most practitioners worked full time as RJ facilitators at: community mediation centres (seven); Devon and Cornwall Police (five);[25] Youth Offender Services (four); NACRO's[26] Restorative Justice Centre (two); schools (two); independent RJ practitioners who

---

[24] As we will see in the next chapter, despite its label as a 'restorative' practice, the restorative disposal in Devon and Cornwall did not strictly administer restorative principles.
[25] Discussed in more detail in Chapter 5.
[26] The crime reduction charity.

had previously worked in the criminal justice system (two); and the probation service (1). Inevitably, the types of RJ practices that were used by the practitioners differed but for the most part practitioners had used victim–offender mediation, FGC, or community mediation meetings based on restorative principles.[27]

The types of hate crime referred to varied, but most common were racially aggravated offences, followed by cases involving homophobia and anti-religion.[28] Interview schedules were semi-structured, though unlike in victim interviews, questions were mostly open ended in order to allow practitioners to fully describe their case examples (see Appendix B). The interviews also asked practitioners about reparation agreements, whether they perceived the victims in their cases to have gained any emotional benefits from the process, and, finally, how they had dealt with issues of prejudice as well as the potential for repeat victimization during meetings (see Chapter 7).

Exploring harm and prejudice

For the most part, the information provided by practitioners concurred with that which had been offered by victims from the HCP. Practitioners were asked both open and closed questions relating to the reparation process (see Appendix B). By far the most common theme relating to emotional reparation was that victims were able to explain how the hate crime had affected them and their families' lives. This finding has already been explored above in relation to mediation, however it is useful to analyse some of the comments provided by other restorative practitioners in this regard in order to reemphasize the significance of storytelling in cases involving hate. In particular, practitioners frequently spoke about the fundamental importance of exploring the issue of 'identity'. For instance, one practitioner interviewee explained: 'In cases where I've worked with homophobia the party has wanted them [the offender] to know... what it's like to be a gay man or a woman in the community, what it's like to experience... homophobic prejudice, so there's a lot of learning that can be gained.' Another practitioner facilitating an anti-Semitic harassment case told me:

---

[27] Just over half (thirteen) of practitioner interviews were carried out face to face with the remaining interviews (twelve) being completed over the telephone.
[28] None of the interviewees spoke of disability hate crime cases.

They [victim and his family] went to great lengths telling me about their own family history and who of their own family members they'd lost during periods of time [referring to the Holocaust], and showing me memorabilia in the house, paintings and things which had been done by relatives who were no longer with us, very personal stuff... Their identity was very, very important to them. And they went to lengths to tell me how proud they were to be Jewish. And they certainly want to maintain and hang on to that identify and those roots.

Having observed restorative meetings with this family myself via Oxford Youth Offending Service,[29] it was clear how important it was for this family to talk about their cultural heritage and for them to emphasize the effects that attacks against them based on their identity had had. The family's Jewish roots and their attachments to those killed during the Holocaust became central to the restorative process of 'storytelling', allowing them to explain not only how the harassment had affected them on a basic level but also why targeting them because they were Jewish had such an egregious impact (see Case Study 2, Chapter 8). In this sense, RJ might be viewed as a means through which victims of hate crime can reassert their identity (a form of essentialism) within a safe and empowering environment. Processes that fail to provide victims with a secure space to talk about their group identity will potentially lack an invaluable tool that enables victims to reclaim, at least in part, the individual security they lose through hate crime victimization.

Reparation: apologies and promises of desistance

Unlike community mediation, the offering of apologies by perpetrators was a common theme amongst interviewees. Most believed that the apologies had been genuine in the hate crime cases they had facilitated. However, concurring with my findings at the HCP was that a significant number of practitioners went on to state that the obtaining of apologies was not sacrosanct to the restorative process. This was explained by one practitioner who stated: 'Apologies are a very adult sign of showing remorse. What was more important was showing the different perspectives in the room. Because by doing that you get to understand the rationale for that person's actions; why they are doing this? And why are they doing this to me?' Such statements emphasized, again, the importance of

---

[29] This case is further explored in Chapter 8, Case Study 2.

'storytelling' as fundamental to the restorative process, rather than any *direct* form of reparation.

Like community mediation, the importance of offenders offering promises of desistance was also frequently mentioned by the practitioners interviewed. For example, one practitioner stated:

> we moved on to questions to the victims [such as] what would make things better for you? They were saying things like, 'I just really want to be happy that you're not going to do this again.'...Just assurance. And at the end of the day, nobody's got a cast iron guarantee that they won't set fire to something in their house again, but...they thought that this was a genuine assurance that he wasn't going to do anything like this again ...

Practitioners additionally stated that victims' acceptance of other reparation could turn on whether they received an assurance that the crime would not be repeated. The common theme of assurances of desistance therefore ran across both datasets, making this aspect of the restorative process one of the most imperative components that aided victims' recovery.[30]

Common themes

The common themes found within and across each dataset have been highlighted throughout this chapter. However before concluding it is worth reiterating them here.

- Storytelling

The importance of 'storytelling' was of particular salience to complainant victims at the HCP and for practitioners who had facilitated hate crime cases. It became evident throughout interviews and during observations of mediation meetings that victims gained considerable emotional release from being able to articulate the harms that they had endured. In many cases this entailed the victim talking at length about their identity and the impact that prejudice, both with regard to the offender's actions and other community members more broadly, had had on them (see further Chapter 8).

- Promises of desistance

The fear of re-victimization meant that promises of desistance became pivotal to most victims' emotional recovery. Although

---

[30] Practitioner data relating to repeat victimization, domination, and inequalities during meetings are analysed in Chapter 7.

active participation and the vocalization of harm helped to reduce levels of anger, anxiety, and fear, it was not until victims obtained assurances of desistance, and in some cases observed that the offender had adhered to his or her promises, that victims could finally move beyond their experience of targeted abuse.

- Facilitator support

One of the unanticipated findings within the studies was the significance that victims put on the support given by restorative practitioners. The most meaningful way support was offered was simply by listening to the victim's side of events. Further support was then offered by co-ordinating meetings with other parties in order to resolve conflict, and finally by re-contacting victims after meetings to check that they were okay. This led to victims feeling that their experience was finally being taken seriously.

- Reparation

At the HCP, direct apologies were infrequently offered. Instead physical gestures such as handshaking, smiling, and laughing were suggestive of a new relationship that indicated a certain level of contrition by one or both parties. Other restorative practitioners spoke of the commonality of apologies as a form of reparation. However, many went on to note that such offerings were not fundamental to the successful application of restorative dialogue.

Conclusion: Understanding Hate Incidents and Repairing the Harms They Cause

The study at the HCP revealed a multitude of hate crimes/incidents, hate harms, and processes of reparation. In particular, two 'types' of hate crime emerged from the data. The first involved ongoing and persistent targeted victimization that had clearly been motivated by identity-based animus towards the victim. This often led to severe emotional trauma among victims who became desperate for local agencies to take their experience of victimization seriously. It was clear in these types of case that one party was a 'perpetrator' of hate and the other a 'victim' of hate crime.

A more common type of hate incident that was observed provided for a less straightforward picture of hate-motivated crime. It became clear very quickly that many hate incidents occurred during intractable inter-personal conflicts that involved community members who were known to each other. Such disputes frequently escalated over a period of weeks and/or months, eventually culminating in the commission of a hate crime/incident. These types of hate crime are highly complex, as not only do they commonly involve numerous disputants, but frequently involve anti-social behaviours that are perpetrated on both sides of the proverbial fence. Thus despite the fact that a 'hate incident' had been committed, it was not always clear who was to blame for causing and/or prolonging the overarching conflict. In these more messy cases, 'the parties' are unlikely to respond well to the imposition of blame via retributive 'justice' measures.

Of course, some caution should be exercised as to the representativeness of the data in this chapter. The small sample of cases researched limits the general applicability of the findings, while the fact that cases were 'difficult' to resolve by other agencies may mean that they do not represent the many incidents which go unreported or which are dealt with effectively by the police (or via the courts) in the first instance. Nevertheless, we need only refer to the growing body of research that shows that the majority of hate crimes are committed by people known to the victim (most commonly neighbours) (see Mason 2005 in the UK context and Cheng 2013 in the US context), for us to consider that the findings at the HCP may well represent a significant proportion of hate crimes/incidents that occur each day between local community members (see Chapter 1). Perhaps most significant to note is that not all hate crimes can be conceptualized as straightforward expressions of bigotry, but are *sometimes* the outcomes of messy social realities which involve socio-economic deprivation, mental health, drug, and alcohol problems and, at least to some extent, shared culpability. It is certainly worth pursuing further empirical research into the situational and social contexts in which hate crimes occur in order to better understand the causal factors associated with hate-motivated incidents.

The other key finding in this chapter was that community mediation *helped* to repair the harms of hate crime. Interviews with RJ practitioners indicated that this finding also applied to other types of restorative practice, so long as restorative values were rigorously administered. In particular, victims must be afforded an opportunity to express to others how the incident/conflict has harmed them and that their 'story' is listened to. In addition, victims will need to obtain an official assurance from the perpetrator that incidents will cease. Only then can *all* the stakeholders of a hate crime move beyond the broader conflict within which each individual has become enmeshed.

Again a note of caution must be added to these findings. The results from the HCP, though encouraging, showed that community mediation could not aid the recovery of *all* victims of hate-motivated abuse. Furthermore, the levels of fear, anxiety, and anger that were documented before and after mediation showed only partial reductions for most victims, meaning that many victims remained, to some extent, angry, fearful, and anxious about their experience of hate crime. The reasons for the failure of community mediation to repair fully the harm of hate crime are complex and multifaceted. First, the fact that in many cases neither party took *full* responsibility for their actions meant that direct reparation was not always possible. This meant that complainant victims did not always receive apologies or material reparation for the harm they had endured. However a second, and more compelling, reason was that most victims continued to face socio-economic disadvantages that were beyond the control of restorative practice. Complex socio-structural conditions will ultimately limit the capacity for RJ practices to repair harm. Moreover, problems with alcoholism and drug abuse may make relationships difficult to rebuild, while mental health issues are likely to inhibit proactive undertakings of restoration. Finally, the fact that many victims living in urban areas reside in Victorian purpose-built apartment buildings (with poor insulation) means that issues of noise pollution will always be difficult to rectify. These multifaceted social issues will mean that for the time being, at least, there is no silver bullet that can cure the intractable hate conflicts that neighbours become embroiled in.

Such socio-structural problems mean that, despite the best attempts by mediators to help resolve individual episodes of hate-motivated conflict, the mediation process cannot undo overarching and systemic prejudices within society or reverse an entire group's socio-economic marginalization. While community mediation may be able to help repair *some* of the harms caused by institutional responses to hate crime (see Chapter 6), restorative practices more generally will not always have the resources or the independence necessary to challenge the harms caused by structural inequality.

If more successful rates of emotional reparation are to be achieved across restorative practices, the principles of RJ must be administered with rigour. The HCP was testimony to how effective restorative practice can be in helping to repair the harms of hate crime. If this is to be replicated, restorative facilitators must understand the complex nature of hate-motivated conflict, including the socio-structural inequalities that influence both the causes and consequences of hate incidents.

5
Restorative Policing and Hate Crime

Introduction

Restorative policing has proliferated over the past twenty years as police forces throughout the world have established new schemes to dispose of minor offences (O'Mahoney & Doak 2013). Many of these initiatives are now implemented as part of a statutory framework that aims to respond more effectively to (mainly youth) offending (see for eg the Young Offenders Act 1993, South Australia). Beyond the legislative framework on RJ, police services have also forged ahead with new restorative interventions for young and adult offenders in cases involving both minor and serious offences (within the UK context see eg CJJI 2012).

This chapter critically examines a restorative scheme established by Devon and Cornwall Police Service, England, which uses street-level RJ and conferencing to respond to (mainly) 'low-level' offences. Fourteen cases were researched where a 'Restorative Disposal' (henceforth RD) was implemented as part of the police's response to a hate-motivated offence.[1] The chapter repeats a similar pattern of analysis used in the previous chapter for community mediation by exploring the harm-repairing qualities of the disposal. The chapter will compare and contrast the findings with community mediation throughout, reflecting on the differing roles that police officers and community mediators undertake and the effect this has on the successful application of restorative values. The chapter then analyses whether police-facilitated restorative justice is an effective and/or appropriate means of resolving crimes which demonstrate, or are motivated by, identity-based prejudice.

---

[1] The fourteen cases made up 50 per cent of all hate crimes that were dealt with via the RD over a twelve-month period.

Part I: Restorative Policing

The emergence of police-led restorative conferencing in the mid-1990s was rapidly followed by empirical research which aimed to evaluate its effectiveness. One of the largest and most significant studies to be conducted has been the Reintegrative Shaming Experiments (RISE) which began in Canberra in 1995. This project was administered by the Centre for Restorative Justice at Australia National University in conjunction with the Australian Federal Police. The long-running study (1995–2000) has provided a large sample of cases and randomized control groups that have enabled the researchers to make statistically significant comparisons between conferencing and court processes. A variety of offences were evaluated including: drink driving (over .08 Blood Alcohol Content) at any age, juvenile property offending with personal victims (under eighteen years), juvenile shoplifting offences detected by shop security staff (under eighteen years), and finally violent offences (under thirty years). The hypotheses of the experiments were that: both offenders and victims would find conferences to be fairer than court, benefits to victims would be greater in conferences than in court, and there would be less repeat offending post conference than after court (Strang et al 2011).

The results of the RISE project have, by and large, been very positive (see Sherman et al 1998, 2000; Strang 2002; Sherman & Strang 2007; Strang et al 2011). Participants of conferences have reported higher rates of fairness and procedural justice compared with those who went to court (Sherman et al 1998). Victims also reported significant reductions in feelings of fear and anger (Strang 2002; see also Chapter 2). Moreover, the police facilitators themselves were more likely to feel satisfied with the outcome of a conference compared with cases that went to court (Strang et al 2011). Such findings have since been replicated within Australia, the US, and the UK. For example, the Bethlehem Police Family Group Conferencing Project in Pennsylvania, US, set up in 1995, has produced generally similar results to those of RISE (McCold and Wachtel 1998). The evaluation of the scheme found higher rates of satisfaction amongst victims, most of whom stated that they felt their opinions were taken into account (see also McGarrell et al 2000). As such, there appears to be growing support for Lawrence Sherman et al's initial conclusion that 'the advantages of increased respect for the police and greater victim involvement suggest that police-led conferencing is a desirable addition to the criminal justice system' (1998: 160).

The positive results from RISE have given credence to the idea that police-facilitated RJ can provide many of the same benefits as those administered by independent restorative practitioners. In many ways police-run conferences may provide additional benefits which independent facilitators cannot. In particular, advocates of police-led RJ have argued that the presence of police in uniform helps victims and their supporters to feel more secure (Hoyle et al 2002). Furthermore, police facilitation of RJ has also been shown to increase the likelihood that any agreed undertakings are carried out (Hoyle et al 2002). The provision of personal security within restorative meetings is particularly relevant to cases involving targeted abuse. Thus the facilitation of conferences by police officers will potentially provide victims of hate crime with a sense of protection against repeat victimization (see further discussion on preventing repeat victimization in Chapter 7).

Yet not all research on police-led RJ has been so equivocal. Carolyn Hoyle et al's (2002) study of the Thames Valley Restorative Caution in the UK provided a more mixed evaluation of police-led RJ. Over a three-year period, Hoyle et al interviewed 483 participants (though only sixty-four victims) in restorative conferences administered by Thames Valley Police. Overall, victims felt that the encounter helped offenders to understand the impact of the offence. Many also reported gaining a sense of closure and that they felt better after the conference. However, a significant proportion of victims also stated that they felt pressured into participating in the meeting, while many also felt that they were not prepared adequately for the process (Hoyle et al 2002: 18–19). In fact, just 13 per cent of participants stated that they met with the facilitator face to face prior to the meeting, with the vast majority of victims receiving only a telephone call (Hoyle et al 2002: 19).

Aggregated, the research findings on police-led RJ suggest that it can be effective at both repairing harm and reducing reoffending, though, as Hoyle et al have shown, improvements may still need to be made in relation to *preparing* victims for *voluntary* participation in face-to-face meetings. Yet neither the RISE project nor Hoyle's research provide us with evidence of whether RJ delivers similar benefits and/or limitations for hate crime. Hence, this chapter now turns to an evaluation of a police-led restorative scheme which has been used to resolve cases involving racially, religiously, and homophobically aggravated offences.

The Devon and Cornwall Restorative Disposal

In 2008, Devon and Cornwall Police Service (England) established a new restorative disposal which all police officers are now trained to use. The disposal is used for minor offences where the victim agrees to participate in either a direct VOM or FGC, or where the victim accepts some form of reparation indirectly. The disposal can be differentiated from the new youth cautions and the conditional caution, as prescribed under the Crime and Disorder Act 1998 (s 66ZA) and the Criminal Justice Act 2003 (ss 22–27) respectively, which are supposed to be based on rehabilitative and restorative principles, but which only sometimes utilize the purpose of reparation (O'Mahoney & Doak 2013: 140). Unlike the youth and conditional cautions, the RD has no statutory basis and does not provide official 'detections'. This means that the implementation of an RD is not recognized within national police records as an 'official' response to an offence. Instead, the disposal is used as an informal intervention which is then included within Devon and Cornwall's internal data on responses to crime.

Disposals are implemented in one of two ways. First, officers may use the disposal at street level by engaging both offenders and victims in an on-the-spot encounter which typically involves the offender apologizing directly or indirectly to the victim (Level One, CJJI 2012). In other cases, the responding officer may decide to arrange a restorative meeting (Level Two, CJJI 2012). This second option is more resource intensive and involves the preparation of both parties for VOM or FGC. Unlike the Thames Valley restorative cautioning model, meetings are not scripted (see Chapter 2). Instead, officers are trained on the principles of RJ and aim to encourage the offender to provide either material or emotional reparation to the victim. In most cases this takes the form of a written apology.

Types of hate crime

The majority of cases researched at Devon and Cornwall involved public order offences (usually offences proscribed under ss 4 and 5 of the Public Order Act 1986), mostly relating to racial abuse that led to the victim fearing violence.[2] In a high proportion of these cases, victims were harassed or verbally abused while at work, commonly in takeaway shops. Although some of the incidents had been ongoing (four), the majority of cases (ten) involved 'one-off' incidents, frequently involving offenders out late at night while intoxicated. This meant that, while some of the cases researched at Devon and Cornwall resembled the types of case that were investigated in Southwark, London, other incidents differed in both context and circumstance. This allowed for a broader range of hate crimes to be examined in relation to RJ.

How restorative was the Restorative Disposal?

An examination of the role that the disposal played (or failed to play) in victims' healing will be discussed below. It is worth exploring first the extent to which the RD could be labelled as a 'restorative justice' measure. Due to the way that the disposal is implemented, I was unable to observe meetings as and when they arose. This was primarily due to the fact that the disposals were frequently used contemporaneously with the reported incident. As I lived in Oxford there was simply not enough time to travel the long distance to observe meetings. Instead, the Force Restorative Justice Support Officer provided me with a list of all cases involving racial or religious aggravation that had been disposed of using the RD over the past twelve months (totalling thirty-two cases). Each victim was then contacted by the Support Officer who provided an information sheet about the study. I then contacted each participant to arrange an in-depth interview about their experiences of the RD and this resulted in fourteen interviews.

The overwhelming majority of interviewees stated that they had not heard of either the term 'restorative disposal' or 'restorative justice' before. My initial conclusion was that officers had simply failed to explain to the victim the purpose and aims of RJ—an intrinsic part of the process (Van Camp & Wemmers 2013). However, later, when interviewing the RJ Support Officer, it was suggested that many victims *may* have heard the term but not registered it due to their limited English vocabulary and the speed with which the disposal was administered. Some may even have forgotten the

---

[2] Though cases also involved religious and homophobic abuse.

term, as some disposals had taken place up to twelve months before the interview. My own experiences of communicating with the victim interviewees gave credence to this suggestion, and most interviewees went on to agree that they had participated in the RD when I explained to them that the offender may have offered some form of reparation, typically an apology, as part of the intervention.

Most interviewees stated that they had received either a written or verbal apology from the offender, indicating that facilitating officers had sought restoration for the victim. Yet on further inspection it became clear that the circumstances in which apologies were offered did not always adhere to key restorative values. For instance, many victims told me that they had been presented with two different options. The first was that the officer could pursue the case by charging the offender, which would involve a written statement from them and potentially a court appearance (several victims stated that it was impressed upon them that this was not desirable). The second option was for the officer to talk to the offender and for him or her to then provide an apology. Some victims felt that they were pressured into accepting this latter option, which in several cases transpired to be a single sentence scribbled on a piece of paper (see Case Study 3; see similar results in Hoyle et al 2002).

At face value, the disposal did appear to include elements of 'encounter', 'repair' and 'transformation'—as highlighted by Gerry Johnstone and Daniel Van Ness (2007a) (see Chapter 2). In my interview with the RJ Support Officer, I was told that officers are trained to spend some time, even if limited, explaining the aims and expectations of RJ. Officers should then attempt to organize a victim–offender mediation meeting where appropriate, placing emphasis on the offender repaying the harms that he or she has caused, either via an apology or through some material or community reparation. During the interviews that were conducted with police constables in Devon and Cornwall, several examples of direct meetings were provided. These interviewees also gave examples of cases where hate victims were able to express to offenders how the offence had impacted them, and where offenders had made genuine attempts to repair the harms caused. I felt confident that these officers, and many others, will have made genuine attempts to adhere to these restorative principles (see also Hoyle et al 2002).

Data from the victim interviews also highlighted that, while the disposal was not always implemented effectively, there were several restorative principles that officers made attempts to administer. In particular, just over half of the victims interviewed felt that they had been given an opportunity to explain to the officer how the offence had affected them and that the offender now had a better understanding of the damage the crime had caused. Still, the failure of the disposal to be fully or even *mostly* restorative was of concern. The study indicated several reasons for this. Most apparent was the lack of training that each officer had received on RJ (see further below). This was evident in cases where officers had specifically asked offenders to apologize (regardless of whether they actually felt sorry or not) (see similarly, Hoyle et al 2002). The failure of officers to establish a dialogue between the stakeholders, based on inclusivity, was perhaps testament to a lack of appreciation and understanding of the aims of RJ. Given the importance of participant preparation (see Chapter 7) and the need for impartial facilitation (Chapter 6), it is difficult to see how on-the-spot encounters that cajole apologies from offenders are truly 'restorative' (Maxwell & Morris 1993; Crawford & Newburn 2003: 187). It is for these reasons that the RD could, at best, be described as 'partly restorative'.

Part II: Could the Restorative Disposal Help Repair the Harms of Hate Crime?

The chapter now turns to an analysis of the harm-repairing qualities of Devon and Cornwall's police-led RD. The relatively small sample means that the results should be viewed with caution. Nonetheless, the qualitative data gained from intensive interviews help to elucidate the experiences of victims and the process variables which most impacted them. These data add to the growing body of research into the use of police-led RJ. Throughout this section, some of the findings will be compared and contrasted with those from the community mediation study (see Chapter 4).

Satisfaction and procedural fairness

A lower proportion of victims in the Devon and Cornwall scheme, although still a majority (eight out of fourteen), were either 'satisfied' or 'very satisfied' with the restorative disposal (RD). Four interviewees stated that they were 'very dissatisfied' with the disposal, while two victims said that they were 'unsure'. Similar results were recorded when victims were asked if they found the

RD to be a positive experience, with the same eight interviewees stating that it had been either 'positive' or 'very positive' (see Table 5.1). Several observations can be made about the lower levels of satisfaction amongst interviewees in Devon and Cornwall when compared to those at the HCP (Chapter 4). First, as mentioned above, most interviewees had not heard of the phrase 'Restorative Disposal', suggesting that officers had not spent sufficient time explaining the purpose of RJ. Further, the majority of victims also felt that officers had not provided them with information explaining what would happen during the disposal. In fact, only five interviewees agreed that the officer facilitating their case had explained to them what the RD disposal aimed to achieve.

Although most victims did not understand what RJ was, a majority agreed that the officer involved in their case had acted fairly when implementing the disposal (see Appendix A, question 24). Nine interviewees also agreed that the officer had tried to help to resolve the problems the incident had caused, or did so at least 'to some extent' (see Appendix A, question 26). Yet when victims were asked questions that were more specifically focused towards the goals of RJ, the results became less favourable. For example, interviewees were asked 'Did the facilitator provide you with an opportunity to explain how the incident had affected you?' As mentioned above, only half of these victims agreed that the officer had done so. One interviewee, slightly irritated by my question, simply responded, 'No Mark, they did not have time to do that!' Two victims also spoke of officers who had wanted to resolve the situation very quickly so they could go off duty. Such statements were indicative of the rushed manner in which RDs were sometimes implemented, with several disposals being implemented late at night at the scene of the incident.

Out of the fourteen cases researched at Devon and Cornwall, only one involved a direct mediation meeting between the victim and offender (all other cases were dealt with indirectly) (see similarly, O'Mahony et al 2002). Two interviewees stated that they wanted to meet with the offender through a direct mediation meeting but were never given the opportunity to do so. The precipitancy with which the disposal was administered was noted by five interviewees, all of whom complained about the lack of effort and time that had been put into dealing with their case. One victim remarked, 'she was very stern and she wanted to get on with her work'.

Part II: Could the RD Help Repair the Harms of Hate Crime?

Table 5.1 Perceived procedural satisfaction and fairness among interviewees participating in community mediation and the Restorative Disposal

Procedural satisfaction	Community mediation	Restorative Disposal
	$N = 23$ (%)*	$N = 14$ (%)
Provided with information about how the process worked	22 (96)	7 (50)
Provided with information on what the process aimed to achieve	22 (96)	5 (36)
Satisfied with process	21 (91)	8 (57)
Positive experience	21 (91)	8 (57)
Facilitator acted fairly	20 (87)	11 (76)
Facilitator helped (or helped to some extent) to resolve the problems caused by the incident	23 (100)	13 (93)
Had an opportunity to explain how the incident/s affected them	21 (91)	7 (50)

* Percentages are used for illustrative and comparative purposes only and are not intended to indicate generalizable data.
See Appendix A, Section 3 for exact questions asked.

Victims were then asked why they chose to take part in the RD—as against pursuing other avenues of criminal justice, such as arrest and caution (see Appendix A, question 22). The answers to this question were particularly troubling. Two victims stated that they had no other choice but to participate in the RD, while several other participants felt that they were pressured into it by police officers. A victim of racist and homophobic intimidation explained: 'The police woman... was like "it keeps kids off the street" and she was very strict... and I was "whoa, ok, well if that's the best way then O.K. I'll go for that one". But it was a bit pressurized. I really wish I had gone for the harassment order straight away.' The lack of free and informed consent given by some victims was concerning given the importance of voluntary participation in restorative practice (McCold 2000). Such responses indicated that some victims were not being presented with an option to participate in a process which is supposed to aim to repair harm through inclusive communication. If this is the case, more broadly, it would mean that a significant proportion of victims are participating in RJ without a genuine willingness to do so. As a result, they are less likely to be engaged fully in what is supposed to be an empowering and emotionally connecting encounter. It was for these reasons that a significant (although minority) proportion of victims stated that they were negatively affected by the disposal.

While some victims were clearly pressured into a process that left them feeling 'let down', it would be unfair to suggest that all victims were coerced into participating in the RD. In four out of the fourteen cases, victims stated that they wished to pursue the restorative disposal because they wanted the other parties to understand the consequences of their actions in order that they would 'learn from their mistakes'. An owner of a petrol station who had been the victim of racist abuse explained: 'I'm quite concerned about their age and their drunkenness and about their future. [If] they will get a chance to go to another country they will know what it is like to be a foreigner.' These few cases suggested that the RD gave some victims the opportunity to help offenders learn about their 'difference' while also understanding the harms caused by hate crime (see further, Case Study 2, Chapter 8).

Emotional wellbeing

Each interviewee was asked whether they felt the RD had improved their emotional wellbeing in any way. Just over half (eight) agreed it had. The remaining six stated it had not helped at all. Several reasons were given by those who agreed that the RD improved their emotional wellbeing, the most common being that they felt that the police officer had tried to 'help' them. One stated that 'I find in this country that the police try and help you if you have a problem'. A young woman who had been subjected to racial abuse by an ex-colleague similarly explained that she felt supported by the fact that the facilitating officer had contacted her again after the disposal to ask if she was still OK.

'Support', as offered by facilitators, was therefore a common factor in both community mediation and the police RD for improving victims' emotional wellbeing. This provides further credence to the importance that must be attached to effective and supportive responses to hate crime by the state (see Chapter 6). For victims participating in the RD, this appeared to be the case especially where facilitators had made an effort to re-contact them in order to see how they were getting on. Related to this was the fact that the

Part II: Could the RD Help Repair the Harms of Hate Crime?   133

vast majority of victims in Devon and Cornwall felt that the officer tried to help resolve, at least to some extent, the problems that the incident had caused, with only one interviewee stating that the officer had not done this. For example, when asked whether the police helped her to resolve her problems, one young female victim answered, 'yes [because]…they explained to them [the offender] that I was hurt and that they had been racist to me'.

Anxiety, anger, and fear

As with those who participated in community mediation, victims were also asked to indicate a level of anxiety and anger caused by the incident on a scale of 1 to 10 directly before and after the RD (see Appendix A, questions 37–40). Thirteen out of the fourteen interviewees indicated a level of anxiety before the RD, with the remaining victim stating that he did not feel it was applicable to his case. Eight victims went on to indicate a lower level of anxiety after the RD. The median level of anxiety before the RD was 8, falling to 4 directly after the RD (p = 0.03).[3] The reduction was experienced by the same eight victims who were both satisfied with the process and who found it to be a positive experience, suggesting that the process itself helped to reduce emotional harm for just over half of these victims. Similar results were recorded for levels of anger, with eight victims indicating a lower level of anger directly after the RD.[4] Despite a majority of victims indicating positive outcomes, two stated that their level of anxiety and anger had increased *directly* as a result of the RD (compared with none at Southwark Mediation).[5] For one victim, this was because he did not want to pursue the RD and felt let down by the lack of attention the police paid to his complaints (see Case Study 1 below).

Using the same six-point ordinal scale as used for mediation interviewees, levels of fear were then examined (see Appendix A, questions 33–36). Just over half of the sample agreed or strongly agreed that they were fearful of the offender before the RD. However, only

---

[3] A Wilcoxon Signed-ranks test indicated that median levels of anxiety were higher directly before mediation (Mdn = 8) than they were directly after (Mdn = 4), Z = 2.204, p = .003. Mean levels of anxiety fell from 8.75 to 5.5.
[4] Mdn = 9 before, Mdn 5 after, Z = −2.504, p = .001. Mean levels fell from 7.5 to 4.9.
[5] The final two stated that their anger was not applicable to the case.

one victim disagreed or strongly disagreed that they were fearful after the RD. A further three victims who had indicated that they strongly agreed before the RD went on to agree after, indicating a small reduction in level of fear. Five victims disagreed that they were fearful before or after and one stated that it was not applicable. This left one victim who stated that they were more fearful after RD, moving from agree before to strongly agree after.

The quantitative data on levels of anxiety, anger, and fear *suggested* that the RD, like community mediation, aided the emotional recovery of a majority[6] of victims. However, qualitative information taken from interviewees offered a more nuanced picture than this preliminary conclusion had conveyed. For example, when asking interviewees why they felt that their anxiety or anger had decreased, only four (half those whose levels had decreased post RD) explained that this was *directly* related to the RD—a less positive finding when compared to community mediation. This left four victims whose feelings of anger and anxiety had dissipated post RD but *not* as a direct result of the intervention.

Three of the four victims who agreed that the RD had helped to decrease their levels of anger and anxiety explained that this was because the disposal had helped to prevent the offence from recurring. This finding concurred with the importance put on promises of desistance by those who had participated at the HCP and again highlighted the need to address victims' fear of being retargeted. The other four victims, whose anxiety and anger decreased but not as a result of the disposal, spoke of the passing of time and support from friends and family as aiding their recovery. For instance, a victim of racial abuse and intimidation told me, 'the reason is not because of the restorative process but because of my friends and girlfriend'.

Interim reliability measures incorporated into the interview schedule ensured that quantitative levels of harm pre- and post-disposal were not attributed to the wrong variable. This part of the study helped to highlight other factors which are important to victims' emotional recovery from hate crime. This had also been illuminated in the data collated in South London, however it remained clear from the qualitative information gained in that study that the mediation process had been central to their emotional recovery. In

---

[6] Although for the RD this was a small majority.

Devon and Cornwall this could not be said to be the case for half (four) of those victims who had indicated lower levels of emotional trauma post RD.[7]

Reparation

One key variation between community mediation and the RD was that the officers who facilitated RDs almost always encouraged offenders to directly repair the harm they had caused. In those cases where reparation was offered (eleven), either a written or verbal apology was provided.[8] A significant difference between the two practices was that the police assigned the roles of 'victim' and 'offender' prior to the intervention. As previously discussed in Chapter 4, and elsewhere in this book, community mediation participants do not arrive at meetings with these labels. Avoiding the label 'offender' at community mediation meant that accused perpetrators were not expected to restore complainant victims to a position that they were in prior to the conflict. It also meant that they were not compelled to accept responsibility for their prejudiced actions prior to the process—an undertaking which many advocates of RJ state is imperative to its practices (Braithwaite 1989). The result was that most complainant victims did not obtain apologies or any other form of direct reparation. Rather, it was the ability of complainant victims to vocalize their experiences of victimization combined with the exploration of harms caused by hate incidents that supported participants' recovery from hate crime (see Case Study 2, Chapter 4). Through their newly found mutual respect for one another, participants then frequently offered more subtle forms of apologetic gesture, such as smiling and handshaking. Essentially, the process often gave rise to a promise by the accused perpetrators to desist from any future hostilities. Such gestures hinted at both responsibility and contrition without formally labelling or shaming participants (see further, book Conclusion).

---

[7] I explore further below why only a minority of victims participating in the RD experienced healing compared with a majority of those who had participated in community mediation.

[8] We will see further in the following section 'Genuineness' how these apologies were perceived by victims of hate crime.

The RD, however, involved clearly defined victims and offenders. Victims were asked to consent to the disposal and offenders were asked specifically by police officers to make reparation for their offence. This meant that, while victims were offered some form of reparation, they were not directly involved in discussions about how the offender should repair the harms caused. It was not uncommon for indirect meetings to be very short, some even taking place over the telephone. This clearly had repercussions for the effectiveness of the disposal and, in particular, the emotional wellbeing of victims.

Genuineness

The eleven victims who had received an apology from their offender were asked: 'How did it feel to hear the offender/other party apologize?' and 'Did you feel the apology was genuine?' Seven out of the eleven interviewees stated that they did not feel that it was a genuine offering of remorse. Of the remaining four, only two felt that it was genuine, with the remaining two stating that they were unsure. The benefits of receiving a genuine apology were explored in Chapter 2. In summary, sincere offerings of contrition relieve victims from feelings of self-blame. The acceptance of an apology additionally helps to bridge empathic divides between stakeholders as they begin to build a new relationship based on trust. In turn, victims relinquish their attachment to feelings of resentment and frustration, allowing them to move more swiftly beyond their experience of victimization. Conversely, offenders who offer emotional reparation that is perceived as disingenuous can exacerbate psychological harms, antagonizing victims' feelings of anger and frustration and ultimately jeopardizing their road to recovery (Daly 2001).

Interviewees frequently spoke of officers who had asked them whether they would accept an apology from the offender in order to resolve their case. It became clear that for many victims this entailed the officer simply asking offenders to write a short note of apology which was then handed back to the victim. Letters typically consisted of one sentence stating that the offender was 'sorry for the incident'. The lack of details and reasons given in letters led victims to believe that it was not a true display of contrition. In two cases the apology was derided for having been made on a 'scrap of paper', while in another case the victim refused to accept the letter. She explained: 'It wasn't genuine. He was a little bit like "it's your fault"... and it was so sarcastic and rude. It wasn't an apology!' A lack of genuineness meant that most acts of reparation did not fulfil their restorative purpose of helping to repair the harms of hate crime.[9] The failure of offender apologies to repair ruptured relationships was intrinsically linked to the arbitrary way in which reparation was sought and then offered back to victims. In particular, the minimal amount of time offenders spent writing letters, combined with the way in which they were then presented, left victims feeling 'let down' by the police and, therefore, by RJ.

It is essential that restorative practitioners do not become enablers of insincere reparation. Facilitators can prevent this by spending sufficient time preparing participants and ensuring that both parties are provided with space to communicate with each other (as was observed at the HCP). In cases where the offender does not wish to apologize, victims may find other aspects of the process reparative (see, for example, Chapter 4, Part II). It is imperative, therefore, that an apology arises organically during dialogue, rather than through facilitators insisting that offenders write letters devoid of genuine sentiment.

The indirect approach to the Restorative Disposal

The indirect approach taken by officers when administering the RD clearly impacted upon the perceived insincerity of offender reparation. This is likely to be due to victims' stories becoming lost when busy police officers tried to articulate the impacts back to offenders. The failure to convey the true impact of the crime will have limited offenders' sense of wrongdoing and, as such, their ability to show genuine contrition.[10] This was evident amongst half of the victims who stated that the officer had not asked them to explain how the incident had affected them (see Appendix A,

---

[9] Conversely, two victims who received what were perceived as disingenuous apologies still felt that they were partially helpful, but not for the reasons restorativists would hope for. One interviewee said 'I guess it was [helpful] in some sense, it wasted a bit of his time which was quite good but it wasn't a big deal.'

[10] Though this was often successfully done by the mediator at Southwark who took detailed notes and spent time conveying how the incident/s had affected the other party.

question 25). Moreover, only one victim participated in a direct mediation meeting with the offender, meaning that most victims could not gauge for themselves whether the offender understood the harms he or she had caused. Even more concerning was that during the one direct meeting, held at a police station, the victim still felt the offenders were cajoled into saying sorry. Several hours after this direct meeting occurred, the victim saw the offenders on the street, one of whom yelled, 'if we see you outside or in an alleyway or any club you're gone'. There was little doubt in the mind of this victim that the offender's apology was meaningless.

Opportunities for direct dialogue

In two cases, interviewees stated that they had hoped to meet with the offender in order to explain how they had been affected and to obtain assurances that their actions would not be repeated but were never given this opportunity. The failure of the police to arrange direct meetings adversely affected victims who felt that officers were uninterested in helping them to resolve their anguish. The wife of one victim, who had experienced racist abuse at his place of work, translated his words for me:

When this was reported to the police we always had hope that there would be face-to-face meeting and there would be some opportunity to explain and to talk and to give both sides the opportunity to tell what they feel, but we never got the opportunity. And then the anger from the [victim and offender's] manager after we reported to the police... was higher and automatically our fear was higher. We are afraid now that he [the victim] will be attacked in the street, not just by the offender but by his friends.

The facilitating officer in this case went on holiday without handing over the details to another officer, leaving the victim feeling helpless and unable to go back to work for fear of reprisal attacks. Failure to give victims, and other affected community members, an opportunity to participate directly in the restorative process inevitably leaves many feeling vulnerable and powerless. Hence, if the RD is to provide a more effective means of supporting the needs of victims, it must focus on providing victims with meaningful participation during either direct or indirect restorative dialogue (see also Hoyle et al 2002; O'Mahony et al 2002).

Case Study 1 Racist intimidation—the effects of poor facilitation

Mr S, an 'Asian Indian' male in his early thirties was racially abused and intimidated while closing up a shop he manages in Devon. Two white men began banging on the window of the shop shouting, 'Fuck off Paki', while using their hands to make a gesture of a gun, indicating that they were shooting at Mr S. The targeting of Mr S in this way had a profound impact on him, he explained:

> You think you are in a place [referring to England] which is safe and which is full of people who treat everyone equally and then this thing happens and I think no I didn't do anything to deserve that, so why? You become sceptical when you are walking and someone looks at you, you feel they might have a go at you as well... are they going to hit you, attack you, harm you?

On the evening of the incident, Mr S dialled 999 and waited for the police. After twenty-five minutes the police telephoned Mr S and asked if the offenders were still there, by which point they had left the scene. Instead of attending to Mr S that evening, an officer arranged to visit him the next day to take a statement and to look at CCTV footage. However, the police failed to arrive at the arranged time and the meeting was rearranged for another day. On this new date the police called again and rearranged the meeting for the following week. On this third date Mr S received another telephone call from a different officer asking why he had not turned up to the police station, even though the meeting had been arranged to take place at Mr S's place of work. By this point Mr S had become frustrated at what he perceived as a total lack of concern about his victimization. He explained: 'I wanted to report it all the way through but they didn't turn up the day the incident happened... and I was really really shocked. I felt like a child who needed someone but no one was there to extend a helping hand.'

Finally, the police received the CCTV footage from Mr S and later arrested the offenders responsible. Mr S was then contacted and was asked: 'Do [you] *really* want to report this incident as it happened over three weeks ago?' [emphasis added]. Shocked by this, Mr S told the officer that he wanted to pursue the case. The officer then told Mr S that the situation would best be resolved by him accepting an apology through the restorative disposal. Mr S did not wish to pursue this but reluctantly agreed: 'It was forced onto me... [the] officers... talk to you in a very nice way but they talk to you in a way and use certain words which make you feel that they are on your side but they were pressuring me into something that I didn't really wanted.' Mr S later received an apology on 'A3 small paper that [had] been torn out of someone's diary'. He did not 'know whom it had been written by, what date it was written and nobody [had] signed it'. I asked Mr S how he felt when he received the 'apology' from the offender and he stated: 'It was a scam, it wasn't really an apology. It made me feel really upset. If someone had really felt that they had done something wrong they would have written something in a way to express their feelings...'. I then asked Mr S whether he would have felt differently had the apology been more genuine. He responded: 'Yes, at least that would have made me feel OK, I understand. But this thing, sending me a piece of paper was like rubbing salt into the wound. I would have been more happy not receiving anything, it was like making fun of it.'

Unsurprisingly, Mr S was extremely dissatisfied with the RD and the apology. He went on to state that the process as a whole increased his levels of anger, anxiety, and fear.

This case illustrates the damaging effects that ineffective application of restorative practices can have on victims of hate crime. Mr S was left feeling helpless when the police failed to meet with him directly after the incident. The constant rearranging of meetings throughout the following weeks indicated to Mr S that they were not taking his report seriously. He then felt pressured into accepting an intervention that he did not really understand. It is unsurprising that victims who experience RJ in this manner fail to appreciate its potential benefits. In this case, Mr S ended up feeling abandoned by the police and ultimately more traumatized by a process that offered little by way of restoration (see further Chapter 6).

Should police officers administer restorative justice?

There are several reasons why police facilitation of RJ programmes remains questionable. Scholars have primarily criticized police-led restorative programmes by arguing that it gives them too much power, leaving individual officers with unwarranted levels of discretion over the resolution of a high number of offences

(Cunneen 1997; Ashworth 2002). Police officers are already tasked with enforcing the law, arresting suspects, collating evidence, and, in some cases, even punishing offenders (such as serving fixed penalties, warnings etc). Any additional discretion may be seen as yet another means through which the police have control over the criminal process (Hoyle 2007: 294–5). In fact, initiatives such as the RD in Devon and Cornwall, rather than effectively resolving 'low-level' conflicts, may simply bring much larger numbers of incidents into 'the system'. This contributes to what Stanley Cohen has called 'net-widening' (Cohen 1985). It is where the state casts its authoritative net over a much wider number of conducts, bringing with it many more offenders into the criminal justice system (see O'Mahony & Deazley 2000; O'Mahoney & Doak 2004). Once there, offenders are more likely to become part of a cycle of offending and reoffending (Matza 1969). Therefore we may wish to remain cautious about any policing scheme that has the effect of pulling large numbers of 'offenders' into the criminal process, especially where previously no criminal sanction would be required (Hoyle 2007: 297; O'Mahoney & Doak 2013: 143).

Whether one agrees with increasing the role of the police in responding to 'low-level' offences or not, it is certainly the case that facilitation of restorative practices by police officers complicates the restorative goal of engaging communities in resolving their own conflicts (Christie 1977; see further discussion on state involvement in RJ in Chapter 6). Officers who exert control over restorative dialogue will inevitably limit community stakeholders' autonomy to determine what they deem is appropriate reparation. Furthermore, without adequate measures in place to ensure that due process is adhered to, there are genuine concerns that officers will abuse their already burgeoning powers, thereby enhancing their social control over communities (Ashworth 2002; see also Cunneen 1997). One might view the increased control of RJ processes by the police as particularly concerning given the large evidence base that suggests continued police bias against certain identity groups (Macpherson 1999; Bowling & Phillips 2002; Lyons et al 2013). If restorative facilitators do not understand the needs and vulnerabilities of minority group victims they will potentially subject them to processes through which dominant cultural norms are imposed upon them (Burke 1993; Bowling & Phillips 2003; see Chapters 3, 6, and 7). This has led to the charge that police-led RJ will become another means through which hegemonic ideals are forced upon already marginalized minority groups (Cunneen 1997).

The comparatively low levels of satisfaction and emotional reparation amongst hate victims interviewed in Devon and Cornwall was evidence, if only limited, of the difficulties that are faced by police officers attempting to implement restorative principles in cases of hate crime. As pseudo RJ practitioners, police officers are unlikely to have the necessary time and resources to prepare adequately, and effectuate properly, restorative practice. Failure to prepare participants for the RD had repercussions for both its validity as a restorative process and its impact on those who participated. Hoyle et al (2002), reflecting on their study into police-led conferencing, had similar reservations:

Inadequate preparation means that participants have no chance to think about what they might want to get out of the meeting; what they want to say; or what they want to ask of the other participants. Nor do they have the opportunity of identifying and asking appropriate supporters to attend with them. Furthermore, if participants do not know what to expect from a restorative cautioning session then what have they consented to?

Hoyle et al's comments are of particular pertinence to the RD in Devon and Cornwall. The domineering approach to restoration taken by many of the officers meant that the police often failed to consider the intrinsic importance of voluntary participation in a process which is supposed to encourage inclusive decision making (see also Hoyle et al 2002). Instead, the pressurized manner in which many officers facilitated the disposal led to reluctant participation and, in turn, to the cajoling of insincere apologies. Inevitably, this limited the disposal's ability to repair the harms of hate crime and instead supported officers' control over the criminal process.

Overall, the data suggested that police services which implement street-level restorative disposals risk harming, rather than healing, victims of hate crime. However, these negative findings do not mean that *all* police services will be incapable of facilitating RJ. Indeed, it was observed at the beginning of this chapter that there is a growing body of research which has evidenced the harm-repairing capabilities of police-led conferencing. Furthermore, for as many victims dissatisfied with Devon and Cornwall's RD, just as many were satisfied. In addition, almost all victims interviewed

Part II: Could the RD Help Repair the Harms of Hate Crime? 143

stated that the police had tried (or tried to some extent) to help them resolve the problems that the offence had caused to them, suggesting that officers had made at least some attempt to help repair the harms victims had suffered. Nevertheless, it was clear from this small study that the RD ran the risk of exacerbating the harms of hate crime victimization. This led to the question: Could the RD be administered in a way that would increase victim satisfaction levels and protect against secondary victimization? Part of the answer may be found in the amount of training that police officers undertook.

The importance of training

If RJ is to fall within the purview of contemporary policing, forces must implement practices using properly trained practitioners who have a firm grasp of the key principles of RJ. Hoyle (2007) notes that despite traditional cultures remaining dominant in many parts of the force, there are many officers who are more than willing and capable of signing up to the values and principles of RJ (see also Mahony et al 2002). She states that 'Those engaged *exclusively* in restorative work are likely, after only a few months, to adopt restorative values and behave in more inclusive and restorative ways' (Hoyle 2007: 301). Perhaps then, the only way to ensure that RJ is administered effectively by police officers is to make sure facilitators work solely or predominantly on implementing restorative disposals. This might be done using a collection of officers within each force who specialize in RJ. Thus, rather than attempting to superficially train an entire force, a smaller group of officers should receive extensive and ongoing training in RJ.

The Restorative Justice Council (RJC), a third sector organization in the UK, currently provides a code of practice and a register for all RJ trainers to sign up to in order to maintain nationwide quality assurance (RJC 2011). Facilitators who register with the RJC must have undertaken twenty hours of face-to-face training before beginning practice (RJC 2011). There are, however, no government-regulated training standards—though the recent Ministry of Justice's RJ Action Plan recommends that the government should develop new standards of practice (MoJ 2012). This means that currently 'restorative' facilitators can continue to practise RJ without a professional qualification, resulting in some practitioners having a lack of knowledge of the fundamental principles of restorative theory. The danger posed by practices that claim to be restorative, but which lack strict adherence to RJ principles, is that they may harm rather than repair those who participate.

A lack of training at Devon and Cornwall Police Service was likely to have contributed to their failure to fully adhere to the values of RJ when implementing the RD. I asked each of the five police constables whom I interviewed to detail the training they had received on RJ. I was told by most officers that they received a three-hour training session on RJ, with one officer stating that she had received only a twenty-minute session on the 'virtues of RJ'. Such a short training period, especially if not followed up with additional learning, is unlikely to promote effective facilitation.

Understanding the dynamics of hate crime

The facilitation of RJ in cases of hate crime will require officers to understand the complex social issues that are central to cross-cultural conflicts (see generally Bell 1997). Institutional cultures may prove inhibitive in this regard (Reiner 2010). Traditional values that have been identified by researchers as making up part of 'cop culture' include (amongst others): a sense of 'fighting crime', pragmatism, conservatism, machismo, and racial prejudice (see Reiner 2010; Macpherson 1999). Prejudices, such as racism, often emanate from wider racial hostilities within society, which can permeate police forces at all levels (Reiner 2000; see also Chan 1997). Of course, prejudice is not just confined to racism. Other criminologists have drawn attention to the homophobic nature of much police culture (Burke 1993) and to the suspicion and vilification of certain 'Others' such as gypsies (James 2007). These pervasive forms of bias have inevitably led to criticisms that the police discriminate against certain minority groups via their practices and processes (Macpherson 1999).

The often strained relations which have developed between the police and minority communities have resulted in a lack of confidence in the police to respond properly to hate-motivated victimization (Chakraborti & Garland 2009: 114–18; see also Smith et al 2012). Unless these cultural barriers can be broken down it seems unlikely that the police, at least at an institutional level, will be responsive to the needs of hate crime victims (see further Chakraborti & Garland 2009: Ch 7). Police restorative facilitators will therefore need further training on the cultural issues intrinsic to cases

Part II: Could the RD Help Repair the Harms of Hate Crime? 145

involving prejudice and identity difference if identity bias is to be challenged and officers are to successfully negotiate the minefield of culturally sensitive topics that inclusive dialogue inevitably stimulates (see Chapters 4, 7, and 8).

It should be noted that a variety of improvements have been made to police training schemes, which deal with community and race relations (CRR, known colloquially as 'diversity training'), a direct result of Sir William Macpherson's (1999) various recommendations after finding that the Metropolitan Police Service was 'institutionally racist'. Other improvements include the development of a more victim-focused response to hate crime, including the establishment of Community Safety Units (CSUs) set up in order to provide specialized investigations into domestic violence and hate crime (Stanko 2001; see further Chapter 6). Beat officers can refer cases to CSUs where a hate crime has been reported. An officer specifically trained in hate crime will then investigate the offence. The police have also increased the use of community consultations and engaged more with multi-agency partnerships in combating hate crime (see Chapter 6).

Yet for all the improvements that have been made since Macpherson, there remains cogent evidence within the extant literature to suggest that racism and other identity-based prejudices remain a persistent and enduring feature of contemporary policing (for an overview see Chakraborti & Garland 2009: Ch 7). Hence, as we begin to move towards a criminal justice policy in favour of offering RJ to all victims of crime at all stages of the criminal justice process (at least within the UK context, see MoJ 2012), we must remain cautious as to whether *all* police officers should provide restorative interventions for 'low-level' hate incidents. If this is to be the case, officers will certainly need extensive training on issues of diversity and minority identity.

Michael Rowe and Jon Garland's (2007) research into the implementation of training recommendations post Macpherson found that officers were highly cynical of programmes which address issues of race. However, once courses were completed, many officers went on to reflect on their usefulness, indicating that such schemes may be of some benefit to officers. One such benefit identified by the authors is that CRR training encourages officers to consider the language that they use and the impact this has on the public, hence avoiding secondary victimization (Rowe & Garland 2007: 50; see also Chapter 6). In order to improve the delivery of such programmes, the authors note that better leadership is required and the inclusion of minority community representatives into course interface sessions should be used to help break down stereotypes (Rowe & Garland 2007).

Unless effective training schemes can be implemented, and this in itself is far from unequivocal, one must remain sceptical about the successful facilitation of restorative justice for hate crime by police officers. At the very least, those forces that do decide to use RJ for hate crime should first consider employing specialized restorative officers who have received extensive training on both RJ and hate crime. These officers must dedicate a significant proportion of their time to preparing and facilitating cases. Forces that attempt to implement street-level RJ without dedicated and trained practitioners will inevitably fail to effectively administer restorative principles. As this research has shown us, ineffective facilitation will have significant consequences for some victims of hate crime, ultimately compounding the process of victimization experienced by minority group individuals.[11]

Conclusion

Findings on the use of the RD at Devon and Cornwall Police Service were more mixed than those from the HCP. Just over half of those interviewed found that the disposal helped their emotional wellbeing, and only in a minority of cases was the disposal helpful at reducing levels of anger, anxiety, and fear. At face value these findings could be used to infer that police-led RJ is not an appropriate method of addressing hate crime. However, further analysis of qualitative data showed that the lack of emotional reparation amongst victims was less a reflection of the efficacy of RJ for hate crime and more cogently linked to the way in which the disposal was implemented by officers. For instance, the extemporaneous approach taken by police officers when implementing the RD meant that participants lacked preparation and information about what the intervention aimed to achieve. Of particular concern was that many victims were denied the opportunity to engage in inclusive dialogue with either the facilitator or the offender. In turn, this led many victims to believe that their victimization had not been

---

[11] It is still unclear what impact the government's spending cuts will have on the training of police officers in restorative justice.

taken seriously, cultivating a sense of being 'let down' (see also Chapter 6). Even more worrying was that the disposal failed to provide *genuine* reparation to victims, with brief letters of apology sometimes acting to exacerbate victims' emotional trauma.

If the police are to continue utilizing restorative interventions for hate crime (or any offence for that matter) a more robust approach to administering restorative principles is required. The sensitive socio-cultural issues exposed by hate incidents give further cause for concern where disposals are implemented 'on the spot' with little preparation by officers who have limited understanding of prejudice-motivated crimes. This book therefore recommends that restorative disposals should not be used by the police for hate crimes *unless* the participants are adequately prepared for an FGC by a facilitator who is sufficiently trained in both restorative values and the causes and consequences of hate crime.

6
Secondary Victimization, State Participation, and the Importance of Multi-Agency Partnerships

Introduction

So far this book has highlighted the far-reaching impacts of hate crime, illustrating how incidents affect not only individual victims, but also their families and other minority community members. In the previous two chapters it has become clear that fundamental to the emotional wellbeing of hate victims, and minority identity groups more generally, is the way in which state and third sector agencies respond to complaints of hate victimization. Within the empirical study, the vast majority of victims reported incidents to a housing association[1] and/or to the local police service, before being referred to a restorative practitioner. It was therefore essential that both housing and police officers treated victims with due care and attention, paying particular regard to the victim's vulnerability.

Agencies that fail to provide adequate protection, support, and advice to hate victims are likely to expose them to what has been termed 'secondary victimization' (Herek & Berrill 1992). Previous research has indicated that agencies who respond to hate incidents frequently compound victims' experience of it (Victim Support 2006; Dunn 2009). For instance, Peter Dunn notes that 'rather than help people regain control, in some instances, criminal justice agencies did the opposite...' (2009: 129), even though many hate crime victims 'wanted to engage with the criminal justice system, perhaps as a way of working out their anger towards the offender'. Linked to the secondary victimization of hate victims are the institutional prejudices found within state organizations.

---

[1] Only in cases where the victim lived in local authority housing. In South London this was the vast majority of complainant victims.

Introduction 149

In Chapter 3 I explored how the state subjugates certain identity groups by unwittingly perpetuating oppressive hegemonic norms (Bowling & Phillips 2002). In some instances, criminal justice agencies themselves pursue discriminatory practices and adopt policies which support what has been famously labelled 'institutional racism' (Macpherson 1999) or other culturally constructed prejudices (Bowling & Phillips 2002).

Within the UK, the state has set about improving its responses to hate crime—partly as a result of the highly critical Macpherson Report (1999) into police racism (see Chakraborti & Garland 2009: 118–21). The literature on the developments since Macpherson has suggested that the police and other criminal justice agencies have become considerably more effective at tackling prejudice-motivated crimes (see *inter alia* Chakraborti & Garland 2009: 118–21; HCHAC 2009). This body of commentary provided an expectation, before the current study was completed, that victims would find state authorities responsive to their reports of hate crime. This was not, however, what my observations of mediation meetings and interviews with complainant victims revealed. In fact, in some cases the involvement of state authorities proved to be highly detrimental to the victim's emotional wellbeing, and in several cases their (lack of) involvement caused heightened emotional turmoil (see Case Study 1 below).

This chapter begins by examining the various forms of secondary victimization that were experienced by the victims interviewed for this book. For the most part, victims were frustrated and angered by what they perceived as apathetic and neglectful responses from the housing officers and police officers who had dealt with their complaints of abuse. Using various case studies, the chapter highlights how the harms caused by secondary victimization can be resolved and ultimately repaired where community mediators implement a multi-agency approach to restorative practice. Such an approach requires additional dialogue between victims, offenders, and the state agencies that they come into contact with.

The chapter argues that these local agencies should be included within the restorative framework as 'stakeholders' by reinterpreting the restorative concept of 'community'. Although not originally envisaged by restorativists as making up part of the notion of 'community' (McCold 2004), such organizations will frequently become important 'community supporters' who can assist in the resolution of hate crime cases. Furthermore, it can be argued that those agencies which cause secondary victimization become direct stakeholders within a conflict and, as such, should be encouraged to engage in restorative dialogue in order to repair the additional harms they themselves have caused.

By broadening out the scope of 'community' to include state and third sector agencies (both as supporters and as wrongdoers), RJ can enhance the likelihood of victims obtaining the support and restoration they require to convalesce, while agencies can also be encouraged to actively prevent hate incidents from recurring. In this sense, the multi-agency approach to RJ, mainly implemented through community mediation centres, may help to repair some of the individual *and* structural harms caused by the process of hate victimization.

Part I: State Responses to Hate Crime: Exploring the Harms Caused by Housing and Police Officers

A high proportion of complainant victims at the HCP were highly critical of the state's involvement in their case. This was especially so in cases that came to the attention of housing officers, who appeared to be the source of much frustration and anxiety. In the UK, housing associations[2] have long been urged to take a more proactive role in tackling the problem of hate-motivated harassment (Netto & Abazie 2012: 678). Over the past thirty years or more, social landlords have increasingly taken on a regulatory role in relation to anti-social behaviour and crime—despite lacking any official remit as 'law enforcers'. For example, landlords can take direct action against tenants by evicting them from their premises, or by making an application to a magistrates' court for an Anti-Social Behaviour Order.[3] In fact, most housing associations now have policies to deal with complaints of hate crime victimization (Netto & Abazie 2012). Southwark Council's own policy was to ensure that victims of hate crime received 'practical and emotional support... within their own home', to improve the confidence amongst victims to report incidents, and to make

---

[2] Housing associations are commonly referred to as local 'councils'. As such, these terms will be used interchangeably.

[3] Soon to be relabelled as Injunctions to Prevent Nuisance or Annoyance (IPNAs) and Criminal Behaviour Orders (CBOs), if and when the Anti-Social Behaviour, Crime and Policing Bill is passed.

recommendations to the local ASBU where necessary (Southwark Council et al 2005).

Unfortunately, such policies are not always effectively administered. Benjamin Bowling's earlier research into racial harassment in East London in the early 1990s found that 55 per cent of those surveyed had reported incidents to a housing department (Bowling 1994). In that study, only 8 per cent of victims were satisfied with the way in which the housing department had handled their case. Bowling noted that most victims felt that the department did 'not do enough, that they appeared uninterested, and that they failed to keep the victim informed about the progress of their case' (1994: 24). More recently, research by Gina Netto and Humphrey Abazie in Glasgow, Scotland found that housing associations were failing to adequately tackle incidents of racial harassment. They note that of particular concern was that not all associations had policies in place to deal with the problem, while those that did have policies still failed to alleviate the distress that was inflicted on victims (Netto & Abazie 2012: 686). They conclude that part of the problem was that associations used an 'events-based' system of prioritization which was linked to the seriousness of hostility demonstrated towards victims. This approach had three major shortcomings. First, it failed to acknowledge the day-to-day reality of living with persistent incidents of racial harassment. Second, housing officers did not take into account the potential for abuse to escalate into more serious forms of personal violence. Third, policies focused on individual perpetrators and therefore failed to consider that groups of people were frequently involved in conflict (Netto & Abazie 2012).

All three of Netto and Abazie's findings concurred with the study carried out at the HCP in London. Interviews with complainant victims at the HCP helped to elucidate the realities of dealing with housing associations in cases involving hate crime. Interviewees frequently spoke of housing officers who had been insensitive, and in some cases negligent, when dealing with their complaints. For instance, when asking one interviewee whether her housing officer helped with her complaints, she responded: 'Oh please! He actually made things worse. He came here and went to the wrong house and started talking to her about the incident. She happened to be her [the accused perpetrator's] best friend. She thought we were complaining about her. It made things worse.'

Other victims felt that housing associations took an indifferent approach to dealing with their complaints, meaning many housing officers failed to discern what amounted to serious forms of hate victimization. The failure to take victims' concerns seriously angered interviewees, leaving many feeling frustrated that nothing was being done to protect them (see similarly Garland and Chakraborti 2006: 18). Such shortcomings in service provision seriously compound victims' experiences of what often amounted to ongoing hate abuse. This resulted in some victims feeling that no one cared about their experiences of victimization. In one case of ongoing racist abuse and intimidation, the victims had made several complaints to the housing association, which, they explained, had largely fallen on deaf ears. It was only when a new housing officer visited the accused perpetrator on an unrelated matter that the victims' complaints of racism were taken seriously. The interviewees explained:

I brought it up with the council... They didn't do anything about it. I called the council again and they [said they had] nothing on record... In January we had a new housing officer, she went up to see him about something and he racially abused her... calling her a 'fucking black bitch, no fucking nigger is going to tell me what to do'... And he physically assaulted her as well... So then I phoned her and she said 'now I know what you have been going through'.

It was lamentable that it took a direct hate attack on an officer before these victims' complaints about hate crime were taken seriously by their local housing association. It was after this incident that the victims were referred to Southwark Mediation. The mediator contacted the local council and facilitated indirect dialogue between the housing officer and the victims. Only then was something done about the victims' constant racial harassment by their upstairs neighbour, and within the space of a week, the offender was removed from his property.

Prejudice, what prejudice?

In Chapter 1 we explored the complex nature of hate, noting that hate offences are committed where an offender demonstrates hostility towards the victim's actual or 'presumed' identity. This means that some victims can become 'hate victims' even if they do not actually belong to the presumed identity group towards which the offender demonstrates his or her hostility. For example, the use of the word 'Paki' was common to many of the racist incidents under research, especially during incidents committed in Devon and Cornwall. However, most of these victims were not of Pakistani descent and it was often noted by them that the word was not an accurate description of their ethnic heritage. Inaccuracy notwithstanding, the label 'Paki' still had a hurtful effect, due to the fact that victims knew their offender had targeted them because of their 'Otherness'.

It is important that state agencies understand the complex dynamics of hate victimization, in particular that hostility, whether directed towards a 'presumed' or 'actual' identity, has a potentially insidious impact on those targeted (see also Garland & Chakraborti 2006, 2007). For the most part, restorative practitioners appreciated the subtle nuances that often exist between different identity groups and that targeting individuals based on a mistaken identity could still have damaging consequences. However, this could not always be said about housing officers. In several cases where the victim's identity did not match the prejudiced language used against them, housing officers had been either dismissive or insensitive about the issue of identity-based prejudice. For example, one victim had complained that her neighbour had been both racist and homophobic towards her, even though she was not in fact gay. She explained:

the first thing they [the housing officer] asked me was, was I gay? I said no. They said why are you bothered by it? I don't think I have to be gay to be bothered by it, it's just ridiculous. When I said he called me a 'half-breed' [referring to her mixed race] they said that's just a 'technical'... so it doesn't count. I said what do you mean, 'well he didn't call you a "nigger" or a "honkey" so that doesn't count as being racial abuse', which makes no sense whatsoever.

The council's failure to acknowledge the presence of hate abuse in this case meant that the victim felt the seriousness of her complaints was trivialized by them. The victim was met with excuses as to why she could not be classified as a 'hate victim' when the officer should, instead, have considered the severity of the racist and homophobic comments made by the accused perpetrator. In other words, because the victim was not gay and because the term 'half-breed' was not considered derogatory enough to be classified as racist, the council was not prepared to treat the case as a 'hate incident'.

Dismissing victims' experience of hate crime victimization has serious implications for both their emotional wellbeing and their continued safety within the community. Housing associations that fail to implement their own hate crime policies will leave many victims feeling isolated and frightened. The duty of care that housing associations owe towards their tenants is not one that can be taken lightly. These are often tenants that remain vulnerable to hate abuse and to the socio-economic disadvantages which lead them to social housing in the first place. Thus, while we cannot expect housing officers to adopt the role of 'law enforcer' or 'social worker', they must remain mindful of the fact that their tenants will need their support when experiencing abuse from other social tenants in their local neighbourhood.

Police responses to hate incidents

The policing of minority communities has routinely been viewed through a lens of suspicion (Reiner 2010: 159ff). Historical studies of the police service have often portrayed it as an institution based on the maintenance of a 'white, straight, middle class and male hegemony' which has supported the practice of homophobia (Burke 1993). Evidence of prejudice amongst the police and the documentation of police brutality towards ethnic minorities and gay and lesbian communities has inevitably led to certain identity groups *viewing* the police as another mechanism through which they are oppressed (see eg Bowling & Phillips 2007; Reiner 2010: 164–71). For example, in relation to LGB communities, Matthew Williams and Amanda Robinson (2004: 214–15) suggest that there is sometimes a 'tendency for working groups of police officers to display hostile, negative and stereotyped views about LGB people. The occupational culture of police officers appears to instil negative attitudes about minority individuals, especially those identifying as lesbian, gay or bisexual' (cited in Chakraborti & Garland 2009: 69).

It was not until the late 1990s that the government officially accepted that prejudice and discrimination affected the work of police services.[4] As noted in Chapter 1, the botched investigation into Stephen Lawrence during the 1990s and the ensuing public inquiry into the police investigation (Macpherson Report 1999) led

---

[4] Despite reports during the 1980s hinting at the extent of the problem, Scarman (1981).

to the assertion that the police were 'institutionally racist'. The report created the impetus for government and police services to make sweeping changes to their policies and practices in relation to the policing of minority communities (see Rowe & Garland 2007).

One of the key outcomes of the Macpherson Report was that it gave prolonged attention to the problem of hate crime. As a result, the Home Office called upon police services to improve their responses to hate-motivated victimization. The Association of Chief Police Officers responded by producing its first set of guidelines on hate crime in 2000, which adopted a clear definition of 'hate crime' and 'hate incidents' (ACPO 2000: see Chapter 1). Better recording practices have also enabled the police to highlight patterns and 'hot spots' where hate crime offences are particularly prolific (Rowe 2004), while the establishment of new CSUs has meant that specialist officers are now tasked with investigating hate crimes reported to the police. Collectively, these policies have been heralded as a success, and the increasing number of victims prepared to report hate incidents is testimony to the increased levels of trust now placed in local police forces (HCHAC 2009; see also Smith et al 2012: 20; Home Office et al 2013: 17).

Yet despite the increased numbers of victims willing to report hate crimes to the police, satisfaction levels with police responses remains low (53 per cent compared with 73 per cent of CSEW crime overall, Home Office et al 2013: 45; see also, Bell 2002). The cases researched at the HCP revealed why this might still be the case. Police officers called by complainants often refused to investigate the case beyond their initial contact with the victim, declaring that the conflict amounted to a 'domestic dispute' and therefore fell outside the purview of traditional policing. Jon Garland and Neil Chakraborti (2007) similarly found in their study into the policing of racial victimization in rural England that officers frequently fail to appreciate the seriousness of 'low-level' racist incidents, tending instead to deal with cases in an informal way, potentially serving only to maintain the process of victimization (see also Bowling 1998). Victim interviewees in this study concurred with such findings. A victim of homophobic harassment and violence in Southwark noted, 'I did call the police and they said it's not our job...that it was a council job...you have a problem with your neighbour you call them and they will deal with it'.[5] Such responses angered

---

[5] See Chapter 4, Case Study 1.

complainants who felt that the police, like housing officers, were not taking their experiences of hate crime seriously. In another case involving the painting of racist symbols on the victim's front door, and later where the accused perpetrator threatened the victim with a hammer, the interviewee told me: 'I said to the police "I am pressing charges" but they never got back to me and they dropped the case without ever letting me know about it, they didn't take the matter further... The police didn't help me at all, they let me down, they let me down!'

A lack of evidence appeared to be a common excuse as to why police officers would not pursue allegations of hate crime. However, some interviewees also inferred that police officers had treated their complaints of racism with suspicion (see also Garland & Chakraborti 2007). In one indirect mediation meeting that I observed, an elderly Caribbean gentleman, aged eighty, had been punched in the face outside a local shop by his neighbour, a much younger white male who was a suspected member of the local Bermondsey Taxi Club (a racist organization). The victim wished to make a statement against the accused perpetrator but was told by the attending police officer that because there was blood on both parties he could not arrest anyone. The local shop owner who had witnessed the incident also refused to make a statement.[6] Notwithstanding the victim's old age, the fact that he had been covered in blood and despite having previously made a series of complaints about the racist behaviour of the offender to the council over a number of years, the attending officer decided that no action could be taken.

The only option left for this victim was to refer *himself* to the mediation service in the hope that a mediator could persuade the offender and his children to leave him alone.[7] Unfortunately, the accused perpetrator refused to engage and therefore the mediator could only work with the victim and his housing officer in order to improve his safety. Yet ultimately, little could be done for this victim without the support of the police or the engagement of the accused perpetrator, meaning that in this case the victim remained vulnerable to future attacks.

---

[6] The victim felt that this was most likely due to the fear of reprisal attacks.

[7] The offender's children had also harassed the victim. On one occasion they had illegally entered his garden and torn down his Jamaican flag. On another they were suspected of removing the numbers from the victim's front door.

Police restorative facilitators

The effectiveness of restorative policing has already been discussed in Chapter 5. It is worth reiterating for the purposes of this chapter that a (significant) minority of victims participating in the Devon and Cornwall scheme were dissatisfied with the way in which the police had treated them. The reasons for this included: pressure put on some victims to participate in the RD; inadequate preparation; a lack of information about the process; and the obtaining of disingenuous apologies. This left some victims feeling let down by RJ and angry that their victimization had not been taken seriously by the police. For many victims, this meant that their levels of anger, anxiety, or fear towards the perpetrator was not reduced post intervention, while in two cases the victims stated that their levels of anger and anxiety had actually increased as a direct result of police involvement.

One victim described how her increased level of anxiety had been a direct result of what she perceived as the trivializing of her case, which she believed led to her re-victimization by the offender. Another victim believed his treatment by the police to be racist. I asked him whether he had ever felt at a disadvantage during the RD. He responded 'yes... because it would have been... different if I was not of a foreign origin... they have not given me all the help and support that they should have or that they have given to other people'. I asked this interviewee whether he felt that had he been white and British he would have received a different level of support. He replied, 'I feel so, yes I do. Unfortunately, yes.' Whether the police had discriminated against this victim based on his ethnicity is uncertain. However, what was evidently clear was that the police had not provided him with the level of support that he required (see Chapter 5, Case Study 1).

Case Study 1, Part 1 Miss J: Long-term racial harassment
Miss J, a 'Black British' female, had been subjected to regular racist abuse by her downstairs neighbour (Miss Y) over a ten-year period. In addition to constant racial slurs, Miss Y repeatedly barricaded Miss J into her home using her own furniture, stole her mail, and made false allegations to the Inland Revenue about her tax status, resulting in a temporary suspension of Miss J's child benefits. Miss J contacted the police to complain about her neighbour's racial harassment. However, when the police arrived to take her statement, Miss Y came out of her flat and told the officer that she was

in fact Miss J. She then proceeded to provide the officer with a false statement. Miss J re-contacted the police a week later to find out why they had not come to take her statement only to be told that she had already given it to them. When she asked the police officer what skin colour the lady was who had made the statement he responded that she was white. Miss J was dumbfounded that having made a report of racist abuse, clearly stating that she was black and her neighbour white, that the police would mistakenly take a statement from the wrong person.

In response, Miss J wrote a letter of complaint to the police about what had happened to her. Another police officer then visited Miss J telling her that Miss Y had made a counter-complaint of harassment against her. He then served her with what was described as a 'harassment order'.[8] He also told Miss J in no uncertain terms that she had to stop making complaints to the police about Miss Y. Unsurprisingly, Miss J was very confused and upset about the police's response to her complaints of hate crime, perceiving their actions to be racist. Miss J sent several other letters to the police and the council, but with little response, after which she became clinically depressed, began to suffer from alopecia, and lost half her body weight. She told me: 'I think it was more the lack of support from agencies that really just made me think, "what is going on here?" The confidence is completely, utterly gone and so it's like that is what it has done to me' [referring to her depression, weight loss, and alopecia].

The police's treatment of Miss J clearly compounded her experience of hate crime victimization, leading her to believe that no one would help. The council's response to her persistent complaints was also to brush them aside. A housing officer asked her to keep a log of all incidents, which she did. Yet when she presented them with the log she was told 'it's a really complicated case and we don't have much funds to deal with it', this only adding to Miss J's frustration and emotional turmoil.

It later transpired that the police officer who had served Miss J with the harassment warning was in fact in a personal relationship with her neighbour, Miss Y, and had falsely imposed the order (see further, Case Study 1: Part 2 later in this chapter).[9]

---

[8] This is likely to have been a 'harassment warning', which is often made by the police in the first instance. Where there is cogent evidence of harassment the police may arrest and charge the accused under the Protection from Harassment Act 1997.

[9] A similar version of this case study appears in Walters & Hoyle (2012).

Sample bias?

It may seem unsurprising that participants of community mediation were generally unhappy with the treatment they received by local authorities, especially given the fact that conflicts typically involved incidents that were referred by the police or housing associations *because* they themselves had failed to resolve the case. In other words, cases that are dealt with swiftly and effectively by the police and other state agencies would not come to the attention of the mediation service and therefore would not be included in this study. Nonetheless, the fact that such high numbers of cases had been referred to mediation involving hate incidents in this local area of London demonstrated that a clear problem existed between state agencies involved in the resolution of hate crimes and minority individuals. The interviewees' responses provide insight into these problems and the failures of police and housing associations to pursue effective hate crime policies. While these responses may not be representative of *all* hate crime cases, they provide useful qualitative information about how and why such agencies failed to support the needs of many hate victims.

Other data gained from the participants of RDs in Devon and Cornwall were less skewed when compared with data collated from those who had participated in community mediation; due mainly to the fact that interviewees made up half of all victims who were dealt with via an RD during a twelve-month period. Although victims participating in the RD reported a lower rate of secondary victimization, the data indicated that the police had failed to provide adequate support to *all* hate victims. This added weight to the suggestion that local authorities tasked with responding to hate crimes frequently cause secondary victimization.

Part II: Reducing Harm Through Multi-Agency Partnerships

In Chapter 4 we saw how a significant proportion of victims relied on mediators as a source of 'support'. The help offered by facilitators was of great relief to those who had felt 'let down' and ignored by the state. When providing this support, the HCP manager often administered a 'multi-agency' approach to mediation. This entailed mediators engaging other agencies such as the police, housing associations, schools, colleges, social services, and/or third sector charities directly in the mediation process. Agency employees participated in the process in a variety of ways including: as stakeholders within group conferences; as participants within direct mediation meetings between one or both parties; or as providers of after care.[10]

The multi-agency approach applied in many of the community mediation cases researched had a clear benefit over and above police-led RJ. This was primarily due to the fact that community mediation was independent of state authority. It was not restricted by government-imposed targets and it is largely devoid of the institutional cultures that have shaped the way in which statutory organizations respond to hate incidents (see Macpherson 1999). Accordingly, community mediators could capitalize on both a dialogic process between complainant victim and accused perpetrator *and* inclusive communication involving the various local organizations that had responded to the victims' complaints of hate abuse. A multi-agency approach to RJ, therefore, consists of both lay members of the community (ie the victim, perpetrator, and their supporters) and professional employees of state authorities (ie housing and police officers).

While multi-agency partnerships within restorative practice build upon the principle of inclusivity, there are a number of implications for other restorative values when taking such an approach. In Chapter 2 I briefly explored the purpose of RJ, noting that restorative practices should aim to empower those directly involved in an offence in order for them to resolve their *own* inter-personal conflicts (Christie 1977; Zehr 1990). In the previous chapter it was noted that police-led RJ often led to criminal justice practitioners taking control of conflict, which had the effect of removing autonomy away from the key stakeholders of an offence. Thus purists are likely to assert that 'professionals' (especially state-employed) should be excluded from restorative processes for fear that they will impose their own rules and norms over and above the needs and desires of the stakeholders (Christie 1977; Cunneen & Hoyle 2010: 162–69).

How then does the inclusion of local state authorities in the restorative process fit within RJ theory? Are multi-agency approaches to

---

[10] Such an approach was less available in Devon and Cornwall as the police acted as both restorative facilitator and at times secondary victimizer (see the following section 'State agencies as "community stakeholders"').

Part II: Reducing Harm Through Multi-Agency Partnerships 161

RJ an aberration of its fundamental values, or can state agencies legitimately find a place within restorative dialogue? As we will see below, we may be able to find part of the answer to this question through reconceptualizing the restorative notion of 'community'. However, before then, we need to explore further some of the potential ramifications of engaging state organizations within the restorative framework.

State agencies as 'community stakeholders'

Scholars sceptical of state involvement in RJ start by pointing out that there is a distinct incompatibility between the functions of conventional state-led criminal justice and that of restorative practice (Boyes-Watson 2004; Cunneen & Hoyle 2010: 162ff). This is primarily because conventional criminal justice processes have focused on enforcing the law by punishing and censuring those who breach its rules, while RJ aims to empower community stakeholders of a crime to resolve and repair their own inter-personal conflicts (Zehr 1990). Restorativists are right to be cautious about the state's involvement in restorative practice. Past attempts by the state to include victims within justice processes have often amounted to little more than paying lip service to their needs. Some have even noted that state institutions increase the risk of re-victimization by involving victims more directly in their practices and processes (central to this chapter) (see Bowling & Phillips 2002; Chapter 3) Yet despite the potential, and perhaps inevitable, pitfalls of state involvement, many have argued that it is necessary for RJ's future development and sustainability (Boyes-Watson 2004; Jantzi 2004). Vernon Jantzi (2004: 190) points out that the role of the state has been multifaceted, acting as 'enabler, resource provider, implementer, guarantor of quality practice—and even offender'. As such, if we are to look critically at restorative practice, 'we see that both law and the state permeate restorative justice completely' (Cunneen & Hoyle 2010: 162).

The state has enabled RJ by legislating for its inclusion into main stream criminal justice, most prominently within the youth justice system (discussed briefly in Chapter 2), and also by providing resources for its practice. Even community mediation services that run within the third sector are often financed by government grants and through council funding. Financial provision is therefore fundamental to the development of restorative practice; for it is the state that has the means and resources to provide the capital required for RJ to become accessible to the masses rather than the few (Jantzi 2004).[11]

If RJ is to become entrenched into mainstream criminal justice it is clear that the state must legislate for its use and fund its practice. It does not necessarily follow, though, that the state must then *administer* such practices. It is this third aspect of state involvement that is of greatest cause for concern. Detractors argue that state-led restorative practices will simply become another means of administrating and taking control of crime, ultimately leading to the marginalization of non-state citizens (Ashworth 2002; Jantzi 2004; see also Hoyle 2007: 294–97). Moreover, such practices may simply perpetuate the hegemony of the law and the more draconian aspects of the criminal process (Cunneen & Hoyle 2010: 164). In other words, RJ may become implicated in the 'racialised, gendered and class-based' effects of the broader criminal justice system (Cunneen & Hoyle 2010: 164; see Chapters 3 and 6).

We have seen some evidence of this, if only tentative, in Chapter 5 when exploring the inclusivity, voluntariness, and reparative capabilities of police-led RJ. Of the fourteen victims who participated in the police-led RD in Devon and Cornwall, only one had been provided with an opportunity to meet directly with his offender. Furthermore, a number of victims felt pressurized into participating in the disposal, while only eight out of fourteen interviewees agreed that the facilitating police officer had provided them with an opportunity to discuss the harms caused by the offence. Of greatest concern was that two victims stated that their emotional trauma increased having been through the disposal, with one stating that he believed the police had been racist towards him.

If the police struggle to apply restorative principles due to their contradictory roles as law enforcer and restorative facilitator, it seems improbable that they can also facilitate restorative dialogue in cases where they have (in)directly caused harm to the victim (see Hoyle 2007: 294–95). How then can state-led RJ help to repair the harms caused by state-led agencies? Although difficult, such a dichotomy has already been played out at a macro level in various jurisdictions across the globe. For instance, some states have initiated restorative programmes as a way of helping to repair the mass

---

[11] However, one advantage of state involvement is that it brings guarantees of quality and adherence together with human rights (Ashworth 2002).

atrocities committed by state institutions in the past (see Llewellyn 2007 on Truth Commissions). Jantzi (2004) refers to the Maori Land Courts in New Zealand, used as a means of redistributing land to Maori communities, as a macro-level RJ initiative. Another more recent example is Australia's national apology in 2010 for the 'stolen generations' and persecution of indigenous peoples throughout Australia's history. Such examples show that despite the state's role as wrongdoer, and providing it has the political will, governments can initiate reparative measures that aim to repair the harms it, itself, has previously caused.[12]

While examples of reparations for mass human rights abuses show that the state may, in some circumstances, attempt to repair some of the widespread harm it has created, this does not necessarily mean that governments will be willing to repair isolated incidents of secondary victimization. In these more micro-level cases, RJ practitioners will not be facilitating reparations by the monolithic state but rather by smaller local agencies who represent, in some form, the various functions of the state. In such cases, it is unlikely that the state will enable, resource, or provide the political foundation upon which its institutions are encouraged to provide victims with reparation. There is little institutional pressure for them to put right the wrongs caused on a day-to-day basis. Given that such agencies represent the autonomy of the state, it might seem that little can really be done by third sector organizations, such as community mediation centres, to engage state-run agencies in restorative dialogue.

One significant barrier to state involvement within restorative interventions is that employees of local authorities will be bound by institutional procedure and rigidly set policies. Constructive dialogue between victims and members of these bodies will be limited by the bureaucracy that is intrinsic to the services they deliver. Part of this bureaucracy is the carefully defined roles of agency employees. Their positions are institutionally constructed and set within the parameters of the organization's social function. As such, the foundation upon which communications with victims is built is not one of equality and mutuality but instead 'service provision'. The service provided is executed through a prism of organizational constraint that is bound by structured policies.

[12] Though the effectiveness of these measures is far from equivocal (Llewellyn 2007).

Communication between victims, offenders, and local agencies is therefore skewed towards the institutional objectives of the organization in question. And although many stakeholders of crime will find the services administered by such agencies helpful, many others will become frustrated and angry at what they perceive as a failure to provide them with adequate care and support. This means that very few agency employees will develop a sense of 'reciprocity, trust and mutuality' with the key stakeholders of an offence (Boyes-Watson 2004: 220). Instead, as Carolyn Boyes-Watson explains, 'Clients are viewed as bearers of deficits and problems rather than valuable sources of knowledge, skill and support' (2004: 220). The impersonal connections that local authorities form with victims and perpetrators of hate crime ultimately limit their ability to provide genuine emotional support to those most in need (Boyes-Watson 2004).

The relationships which develop between state agencies and the stakeholders of hate crime will inevitably become strained where institutional practices create barriers to mutuality and trust. Restorative dialogue, however, is unlike other forms of inter-personal communication. Restorative practices that are administered externally from state-based agencies, allow professional participants to be removed from their social or institutional settings. This physical relocation means that stakeholders are invited into a new environment, away from their bureaucratic surroundings, which emphasizes equality and reciprocity between discussants. Restorative meetings, if managed by an impartial practitioner, additionally help to facilitate dialogue that is based on non-domination (Boyes-Watson 2004). The fact that restorative dialogue is focused on harm and restoration, as against blame or service provision, means that participants will be better able to form genuine emotional connections (see Chapters 7 and 8 on emotional connections in RJ). The process of storytelling, as we have already seen, helps to break down pre-existing obstacles to empathy by exposing the humanity of each stakeholder. It is through galvanizing these visceral connections that RJ can transcend the bureaucratic barriers to communication which limit agency/victim relations.

Pivotally, agency employees who participate in restorative processes may need to assume two key roles. First and foremost, they must attend discussions as professional service providers ('community supporters') who are there in order to support the key stakeholders of the offence/conflict (ie victims and offenders). However, simultaneously they may also need to be involved by restorative facilitators as 'community stakeholders'. This latter role is explained more fully below. For now it is sufficient to note that, together, the stakeholders (including agency employees) should engage in dialogue and 'storytelling', which helps to humanize each of the participants. In turn, this will encourage agency employees to offer support and reparation (where required), rather than treating stakeholders as a 'problem' that needs to be 'dealt with' (Boyes-Watson 2004; see Case Study 2 and Case Study 1: Part 2).

Essential to this more inclusive process is that restorative facilitators remain impartial (as briefly mentioned above). Conflicts of interest inevitably arise in cases where a restorative facilitator is employed by the same institution that is required to then repair harm. Impartiality is therefore best ensured where the facilitator remains detached from the state altogether (as in community mediation for example).[13] Facilitators independent of state control are also less likely to be curtailed by institutional bureaucracy or subject to government targets. For these reasons, restorative practitioners are more able to facilitate a process that holds those who have harmed to account. As Declan Roche expresses, 'if state accountability is to be nurtured, the convenor must be independent as much as possible' (2003: 137, cited in Hoyle 2007: 297).

However, this does not mean that RJ practitioners employed by the state cannot successfully facilitate practices that include *other* state agencies. Rather, what is of most importance is that restorative facilitators are not *directly* employed by the agency that they wish to include within reparative dialogue. This is to avoid a conflict between their impartiality as facilitators and the institutional responsibilities they have as service providers (Hoyle 2007: 297). For instance, a restorative practitioner employed by a YOS is not directly constrained by the bureaucracy and administration of the police service or the local housing association. As such, YOS restorative facilitators who invite police officers or housing officers into FGCs do so with a greater level of objectivity than that which would exist within a police- or housing-led restorative practice.[14]

---

[13] The fact that community mediation is often funded by the government and local councils can complicate this independence.

[14] Since this research was carried out, Southwark Mediation has seen huge cuts to its services. The local council has expressed the view that mediation services should be taken 'in house' and facilitated by housing officers. This is of serious concern considering the secondary harms caused by housing officers reported by most interviewees.

Practitioners who engage local agencies as 'community stakeholders' must also ensure that their involvement does not provide a mechanism through which the victim feels dominated. Facilitators must therefore limit the power inequality between the parties by preparing agency employees before meetings and explaining to them what their role will be during restorative dialogue (see Chapter 6). Ground rules set at the beginning of the process, which outline the manner in which participants should address each other, equally help to reduce the likelihood of state employees bringing their own agenda to the table. Sufficient preparation, as we will see in Chapter 7, is fundamental to the prevention of domination during dialogue. Only when adequate preparation of all the parties has been carried out should practitioners invite local agencies into direct mediation meetings.

The involvement of state agencies directly within restorative processes may appear contentious given RJ's focus on empowering community members to take control of their own conflicts. However, the state's role as social services provider within most local communities means that 'the state' will continue to dominate local responses to crime and victimization. This means that the state and other community agencies will continue to be implicated in the vast amounts of hate crime that occur throughout society. And, as such, state authorities will continue to be involved in hate crime cases, be it as victim supporters, victim protectors, or as secondary victimizers. It is in this sense that local agencies, as stakeholders of hate offences, should be brought within the scope of RJ in order to support victims and to help repair the secondary harms they themselves so often cause. The next section explores further the role that local agencies should play in restorative dialogue, arguing that, despite their attachments to the state, they can also constitute part of the notion of 'community'—central to RJ theory.

State-run agencies as 'community'?

'Community' is a central concept within the theory and practice of RJ (McCold 2004). It has long been heralded as the platform upon which the stakeholders of a crime should resolve inter-personal conflicts (Christie 1977; Braithwaite 1989; Zehr 1990). Restorativists argue that the positive role of community is that it is a definable social entity (Weisberg 2003), upholding a strong moral authority through which particular groupings of people are bound (Braithwaite 1989). The notion of community has therefore been envisaged as an entity for good (Pavlich 2004). And as such, it has been promulgated as the antidote to the self-serving individual and to the remoteness of the monolithic state (Weisberg 2003).

Restorative justice scholars have conceptualized 'community' in both broad and narrow terms. For example, John Braithwaite (1989: 85) states that community is a set of 'dense networks of individual interdependencies with strong cultural commitments to mutuality and obligations', while Lode Walgrave (2002: 74) states that a community is 'an "area", delimited mentally, structurally or territorially'. Essentially, community can be defined both in terms of location and space but also through 'subjective feelings' (Walgrave 2002). At its most basic level we might say that community is simply a 'perception of togetherness' (McCold & Wachtel 1997 cited in Walgrave 2002: 74).

Such analyses draw heavily from sociological conceptualizations of community. The sociologist Scott Lash (1994), for example, argues that communities do not necessarily share common interests or assets, but instead share an essence through which members form a bond with each other. Paul Kennedy and Victor Roudometof (2004: 6) similarly define community as 'units of belonging whose members perceive that they share moral, aesthetic/expressive or cognitive meanings, thereby gaining a sense of personal as well as group identity'. Accordingly, while 'communities' frequently share spatial locations, they are not necessarily bound by territorial space (Spalek 2008). In fact, communities are often transitory in nature, constantly transgressing previously prescribed moral, essential, and mental boundaries (Spalek 2008). Individual members, likewise, transcend communities' prescribed borders, forming new identity groups, and/or subscribing to a multitude of different communities.

The application of community in restorative justice practices

The concept of 'community' is clearly subject to metamorphosis and its definition is largely context specific. How then does such a fluid notion apply to restorative practice? Initially, theorists argued that 'community' simply provided a forum within which harms could be discussed (Christie 1977). Community members are encouraged to explore how they have been impacted by the crime and how the offender/s might go about repairing the harms caused. Under this construction, community is conceptualized within a vacuum, it merely being part of the apparatus through which stakeholders take control of their own conflict.

Other scholars have since developed a more sophisticated analysis of the role of community. For instance, Paul McCold (2004) argues that there are two distinct forms of 'community' that apply to the practice of RJ. The first is the 'micro-community', and refers to those who have been directly affected by an offence. Micro-communities also comprise what has been labelled as the 'community of care' (McCold 1996) ie family members, friends, and other individuals who have meaningful relationships with the victim and/or the offender. Micro-communities play an important role in providing emotional and social support to those directly involved in an offence (Schiff 2007). They can also participate in dialogue helping the stakeholders, collectively, to understand the harms that have been caused to the victim and to his or her broader 'community of care'. RJ processes that involve micro-communities include FGCs and community mediation.

McCold's second type of community is the 'macro-community' and is defined by geographical space or through identity membership (for example, the 'gay community' or the 'Muslim community'; see also, Weisberg 2003). Macro-communities have little emotional or personal connection with the victim or offender. Instead they are more concerned with the harms that are aggregated to neighbourhoods, a particular identity group, or society more generally. Individual members of the macro-community can engage with restorative practices in order to convey social condemnation for the harms caused (Braithwaite 1989). They are also encouraged to explain how the offender's actions have affected the broader community into which he or she must later be reintegrated. An example of a restorative practice that involves a macro-community is the youth offending panel (see Chapter 2).

While 'community' has been considered as both a physical forum and as a collection of different types of individuals, it has also been developed as a metaphysical phenomenon. By this I mean that it is conceived as a way in which things ought to be. 'Community' is understood, in this sense, as serving a normative function that helps to develop, communicate, and uphold 'the standards to which its members are expected to adhere as well as the values that undergird those norms' (Schiff 2007: 236; to what extent these standards and norms are homogeneous is explored further below and in Chapter 7). Community is therefore value laden. It is to these community values that we should aspire and through which RJ can be advanced.

Linked to community's normative function is that it then becomes a 'tool' through which restorative goals can be achieved (see Walgrave 2002: 75). For instance, a community can provide the context needed for restorative practice, such as reintegrative shaming (Braithwaite 1989). Its purpose therefore moves beyond that of supporter or stakeholder of harm to that of a mechanism of reform and rehabilitation (Braithwaite 1989). Accordingly, 'community' becomes a 'goal' of RJ. For example, restorative meetings help to rebuild the 'community' by healing damaged relationships and reintegrating offenders who are now less likely to offend (Walgrave 2002). In this sense, the betterment of community is an aim to be achieved via dialogic processes that engender the reparation of damaged relationships.

State agencies as 'community supporters'?

The concept of community within RJ is clearly one which is broadly conceived, fluid, and intersecting. Yet despite this, an analysis of the varied roles that local state (and third sector) organizations play within the various guises of community has remained largely outside RJ scholarship. Neighbourhood policing teams, schools, colleges, housing associations, anti-social behaviour units, victim support groups, social care units, citizens advice bureaux, and many more have the duty and responsibility of responding to and supporting the needs of both victims and perpetrators of hate crime. Their role in tackling the causation and harms of hate victimization is pivotal. In spite of this, such organizations appear to remain absent from many discussions on what 'community' is within RJ literature. This is likely to be due to the fact that local agencies are primarily state-run, leading, as I suggested above, to their rejection by restorativists as potentially taking control away from the community and hence from the stakeholders of a crime (Christie 1977; White 1994).

Those who have written about the role of community groups and/or local agencies in the restorative context have usually done so in terms of their working in addition to or in parallel with restorative practices. For instance, Susan Herman (2004: 77) argues that the complex socio-economic problems underlying victimization and its long-term effects may require redress by state, local, and charitable organizations that are better placed (compared with RJ practices) to deal with such problems (Herman 2004). A number of social services may be required to assist in supporting victims. Such organizations are better resourced with the means to address the victim's long-term needs (Herman 2004). However, instead of arguing that these organizations should work collectively within a restorative framework, Herman suggests that a parallel system is required where the victim is treated separately from the offender, thus creating 'two systems' of justice.

Lorraine Amstutz (2004) similarly emphasizes the importance of victim support groups in helping victims to recover from crime. She highlights several action steps taken from a 'listening project' that can help with the forming of partnerships between restorative practitioners and victim groups, including establishing ongoing dialogue between restorative practitioners and victim support practitioners, and working in partnership with other agencies to advocate the requisite justice resources required to support the needs of the victim. However, like Herman, Amstutz still falls short of arguing that victim support groups should be included within restorative meetings. Instead, she argues that practitioners can learn about the needs of victims by engaging more with victim groups before referring victims to their services post RJ.

While both Herman (2004) and Amstutz (2004) argue for greater support for victims, neither a parallel system of justice nor the forming of better partnerships with victim support groups *fully* utilize the inclusivity and flexibility of RJ. The failure to include local organizations within RJ theory is, to a certain extent, shortsighted. I have already alluded to this above, suggesting that local authorities become stakeholders of hate conflicts as and when they respond to complaints about hate incidents. As such, it can be asserted that local organizations fall within the notion of community in several ways. First, community agencies constitute part of the local geographical territory. They exist within certain spatial boundaries to serve the citizens who reside in particular neighbourhoods (making up part of McCold's (2004) macro-community). The purpose of both organizations is to protect, support, and respond to the needs of those who live in the local area. Such organizations can therefore be viewed as part of the social fabric of *most* geographically defined communities.

Second, local agencies often become part of victims' and offenders' 'community of care' (making up part of McCold's (2004) microcommunity) when an offence is initially reported to them and/or when they are contacted in order to provide victim support. For example, the housing officers involved in most community mediation cases researched became directly associated with the direct stakeholders upon providing them with advice on their rights and responsibilities as council tenants. Officers were called upon to assist victims to recover from experiences of hate abuse, while also ensuring that offenders did not repeat their prejudice-motivated behaviours. Their intimate involvement in many hate cases (see also Bowling 1994) meant that they became a central part of the stakeholders' immediate support network (see Case Study 2 and Case Study 1: Part 2).

Finally, linked to their role as supporters is that local agencies can also be viewed as a community 'tool' (Walgrave 2002). Agency employees help victims to move on from their experiences of crime (for example, Victim Support or social workers assisting victims during the restorative process) and/or additionally provide resources to help offenders reintegrate into the community (for example, drug and alcohol rehabilitation, anger management, support with housing etc). Both lay members of a community and the local organizations that constitute part of its territorial space and group identity collectively represent and uphold the moral obligations by which it is bound. Hence, neighbourhood policing teams and housing associations are not aberrations of the community but fundamental constituents of it. They are local organizations consisting of employees who often reside in the neighbourhood that they serve. Accordingly, local agencies should be included within RJ meetings where it is determined that they can provide additional emotional support to victims while also encouraging offender reformation.

State agencies as 'community harmers'

Broadening the scope of 'community' to encompass local third sector and state organizations will potentially enhance the healing process for victims, central to RJ theory. However, such an assertion presupposes that 'community', including its constituent parts, is a benevolent entity. The assumption is that community will provide expedient support and assistance to stakeholders where needed. At face value, such a proposition seems fair given that a central aim within the mission statements of state agencies will be to support, protect, and assist community residents. The police, housing, and other such organizations have moral obligations towards those they are tasked with serving, and in this sense they exist for the sake and betterment of the community.

Nevertheless, as we have seen in Chapter 3 and within this chapter, members of many communities (including employees of state institutions) frequently act to victimize, re-victimize, and cause secondary victimization to those who do not follow hegemonic community ideals. One of the main findings presented during this chapter has been that housing associations and police officers often demonstrate a lack of care towards stakeholders of hate crime and/or fail to convey adequate social condemnation of the harms caused by certain prejudices. A paradox therefore exists between the *assumed* benevolence of community (including that of individual members and community agencies) and the *actual* effects it has on victims of hate crime. A notion of community that remains confined to a romanticized vision of homogeneity, in which its members are bound by a unified voice, may potentially expose some victims to further harm in cases where the community's sense of 'togetherness' does not include certain 'Others' (Crawford 2002; a more detailed critique of community as a homogeneous entity is provided in Chapter 7).

A more nuanced understanding of community is therefore called for which considers both its benevolent and malevolent effects. First, we need to acknowledge that while some communities represent a sense of unified 'togetherness', others will ultimately be more fragmented, both in terms of their *supporting* and *harming* roles (Crawford 2002; Cunneen 2003; see Chapter 7). In other words, some communities will embody a homogeneous representation of mutuality, obligation, and righteous social condemnation. Yet in others, the community may simply act to uphold prejudiced views, and if given a large role in repairing the harms of hate crime may potentially leave an insidious residuum (see further Chapter 7).

Practitioners of RJ must be careful not to expose victims to re-victimization through a dialogue involving community members who attempt to impose upon victims norms and values that are an affront to their minority identity (see Chapter 3). A more realistic interpretation of community must consider the roles played by other stakeholders in both repairing and exacerbating harm.

Put another way, if 'community' is viewed *only* as a repairer of harm it will ultimately frustrate RJ's potential to effectively resolve the complex conflicts which are manifest in multicultural communities.

Restorative practitioners must therefore appreciate the different but intersecting roles of community in order to enhance RJ's capacity to help repair the harms caused by hate victimization (and secondary victimization). I have already alluded to the fact that in cases where a local agency has *not* caused secondary victimization, its representatives can participate as part of the victim's 'community of care'. In such cases, representatives are invited into the restorative process, either as participants in group conferences or direct mediation meetings with the victim, during which they are encouraged by the facilitator to provide the support their organization is most equipped to offer (see examples below).

Yet, as we have seen in Part I above, local agencies frequently cause secondary victimization. In such cases, their role as community participant becomes complex. By causing harm, the agency subverts its role as community supporter and consequently assumes another part of community—that of perpetrator of harm (and in turn conflict stakeholder). This means that in cases where a local institution has caused secondary victimization, representatives from that organization must engage in restorative meetings in several ways:

1. The agency is invited to join dialogue as a *renewed* 'community supporter', in which its representative is encouraged to offer the professional support the organization previously failed to administer.
2. Agency representatives are included as 'community stakeholders'. They are then provided with an opportunity to take responsibility for the secondary victimization their organization has caused. This is best achieved by encouraging agency employees to offer direct reparation to the victim, most commonly by apologizing for their mismanagement of the victim's case, but also by promising them to provide the support they are entitled to in the future (see Case Study 1: Part 2).

The multifaceted role that community-based agencies will frequently play in repairing the harms of hate crime is clearly complicated by their dual roles as *state* and *community* as well as *supporter* and *harmer*. The next section therefore provides qualitative data that illustrate how, in practice, the inclusion of community/state agencies during restorative dialogue can help to support victims of hate crime and repair the harms of secondary victimization.

Multi-agency approaches: supporting the needs of victims and preventing repeat victimization

The need for multi-agency partnerships between local agencies when tackling hate crime first arose during the 1980s after the publication of the 1981 Home Office Report, *Racial Attacks*, explicitly expressed the need for greater co-operation between state institutions (see Bowling 1998). However, it was not until the publication of the Macpherson Report (1999) that multi-agency working was established as a key method of attending to the problem of hate victimization (Iganski 2008: 100–1). In supporting the multi-agency ethos, the London based Race-Hate Crimes Forum was launched in 2003. The Forum was made up of key agencies that have within their remit the task of dealing with racist hate crime. Forum meetings provided an arena through which state agencies could present on the progresses they had made in relation to tackling hate crime and for the Forum to then scrutinize their policies and practices (Iganski 2008: 101). Paul Iganski, reporting on these presentations, found that while state authorities were prominently vocal during meetings, victims and victim support groups felt that they were denied a voice (2008: 106). Multi-agency partnerships have also been accused of lacking coherent communication and commitment by some individuals and agencies (Garland & Chakraborti 2006: 19). One of the problems faced by multi-agency working is that there is rarely a single organization or person galvanizing the collective work between the agencies.

Within the area of Southwark, community mediators frequently became the driving force behind multi-agency partnerships, ensuring that local organizations came together to discuss how they should best move forward with individual cases. The involvement of local organizations such as housing associations, neighbourhood policing teams, schools, and social services was key to resolving six of the nineteen separate cases researched at Southwark Mediation (though in most cases, local agencies were included in restorative dialogue at some point during the process). The manager of the HCP explained how the multi-agency approach to community mediation works in practice:

The multi-agency approach is very much a restorative approach... it's about people being included in a process which can enable change, it's about giving people the opportunity to say why they're doing what they do... it's about understanding what informs what they do... But it's also about getting support, so if I feel that people need additional support or counselling support—it might be something to do with their home, with their education, something that will help them in their own environment... I contact schools, I work with community groups, social services—it can be a whole range of people.

In some cases, employees from these agencies took part in group conferences where both complainant victims and accused perpetrators were present. In other cases, mediation meetings included the complainant victim and his or her supporters, together with agency employees. The HCP manager further explained:

it may need a case conference... And by that I mean bringing all the agencies together to talk about this issue and come up with some outcomes. And that may be because the person concerned isn't able to take charge of the situation themselves... it may be to support... but it is also [about] risk assessment.

An interviewee who had been subjected to persistent racial abuse explained how such an approach was important to resolving his case:

she brought my wife and I and the other gentleman in question and the authorities, the council and the police [together], which I thought was the most important thing. Without the council and ourselves or without [the mediator] I don't think we would have been able to solve this.

In this case the inclusion of a housing manager and two other housing officers in a group conference provided both husband and wife the opportunity to directly explain to the perpetrator and the council how racial abuse had affected their lives. During this meeting the complainant victims were visibly upset at what they felt was a tirade of racial harassment against them by their neighbour. The mediator explored the issue of racism in detail with the group and the impact that racial slurs had had on the complainant victims. At the end of the meeting the mediator formed a mediation agreement—also signed by the housing manager, the complainant victims, and the accused perpetrator—which stated that in no circumstances should racial slurs be used. If the agreed terms were reneged upon, the accused perpetrator could be found in breach of his tenancy agreement. Although not directly stated, this could have led to the accused perpetrator's removal from the council's property. Such a process therefore included both restorative dialogue and a potentially punitive penalty for breach of the agreement. Six months after this meeting took place the complainant victims told me that they were very relieved that their neighbour no longer abused them.

Case Study 2 Persistent disablist abuse—the support of school teachers

Mr L is a young 'Black British' man living in South London who suffers from a 'speech impediment' and minor 'learning difficulties'. His ordeal began in 2007 when a group of local school children noticed that he had a disability. Soon after, the group began to taunt Mr L, shouting obscenities at him in the street including calling him a 'paedophile' and a 'devil', while also verbally abusing his girlfriend, a young white woman who suffers from autism, in particular calling her a 'white bitch'. This went on for over a year until Mr L finally contacted the police about the abuse. This resulted in the arrest of one of the perpetrators who was warned about his behaviour. However, the harassment continued and the boys began to throw stones at the couple when they saw them in the street. Mr L and his girlfriend's ordeal worsened when the group started a rumour among the local community that Mr L was a paedophile. As a result, Mr L felt that he could no longer leave his house for fear of being attacked.

Mr L's case was eventually referred to the HCP by a neighbourhood police officer. The mediator arranged to meet with Mr L and the other parties involved in the case. After several indirect meetings the mediator decided that the best way forward would be to arrange a direct meeting between Mr L, the young perpetrators, and the head teacher at the perpetrators' school. During this meeting, Mr L was able to explain how the incidents had affected him, while the head teacher played a central role in demonstrating appropriate social condemnation of his students' disablist actions. Mr L commented, 'At first I was worried that the school teachers would take the school kids' word, but when it turned out well I was really relieved.' A mediation agreement was drawn up in which the young perpetrators apologized and promised to desist from any further abuse.

Unlike the previous police intervention, the mediation process provided Mr L with immense emotional relief; he commented, 'I had anxiety, it sent me paranoid and I would have flash backs and when I see them they would laugh at me...but after [mediation] I was more relaxed and they left me and my girlfriend alone.' He went on to state that 'I'm more happy, me and my girlfriend can walk in the street. If it wasn't for [the mediator] helping out I might not be here.'[15]

The inclusion of the offenders' head teacher in this case not only provided appropriate social condemnation of the students' disablist actions but it also provided the victim with emotional and social support, allowing him to feel more confident that he would no longer be targeted by his abusers.

Repairing the harms of secondary victimization

Case Study 2 highlights the benefits of including community organizations (such as school teachers) within the restorative process. By participating in restorative dialogue, agency employees are more likely to offer emotional and social support to victims, thus aiding their recovery from hate incidents. Moreover, their inclusion within the process reduces the likelihood of repeat victimization. The prevention of repeat victimization is primarily achieved by local organizations demonstrating social condemnation of the offender's prejudiced behaviours. It is also achieved where agencies present the offender with potential repercussions if they break mediation/reparation agreements.[16]

Notwithstanding the potential benefits that can be gained by implementing a multi-agency approach to mediation, we have yet to consider the need for harm reparation by state authorities themselves. After all, as we have seen at the beginning of this chapter, local agencies frequently cause secondary victimization when responding to reports of hate incidents. The reparation of secondary harm can be a complex undertaking. Persuading agencies to admit that they have caused harm and/or that they should actively repair this is no easy task. Practitioners may find in such cases that they begin to become victim advocates as well as restorative facilitators.

Whether restorative practitioners should seek to provide additional support for victims is questionable, given the emphasis that is placed on practitioner impartiality (Strang 2002). However, in

---

[15] Case study also used in Walters (2012).
[16] Such as the threat of expulsion from school, or the threat of eviction by housing officers.

some cases mediators may well need to stretch beyond their role as facilitator of dialogue between victim and offender and actively seek to enhance the victim's wellbeing by encouraging state and community agencies to participate in RJ (see generally Amstutz 2004). The HCP manager asserted:

> some people have said, 'Is it your business to inform people about other agencies? Is it your business to be telling people about legislative or police services?' and I say, 'Yes, it is' because mediation isn't just about mediating people in a room or writing agreements. It's a very essential process and a very holistic one, and that for me, is a function of mediation. It isn't just one-dimensional. It can do all of those things!

In order to illustrate how restorative practitioners can facilitate a multi-agency approach to mediation that helps to repair the harms of secondary victimization I provide further examination of Case Study 1.

Case Study 1, Part 2 Repairing the harms of ineffective state intervention

In part one of this case study we saw how Miss J had been subjected to years of racial harassment, abuse, identity theft, investigations by the Inland Revenue (which temporarily resulted in the stoppage of child support payments), the failure of the housing association to take any action against Miss Y (the perpetrator), and several botched dealings with Southwark police. Finally, after twelve years, Miss J was referred to the HCP at Southwark Mediation who initially set about arranging a direct meeting between Miss J and Miss Y to explore what had been happening over the past decade. During this meeting it became clear to all parties present that Miss Y would not desist from her hate-motivated behaviour. Miss J remarked, 'It had gone beyond—you know—shake hands make up; it's way past that to an issue of us being moved.'

Although the face-to-face mediation meeting did not directly resolve this case, it did allow all parties involved (in particular the housing association) to appreciate that something needed to be done in order to prevent the further victimization of Miss J. After this initial mediation meeting, the role of the mediator shifted from mediating between victim and accused perpetrator to working with Miss J and the various organizations that had exposed her to secondary victimization. These meetings allowed Miss J to explain not only how her ongoing victimization had impacted her, but also how the council's and police's apathetic responses to her complaints had damaging repercussions. Three separate mediation meetings between Miss J and her housing officer were arranged during which the housing association was held to account for its own hate crime policy. Eventually, Miss J was relocated into a new apartment. The mediator told me:

> I held the meetings because I wanted to check if [the housing association] was aware racism was an issue. [Miss J's] housing officer was black, the support worker was mixed race. They were acutely aware of it. To not effect measures is to by default effectively re-victimize [Miss J]. [Miss J] was constantly told by [the housing association] that there was nothing they could do about her neighbour as there was no impartial evidence, what she was told was utter nonsense! (The names of parties involved have been replaced.)

Miss J also commented at interview:

> the police couldn't really get her [Miss Y]... but with the mediation she realized that 'hold on for a second my housing people are now aware of this'... so now when I complained about it instead of them saying oh [Miss J] this is a trivial matter they had to write a letter to her saying it has been brought to our attention... and to please stop it. So she now found herself being accountable... I suffered for 12 years and no one did anything about it and then we got all of these agencies involved through mediation I got moved away...

Following these meetings the mediator then facilitated a meeting between Miss J and the local Community Safety Unit (the police department tasked with investigating hate crime). After this meeting the Unit investigated Miss J's complaints and discovered that the officer who had previously served her with a harassment warning was in fact in an intimate relationship with Miss Y. The officer was subsequently suspended, Miss J's harassment warning was withdrawn, and a letter of apology was sent to her. Finally, the mediator then worked with Miss J's family support officer who went on to obtain medical and counselling support for Miss J.

This case was socially, emotionally, and logistically complex and during my interview with Miss J it was clear that she was far from fully recovered from her experience of inter-personal and institutional racism. She is, however, much happier in her new life and has regained her lost weight. The case is demonstrative of the extent to which hate victimization can damage a person's/family's life if the incompetence and neglect of state-run agencies goes unchallenged (see also the Pilkington case, Chapter 1). The dedication and hard work of the mediator in facilitating the various restorative meetings in this case are commendable. It illustrates how mediators using multi-agency partnerships in complex hate crime cases can help victims to move on with their life, free from hate abuse. In this case, both housing and police officers were held to account for their failures to support Miss J. Both organizations, by participating in direct mediation meetings, became aware of the harms they had caused. It was through this dialogical process that the agencies went on to offer the support they had previously failed to administer, as well as reparation for the secondary harms they themselves had caused.

The cases left unresolved

The inclusion of multiple agencies within community mediation significantly strengthened its capacity to aid recovery and prevent future incidents of hate crime. Out of the nineteen ongoing cases of hate conflict in South London where complainant victims were interviewed,[17] seventeen were judged to have been resolved through community mediation—eleven primarily through victim–offender mediation and six only after a multi-agency approach had been implemented. In total, this meant that the complainant victims of seventeen separate cases were no longer subject to hate victimization by the accused perpetrator/s.

This left two cases unresolved.[18] In the first case the victim had experienced racial abuse, including dog faeces being disposed of through her letter box. The mediation process was judged to have failed for two reasons. First, the mediator could not engage the accused perpetrator and therefore could not facilitate direct dialogue between the parties. Second, the police officer referring the

---

[17] A total of twenty-three interviewees referring to nineteen separate cases.

[18] At the beginning of this chapter I also highlighted a mediation meeting involving the racially motivated assault of an elderly African-Caribbean gentleman (see under 'Police responses to hate incidents'). I was unable to interview this victim and therefore his case does not make up one of the nineteen separate cases fully researched at the HCP. However, it should be noted that the failure of the accused perpetrator to engage in the mediation process in this case meant that the victim remained vulnerable to racial abuse.

case to mediation had communicated to the mediator that the complainant victim had been socializing with a known drug dealer. The mediator mentioned this during an indirect meeting with the complainant. This upset the complainant who felt that the mediator was judging her credibility based on her association with someone else. The victim also made it clear to me during interview that she would no longer engage with the mediator unless she could persuade the housing association to relocate her. This was, of course, not the primary role of the mediation service and as such this case was aborted.[19]

In the other case, a combination of racial, homophobic, and disablist incidents had been committed by the victim's neighbour. During a direct mediation meeting, the perpetrator apologized for his behaviour and subsequently stopped harassing the victim. However, three weeks after mediation took place the offender began to abuse the victim again. Mediators were called in several times and on each occasion the offender apologized and temporarily desisted harassment, only to start again some weeks later. This continued despite letters from the housing association stating that he would be in breach of his tenancy agreement if he did not refrain from such behaviours. Finally, the tenant moved of his own accord leaving the victim in peace.

These cases demonstrated that even with the involvement of complainant victims and community agencies within restorative meetings, the process cannot always help to repair the harms caused by hate crime or prevent abuse from recurring. In some cases, the failure to find resolution could be directly correlated to the perpetrators' refusal to participate. In such situations mediators will struggle to facilitate reparation for the victim. Even in cases where perpetrators do participate, there will inevitably be some occasions where community mediation is unable to help resolve conflict. In these few cases there will be no other alternative but for the state to administer a punitive response to hate crime offenders.

Conclusion

This chapter has illuminated the problem of secondary victimization faced by many of the individuals who contacted local authorities to

---

[19] Although in other cases the mediator had engaged housing officers in mediation who then went on to relocate victims.

report incidents of hate. In the case of housing associations, housing officers tended to exacerbate victims' experiences of hate crime/incidents by failing to take adequate measures against accused perpetrators, or simply by portraying to the victim a sense of indifference about their complaint/s. Similarly, police officers called to victims' home addresses rarely investigated reports of hate abuse beyond their initial response, instead often telling victims that their complaint related to a 'domestic' matter. A lack of concrete evidence also led to officers dropping cases, commonly without telling victims, much to their frustration. The failure of local authorities to take any concrete action against those accused of hate crime inevitably led to the continuation of 'low-level' but persistent abuse of victims.

The apathetic and neglectful responses by local authorities, as relayed by interviewees, resulted in what was often phrased as their feeling 'let down' by the state. Nevertheless, it would be wrong to conclude that all interviewees experienced secondary victimization. It must be noted that in some cases, victims found local agencies to be very helpful and supportive—particularly those who had recently moved to Devon and Cornwall from Eastern Europe. While in other cases, agency employees were not deemed to have been neglectful but instead, despite their statutory powers, were simply unable to resolve the often intractable conflicts in which community members become involved (see Chapter 4, Case Study 2). Either way, this often meant that victims continued to suffer at the hands of their abusers. Resolving such complex long-term cases of hate victimization frequently required mediators to implement a multi-agency approach to restorative dialogue. This involved the participation of both complainant victims and accused perpetrators, as well as various other community and state organizations seen as pivotal to the resolution of conflict and to the reparation of harm.

This chapter has asserted that the inclusion of local agencies within restorative dialogue is intrinsically linked to the notion of 'community'. I have argued that local agencies constitute part of what is understood as 'community' in a variety of different ways. For example, agencies frequently became an important component of the victim's 'community of care' (McCold 2004), providing them with the necessary emotional and social support that was required for victims to feel safe again in their local neighbourhood (see Case Study 2). Moreover, their involvement often conveyed appropriate social condemnation of prejudice, thus helping to prevent the recurrence of hate incidents (Braithwaite 1989). In other situations, authorities also needed to be included within the process as a 'secondary harmer' bringing them within the meaning of 'community stakeholder'. This latter role required agencies to take responsibility for the secondary victimization they had caused and then to repair the harms they had subjected victims to.

Agencies were actively encouraged to repair harm in two main ways: first, by administering a level of support that they had previously failed to deliver and/or second, by offering direct reparation to the victim, such as a written apology (see Case Study 1: Parts 1 and 2). In either case, the role of local agencies within RJ was transposed from one of state authority to that of community participant. The dialogical emphasis placed on restoring harm and supporting the victim helped to break down the agencies' bureaucratic and professional responses to hate incidents and instead encouraged emotional connections amongst the participants. Providing that mediators remain outside the agencies' autonomy, such processes could be facilitated based on the values of mutuality and non-domination.

To this end, we might begin to consider how RJ practices, such as community mediation, counter some of the structural disadvantages that I began to highlight in Chapter 3 and which were more fully explored at the beginning of this chapter. In particular, agencies that were held to account for their own hate crime policies and that were encouraged to offer the support they had previously failed to provide were, in effect, repairing some of the harm caused by institutional and structural prejudice. This went some way to restoring the institutional inequities that are frequently experienced by victims of hate crime. This means that community mediation is able to reach further along the continuum of hate victimization by helping to repair both social as well as individual harms. Perhaps in time, the benefits of multi-agency partnerships will encourage restorative practitioners within other parts of the justice system to engage local agencies during the dialogic process. As community mediation has shown, the engagement of 'community' in all its guises can promote additional emotional support for victims and help repair the harms of secondary victimization, while simultaneously improving the safety of minority victims within their local neighbourhoods.

7
The Perils of 'Community': From Theory to Practice

Introduction

In Chapters 5, 6, and 7, I presented data which suggested that, if used in accordance with restorative values, RJ practices *help* to alleviate the distress caused by the 'process' of hate victimization. In essence, we have seen that victims' vocalization of their experiences of harm (including those directly relating to prejudice), the support offered by facilitators, and, pivotally, assurances of desistance, combined to aid the emotional recovery of *most* hate crime victims. A multi-agency approach to restorative dialogue, involving the active participation of local agencies, further enhanced the reparative capabilities of restorative practice. This chapter builds upon the previous chapter by providing further analysis of the concept of 'community', central to RJ theory and practice, while also examining the risks that community participants pose to the reparative process.

As we saw in Chapter 6, the theoretical 'promise' of community is that it provides both social condemnation for wrongful behaviour and a positive environment to which the offender can return (see further Chapter 8). In cases involving hate, the value of 'community' is that it will help to bridge the cultural disconnect that exists between victims and offenders by breaking down the 'differences' which previously polarized stakeholders. The same dialogical processes that have been identified in the preceding chapters as supporting victims' emotional wellbeing are intrinsic to this task. Principally, the exploratory methods that focus on harm not only help to *repair* the traumas of hate, but provide a pivotal mechanism through which individuals' 'difference' is *humanized* (McConnell & Swain 2000; Walters & Hoyle 2010; see further Chapter 8). The uniting force of 'community' therefore allows RJ to focus on the commonalities which exist between participants rather than those traits which differentiate them. The common goals of peace and resolution, for example, help to bring forth a common morality that resists hate and instead encourages social harmony.

The restorative process, when conceived in such terms, appears almost panacea-like, it seemingly being ideally suited to bringing about community cohesion. Yet we must not be too quick to overstate the potential of RJ for hate crime. A multitude of risks to the reparative qualities of RJ are exposed by participants' identity and cultural differences, consequences which must be fully explored before restorative practice is 'rolled out' for hate crime. In particular, critics have pointed out that far from being cohesive and harmonious collectives, communities are often fragmented, hierarchical entities which, like state institutions, perpetuate hegemonic norms and values that can oppress the identities of certain minority groups (Crawford 2002; Cunneen 2003; see Chapters 3 and 7). A major concern, therefore, is that if criminal justice practices blindly apply a benevolent notion of 'community', they may actually perpetuate the elitist norms which give rise to minority group marginalization. For instance, the inclusion in restorative processes of community members who are affected by a culture of racism (Sibbitt 1997; Spalek 2008) may actively neutralize, rather than condemn, the behaviours of racist offenders. In fact, there is a genuine risk that an offender's 'community of care' will subject victims to further expressions of animosity, thereby re-victimizing the victim and his or her supporters (Pavlich 2004; see also Stubbs 2007).

The paucity of empirical research into RJ and hate crime means that a disjuncture exists between the normative assumptions made about RJ (outlined in Chapter 2) and the possible risks that dialogic processes expose victims to. Using the three main datasets collated for the book, this chapter aims to reduce the gap between theory and practice by empirically exploring the role of community participants and their re-victimizing potential within restorative practice, as applied to hate crime.

Part I begins this examination by re-analysing the notion of 'community'. Several concerns are illuminated, including whether divided communities will provide adequate social condemnation of hate incidents. The potential for offenders—along with their 'communities of care'—to dominate proceedings by manipulating dialogue and re-victimizing victims is also highlighted. Part II then explores whether the risks of re-victimization and domination during meetings occurred in practice. Using data from victim interviews, I document the very low levels of perceived disadvantage reported by victims. Then, using data obtained from observations and interviews with restorative practitioners, I analyse the methods that were used to avoid domination and repeat victimization. In general, two consistent themes were articulated by practitioners as minimizing the risk of domination and re-victimization during meetings. The first factor consistently articulated by RJ practitioners was that participants were well prepared before meetings, ensuring that they understood the purpose of RJ and the subject matter which would be explored during any further (in)direct meetings. The second common theme related to risk management and involved the setting of ground rules at the beginning of meetings, thereby reducing the likelihood of hostile language being directed at participants. Finally, I explore the value of including 'appropriate' community supporters within restorative meetings, noting that restorative facilitators may at times need to challenge prejudice themselves if RJ is to limit the moral impunity imparted by some 'communities of care'.

Part I: The Perils of 'Community'

In Chapter 6 I began to reconceptualize 'community' by challenging overly simplistic conceptions of the notion that exist within the extant literature. In particular, I argued that rather than being aberrations of a community, local state authorities (and charitable organizations) are fundamental components of a community as they are intrinsic to its social fabric. We also saw how state agencies frequently become part of stakeholders' 'community of care' as and when they are asked to respond to incidents of hate crime. It was during such responses that local authorities were called upon to offer support to victims. However, for many victims, their interaction with agency employees left them with a sense of secondary victimization. At this stage of the book I therefore highlighted the harm-*repairing* and harm-*causing* qualities of various aspects of 'community'.

It is worth analysing here how the notion of 'community', central to restorative practice, becomes further complicated by the sociocultural factors that are causal to hate crime incidents. A simple recap of the purposes of 'community', and the sociological causes of hate crime, will help for these purposes. Community is conceptualized in myriad ways and is linked to both geography and identity (Pavlich 2004; see Chapter 6). Originally envisaged as a benevolent entity, restorative scholars have advanced the notion and role of 'community' as one through which individuals can resolve and repair their inter-personal conflicts (Chapter 6; Christie 1977; Braithwaite 1989; Zehr 1990). John Braithwaite (1989) argues that in communitarian societies individuals are densely enmeshed in interdependent networks which are bound by mutuality and obligation. Interdependencies give rise to a symbolic attachment to personal obligations to others in any given community (Braithwaite 1989). Those who breach social rules (laws) fall outside the moral boundaries of their community by becoming an aberration of its collective good. Restorativists have accordingly asserted that the 'community' becomes fundamental to correcting transgressors of the law by providing social condemnation (inducing shame) of criminal behaviour, as well as supporting reintegration of the offenders back into its sphere, minus any negative stigmatization (Braithwaite 1989, 2002).

Critics, however, have argued that such a conceptualization is overly simplistic and fails to grasp the complex socio-cultural structures of modern communities. Indeed, as we have seen, a community not only helps to uphold the moral obligations of its members, but simultaneously wields a persecutory axe over those who fall outside its subjective feeling of 'togetherness' (see Chapter 3; see also Perry 2001; Cunneen 2003; Pavlich 2004). Various scholars have criticized restorativists for having romanticized the notion of community and idealistically applying it to restorative practice (Crawford 2002; Cunneen 2003; Pavlich 2004). Adam Crawford opines that the portrayal of 'community' has been almost mythological, containing a rhetorical force that 'collapses diversity and irons out important contradictory evidence...for the sake of a coherent "story"' (2002: 109).

In Chapter 3 I suggested that communities (and society more broadly) are hierarchical entities that have historically been structured through gender, race, sexual orientation, and other identities (see Perry 2001 in relation to hate crime; Crawford 2002 in relation to RJ). Barbara Perry (2001), for instance, states that within modern society, power hierarchies are now constituted by dominance over 'difference'. Difference has been used to construct intersecting social hierarchies pertaining to gender, race, sexuality, and class, amongst others (Perry 2001: 46; see also Spalek 2008). Paradoxically, the notion of 'difference' results from people 'belonging' to groups whose members they see as having the same or similar identity characteristics as themselves. People often form bonds with those who they feel share similar cultural and ethnic traits. Groups will coalesce around similar identity characteristics, including ethnicity, religion, sexual orientation, or other such characteristics (forming 'in-groups'). Categories of identity often assume binary classifications. An individual is either white or black, white or Asian, gay or straight, Christian or Muslim (Perry 2001: 47). In forming 'in-groups' we seek out the 'Other', ie the person who is most definitely not like 'us'.

The creation of dominant groups (the majority community) entails the creation of hegemonic identity traits, norms, and values which all 'in-group' members should aspire to (Perry 2001: 47). Inevitably those who fall outside society's construction of identity are seen as 'different' (Perry 2001). Communities therefore become bound by dominant identity characteristics. Individuals who diverge from these group norms are perceived as a threat to the identity ideal. It may be difficult for some people to understand what they do not know or that which they are not used to. The presence of 'difference' therefore threatens dominant group members' sense of social and cultural security (Perry 2001). Individuals fear those who they do not understand and that which threatens their own socio-cultural position within society (Ray & Smith 2002). In particular, dominant members may become fearful that 'Others' will encroach upon their 'in-group's' ways of life, potentially changing who they are as a group of people (Gadd et al 2005). I have previously noted that '[i]n response to these negative emotions, people frequently transpose their feelings of helplessness into those of animosity. This is little more than the projection of angst which is used to gain a sense of control over those who they see as causing their insecurity' (2011: 318). This emotive reaction temporarily relinquishes their original negative feeling of fear and instead fills them with a determination to suppress the threat (Ray & Smith 2002; Ray et al 2004).

Within some communities, 'Others' who continue to transcend identity ideals will be seen as a direct threat to the dominant groups' existence (Levin & McDevitt 1993). As a result, members of the dominant group will directly and indirectly act to subordinate 'out-group' members (Perry (2001) refers to this as 'doing difference').

Part I: The Perils of 'Community' 189

This ultimately leads to certain minority groups, often those viewed as the most transgressing of dominant norms, receiving unequal distributions of wealth and access to housing and education (Perry 2001; see also Home Office 2005a, 2005b). Subordination is also enforced via the practices and policies of private and state agencies (including the criminal justice system) that systematically discriminate against certain 'Others' (Macpherson 1999; Phillips & Bowling 2007; explored further in Chapter 3). For example, gay people who make public their sexual orientation through visible displays of affection or by opening establishments patronized predominantly by gay people threaten the heteronormativity of civilized society (Bibbings 2004). In response to this blatant deviation from society's sexual norms, some individuals will act to suppress gay people for fear that they will increasingly encroach upon society's sexual identity. In some cases people will believe that 'gayness' will pervert their children and lead to the degradation of society. Violence and other forms of intimidation are therefore used to vanquish gay people and various 'Others' for having overstepped social and cultural boundaries (Perry 2001: 59). Members of many minority groups are therefore frequently pushed to the outer edges of local communities for having disobeyed the hegemonic norms that are prescribed by dominant elites (Sibbitt 1997; Perry 2001; Walters 2011). 'Others' consequently become subjugated by those who fear that their 'difference' will encroach upon the dominant values that form Britain's (and other nations') social milieu.

If communities are no more than hierarchical entities that are structured through identity, and delineated by processes of 'difference', restorative practices risk becoming yet another means through which the objects of dominant groups' hate is subjugated. The problem is that 'restorative justice can become what it opposes: a practice which excludes individuals because they are without community or without the *right* community' (Cunneen & Hoyle 2010: 175). Such a situation may be played out during dialogue where offenders who are reassured by a sense of grievance against certain identity groups remain hostile towards them (Smith 2006; see also Byers et al 1999). Offenders may also attempt to rationalize their prejudiced actions by seeking refuge in 'techniques of neutralisation' (Sykes and Matza 1957; Byers et al 1999). Such techniques can involve offenders denying or underplaying the seriousness of their offence or their own culpability. They might refuse to accept full responsibility by blaming the victim for their behaviour; or admit that they have broken the law but not that they have caused any real harm; or—and of particular relevance here—assert that the victim is undeserving or illegitimate, or even less human (Byers et al 1999; Perry 2001). For example, Bryan Byers et al's (1999) research into hate crimes against the Amish in Fulham County, USA found that hate offenders often attempted to play down their prejudice in an attempt to neutralize their behaviour. They often viewed their victims as deserving of victimization, a view held by other community members who supported attacks against the Amish as 'fair game' (see also Sibbitt 1997).

The vulnerability of certain victims and their pre-existing unequal relationship with their abusers certainly complicates the RJ process. For instance, Julie Stubbs (2007), referring to domestic violence cases, argues that the state may inadvertently put victims' welfare at risk by bringing them together with their offender. Many abused women wish to escape their abusive partners but fail to do so for fear that they do not have adequate means (emotional and/or financial) to leave (Busch 2002). Instead of offering such victims separation, RJ could bring victims and offenders closer together in an attempt at repairing their relationships and restrict the victim's choice about leaving their partner. Of most concern is that abusive partners may regain or maintain control over the victim's life by simply offering an apology (Busch 2002). In this sense, Stubbs (2007) asserts that RJ is unlikely to change the future behaviour of domestic abusers and therefore acts to maintain gendered control over female victims (see also Coker 2002).

In communities throughout society, a general culture of prejudice is cultivated via both structural processes of 'doing difference' (Perry 2001) as well as being nurtured within families and friendship circles and by neighbours (Sibbitt 1997; Byers et al 1999). This will mean that many offenders' 'community of care' will validate their negative views on race, religion, and sexual orientation (and other identities). As such, there is a genuine concern that some offenders may use their perceived moral authority to manipulate the more informal restorative process. Offenders emboldened by a sense of justification (Byers et al 1999) may manipulate the more informal restorative process to diminish their guilt, trivialize their prejudice, and potentially shift the blame onto the 'Other'. In such circumstances, ineffective facilitation by practitioners who do not fully understand the cultural tensions that exist between the parties or, worse still, sympathize with their fears of 'difference', will fail to prevent repeat victimization (Smith 2006). In turn, victims may feel compelled to accept disingenuous apologies in an attempt to appease the offender and reduce the likelihood of reprisals (Coker 2002; Stubbs 2007). If this occurs, RJ will not only fail to provide a pathway to authentic reparation but will ultimately add to the process of victimization.

The 'social distance' that will exist between stakeholders of hate crime, combined with pervasive cultural prejudices within communities, has serious implications for the application of RJ. Cultural and identity difference has therefore led some to question the potential efficacy of RJ for those without a shared community if, for example, minority groups are viewed with scepticism or as deserving of discrimination (Kelly 2002). Restorative scholars who have presented 'community' as a harmonious collection of social and political relations may consequently help to mask conflict, power divisions, 'difference', and inequalities (Crawford 2002; Cunneen 2003: 186). Chris Cunneen (2003) asserts that the application of a notion which silences those who are marginalized means that RJ may become complicit in the oppression and victimization of 'Others'. George Pavlich similarly opines that structural inequalities mean that 'a perilous totalitarian threat haunts every attempt to ground restorative justice in community' (2004: 177). Communities and perpetrators who favour a white, heterosexual, able-bodied hegemony may fail to adequately recognize the individual and social needs of ethnic minority, gay, lesbian, and disabled victims. The affirmation of dominant values within restorative dialogue will act only to compound the social harms that victims of hate crime have already endured (Kelly 2002; Cunneen 2003). Consequently, practices that give implicit support to the structured boundaries of 'community' will become implicated in 'its totalitarian effects' *if* facilitators fail to counter the power imbalance between offenders and those deemed as 'different' (Pavlich 2004; see also Daly 1999).

Recognizing community as good and bad

Conceptualizing community as a despotic entity that marginalizes, oppresses, and victimizes the 'Other' provides an internal antithesis to the restorative ideal. Taken at face value, it suggests that RJ, rather than healing and empowering victims of hate crime, potentially leads to the domination and re-victimization of minority individuals (Kelly 2002). However, to a large extent such analysis is based on theoretical assertions about the structural dynamics of 'community' and normative assumptions about the processes involved in restorative practice. Although I have argued elsewhere that dominant socio-cultural structures are causal to minority group marginalization and ultimately to the commission by some individuals of hate crimes (Walters 2011; see also Perry 2001), I do not contend that 'community' in its entirety is a myopic entity. Rather, I suggest that community has both *benevolent* and *malevolent* qualities within its sphere. In other words, there are macro and micro aspects of 'community' that can be harmful to certain individuals, but equally there are elements which strive for equality, equity, and justice.

In fact, in many respects, the criticisms made by scholars such as Cunneen and Pavlich about 'community' are open to the same accusations that they have themselves made about the over-simplification of the concept. By this I mean that while it is true that advocates of RJ have painted a notion of community in overly benevolent terms, its critics may have equally overstated its potentially divisive and harmful qualities within the restorative context. Perhaps then, restorative scholarship is better served by appreciating a more nuanced understanding of 'community', one that understands and appreciates both its healing *and* harming qualities. These dichotomous qualities are not mutually exclusive. Restorative practice must therefore be able to recognize when 'community' is of benefit to the justice process, while simultaneously building in protections against those aspects of the notion (and its members) that are likely to have a more insidious effect.

For example, both the offender's and the victim's 'community of care' make up an important part of 'community' within restorative practice (as seen in Chapter 6). While the victim's 'community of care' are likely to provide him or her with important emotional support, the offender's 'community of care' might simply act to uphold his or her bigoted views towards the victim. In such cases, some community stakeholders provide a positive influence over the restorative process, while others act only to infuse negativity into its reparative and reforming potential. Balancing out these, and various other, aspects of 'community' is necessary if practitioners are to facilitate effective reparation. As this chapter will illustrate, this is by no means easily achieved.

There remains a paucity of empirical research on whether effective restorative dialogue can be maintained within multicultural settings (Daly 1999; Albrecht 2010); less still on how effective restorative practices are when cultural and identity difference is at the heart of conflict (see Umbreit et al 2002; Walters & Hoyle 2010, 2012). Evidence already outlined in previous chapters suggests that restorative practices, if implemented in accordance with restorative values, can *help* to repair the harms caused by hate crime. The data showed that dialogue with the offender (directly or indirectly) often reduced (although only partially) victims' feelings of fear, anger, and anxiety (Chapter 4). Moreover, facilitators with proficient knowledge of hate crime who adopted a multi-agency approach to restorative practice were able to ensure victims received the emotional and social support they required, while secondary harms caused by the institutional practices of state organizations could be repaired where mediators engaged agency employees within the restorative process (Chapter 6). A corollary of these findings is that the restorative practices researched avoided some of the most potent risks 'community' posed to victims of hate crime. Indeed, it is unlikely that victims would have stated that the process helped to repair their emotional harms, as well as preventing repeat victimization, if in reality their participation served only to sustain their marginalization and led to re-victimization. Still, in many respects we are left unsure as to what aspects of restorative practice helped to avoid the risks posed by 'community' and the invidious forms of discrimination that frequently pervade it. The next section therefore delves deeper into the dynamics of cross-cultural dialogue by exploring whether, in practice, the perils of 'community' inhibit the goals of RJ for hate crime.

Part II: Avoiding Domination and Re-victimization

An appreciation of the theoretical concerns articulated above is fundamental to the successful application of restorative practices for hate crime. When carrying out the empirical study, I therefore assessed whether the meetings observed resulted in any form of re-victimization and/or whether the offender attempted to dominate proceedings. In addition, I asked each victim interviewee whether they ever felt 'disadvantaged' at any point during the restorative process because of their race, ethnicity, sexual orientation, religious beliefs, or disability. Practitioner interviewees were also asked to describe whether the offender/s involved in their case examples had made any direct or indirect attempts to re-victimize victims during the process. Practitioners were then asked whether the risk of domination and re-victimization could be avoided during the restorative process and, if so, how.

During the five observations of face-to-face meetings between the victim and offender, at no time did the offender (or his or her supporters) verbally abuse the victim (or his or her supporters). This meant that victims were not subjected to any direct form of racial, religious, homophobic, or disablist vilification—one of the main concerns of bringing hate offenders face to face with their victims (Kelly 2002). This finding concurred with other research, including Kathleen Daly's (1999) study into gendered violence at the South Australia Juvenile Justice project. She found that 'instances of explicit expressions of prejudice and power, or felt disadvantage, were rare' (1999: 179; see also Albrecht 2010). Such findings hint at the improbability of serious forms of hostility being evinced towards victims during restorative meetings.

Nonetheless, it cannot be asserted that perpetrators' dialogue will not, at times, contain expressions that are derogatory towards or biased against certain identity groups (see eg 'Challenging prejudice', Chapter 8). For instance, in one mediation conference observed in Southwark, the accused perpetrator spoke of African people in largely derogatory terms, he made several references to his neighbours talking in a 'foreign' language, and at one point remarked, 'some Africans speak blah blah blah [he makes up a pretend foreign language]. The majority of African people are always on the phone'. This indicated that he felt negatively towards non-white and non-English-speaking people. During this direct meeting, the mediator and another participant from the local housing department challenged the offender's comments suggesting that not all African people speak loudly, for which the offender apologized, saying that he might not have worded the sentence appropriately.[1] Yet his comments had clearly been either an intentional swipe or unwitting undermining of people of African descent while, simultaneously, his denials of racism communicated to the group his incredulity of the victims' story.

---

[1] See further below, 'Including "appropriate" supporters and condemning prejudice'.

The offender's body language had also been defensive. For most of the meeting he failed to maintain eye contact with the complainant victims. In addition, he tutted when the victims spoke about their experiences of racial harassment and at other times audibly chewed gum (see further details in Chapter 8, Case Study 1). Although the accused perpetrator went on to apologize for his remarks and made an offer for the parties 'to start again', there had been various communicational cues that could be perceived as a physical dismissal of the complainant victims' emotional trauma. Together, the various facets of communication that I had observed within this meeting could be perceived as potentially harmful to the victims, whom I had anticipated before interview would indicate that they felt disadvantaged—at least during some stage of the meeting—because of their ethnic identity and/or language skills.

However, contradicting my own interpretation of the meeting, the complainant victims later told me that they found the process to be of great emotional benefit to them. At interview, Mr V-D (the complainant victim) stated that he and his wife never felt disadvantaged during the meeting. I queried further whether translating for his wife made the communication difficult for them both. He remarked, 'No I think it was fine because they managed to get the message, what my wife meant'. The interviewee went on to state that the mediator had acted fairly and impartially throughout and that without the conference they would never have been able to resolve their constant fear of racial victimization. Though informal, the meeting was structured, with firmly set ground rules at the beginning and several meetings and phone calls with the participants beforehand to prepare them (see further below 'Avoiding re-victimization: preparation, preparation, preparation'). The parties were told at the beginning of the meeting that they would have an opportunity to talk but that when doing so they should be respectful (see further below 'Ground rules'). The parties were then asked to talk in turn without interruption. On the two occasions when the accused perpetrator did attempt to interrupt the victims' dialogue, the mediator firmly asked him to wait until they had finished. This firm but fair approach to discussion ensured that all parties had the same amount of time to talk about the conflict, while also helping to ensure that the meeting did not descend into another altercation between the parties. Mr V-D went on to tell me he believed that Mr H (the accused perpetrator) was now better able to understand how his actions had affected him and his wife.

In turn, the mediation process was directly responsible for improving the emotional wellbeing of the victims who are no longer fearful of Mr H abusing them.

I spent much of my time during observations paying critical attention to participants' dialogue and their body language. I struggled, elsewhere, to find any direct displays of prejudice, or even more subtle communicational cues indicating identity-based animosity. I had at the start of the research process envisaged that, at least in some cases, expressions of prejudice would be communicated. After all, a substantial proportion of the cases researched involved ongoing hate crime victimization. This was therefore, to some extent, a surprisingly positive finding. It should be noted, however, that the limited number of direct and indirect observations conducted for the study means that I am unable to make any credible generalizations about non-domination and re-victimization for hate crime. That said, as we will see below, the findings made during observations were well supported by both victim and practitioner interviews.

Victims' perceptions of disadvantage

In addition to observing restorative meetings, all victim interviewees were asked whether at any point during the restorative process they had participated in they ever felt at a disadvantage because of their identity traits. Thirty-seven out of the thirty-eight interviewees[2] stated that they did not feel disadvantaged at any stage of the process because of their race, religious beliefs, sexual orientation, or disability, ie those identity traits causal to the hate incidents researched.[3] This inferred that the vast majority of victims did not experience domination or re-victimization during either community mediation or the restorative disposal. A victim of ongoing racial harassment at Southwark commented: 'No definitely not. No I felt comfortable. I felt comfortable because I had a space where

---

[2] Twenty-three from the HCP, fourteen from Devon and Cornwall, and one from Oxford YOS.

[3] It should be noted that two interviewees did feel disadvantaged but for reasons other than their minority identity status. One interviewee stated that the fact he had attended by himself while the accused perpetrators were two strong made him feel at a disadvantage to start with. A further victim stated that her age (twenty) made her feel vulnerable without her parents being present.

I could say how I was feeling.' Another interviewee remarked that he had felt at a disadvantage before the first direct mediation meeting because of his learning difficulties, his main concern related to the fact that the other parties (including the headmaster of a school) would not believe that he had been targeted by several students from the school. However, this feeling soon dissipated during the actual meeting. He commented, 'At first... I was worried that the school teachers would take the school kids' word but when it turned out well I was really relieved.'[4] Similar comments were made by many interviewees in Southwark who stated that the mediator had provided both parties with an opportunity to talk about the incident, while her impartiality had ensured that the dynamics of meetings remained fair.

This left just one interviewee who stated that his race, causal to the hate incident, put him at a disadvantage throughout a restorative disposal implemented by Devon and Cornwall Police. In this case, the victim's feeling of disadvantage was not directly related to the actions of the offender (as already highlighted, most victims and offenders were involved in indirect meetings at Devon and Cornwall), but rather was the result of how the facilitating officer had treated him. The interviewee stated that he had not been provided with any emotional support, that the officer had failed to provide adequate information as to what RJ aimed to achieve, and had then gone on to pressurize him into accepting an apology from the offender. He told me at interview, 'it would have been... different if I was not of a foreign origin... they have not given me all the help and support that they should have or that they have given to other people.' The interviewee went on to say that had he been white and British he felt he would have received a different level of support (see Chapter 5, Case Study 1).

This single case appeared to be the exception to restorative practice, rather than the rule. Still, it demonstrated that practices which fail to properly incorporate key values of RJ risk subjecting participants to additional emotional harm. At no point during the Restorative Disposal did the victim feel empowered by his involvement, or in control of his part in the justice process. He was never asked to explore verbally the suffering he had experienced or to explain how the offender might repair the harm that the racial

---

[4] Case also referred to in Ch 6.

abuse had caused him. Instead, the police involvement in this case was a clear example of a state authority maintaining control over an offence through which they exerted their own values as to how it should be resolved (Chapter 5). Such recourse was to this victim's emotional detriment and the case re-emphasized the dangers that exist in poorly administered RJ for hate crime.

Avoiding re-victimization: preparation, preparation, preparation

Both observations and victim interviews suggested that domination during meetings or attempts to re-victimize the victim were almost non-existent. This finding was supported by practitioner interviewees who stated that the offender involved in their cases had not made an attempt to re-victimize his or her victim during direct meetings.[5] In two cases practitioner interviewees explained that the meeting had broken down but that there had been no specific use of biased language or intimidation during the meeting. Such a finding is somewhat surprising considering the risks posed by 'community' as outlined above. So why were expressions of prejudice or demonstrations of domination so rare during restorative meetings?

A clear and recurring explanation was that all parties were thoroughly *prepared* before participating in restorative meetings. This entailed practitioners talking to each of the parties about the incident and asking them to explain how and why it occurred. It was here that many interviewees stated they held 'mini conferences' whereby they would ascertain how the offender was feeling about his or her actions and further explore the prejudices which gave rise to his or her offending behaviour (see also Chapter 7). One practitioner explained:

in the preparation you go through the whole process of the conference with the offender, you say 'well what are you going to do if the victim gets really angry with you? What are you going to do if you feel angry at something the victim says?' You talk that through with them so you try to preempt, get them ready and also suss out whether they're going to be able to manage these very difficult emotions. Because if you have any sense that they could cause harm...that can re-victimize people.

---

[5] Concurring with findings from victim interviews.

Preparation is not just about ensuring participants are *aware* of what RJ is or rehearsing the types of questions which will be asked during direct meetings. Initial meetings are also about ensuring that offenders are *willing* to engage in a process of reconciliation with the 'right' reasons. A practitioner explained:

> you need to do really good preparation with both offender and victim... I think you need to make sure that both parties are willing to participate and willing with the right motives. In terms of that... you need to make sure very clearly that the offender is not going to come out with similar comments or whatever the offence was... By the time you get to a face-to-face meeting, every participant is so aware of what's going to happen. It's a voluntary process, they're happy to be there, they're reflecting anyway on what's happened. In my experience the chances of re-victimization are very, very small by the time you get to a face-to-face meeting.

During my interviews it became clear that comprehensive preparation was the key to avoiding and/or challenging power domination and re-victimization within meetings. Every practitioner spoke of its fundamental importance to the process. Many interviewees pointed out that participants who were thoroughly 'prepped' before direct dialogue had time to digest the purpose of the meeting and what their role would be in helping to resolve the conflict, while those who remained vociferous about their dislike of certain minority groups and who showed little accountability for their actions were more likely to be asked to participate in indirect dialogue. Practitioners hinted that offenders who refused to take any responsibility for their actions were very, very rare (see also Shapland et al 2006).[6]

Despite the fundamental importance of participant preparation, scholars within the field have almost completely ignored this part of the process when theorizing or researching the utility of restorative interventions.[7] In neither of the main RJ handbooks on the

---

[6] In community mediation, where perpetrators have been accused rather than convicted of a hate crime/incidents, mediators will need to focus less on individual responsibility before direct meetings and more on how the parties might be able to help resolve the conflict they have become embroiled in. The parties will need to know that each will have an opportunity to express their feelings about the conflict and that the issue and effects of prejudice will be explored (see Chapter 5).

[7] Restorativists have often simply asserted that offenders must accept responsibility before participating in direct meetings (Braithwaite 1989). Researchers also frequently ask whether participants were told of the purpose of RJ before direct meetings (Strang 2002). Yet theorists or researchers rarely go on to examine the practicalities of preparatory meetings.

market do any of the chapters examine in any detail the practicalities or the significance of preparatory meetings (Johnstone & Van Ness 2007b; Sullivan & Tifft 2008a). For instance, in one chapter by Barbara Raye and Ann Roberts (2007) entitled 'Restorative processes', the authors describe and examine the most common models of restorative practice, comparing and contrasting VOM, conferencing, and circles. At no point do the authors detail the logistics involved in preparing participants or how intrinsic this task is to the successful application of each model. Considering the key relevance of these meetings to the successful application of RJ, this is indeed a noteworthy omission. With the use of RJ proliferating across the globe within complex social and cultural settings, the practicalities involved in preparing participants for RJ must be emphasized and examined further by criminologists.

Ground rules

While preparation was clearly central to avoiding re-victimization, practitioners frequently spoke of a secondary way of managing risk by employing ground rules. The setting of ground rules at the beginning of meetings helped to ensure that participants adopted appropriate language during dialogue. Additionally, the rules outlined the ways in which individuals should address each other, including avoiding certain physical gesticulation such as pointing fingers. For example, during one observation a community mediator told the parties:

This isn't Jerry Springer...do not tell people what to do...Any points made can be noted down and used to help form the mediation agreement...You will hear different views today, be respectful of those different views...please ask questions in a polite and respectful manner. It is not always easy to talk...My role as mediator is not to point the finger or to judge or blame...This is a place of respect for communication.

These simple but firmly set rules helped to structure communication between participants, thereby reducing the risk of meetings descending into 'slanging matches'. Nevertheless, raised voices and finger pointing were common occurrences in the meetings observed. During several observations, communication became so fraught that I anticipated the meeting would be terminated. Yet each time dialogue descended into lively disagreement, the mediator interjected, reminding participants of the rules before highlighting the common goal of resolution. I was surprised each time how this method of facilitation changed the direction of communication and ultimately the atmosphere in meetings. Both my observations and practitioner interviews revealed that despite participants often beginning meetings refusing to even look at each other, and where voices were frequently raised during discussions, by the end of a meeting participants were typically smiling and shaking each other's hands (see examples in Chapter 4).

Including 'appropriate' supporters and condemning prejudice

I have discussed above and in Chapter 6 how 'community' can be both a benevolent *and* malevolent force. In relation to the offender's supporters, the concern is that his or her 'community of care' will fail to offer adequate social condemnation and instead provide moral impunity for his or her hate-motivated actions (Maxwell 2008). If this is the case, facilitators will struggle to create a platform from which to effectively challenge prejudice (Chapter 8), instead leaving face-to-face dialogue open to opportunities for domination and re-victimization. Facilitators must therefore endeavour to include individuals who provide appropriate social condemnation for the wrongs committed (Braithwaite 2002). This is clearly problematic in cases involving young offenders whose parents or friends are themselves a source of animus. In such cases, the facilitator must determine whether inclusion of the offender's parents will antagonize the victim and/or help to neutralize the offender's wrongdoing (Sibbitt 1997; Byers et al 1999).

Preventing community supporters from harming victims will require facilitators to 'vet' potential supporters prior to a meeting. It may also require them to exclude any co-offenders, holding separate meetings for each (McConnell & Swain 2000). Of course, while safe options, these measures challenge one of the key aims of RJ—to engage communities. In some cases, facilitators may manage to locate appropriate pro-social supporters for offenders—whether grandparents, teachers, social workers, or local football coaches. Shadd Maruna et al (2007) also suggest that ex-participants of restorative conferences, drawn from the same neighbourhoods and same age groups as the offender may prove helpful as supporters. These individuals could play a mentoring role through all stages of the restorative process (Maruna et al 2007: 64).

However, while these people can effectively challenge the offender's prejudices and then provide avenues for reformation, they may not so easily be able to provide reintegration into the most crucial communities for offenders, most typically kinship or friendship groups. Thus if offenders are to be truly reintegrated into a community that does not support their prejudiced attitudes, practitioners may need to include offenders' parents and friends in the hope that dialogue on harm, prejudice, and identity difference helps to challenge the negative views of both offender and his or her 'community of care'. As Gabrielle Maxwell remarks, 'It is those who are connected to the offender and the victim who need to be involved in the restorative process if it is to find solutions that truly make amends and achieve the reintegration of offenders and victims [into] the social group' (2008: 93). One practitioner explained the importance of parental involvement in hate crime cases at a practical level:

very often we'll have two parents who will look at each other and talk, and the young people listen to this and that can often go a long way to being restorative, parents saying 'I'm truly sorry for what my young person's done, I can totally see from a parent's point of view', that makes the victim's parent feel better and in turn I think then has a knock-on effect on the victim.

Inevitably, though, there will be circumstances where the offender's 'community of care' remain a source of hostility. In such cases it may become appropriate for facilitators themselves to challenge some of the norms and values of the wider community in order to avoid repeat victimization and so that offenders are encouraged to reflect on and account for their behaviour (Maxwell 2008; see also, Case Study 1 and further Chapter 8, 'Challenging prejudice'). Such an approach is contentious, especially if we consider that restorativists have argued that the facilitator's role is to facilitate dialogue and not to add to it (Christie 1977; see in relation to cross-cultural mediation Albrecht 2010).

Nonetheless, there will remain some cases where victims (or their supporters) do not feel confident enough to challenge hostile remarks. This may well be a result of participants' prior experiences of marginalization (Chapter 3). Facilitators who fail to broach issues of identity prejudice during meetings risk neglecting a key causal mechanism of the offence/conflict. Facilitators must therefore feel confident and be experienced enough to ask the participants to discuss and explain the harmful consequences of prejudice if the stakeholders are to collectively repair the harms of hate crime.

When facilitating dialogue on identity prejudice, practitioners must be careful not to berate or stigmatize offenders (direct disapproval) as this will only serve to antagonize them further,[8] providing additional internalized proof that they are under attack from the 'Other' (see further Chapter 7). Rather, practitioners must attempt to encourage constructive dialogue on the harms of prejudice and, where necessary, actively question spurious assertions made by offenders regarding the victim's identity difference. Facilitators should not approach the issue of prejudice or identity difference in direct meetings without preparing the participants beforehand (as we have seen).[9] Participants who are unprepared for such discussions may turn hostile towards the victim as a form of defence. Preparing participants for such discussions therefore helps to defuse possible tensions and allows the parties to engage in constructive dialogue about the causal mechanisms and deleterious consequences of hate crime. Of course many offenders will still deny they are 'racist' or 'homophobic' but, having been prepared for direct dialogue, will be open to engage in discussions on the topics of prejudice and identity. Those who go on to provide reparation and promises of desistance hint at their willingness to take responsibility for their hate-motivated actions, even if they remain unwilling to admit this directly.

Clearly, practitioners will need extensive training on all aspects of cross-cultural dialogue and the socio-cultural factors relevant to hate crime. This is not an easy undertaking. Attempts at training national agencies, such as the police, on issues of diversity have been fraught with difficulties (Rowe & Garland 2007). Deeply embedded institutional cultures and the bureaucratic organization of some agencies will make effective learning about 'difference' challenging (Reiner 2000; see further Chapter 8). Whether such organizational constraints persist in relation to RJ practitioners is less clear. Perhaps the emphases on 'community' and 'repairing harm' that initial RJ training programmes encompass, as well as a general ethos of 'transformation' and 'healing' embraced by those interested in practicing RJ, will mean that restorative practitioners

---

[8] A potential result of negative shaming, see Harris et al 2004.
[9] I observed the mediator at Southwark preparing participants for dialogue on prejudice/identity difference in several cases.

are more receptive to learning about the socio-cultural dynamics of hate victimization and less susceptible to institutional forms of prejudice. Nevertheless, it will be essential that restorative practitioners receive training on cultural diversity issues.[10] Only those facilitators who have a genuine understanding of prejudice and its effects will be able to effectively negotiate the complex social factors that are pertinent to the resolution of hate-motivated conflicts (see further Chapter 8).

Conclusion

The exploration of the aetiological determinants throughout this book and analysis of the potentially harmful effects of 'community' at the beginning of this chapter have provided the theoretical grounding upon which empirical analysis of the risks posed to hate crime victims has been made. The potentially invidious nature of fragmented and hierarchical communities poses the greatest barrier to the successful application of RJ (Crawford 2002). Cultural disjuncture, and the pernicious stereotypes that prejudices often give rise to, amalgamate to create genuine threats of re-victimization within restorative meetings. Such risks threaten to re-traumatize hate victims, while facilitating the offenders' retreat back to their own communities, further emboldened by their disdain of the 'Other'. This theoretical analysis led to the assertion that restorative practice *could* become just another means through which minority groups are subjugated by the hegemonic norms promulgated by white middle class justice (Cunneen 2003; Stubbs 2007).

Yet, in many respects, the preliminary analysis of socio-structural domination presented at the beginning of this chapter had already been partially thwarted by the preceding chapters. Essentially, the findings in Chapters 4 (and to a lesser extent Chapter 6), that restorative practices *helped* to repair the harms of hate crime, already hinted that RJ, at least for the most part, avoided re-victimization and domination. Despite this, it remained unclear how restorative practices ensured that victims did not feel re-victimized. This chapter suggests that restorative practices are well equipped to deal with power imbalances and the cultural differences which

---

[10] Training schemes for practitioners on the use of RJ for hate crime have been provided in the past by the charity Race On the Agenda (ROTA).

exist amongst participants. Key to bridging cultural divides is that restorative dialogue focuses on a *common understanding* between stakeholders of hate crime. Focusing on what is common amongst participants, such as the fact that they both live in similar housing conditions, or that they have young families, or simply that they both desire to have a peaceful life, are key to avoiding the perils of prejudice. In doing so, facilitators ensure that the parties form emotional connections that reveal each other's humanity. As we will see in the next chapter, it is the empathic responses induced by restorative dialogue which can engender changes in future behaviours.

Significant to the theoretical concerns espoused at the beginning of this chapter was that almost all victims interviewed stated that they did not experience any form of targeted victimization or feel disadvantaged as a result of their ethnicity, sexual orientation, religious beliefs, or disability at any point during the restorative process. This finding was additionally supported by practitioners who asserted that victims were highly unlikely to face victimization during restorative meetings. This was consistent both for victims who had participated in direct meetings and for those who had participated in indirect dialogue. In fact, only one victim in Devon and Cornwall spoke of feeling at a disadvantage because of his ethnicity. Although clearly an exceptional case, it provided further concern as to the implementation of RJ by police officers (see Chapters 5 and 6; Hoyle 2007).

The finding that most victims do not experience domination or re-victimization during restorative meetings begged the question, why not? Especially when we consider the fact that most victims of hate crime face subjugation in many aspects of their lives (see Chapter 3). Practitioner interviews uncovered what appeared to be the central most important factor in this process—*preparation*. It became clear that each and every participant must be comprehensively prepared for the process, while additional time must be spent exploring the harms and emotions behind hate offences for those who were participating in direct dialogue. Hence, preparation is not just about managing risk, it is about imparting amongst participants the restorative values which become central to any ensuing dialogue. With adequate preparation in place, willingness by the participants to take part, and firmly stated ground rules at the beginning of meetings, incidents of domination and/or re-victimization became rare. Aggregated, the findings suggest that in more cases than not, restorative dialogue can effectively break down cultural barriers to communication, exposing offenders to the true humanity of victims. Nonetheless, in facilitating this process, restorative practices must remain alive to issues posed by cultural and identity difference. Indeed, if progress is to be made towards the adaptation of RJ frameworks more widely for hate crime, practices must become sensitized to the cross-cultural issues which characterize such cases.

8

Humanizing 'Difference' and Challenging Prejudice Through Restorative Dialogue

Introduction

In the last chapter I explored the potential risks that fragmented and hierarchical communities pose to the successful application of RJ. We saw how pervasive cultures of prejudice pose particular dangers to the restorative process, especially where participants' 'communities of care' are included within restorative dialogue. The empirical findings, while far from equivocal, suggested that restorative practice appeared well equipped to manage risks such as re-victimization and domination within meetings. This was partly achieved by facilitators using preparatory meetings to explore the underlying reasons for offending, while simultaneously ensuring that participants were willing to participate in dialogue that focuses on harm. Additionally, the risks posed by potential power imbalances were carefully managed via the setting of ground rules at the beginning of every meeting—rules that would often be reiterated throughout discussions. Yet, despite these findings we are, to a large extent, still left unsure as to:

1. whether cultural and identity differences inhibited restorative dialogue in any way between participants; and
2. whether restorative dialogue helped to *challenge* prejudice and modify the behaviours of hate crime offenders.

Part I of this chapter begins by examining the crucial role that emotions play in forming connections between participants, including how feelings such as shame, guilt, remorse, and empathy can be utilized to encourage behavioural change. The chapter then analyses how dialogue may be stifled by diverging cultural and dialectical styles of communication. The methods used by restorative practitioners to limit barriers to communication and encourage the formation of emotional connections are then considered. The datasets (in particular data gained from observations) are further assessed to see whether, in practice, participants were able to engage in empathic communication during the restorative process, thereby breaking down empathic divides.

Part II of this chapter then moves on to explore RJ's capacity to effectively challenge prejudice and modify hate-motivated behaviour. Here I illuminate the importance of 'storytelling', demonstrating how active participation helps to humanize victims. Using the only case taken from Oxford YOS, I illustrate how reparative work can be utilized to promote 'moral learning' about the harms of prejudice. The limitations of challenging deeply imbedded prejudices through restorative meetings are also conceded.

Part I: Negotiating Cultural and Identity Difference: Overcoming Empathic Divides?

Restorativists have long argued that the exploratory methods used in restorative practice not only help to repair the harms of hate, but also provide a pivotal mechanism through which individuals form emotional connections. It is these connections that allow the formation of renewed relationships to emerge (Braithwaite 1989, 2002). The promise of RJ for hate crime, in this regard, is that the stereotypes which once divided participants are dismantled, allowing those from diverging identity backgrounds to form more positive relations (McConnell & Swain 2000; Walters & Hoyle 2010; Gavrielides 2012). Scholars have asserted further that victims who are provided with an opportunity to tell their 'stories' will expose offenders, perhaps for the first time, to structured communication about the impacts of prejudice (McConnell & Swain 2000). In turn, offenders who are directly confronted with the consequences of their actions will be more likely to feel genuine remorse for their hate-motivated behaviours (Maxwell & Morris 2002; Van Stokkom 2002; Harris et al 2004). Offenders subsequently become more inclined to offer sincere gestures of contrition (Braithwaite 1989). It is through such discourse that offenders and their 'community of care' are encouraged to reflect on the true humanity of their victims, as well as other community members who share similar identity characteristics. This empathic process assists the rebuilding of relationships, allowing the parties to better understand the 'differences' that have previously divided them (Maxwell 2008).

Understanding 'difference': the role of shame and guilt

John Braithwaite's (1989) seminal thesis on reintegrative shaming asserts that social disapproval is crucial to challenging offenders' behaviours and, in turn, modifying their future conduct. However, it is not the denunciation by the state which is central to any conveyance of moral disapproval. Instead, condemnation is more effectively expressed via informal, but structured, dialogue that involves the stakeholders of a crime. It is expressed *indirectly* through being asked to participate in a restorative practice that focuses on harm reparation (Braithwaite & Braithwaite 2001, as well as *directly* by those who participate in restorative dialogue. In particular, social condemnation displayed by those who are personally connected to the offender is likely to have the most positive effect on his or her sense of wrongdoing. Participants who display disapproval for the wrongdoing (rather than for the offender him or herself) give rise to feelings of *shame* that, consecutively, lead to genuine feelings of remorse. Hence, rather than stigmatizing the offender, the restorative process gives rise to what Braithwaite calls 'reintegrative shaming', whereby the offender is assimilated back into the community where he or she is now less likely to reoffend.

Interlinked with the emotion of shame is that of guilt. Nathan Harris et al explain the difference between these two connecting feelings, stating that 'shame...occurs when one feels disapproval in the eyes of others (imagined or real disapproval)' whereas 'guilt occurs when one disapproves of one's own behaviour (disapproval by one's own conscience)' (2004: 193). Thus for shame to occur, the offender must be aware that others are disapproving of him, whereas guilt will be felt where the offender realizes that what he has done is wrong (Van Stokkom 2002: 340).[1] Bas Van Stokkom asserts that shame and guilt cannot be disentangled as they both imply 'a negative evaluation and are of a painful nature' (2002: 340). Harris et al (2004) accordingly join the words to create the term 'shame-guilt'.

For shame-guilt to work restoratively, meetings must be carefully *managed* in order to prevent 'reintegrative' shaming turning into 'stigmatic' shaming (Braithwaite & Braithwaite 2001). Facilitators

---

[1] Though see others such as Tangney (1991) who argue that shame and guilt are completely separate emotions that work in different ways to challenge the offender's sense of 'self'.

must avoid scenarios whereby participants mock and/or make chastising gestures towards the offender (Maruna et al 2007). They must ensure that the offender has a chance to explain his or her behaviour, while also receiving positive messages that he or she is fundamentally a good person, capable of pursuing a moral and law-abiding existence (Harris & Maruna 2008). If participants heap uncontrolled levels of shame and stigma onto an offender he or she is likely to feel embarrassment, humiliation, and a sense of injustice (Retzinger & Scheff 1996; Harris & Maruna 2008). This will inhibit empathy between stakeholders and any feelings of remorse that are crucial to encouraging positive transformations (Retzinger & Scheff 1996; see further sections below).

Whether an offender experiences 'reintegrative shaming' will therefore depend heavily upon the communications offered by those participants included in any given restorative process. I have already suggested in Chapter 7 that an offender's 'community' may in certain contexts fail to provide the requisite moral denunciation for hate crime, thus failing to demonstrate effective social condemnation. This is especially the case where the offender's kinship is a source of his or her hostile feelings. Harris et al point out that 'moral standards are learnt from various significant others' (2004: 194). The 'self' and the values that each individual acquires come from those who are closest to that person. An offender's kinship is likely to have immense influence over his or her moral judgements and social ideals. The beliefs that we have about the world and those who inhabit it will be heavily influenced by others who share our social and cultural identity (Mackie 1986). Moral beliefs are therefore intrinsically intertwined with the social contexts that individuals live in. People rely on those closest to them to provide moral guidance, whether consciously or unwittingly. It is these community members, particularly friends and family, who help individuals to make sense of the world.

We are more likely to reassess our own beliefs and question our judgements where disapproval is demonstrated by those individuals we most respect. Of particular significance to restorative encounters that involve cross-cultural dialogue is that studies have shown that social influence is of greater potency when exerted by those who share a common social identity or cultural heritage (see eg Mackie 1986). Harris et al point out that 'for social disapproval to result in feelings that what one has done is wrong (shame or guilt) it must have some validity in the eyes of the person being disapproved of' (2004: 195). This is where Braithwaite's theory of reintegrative shaming, and others who subscribe to the role of 'shame-guilt' (Harris et al 2004), may exhibit limitations. In hate crime cases, the offender will not share an important social or cultural identity which is of essence to the victim. Not only will his or her 'community of care' identify with a different social/identity group but they will typically be the source (or a reinforcing source) of much of the offender's animus towards the victim's identity. The socio-cultural divergence that will inevitably exist within restorative meetings in hate crime cases and the prejudiced beliefs and attitudes of some stakeholders must not be understated. A huge question mark therefore quickly appears over any theoretical assertion as to the capabilities of restorative dialogue to induce feelings of shame and/or guilt in hate crime offenders (and of course other cases involving cross-cultural conflict).

Encouraging remorse through empathy

Rather than focusing on the emotions of shame and guilt, Gabrielle Maxwell and Allison Morris (2002) argue that restorativists must concentrate on the more constructive emotion of remorse. Van Stokkom states that 'remorse points to self-alienation (and horror at one's deeds) and thus puts the self in question' (2002: 350). It frequently results in feeling sorrow and compassion for the victim, whereas guilt 'is more directed at repairing the gaps in the self's defensive walls that keep a deepened and lucid sense of oneself at bay' (Van Stokkom 2002: 350; see also Retzinger & Scheff 1996; Maxwell & Morris 2002). It is the emotion of remorse and the propensity for humans to demonstrate contrition when they feel sorrow that provides genuine potential for attitudinal or behavioural change in hate crime offenders. Remorse indicates that the offender intends to rebuild him or herself by strengthening the more positive aspects of the personality (Van Stokkom 2002). Maxwell and Morris (2002) contend that feelings of remorse are more closely correlated with reductions in recidivism. Lower rates of reconviction are predicated on the fact that offenders are less likely to repeat their harmful actions where they acknowledge that their actions have damaging consequences and they feel contrition for this.

Intrinsic to whether an offender experiences remorse will be his or her ability to empathize with the victim and other participants within restorative processes. Empathy also becomes the catalyst by which other reforming emotions such as shame and guilt (shame-guilt) are galvanized (Maxwell & Morris 2002; Van Stokkom 2002; Harris et al 2004). Empathy may be broken down into four basic dimensions. Arrick Jackson (2009), referring to Mark Davis's (1983) work, highlights these as:

1. 'fantasy', where individuals transpose themselves into the feelings of another character;
2. 'perspective taking', whereby the individual puts him or herself into another's situation and comprehends the other's circumstances;
3. 'empathic concern', where, following on from 1 and 2, individuals become concerned about the welfare of the other as they share in his or her pain;
4. 'personal distress', where the individual develops emotional anxiety upon hearing or learning of the suffering of the other (Davis 1983; cited by Jackson 2009: 189).

Dimension 2 is commonly used as a definition of empathy in restorative literature (Jackson 2009). However, it is the amalgamation of all of these elements of empathy that must be appreciated if we are to truly understand both how empathy is induced in restorative practice and how it may be utilized to greatest effect.

Levels of empathy will differ between participants and may depend upon both contextual and personal variables, including where the incident happened, whether a prior relationship with the offender exists, who else was involved, the age, gender, race, sexual orientation, and social class of the parties (amongst various other background characteristics), and the personality traits of each of the stakeholders. Participants from diverging cultural backgrounds may also have different ideas of what 'justice' should entail, with some cultures nurturing more punitive means of addressing crime (see Albrecht 2010: 18; Umbreit & Coates 2000). Each of these variables will impact upon the ability of participants to form emotional connections during meetings, and it is these connections that ultimately impact upon the successfulness of the restorative process.

Outside of the hate crime context, restorative theorists have often presupposed that individuals are capable and ready to empathize with each other (Crawford 2002). This has led some critics to argue that theories of empathy, shame, and reintegration have neglected to adequately analyse how the social diversity of most communities will impact upon participants' ability to identify with the feelings of another (Crawford 2002; Cunneen 2003; Chapter 7). Dialogical variances across (and sometimes within) different communities, such as those already highlighted, inevitably give rise to what has been labelled as an 'empathic divide' (Haney 2005: 189–210). Diverging social norms between community members can create 'social distance', meaning that the stakeholders of a hate crime may not immediately identify with each other's identity backgrounds and may therefore struggle with 'perspective taking' (see Smith 2006). Participants may live in different neighbourhoods, hold different beliefs, and will typically socialize in different groups (Smith 2006). If social distance is too extreme, the participants may fail to show 'empathic concern' for each other, ultimately restricting their ability to feel any distress by what they see and hear from other participants.

Communicational barriers to emotional connection

Communicational differences between participants can become pivotal to whether participants understand the victim's articulation of trauma and, subsequently, to whether emotional connections are made between the stakeholders of an offence. Communicational coherence is important as it drives the reparative responses that follow. Barriers to cross-cultural dialogue will be vast and varied, especially where participants speak different languages and/or use disparate modes of non-verbal communication. In cases where the participants speak different languages, facilitators may need to use interpreters in order to include all participants in the dialogue.

Five observations of direct communication were made for this study. An additional thirteen meetings were observed between victims and restorative practitioners, with the bulk of these involving participants whose identity differed from that of the facilitator. Within each of these observations, detailed notes were made about what was said during meetings, the body language of the participants (especially in direct meetings)—including the physical gestures that were made—and whether either party signalled that they understood and appreciated the other party's feelings.

In two of the direct mediation cases observed, difficulties with language prevented participants from directly addressing each other. In one case, two children acted as interpreters for their father, a participant originally from Iraq. This was not ideal but their confidence when doing so allowed the parties to engage with each other with minimal interruption. In one other case the husband of the victim spoke on her behalf, translating her words when she was asked to explain how the incident had affected her (see Case Study 1 below). However, in cases where family members are not present to translate, professional interpreters may be required. Inevitably, the need for translation will restrict the fluidity of dialogue (Albrecht 2010). The emotion behind what is being said can be lost and reactions to participants' stories may seem skewed when compared with the immediacy of typical response. As one practitioner put it: 'You can run conferences with interpreters, and I've done several of those, but it doubles the length of conference...and...you lose a lot of the emotion in the talking'. Whether interpreters help or hinder the flow of dialogue is debatable. More problematic is that minority individuals often refuse their services (Albrecht 2010). In such cases, dialogue can become frustrated altogether, ultimately preventing any mutual understanding. Facilitators may need to insist upon the use of interpreters if they are to ensure that all participants have an opportunity to engage in dialogue and so that offenders, and their 'community of care', can fully appreciate the harms caused by prejudice. A practitioner interviewee explained:

I said we'd need an interpreter, but they said no...The grandfather spoke to me in quite haughty English, the grandmother just smiled and served cakes. I thought, is this just the cultural assumptions that people make—that the women just smile and serve and take a backseat, or is it that she doesn't understand a word we're saying. So I said we needed an interpreter...and the grandmother had plenty to say. Sometimes you can make assumptions that aren't true.

There are several reasons why minority individuals might initially refuse interpreters. Berit Albrecht (2010) suggests that some participants refuse because of personal pride or because they do not want other 'in-group' members knowing they are in conflict. Research conducted for this book also suggests that refusals might be due to participants not wanting to be seen as 'trouble makers' who were causing additional costs to the state. Such sentiments were noted by several victims who had immigrated to the UK. These interviewees stated that, as immigrants, they did not want to be perceived as a burden on the justice process or as taking resources away from the state (see generally Levin & McDevitt 1993, 2002). A Polish victim and his wife commented: 'We don't have any family in England and we never told our children, it is *our* problem. No one knows apart from police and people from charity. We don't want our English friends to think that we think that here is so bad and terrible...'. Such sentiments provided some evidence, albeit very limited, that victims of anti-immigrant hate crimes were aware of societal perceptions that 'foreigners' are 'unfairly' taking British jobs, social welfare, and state resources away from those who are 'genuinely' in need. In response, they were keen to resist contributing to that perception (see also Levin & McDevitt 2002; Ray & Smith 2002).

Paralanguage

Paralanguage and/or a person's density of language are also likely to differ between identity groups. The use of inflections, pauses in speech, silences, timbre, volume, and speed of articulation provide opportunities for misinterpretation (Umbreit & Coates 2000). The way in which a person speaks can be idiosyncratic to the identity group to which they belong. To outsiders, subtle differences in language can cause misunderstandings, potentially offending those unfamiliar with certain tones and inflections. Where differences in paralanguage are most stark, points of common understanding will be more difficult to form, leading to potential dissonance (Albrecht 2010). A practitioner interviewee remarked:

You often don't have time to educate some people about certain elements... for example, a number of Indian dialects, the emphasis is in such a different place when they speak in English that it can make the language sound abrupt. And it's nothing actually to do with the fact that they're being abrupt or dismissive, it's just the emphasis of using shortened words or a slight raise of volume is in a different place to where we put it in English.

There are various other modes of communicating information from one person to another which can also lead to confusion. Physical posture, facial expressions, eye contact, and laughing can all be used as a means of communicating, or signalling to another, certain information (Umbreit & Coates 2000; Albrecht 2010). The use of facial expressions, hand and arm gestures, and other body movements help to display certain emphases when conversing. As with verbal communication, physical gestures can differ markedly depending on cultural background. For example, in some cultures, individuals are discouraged from showing physical emotions publicly or from maintaining eye contact with those deemed to be in a position of authority (see Umbreit & Coates 2000: 8 for examples). These individuals may be perplexed when confronted by a person showing high levels of physical emotion, especially towards their elders. On the other hand, a person who is used to physical displays of emotion may find a person who maintains minimum facial expression and/or who lacks eye contact to be reticent or even cold.

Bridging the empathic divide?

Although a multitude of contextual and personal variables will impact upon the successful facilitation of restorative dialogue, the ability of individuals to share common emotions such as shame, guilt, remorse, compassion, and empathy will equally provide opportunities to find inter-personal congruence. Harris et al assert that 'most offenders will *not* ultimately be indifferent when confronted directly with the suffering of their victims, even if they are indifferent initially' (2004: 201, emphasis added). Offenders are like any other human being in that they 'feel a deeply rooted sense of empathy for other humans', especially when that other person is suffering (Harris et al 2004: 200). Maxwell and Morris (2002: 280–1) additionally explain that offenders who are confronted with the consequences of their actions, knowing that the suffering has been caused by their own actions, naturally experience feelings of remorse. This is likely to be the case whether the victim is perceived as 'different' or not. If this process is managed sensitively, both victims and offenders can return to their family units with a renewed sense of 'self' (Van Stokkom 2002; Harris et al 2004). In turn, the collective acknowledgment of feelings of shame, guilt, and remorse within the offender's 'community of care' may provide for broader community edification.

In fact, the majority of practitioner interviewees were confident that the restorative process could overcome cross-cultural differences. The following practitioner interviewee provided a typical example of an empathic connection:

I had a meeting with two lads where one was from a kind of gypsy background and he had assaulted a boy who was...gay...It started off as different as you could imagine but actually during the meeting...I think the offender realized he had also been experiencing bullying himself on account of his background and there was a little bit of chink of light in him recognizing that his experience of being bullied was also the one that he had kind of created on to this young man.

The capacity of restorative practices to break down the empathic divide *despite* cultural differences is predicated on its flexible and inclusive approach to dialogue that is focused on experiences of emotional harm and inequality (Daly 1999; Albrecht 2010). Most practitioners will be trained to be responsive and reactive to the needs of participants. This will sometimes require the inclusion of interpreters to aid communication. Most important though, is that practitioners provide a safe space for all stakeholders to vocalize their experiences of hate and for participants to listen to each other's stories.

Nonetheless, there will inevitably be some cases where stakeholders fail to form the empathic connections which give rise to truly transforming emotions. Yet even this does not mean that restorative dialogue becomes futile. Indeed, as we will see in the next case study,[2] inclusive dialogue may still generate feelings of shame-guilt and lead to a common understanding between stakeholders, despite participants never really closing the empathic divide.

Case Study 1 Mr and Mrs V-D: 'It's a cultural thing'
The complainant victims (Mr and Mrs V-D, a young black couple originally from South America) had accused their neighbour (Mr H, a white British male of middle age) of persistently racially abusing them. Together with two housing officers and their housing manager the parties were invited to take part in a group conference. (A police officer from a local neighbourhood policing team was invited to the conference but did not show up to the meeting.) Mr and Mrs V-D began the meeting by explaining how they had been racially abused by Mr H over the previous six months. As Mr V-D spoke, Mr H sat with his arms behind his head while tilting his chair back on its hind legs. Mr H's physical displays of communication could be judged as defensive and at times passive aggressive. His communicative displays were clearly intended to send a message of incredulity about Mr and Mrs V-D's allegations, while simultaneously demonstrating that he lacked any respect for what they had to say.

As Mr V-D continued, Mr H made only fleeting eye contact with him and kept his arms crossed. Mr and Mrs V-D on the other hand maintained eye contact with those whom they spoke to during the meeting and sat forward with their hands cupped in front of them.

---

[2] The facts of which are already summarized in Ch 7, pp. 194–6.

Although their body language appeared relaxed, their spoken communication was more strained. In particular, Mrs V-D struggled with English and frequently spoke in a foreign dialect. This was then translated by her husband who spoke fluent English. Both Mr and Mrs V-D spoke with heavy accents, which at times made it difficult to follow what was being said. This slowed proceedings but did not prevent Mrs V-D from explaining how the incident had affected her.

It was clear, however, that Mrs V-D's inability to speak English riled Mr H. He frequently repeated during the meeting that 'they don't speak English, it's always another language'. It was also mentioned by Mr H that Mrs V-D spoke 'too loudly'. This latter point was clearly evident during the observation where it was clear that the volume and speed at which Mrs V-D spoke was significantly louder than other participants at the meeting.

The mediator probed the issue of foreign language further. Mr H remarked 'It's a cultural thing'. The mediator then remarked, 'if your neighbour had been white would the allegation [referring to his counter-allegation of noise] have been made?' Mr H responded, 'They don't speak English, it's always another language...It could be. Who knows?' Still looking for a resolution, the housing manager then asked, 'What is triggering [Mr H's] behaviour? How can we move on?' Mr H replied that he would stop shouting and banging on the walls and then proposed—referring to his relationship with his neighbours—'Let's try and start again'. At this point the body language of both participants softened, if only slightly, and Mr H held eye contact with Mr and Mrs V-D. An agreement was drawn up that Mr H would not hammer on Mr and Mrs V-D's wall or use racist language towards them. Mr and Mrs V-D agreed that they would not make any unreasonable noises.

After leaving this meeting I could not help but feel that the empathic divide between the parties, while at times drawing closer, was never really bridged. The social distance between the participants clearly created a substantive barrier to effective dialogue. Difficulties with language, accents, timbre, and the speed at which Mr and Mrs V-D spoke, combined with the defensive physical gestures made by Mr H, collectively stifled the free flow of dialogue, inevitably limiting mutual empathy.

Somewhat surprisingly, however, Mr V-D stated at interview that he was very happy with the outcome of the meeting and that the process had aided his and his wife's emotional wellbeing. In fact, six months after the mediation agreement was signed Mr and Mrs V-D have had no further problems from Mr H, leading Mr V-D to believe that the mediation process was highly effective at preventing further victimization. This suggests that even where dialogue is strained and empathic responses restricted, inclusive dialogue which led to a mediation agreement could still bring the parties to a *common understanding* that allowed them to move beyond conflict.

Despite the various cross-cultural barriers to communication, Mr V-D and his wife were still able to engage in a process that provided them with a voice. And although the participants displayed little empathy towards each other's stories, the careful facilitation of the meeting ensured that the parties came to an agreement and at least *some* common understanding as to how the incident had affected them. The fact that the perpetrator agreed to participate in the conference, where several of the participants challenged his racially motivated conduct, suggested that he was likely to have experienced a sense of shame for his conduct. The victims' story of trauma may have additionally led to a feeling of guilt about the pain he had caused them. The combined emotion of 'shame-guilt' was carefully managed by the facilitator who did not stigmatize the accused perpetrator as a 'racist', instead offering him an opportunity to reflect upon his behaviour by appreciating how this had affected his neighbours. The mediation agreement further offered him a chance to become a 'good neighbour' by desisting from racially abusing his neighbours. The fact that the complainant victims were happy with the outcome of the conference, and that six months after their ordeal no further incidents had occurred, suggested that the parties' common understanding had had a lasting effect.

PART II: Humanizing 'Difference': the Importance of 'Storytelling'

It is not just communicational style, linguistic difference, and cultural variance that limit empathic connections. Practitioners must also contend with perpetrators' bigotry and the destructive stereotypes that give rise to beliefs about the worthiness of minority group individuals. Thus if the empathic divide is to be truly bridged, restorative practitioners must find ways of challenging prejudice *and* humanizing 'difference'. This next section explores further whether restorative practices are equipped to effectively challenge the prejudiced beliefs that give rise to hate-motivated behaviours.

Stereotyping and the pernicious labels that it can give rise to means that participants will inevitably attend meetings with preconceived ideas about the social worthiness of the other party (Hoyle 2002). Participants' animosities may vary in degree ranging from a merely superficial dislike of someone based on little more than a spurious stereotype to deep-seated feelings of hatred held on ideological grounds (Levin & McDevitt 1993; see 'Challenging prejudice' below). The likelihood of successfully challenging someone's negative notions of 'difference' will vary depending on the levels of prejudice held by the offender, but also on other variables such as the offender's age, previous exposure to people of the identity group they have expressed animus for, their educational level, and their general willingness to accept responsibility (amongst various other factors). Only in cases where genuine attitudinal change is galvanized will RJ pave the way for longer-term reductions in recidivism. In other words, if RJ can help to change an offender's bigoted views it may have a legitimate role in challenging the ubiquity of hate incidents.

This chapter does not contend that RJ is a panacea for hate crime. It would be somewhat idealist to assume that years of learned bigotry, compounded and confirmed through the structural inequalities that are perpetuated via social mechanisms of subjugation, can be undone by a single restorative intervention. Yet this does not mean that the emotional dynamics nurtured within restorative practices cannot induce a genuine change in *some* hate offenders. Accordingly, the success of restorative dialogue may depend on a variety of variables that will differ in each case. This means that restorative practitioners must be flexible in their approach to dialogue as well as to their thinking around suggesting appropriate reparation. Above all, if RJ is to provide victims with genuine reparation, the process should attempt first to humanize victims and their communities to the offender and his or her 'community of care'. A practitioner interviewee explained:

The [restorative process]...is a powerful engine for empathy and wherever people get empathy you humanize each other and you may not change that person's world view on things but it might change the view of the person they're in conflict with. That's where you may get a shift. How people capitalize on that afterwards is a different story.

Direct interactions with gay, disabled, or minority ethnic individuals that are structured around restorative values will help to normalize the 'otherness' of these participants. Dialogue that is focused on reconciliation provides an opportunity for participants of diverging cultural and identity background to focus on common goals. In doing so they are exposed to each other's individuality as well as the socio-cultural idiosyncrasies that make them 'different'. Many of the spurious stereotypes that are held by participants begin to fall away as each party observes the humanity of the other. In this sense, victims' stories aid not just offenders' understanding of the harms they have caused, but also their appreciation of the cultural and identity differences of those involved. In turn, there is scope for reducing the likelihood that offenders will repeat their hate-motivated behaviours.[3] One practitioner remarked:

> The only way to deal with it is to air it. Like the case from Ashfield young offenders unit, someone setting fire to a mosque—[the offender] would never have understood if the people from the mosque hadn't come and talked to him. It strikes me that this is the only way...And you have to worry whether [the victim will] be re-victimized again. [However] once people understand a bit more they're much less likely to be racist or homophobic.

The empathic process is most potent where individuals have opportunities to directly address each other and for dialogue to form organically between the participants. Empathy will be more limited where stakeholders communicate indirectly as the sharing of emotions can be lost through translation (Hoyle 2002). Indirect communication will mean that the parties do not hear or see each other's account of the incident/s. In fact, emotional disconnection was most evident in cases in Devon and Cornwall where thirteen out of the fourteen victims interviewed stated that they were not offered a direct mediation meeting. A significant number of victims (six out of fourteen) stated that they did not have an opportunity to convey the harms they had suffered. A majority of interviewees also stated that they did not feel the offender had a better understanding of their identity background having been through the RD.

Although emotions are clearly more difficult to convey through indirect communication, the study suggested that shuttle mediation

---

[3] For further analysis of moral education in victim–offender conferencing see Schweigert (1999a, 1999b).

could still aid the empathic process in some cases. Information about the harms caused by hate and knowledge about the victims' identity can be conveyed to the offender via restorative facilitators. Facilitators must interpret the harms caused and the reasons for offending and then relay these factors to each of the parties. This was observed many times at Southwark Mediation where the mediator conveyed the victim's sentiments with dexterity. We will see below how facilitators can build additional moral learning into reparation agreements, further enhancing offenders' understanding of cultural and identity difference where the participants do not directly meet (see Case Study 2 below).

Challenging prejudice: 'superficial' prejudices, victim–offender relationships, and the denial of hate

The types of animosity and levels of hatred that gave rise to incidents under investigation differed markedly between cases (see Chapters 4, 5, and book Conclusion). From the cases researched, and those that were relayed to me by practitioners, it appeared that very few offenders could be classified as holding an ideological hatred of the victim's identity group (see similarly Sibbitt 1997; Ray & Smith 2002; Iganski 2008).[4] More likely was that offenders had unwittingly learned their prejudices over their life course, a result of pervasive stereotypes about those who fall outside the prescribed boundaries of dominant culture (Perry 2001; Levin & McDevitt 1993, 2002). For many offenders, their bigoted views will have been based on little other than these fallacious stereotypes, which in turn had given rise to a heedless fear of 'difference' (Perry 2001; Walters 2011). In other words, from the cases observed and from data collated from victims and practitioners, offenders appeared to be ignorant of the humanity of certain identity groups rather than deeply hateful of them (Iganski 2008).

As we have already seen in Chapter 4, many incidents were sparked when issues such as noise pollution,[5] inconsiderate disposal of refuse,

---

[4] The analysis of hate offenders is made from the perspective of victims and practitioner interviews as well as from observations of restorative meetings. Offenders were not interviewed as part of the book and therefore assertions made about their beliefs and levels of prejudice should be viewed cautiously.

[5] The majority of HCP cases involved complaints and counter-complaints about noise.

or smelly 'foreign foods' near to an offender's home incensed offenders, later triggering a demonstration of hostility towards the victim based on the victim's race, religion, sexual orientation, and/or disability.[6] Such cases can be linked to Paul Iganski's (2008) situational perspective of hate crime in which he argues that most hate offences occur during people's routine activities. The gay neighbour who plays his music too loudly, or the Indian family who speak too loudly in a 'foreign' voice at the bus stop can induce a sense of grievance that triggers a (partly) hate-motivated response by an offender (Chapter 4; see also Iganski 2008; Walters & Hoyle 2012).

The empirical research carried out for this book exposed further the day-to-day realities of hate crime victimization. Incidents were often committed by people known to the victim—individuals who lived within their local neighbourhood. Offenders were typically neighbours, colleagues, and in some cases they had even been close friends. In cases where the victim had no prior contact with the offender, a relationship had commonly been created via a customer/service transaction (cases included taxi drivers/passengers and shop assistants/customers). These relationships often become strained after a perceived grievance sparked what in most cases became a volatile conflict between the parties.

The cases researched suggested that a high proportion of offenders' prejudices were of a low to medium level and their causal relationship with the incidents only partial (see Jacobs & Potter's 1998 infamous table, cited in Chapter 1). A practitioner commented:

It can be quite superficial in all the cases I have mentioned...If you think about the context...there is an opportunity for young people where they may be saying something quite flippantly but don't actually mean it if they are encouraged to think it through and how it was perceived.

Another explained:

She [the offender] was asked the question, 'What were you thinking about at the time you did it?' And her answer was simply that she'd had a few to drink and that she was angry at the situation and just lashed out in the first way that came to mind. That it wasn't actually intended to be an indication of her feelings toward his race...she hadn't meant it in that way and she had lots of friends who were white and didn't have any issues of race but was just angry at the time and that was the way it manifested itself.

---

[6] This is not to deny that some cases were caused by a clear hatred of the victims' identity.

The fact that many hate incidents occurred during complex interpersonal conflicts that had created a (or several) trigger event/s meant that offenders had ample opportunities to deny that they were prejudiced (see also Gadd et al 2005; Gadd 2009). One practitioner remarked: '[What] I find with many of these cases is the...person admits to an offence but won't admit to a racist element of it. So they say they made remarks or something or they were violent but kind of guard against the racist bit.' Instead, many offenders focused their explanations as to why they acted as they had on other issues, such as being angry about the noise their neighbour had been causing. Other offenders were often at pains to explain that they did not mean their actions as an expression of hatred towards an entire identity group. Taken at face value, such explanations suggested that some hate incidents were not conscious attempts to subordinate victim groups at all, but rather were expressions of a more individualized form of hatred, often born out of frustration. Incidents were triggered by circumstance and were then vented as a means of hurting the victim individually, rather than as a symbolic message to a collective identity (see Case Study 2 below). This insinuated that the hate element of these offences/incidents came not from a genuine feeling of prejudice, but through an opportunity to use the victim's 'difference' and their perceived vulnerability as means of harming them (see also Gadd 2009; Chakraborti & Garland 2012: 5). A typical practitioner response elucidates this point:

> I've heard racist language used, the kids would say: 'I wasn't thinking.' And you look at them and you try and arrange perhaps a little meeting and they bring along black friends, and quite often it's actually that they don't like the individual and it's nothing to do with the fact that they're black or not...it's just another way of bullying. So it's less about racism, it's more about just, if you like, individual hate which leads to bullying.

Despite the common denial of bigotry amongst those offenders who 'lash out' in the heat of the moment (Gadd 2009), it remains difficult to completely refute the assertion that such conduct is not at least *partly* motivated by prejudice (see Chapter 1; Walters 2013a). This is not to suggest that feelings of prejudice will make up part of the offender's world view, far from it (Iganski 2008). However, the fact that an offender chooses to express racial or anti-religious animosity generates a presumption that he or she intends to subjugate the victim's identity. The offender's intention does not necessarily extend to subordinating entire identity groups, but will frequently be aimed at hurting the victim in the most potent way possible. Yet unless the offender is completely unaware that racially abusing (for example) someone during the commission of an offence would be perceived by others as an act of racism, it is difficult to conceive of such demonstrations as anything other than an expression of group-based animus (Walters 2013a). This is mainly because the offender is likely to be *aware* that his conduct/words will be perceived by others as racist, even if he or she does not consciously wish to subjugate non-white people (Walters 2013a). Moreover, the offender's actions must be understood in terms of the types of harm which they cause. This means the expression of prejudice—whether intentionally directed at an entire group or not—must be considered in order that offenders acknowledge the likely impacts that their conduct will have on other members of the victim's group (Perry & Alvi 2012; see Case Study 2 below). It is therefore important that criminal justice practitioners appreciate the prejudiced component of *all* 'hate' incidents if they are to effectively deal with the multifaceted causes and consequences of such actions.

Be that as it may, the task of responding to hate incidents will inevitably be obfuscated by offenders who refuse to acknowledge the bias nature of an incident. For example, David Gadd notes that

[b]ecause [offenders] know that racism will not be tolerated by the probation service, and because they know that being regarded as 'a racist' is morally stigmatizing…many of those on probation are reluctant to talk about issues to do with race…This has meant that racism often goes unaddressed in intervention work: some probation officers avoid the subject altogether; others perceive only the very small minority of offenders who are overtly interested in the far-right as 'real' racists; much everyday prejudice goes unremarked because practitioners are quite understandably afraid of compromising a viable working relationship with a typically unwilling client group troubled by complex social and psychological difficulties (2009: 759).

Meaningful discussion between offenders and probation officers on the causes and consequences of hate crime is certainly hampered by outright denials of prejudice. However, unlike probation officers, restorative practitioners are better equipped to facilitate lengthy discussions on the effects of prejudice. This is primarily because facilitators include victims and other stakeholders who are encouraged to convey not only the harms of prejudice, but also what it is like for them to be 'different' in the community. The role of the restorative facilitator is not to supervise the offender or to chastise him for his hate-motivated behaviour. The greatest hope for offender edification therefore comes not from criminal practitioners' words, but from the emotional connections formed between the stakeholders of an offence and the resulting social condemnation that is conveyed via restorative processes.

In fact, with what seemed like a majority of offenders demonstrating prejudice in a perfunctory manner, many practitioners felt that the restorative process could transform offenders' superficially held animosities. In particular, discussions that centred on the impact that hate speech has on individuals, and other community members, helped offenders to appreciate both the wrongfulness and harmfulness of their prejudice (see further Case Study 2 below). A practitioner involved in facilitating a racist assault against a taxi driver explained:

> the offender [had] always taken some responsibility and was ashamed for what he had done because he didn't see himself as a racist or as prejudiced to that degree... You often see it. In fact, all through the cases that I have done down here, which are all different, the offenders did not see themselves as racists... but they felt ashamed and they wanted to take responsibility for that and put that straight.

My observations of restorative meetings also highlighted the ability of practitioners to facilitate discussion on hate, despite offenders frequently denying they were prejudiced. In Chapter 4, Case Study 2, the complainant victim provided a lengthy account of his past experiences of homophobia and spoke in detail about how the behaviour of his neighbours had made him feel that they were targeting him because of his sexual orientation. The accused perpetrators engaged in discussion about homophobia and spoke about one of their own family members who had come out as gay. Thus, unlike other justice interventions, the victim-focused approach taken in RJ encourages the parties to examine, together, the harms caused by racism, homophobia, anti-religion, and/or disablism. As Chapter 4 highlighted, such a process frequently elicits a promise from offenders that they will not engage in any future racist/homophobic/anti-religious, and/or disablist behaviours. Such promises hint at the acceptance of responsibility, even if there is not outright acknowledgement by the offender that they acted in a biased way.

Notwithstanding RJ's capacity to effectively challenge prejudice, the constant denial of racism (and other prejudices) by offenders meant that offenders failed to take *full* responsibility for the hate element of their actions. As such, restorative dialogue could not always comprehensively address the social-psychological mechanisms that had given rise to the offender's behaviour. This is ultimately a limitation that all justice processes will face. It is illustrative of the very sensitive and complex nature of prejudice, including how many of those who demonstrate hostility based on the victim's identity do not see themselves as 'hate offenders' (Gadd 2009).

Deep-seated prejudice

While most (especially young) offenders held *superficial* prejudices, inevitably there were some offenders who exhibited more deeply rooted hostilities against certain minority groups. Their dislike of 'Others' will typically have stemmed from a growing fear that minority groups are beginning to encroach upon dominant social norms and values, potentially destabilizing the offenders' ontological security (Perry 2001). For others, the presence of such groups will threaten 'their' geographical space (Green et al 1998; Levin & McDevitt 2002), socio-economic security (Ray & Smith 2002), or a combination of these (Walters 2011). Together, these fears give rise to the belief that minority groups are trying to take over dominant cultural identity and geographical space, while also taking away 'British' jobs and social welfare from those who really deserve them (Levin & McDevitt 2002; Ray & Smith 2002; Gadd et al 2005).

In seven out of the nineteen cases researched at Southwark it became clear that the perpetrator had persistently demonstrated severe forms of prejudice towards the victim over a protracted period of time (see Chapter 4, Case Study 1). In such cases, effectively confronting what is likely to be many years of growing bias becomes a complex task. It is unlikely that a brief restorative intervention will generate any meaningful transformations to most of these offenders' world views (Gavrielides 2007). One victim commented:

the lady [accused perpetrator] never really knew where I came from. She knew I was black but she didn't know whether I was West Indian or whether I was African...I don't think it would have made any difference...it was the mere fact that I was the colour I was, that was it for her.

Distinguishing between those who hold superficial (ie low–medium) prejudices and those who feel greater levels of hatred is a task that facilitators will be required to perform during their preparation (Chapter 7). Practitioners will need to spend additional time preparing cases and exploring with the offender his or her feelings towards the victim (Maxwell 2008). Only then can the facilitator gauge the offender's level of animosity and whether he or she is likely to repeat his or her hostilities during direct meetings.

It is unlikely that RJ will miraculously change the entrenched prejudices of offenders, especially in cases where offenders are resolute in their disdain of the victim's identity. Several practitioners spoke of situations where participants had remained indomitable about their views of victims during preparatory meetings. In such cases, the practitioner stated that they had to make a judgement call as to whether they felt the offender would be antagonistic during a direct meeting with the victim. Most interviewees stated that in such cases they focused on 'indirect' restorative meetings in order to prevent repeat victimization. Others, however, said that they left the decision to take part in direct communication up to the victim, but prepared them for the possibility that hostile comments might be made within the meeting.

In one case explained to me, a young offender who had burnt down the victims' shed had communicated to the facilitator that he believed immigrants should not come to the UK. The facilitator relayed this to the victims, an older couple of Indian heritage, who decided that they still wanted to meet with the young offender directly. During the direct meeting the offender went on to regurgitate statistics about immigrants and 'foreigners' taking British jobs. Having been prepared for this, and as older participants, the victims were able to reply to the young offender calmly and empathically. During the meeting the offender also used the word 'Paki'. The practitioner remarked:

Some victims will challenge it [racism] and in that particular meeting...he [the offender] mentioned the word 'Pakis'...and she [the victim] challenged him and said: 'We're not "Pakis"! We were born in this country.' And she said, 'My mother, my father and my husband's mother and father were born in India, so they weren't "Pakis" either.' And there was the get-your-facts-straight challenge...and I thought that was far better coming from them than it is from me.

The young offender, while clearly hostile towards non-British people, went on to apologize to the victims, stating that he was sorry for the harms he had caused. The practitioner believed the apology to be genuine and the victims later commented that they found the process to be of immense emotional relief. Together, they made the decision that the effort made by the offender to engage in dialogue, combined with his apology, was all that they wanted from him in terms of reparation. Whether this encounter carried forward any longer-term impacts on the young man's behaviour is far from clear.

Such cases suggest that even where learned hostilities run deep into the offender's world views, RJ may still have a place—if only peripherally—in challenging prejudice. This belief was also reiterated by several practitioners who stated that restorative meetings could still have a positive influence on hate offenders despite not being able to bring about a complete change of attitude. A victim of long-term targeted homophobic and disablist abuse also illuminated this finding when he remarked:

[Mr X] automatically presumed that all gay men are also paedophiles… I think that was one of the issues and once all those issues were put to him in sensible conversation, while he's not going to change his opinion totally, I think it led to him realizing that everything was not as black or white.

A practitioner similarly summed up both the benefit and limitation of RJ in this regard:

Everyone's entitled to their own views, whether it's somebody's sexuality or cultural beliefs or religion, it's about letting the perpetrator know or understand the effects that when it's said out loud…you can't necessarily change someone's views about a certain subject, but it's about what they do with it and how they keep it to themselves.

Moral learning

One way of improving the likelihood that offenders will gain a greater appreciation of the effects of prejudice is to build direct forms of 'moral learning' into the restorative process. Although not necessarily a central goal of RJ, reparation may help to rehabilitate offenders by offering them a form of education (Braithwaite 1999; Schweigert 1999a, 1999b). Restorative justice meetings are an excellent platform upon which participants can rise to a higher level of 'moral thinking' (Schweigert 1999b: 35; see also Gavrielides et al 2008: 38–9). Conferencing, in particular, can be educative and liberating for stakeholders by freeing them from stereotypes that encourage feelings of anger, fear, and distress (Schweigert 1999a: 174). This is best achieved by bringing '...the moral authority in personal communal traditions and the moral authority in impersonal universal norms together in a mutually reinforcing combination' (Schweigert 1999a: 174). Universal norms such as equality, dignity, and respect will become significant moral values in cases involving hate crime (Walters 2012). However, as I have already noted, these values may well be in conflict with 'community traditions'; those which give rise to hostile attitudes towards 'difference'. Yet, as Francis Schweigert notes, 'Universal moral principles, unlike communal norms, represent attempts to transcend particular communal identities and worldviews, to speak to the common human condition everywhere and at all times' (1999a: 174). Hence, the promotion of overarching values such as 'dignity' and 'respect' within restorative practice may be of particular significance if RJ is to effectively challenge both the individual prejudices and community norms that give rise to hate-motivated behaviour (Walters 2012).

As we have seen, such values are promoted through direct forms of dialogue which expose participants to the harms of prejudice and to the humanity of each individual. However, moral learning can also be incorporated into reparation agreements. Agreements often include direct work for the victim (eg cleaning graffiti off a fence or painting a shed), work for a community cause selected by the victim (eg volunteering for a local charity), specific undertakings (eg attending a counselling course), or a mixture of these (Marshall 1999: 11). In the context of hate crime, RJ facilitators will need to find innovative ways of including both reparation and moral learning into such agreements. The next case study illustrates how restorative practitioners can facilitate such moral learning, potentially enhancing the likelihood of offender edification.

Case Study 2 Anti-Semitic harassment—exploring the harms of the Holocaust

Mr K, a seventeen-year-old Jewish male, lives in a small town in Oxfordshire. Mr Y, a seventeen-year-old white British male, began to harass Mr K because of his Jewish heritage. The first incident involved Mr Y coming from behind Mr K and pushing him to the ground. During this episode of violence Mr Y repeatedly yelled, 'you fucking Jew'. Mr K ran from the scene as Mr Y and a group of his friends threw rocks at him, one closely missing his head. Mr K reported the incident to the police. However, the offender continued his victimization of Mr K, including one incident where he racially/religiously abused him and his mother when walking in town. Mr K's mother, shocked by the abuse, reported the incident to the police, after which Mr Y was arrested and following an investigation and prosecution he was convicted of racially and religiously aggravated harassment under section 32 of the Crime and Disorder Act 1998. As a first-time offender, Mr Y was sentenced to a Referral Order and later referred to Oxford YOS where an RJ practitioner was assigned to his case.

The RJ practitioner met with Mr K and his father who spoke at length about how the incident had affected them and how important their Jewish roots were. The facilitator asked Mr K how the offender might help to repair some of the harms he had caused. Mr K told me at interview: 'I personally said I don't want him to be punished by clearing the side of the roads because that will get you nothing, it was my suggestion for him to see on the internet about what happens when you hate Jews.' This suggestion led to the offender being asked to undertake a research project into the rise of the Nazi party and the effects that anti-Semitism had on the Jewish race during WWII. The offender manager, herself Jewish, supervised the project which was completed over a two-week period. The report was then presented back to the victim and his family by the RJ facilitator. At the end of the six-page report[7] the offender reflected:

Since I have had my reparation [the completion of the research project] I feel that I understand why incidents involving racial abuse against Jewish citizens and all over races are taken so seriously. As I have been doing this timeline and reading about what actually happened around the time of the Holocaust before it wasn't clear to me but now it is and I realize the seriousness of the offence I committed. I also understand the hurt and pain the victim and his family must of felt when I said what I said to him as it was obviously a terrible time for there race from the earlier 1930's and I shouldn't of used that against him to hurt his feelings as it is not just him that it relates to but a whole race of people and that's not what I intended to do.

---

[7] The report is copied verbatim and therefore I have not corrected any spelling or grammatical mistakes.

On reflection of my actions I now feel that I will be able to use language more appropriately towards over people and not to talk about peoples religions and believes in such a way that I did before as it is not nice and I would not want people to talk about my family and there racial believes the way I commented about the Jewish religion as it is unacceptable because of the pain it causes to the people it happens to and because language like that is not acceptable in public areas because it could offend more than one person even if it is not directly aimed at the public they still would've had to hear it.

To begin with, both father and son appeared sceptical as to the genuineness of the report. In particular, the victim's father was concerned that the offender had missed out important information about concentration camps during WWII. However, after several minutes of digesting what the offender had written, the father of Mr K commented: 'What he has written...he shows what a personal hate can do when you gain power. What would happen...it's a start, this is better than painting a fence or something!' Mr K then responded: 'Let's hope this shocks him into changing his ways. This is really a cross roads for him. Maybe he will benefit from it...'.

At interview, Mr K went on to say that, 'It's definitely helped me a lot more than if I wouldn't have had it.' Whether or not the offender in Mr K's case genuinely had a new-found respect for the victim and other people of Jewish descent remained uncertain. The fact that the victim opted for an indirect approach to RJ meant that he could not witness first-hand how sincere the offender was. Still, when asked whether he believed the offender now had a better understanding of his identity background, Mr K replied: 'Somewhat I think, well the fact that he had to do this [referring to the report]...he's looked into some things that hatred can do...the bad times of the Holocaust...'.

The victim went on to state that he had not experienced any further forms of harassment from Mr Y. One can only hope that the words written by the offender were a sincere offering of sorrow, such that in the future he desists from hate-motivated behaviours. Mr K's case is just one example of how reparative work may help offenders to learn more about cultural and identity difference, and more broadly the harmful impacts that racial and religious hostility has, not only on the primary victim, but on entire groups of people.[8]

---

[8] A summarized version of this case appears in Walters (2014).

Desistance

It is difficult to show with any certainty whether the offender in each of the cases researched at Southwark, Devon and Cornwall, or Oxford had a better understanding of the victim's identity post RJ, especially considering that offenders were not interviewed for this book. It is certainly unlikely that offenders who hold deeply ingrained hatred will be miraculously reformed over the course of a short-term restorative intervention. The study was, however, able to identify in each case whether the victim was subjected to any further abuse post restorative intervention.[9] In seventeen out of the nineteen cases researched at Southwark Mediation the accused perpetrator ceased abusing the complainant victim having completed the mediation process. It has already been noted in Chapter 6 that eleven of these seventeen cases were resolved primarily through direct or indirect dialogue between the main parties. The remaining six cases were resolved and incidents ceased only after a multi-agency approach was adopted. These latter cases often involved a threat of eviction made by housing officers, bringing a potentially punitive element within the restorative framework.[10] Of particular significance was that the vast majority of offenders who had persistently victimized the victim over a prolonged period of time desisted post mediation.

A majority of victims in Devon and Cornwall (eleven out of fourteen) also stated that they did not receive any further victimization from the offender post RD.[11] However, only some of these cases can be directly linked to the effectiveness of the disposal. In eight cases the victim did not have a prior personal relationship with the offender.[12] In most of these cases victims were abused at work by customers/service users. It is less likely that the stakeholders of the offence will cross each other's paths again in cases where the offender has no prior relationship with the victim. In fact, many noted that they had not seen the offender/s since the original incident. Hence, in Devon and Cornwall it could not always be ascertained whether the offender desisted because of the RD or simply because

---

[9] Victims were interviewed up to twelve months post RJ in Devon and Cornwall and eighteen months in Southwark, London.

[10] It is outside the scope of this book to examine the effects of coercion on offenders' participation in RJ and its effect on their adherence to mediation/reparation agreements, see generally Walgrave (2007).

[11] Four cases involved 'one-off' incidents.

[12] This still amounted to a minority of cases across the datasets.

he or she had no further contact with the victim. Nonetheless, collectively, the findings on desistance suggested that restorative practices can help to reform the behaviours, if not the beliefs, of many hate offenders.

Conclusion

Cultural and linguistic dissonance between stakeholders of hate crime is clearly a barrier to fluid and empathic communication during restorative processes. Yet this does not mean that offenders cannot form emotional connections and/or find common understandings with those they perceive as 'different'. Rather, it suggests that restorative practitioners will need to find solutions to empathic divides by supporting inclusive dialogue. We have seen throughout this chapter how such connections can be formed. Indeed, the flexibility of restorative processes means that dialogue can be adapted in order to overcome variations in identity, culture, and language. Ultimately, practitioners who focus on harm and conflict resolution will support mutuality between participants. In so doing, restorative practices provide genuine opportunities to humanize 'difference', thereby helping multicultural communities to move closer together.

Restorative interventions that open up cross-cultural dialogue, while simultaneously protecting against domination, create meaningful space to effectively challenge and modify the hate-motivated behaviours of offenders. The edification of hate offenders was, unsurprisingly, easiest in cases where victims had demonstrated 'superficial' prejudices towards their victim. In these cases it appeared that restorative dialogue provided a cogent means through which social condemnation of the offending behaviour could be expressed and thus feelings of shame, guilt, and remorse more readily experienced. Offenders that hold more deeply rooted hatred will clearly be more challenging. In such cases it was less likely that RJ could effectuate a genuine long-term change in the offender's hostile beliefs. This is to be expected considering that the restorative process is often only a short-lived justice intervention. Even so, some practitioners and victims still believed that restorative dialogue could play a positive role in challenging the offender's attitudes towards 'difference'. And although unlikely to change their world views, it was hoped that the process might induce a 'chink of light' in some offenders. Within these more thorny cases, restorative practitioners should consider more creative ways of furnishing 'moral learning' (see Case Study 2). Using reparation agreements to include victim or community work may help offenders to reflect further on the deleteriousness of their actions and the harms caused by prejudice. Such work will also allow offenders to process their emotions of shame and guilt more positively, increasing the likelihood that they will modify their behaviours in the future.

Supporting the tentative findings about offender edification were the more conclusive results on offender desistance post RJ. The findings from Southwark Mediation were particularly encouraging here, showing that community mediation was able to prevent further hate victimization in the vast majority of cases.[13] This was an important finding considering the damaging impacts that continuous forms of hate-motivated abuse have on victims (Chapter 3), and it suggested that restorative practices may have an important role to play in reducing overall levels of hate crime.

---

[13] Though it remains unclear whether the accused perpetrators went on to victimize other individuals who displayed certain identity characteristics.

9
Conclusion: Uncovering Hidden Truths

The Need for a Restorative Approach to Hate Crime

The impetus for this book arose from the proposition that conventional justice measures fail to address effectively both the causes and consequences of hate crime. The most prominent concern is that the current emphasis on enhancing the punishment of hate offenders does little to aid the emotional or physical recovery of victims. Furthermore, the retributive (and punitive) principles upon which such penalties are based do little to engender greater acceptance of 'difference' (Moran et al 2004a). The state's focus on retribution, as against reparation or rehabilitation, means that offenders are generally separated from their victims, further polarizing the stakeholders of hate crime. This prevents offenders from gaining greater insight into the cultural backgrounds of those they fear, while increasing penalties does little to placate offenders' erroneous perceptions that minority identity groups are given preferential treatment by the state (Jacobs & Potter 1998; Dixon & Gadd 2006).

Notwithstanding the limitations of criminalizing hate, it would be unfair to suggest that the retributive approach to tackling hate crime is entirely counterproductive. Hate crime laws are based intuitively on the principle of proportionality; if hate crimes hurt more (or at least the *risk* of harm is greater, as empirical evidence suggests they do, see Herek et al 1997, 1999, 2002) offenders should be met with a harsher punishment (Iganski 1999; Lawrence 1999; Levin 1999). The criminalization of hate certainly helps to censure prejudice-motivated offences, and I am persuaded by the argument that symbolic denunciation of such conduct has an incremental macro-level influence on societal views on the (un)acceptability of racism, homophobia, anti-religion, and disablism (Iganski 2008). Furthermore, legal proscription ensures that the hate crime policy

The Need for a Restorative Approach to Hate Crime 237

domain is given greater attention by police and prosecution services, both of which must specifically identify incidents and attend to them. Without the legal framework for hate crime, it is much less likely that criminal justice agencies will dedicate the amount of time and resources that they now do to tackling this type of offending.

Notwithstanding the pros and cons of proscribing hate-motivated crimes, it remains of particular concern that *most* perpetrators continue to evade any form of criminal prosecution (Burney & Rose 2002; Gadd 2009; Home Office et al 2013). This is partly because many victims do not report incidents to the police (Garland & Chakraborti 2009: 68–9). However, as this book has shown, there are many cases that are reported to state agencies but that do not result in criminal prosecution. This is often the result of police officers failing to collate sufficient evidence to successfully prosecute and convict hate offenders (see Burney & Rose 2002). In various other cases, reported hate crimes are not pursued by the police because incidents are viewed as 'low-level' or 'domestic disputes', ie conflicts which fall outside the purview of traditional policing.

The social complexities present in most hate-motivated conflicts must not be forgotten, brushed aside, or deemed to be either too multifarious or too trivial for the state to address (see Table 9.1 for further details of 'types' of hate crime). Left unchallenged, 'low-level' incidents often become daily occurrences that gradually shatter the lives of those targeted (see, for example, the Pilkington case, Chapter 1). So-called 'domestic' disputes frequently escalate over protracted periods of time, resulting in violent outbursts that cause immense emotional and physical damage. The manager of the HCP at Southwark Mediation summed up the problem of local authorities' failure to effectively respond to hate incidents:

You can prosecute someone but often…they fall at the last hurdle, the CPS don't make the charge and people are left disappointed and they're not given answers and things might reoccur, and that all spirals…[leaving victims asking] 'What the hell are these agencies here to do, they're not protecting me?'

Such comments were representative of many of the cases researched for this book. It means that many hate crimes go unchallenged by the state, while victims are left unprotected and subject to repeat victimization. The current focus on criminalization, while helpful, is simply not enough. As such, we must seek out new ways of effectively attending to the causes and consequences of hate crime.

Empirical findings on harm reparation

The theoretical framework outlined in Chapters 1, 2, and 3 of this book provided the basis upon which the empirical examination of RJ for hate crime was carried out. Chapters 1 and 3 marked out the conceptual complexities of hate crime, highlighting, in the main, how hate-motivated incidents of all types and severities permeate communities throughout the world. Research has shown that while some violent attacks are marked by extreme brutality, most other hate-motivated crimes form part of a more insidious 'process' of victimization, often involving ongoing 'low-level' incidents. The process of hate victimization also needed to be set against a context of structural marginalization which served only to exacerbate the harms of each isolated act of hatred. Only through understanding the relationship between micro-level hate incidents and macro-level social harms can we begin to appreciate the depth of trauma which victims of hate crime are likely to experience.

In Chapter 2 I began to explore whether RJ can help to repair the harms caused by crime. Both normative assumptions and empirical research were evaluated in order to establish which variables aided the recovery of victims. In particular, it was noted that inclusive dialogue, central to RJ, helped to reorientate victims from a position of vulnerability to one of empowered stakeholder within the justice process. However, it was not until Chapter 4 that we observed whether the benefits of RJ extended to victims of hate crime. The analysis provided in that chapter suggested that community mediation was by far the most successful restorative intervention researched for this book in terms of both reducing emotional harm and preventing further hate incidents from recurring.

The majority of victims at the HCP stated that the process had improved their emotional wellbeing as well as reducing feelings of fear, anxiety, and anger. Three key process variables were identified by interviewees as pivotal to their emotional recovery. The first was that mediation provided them with an opportunity to 'take part' in their *own* conflict resolution. Having been ignored and neglected by various local agencies (see Chapter 6), it came as a great relief to victims that the mediation service was prepared to *listen* to them and *support* their case. Central to this part of the process was that victims found a voice, having previously been silenced by the police, housing officers, and the community members who sought to victimize them. Mediation meetings allowed participants to develop their own narrative via a process of storytelling. It was this dialogical aspect of mediation that promoted greater emotional wellbeing amongst participants. The additional support offered by mediators, by way of service referral and, later, telephone calls to check that the victim was still OK, further enhanced victims' recovery.

The final, and perhaps most important, factor relevant to victims' emotional recovery was the promise of desistance that offenders (accused perpetrators) frequently provided within mediation agreements. It was clear throughout the study that such promises contributed significantly to the victims' emotional reparation. However, for many victims, it was not until they had observed first hand that the promise was kept that they could move on with their lives, free from the constant fear of repeat victimization. As was highlighted in Chapters 1 and 4, the ongoing nature of much targeted abuse, and the regularity of incidents, meant that many victims were desperate to be free from the threat of repeat abuse.

The generally positive findings from Southwark Mediation were not replicated in Devon and Cornwall. Despite certain methodological limitations—in particular the use of telephone interviews (instead of face-to-face interviews) and the lack of any direct observations of police disposals—it soon became apparent that interviewees were less satisfied with this type of restorative process and consequently were less likely to report emotional reparation. In fact, only four out of the fourteen victims interviewed stated that the RD had helped to reduce their levels of fear, anxiety, and/or anger; while in two cases the victims reported that they felt worse having participated in the disposal. The main shortcomings of the disposal were identified as the following: a failure by officers to adequately explain the purpose of RJ to victims; a failure to adequately prepare victims for the process; a failure to offer victims a direct meeting with the offender (with only one participating in face-to-face dialogue); and a failure to offer some victims an opportunity to explain how the incident had affected them.

Compounding all of these deficiencies was the fact that victims also felt that officers had cajoled apologies from offenders, many of whom had written single sentences on a piece of paper by way of reparation. Consequently, most victims felt that their reparation had been disingenuous, leading to further feelings of frustration and anger. These findings resulted in a tentative conclusion that, despite the disposal being labelled as 'restorative', the intervention appeared to be another means through which the police exerted almost full control over how the offence was dealt with. As a result, the intervention failed to incorporate key restorative principles, leaving many victims feeling that the justice process had 'let them down'.

If police services are to utilize restorative interventions for hate crime (or any other crime for that matter), they must fully understand, and rigorously implement, the principles that govern RJ theory. This will entail the use of restorative practitioners who are sufficiently trained and fully committed to the practice of RJ. More broadly, restorative practices that are used to support hate victims must ensure that they do the following:

1. thoroughly prepare both victims and offenders by providing them with information about the aims and objectives of RJ;
2. use preparatory meetings to explore all the factors causal to the incident/s and any broader conflict that the parties are involved in;
3. provide several opportunities for victims to express their experiences of hate victimization, the impacts of being 'different', and the effects that identity-based prejudice has on them and other community members;
4. listen to the victim's 'story';
5. include victims in the decision-making process on how offenders (accused perpetrators) can best repair the harms caused;
6. provide offenders with an opportunity to explain the reasons behind their actions—it will be important for facilitators to resist chastising or labelling offenders as 'haters';
7. encourage offenders (accused perpetrators) to offer genuine reparation—importantly, facilitators must not coerce offenders into providing insincere apologies;
8. establish ground rules for direct communication that emphasize mutuality and respect while limiting opportunities for adversarial debate;
9. include 'promises of desistance' in reparation/mediation agreements signed by both parties;
10. provide additional support, including referrals to other agencies who can provide social/emotional support, and making periodical telephone calls to check on victims' progress.

11. include local agency employees (such as police and housing officers) within restorative conferences (or separate meetings) in order to ensure that participants receive the support they are entitled to and/or receive reparations for any secondary harms previously caused by an agency.

The limitations of restorative justice for hate crime: repairing structural harm?

Despite RJ's healing potential, the restorative practices examined could not *fully* repair all the harms caused by hate crime victimization. The findings indicated that, in most cases, the levels of fear, anxiety, and anger experienced by victims were only *partially* reduced post RJ. There were several reasons why RJ could not provide full reparation for hate victims. First, the regularity and prolonged nature of much hate abuse caused deeply embedded emotional and physical traumas that had accumulated over protracted periods of time. Although mediation had often provided victims with a voice and support, and had finally put a stop to the abuse, much of the emotional damage could not be totally reversed by a restorative encounter; at least not in the short term.

Second, the long-lasting impacts of hate crime could be intrinsically linked to broader socio-structural inequalities and to the myriad social harms experienced by certain minority groups (Chapter 3). The fact that hate crimes often made up just one part of a 'process' of victimization meant that isolated incidents had to be set against a broader context of structural marginalization. Social disadvantage and the lack of support offered by state agencies inevitably heightened the vulnerability of many minority group individuals interviewed (Chapter 6; see also Perry 2001). These socio-structural inequities were left largely unchanged post RJ. Hence, despite aiding victims' emotional recoveries, restorative processes could not alleviate the broader socio-cultural and socio-economic disadvantages which are manifest in contemporary society.

Despite the failure of most restorative interventions to repair the structural harms faced by hate victims, some attempts at reducing the vulnerability of victims and enhancing state-based support for them was observed at the HCP. Secondary harms were often caused by local agencies when responding to reports of hate crime/incidents (a part of the process of victimization). This was an unanticipated finding in the study. Although in Chapter 3 I had presented a social harm perspective of hate crime, I had expected the responses to hate crime by state agencies in England and Wales to be generally well received by victims, particularly considering the large-scale policy changes that had been effected since Macpherson (1999). However, many victims at both the HCP and Devon and Cornwall stated that housing officers' and police officers' responses to their complaints were apathetic, while in some cases their dealings with the victim were marked by neglect. Others who had directly contacted the police were often told that nothing could be done due to the 'domestic' nature of the incident/s, replicating past criticisms about the police's response to domestic abuse. In other cases, victims were not contacted again after the police dropped the case due to a lack of independent evidence. Of greatest concern was that in a couple of cases the actions of agency employees suggested that they had ostensibly discriminated against the victim (see Chapter 5, Case Study 1 and Chapter 6, Case Study 1). Collectively, the failure of either the police or housing associations to take victims' complaints of ongoing victimization seriously led to the exacerbation of their emotional trauma.

In Chapter 6, we saw how the inclusion of local agencies—through what was labelled a 'multi-agency approach' to RJ—ensured that victims gained access to local services that they had previously been denied. Important to the multi-agency approach was that restorative practitioners appreciated how local agencies became important 'community supporters', providing essential social services to victims and offenders alike. Facilitators also had to consider the fact that agencies sometimes caused secondary victimization and as such needed to repair these harms.

An understanding of the dichotomous roles that local authorities play in hate crime cases will aid the effective facilitation of RJ. The fact that community mediators were able to engage agency employees in the restorative process meant that victims not only received the support they clearly needed, but in some cases received reparation for the damage state organizations had themselves caused. It was here that we began to see how *some* restorative practices can help to repair not only the individual harms caused by hate crime, but also some of those caused by socio-structural processes of victimization.

The Need for a Restorative Approach to Hate Crime 243

Avoiding risks and challenging prejudice?

In Chapter 7 the book explored, in greater detail, the risks that RJ can expose victims to. As with Chapter 6, this looked at both the potentially healing and potentially harming effects of 'community'. The perils of community were that the dominant norms and cultural values inherent in most communities would be imposed on 'Others' via the dialogical processes central to restorative encounters. Worse still was that cultures of prejudice that are cultivated within certain locales would prevent RJ from conveying the required social condemnation for hate-motivated incidents. The fear was that offenders, emboldened by their sense of righteousness, would manipulate the process, trivialize the victims' experience, and subject them to re-victimization.

Such concerns are real and must not be underestimated. Accordingly, the study endeavoured to explore whether the risks of community were experienced by participants in practice. Both practitioners and victims were interviewed about their experiences of domination and re-victimization at all stages of the process, while during observations of direct meetings I paid close attention to these concerns. Encouragingly, the responses from victims and practitioners indicated that repeat victimization during the restorative process was rare. It became clear during observations and when interviewing practitioners that this was mainly due to the preparation that was undertaken at the start of the process. The greater the preparation, the less likely it is that victims will be exposed to domination during meetings. This aspect of restorative practice was reiterated time and again by every practitioner I interviewed. Most noted that offenders who willingly participated and who understood the nature of the restorative process were highly unlikely to repeat their previous demonstrations of hostility. The setting of firm ground rules and including appropriate supporters during meetings also helped to ensure that the focus remained on *repairing* and not *causing* harm (see below 'What did hate crime tell us about the practice of restorative justice?').

In the final substantive chapter of the book I moved on to an examination of the potentially reforming effects of RJ for hate crime. Following on from some of the concerns raised in the previous chapter, I illuminated the various hurdles that are faced when bringing participants from divergent cultural backgrounds together to discuss the complex hate conflicts that they became embroiled in. Differences in language, paralanguage, and physical gesticulation clearly inhibited the free flow of direct dialogue. However, the flexibility and inclusiveness found within restorative practices—in particular community mediation—allowed facilitators to overcome these variations, thereby helping the parties to form emotional connections and eventually common understandings.

Still, the cultural differences and the prejudices that were intrinsic in hate crime cases clearly proved inhibitive to forming empathic connections in some cases. In order to really challenge the prejudiced behaviours of hate offenders, practices therefore needed to actively seek to humanize the 'differences' that divided stakeholders. Most restorative practitioners felt that the animosities held by offenders could be challenged using inclusive dialogue that focused on the harms caused by hatred. And although in many cases offenders denied that they were racist or homophobic (for example), the exploratory nature of the process allowed the parties to talk at length about the impact that prejudice had on the victim as well as discussing what it was like for him or her to be 'different' in the community. Such discussions often had a positive impact on offenders' understandings and acceptance of 'difference'. Furthermore, practitioners who facilitated reparation work that contained an element of 'moral learning' were able to additionally bolster offender edification and, in turn, reduced the likelihood of repeat (hate) offending (Chapter 8, Case Study 2).

The research indicated that restorative practices could provide sufficient scope to challenge the superficial to medium-level prejudices held by most hate offenders. Yet it is important to note that restorative dialogue could not always alter the views or behaviours of offenders whose animosities had become deeply ingrained, especially in cases where prejudices had been learned over many years. In these more challenging cases, practitioners had to judge whether direct dialogue would leave victims open to possible re-victimization, and if so, whether an indirect approach to RJ would prove more effective. One can only really hope that restorative dialogue in such cases will offer *some* edifying influence over hate-motivated offenders.

What Did Restorative Justice Tell Us About the Nature of Hate Crime?

During the empirical stage of this book I was given access to the case details of fifty-five separate hate crimes/incidents from which

I went on to interview thirty-eight victims. In addition to this, I interviewed twenty-three practitioners who relayed twenty-eight hate crime case examples to me[1] and I observed eighteen separate restorative meetings. In total, I came close to analysing information on ninety hate crime/incident cases that had come to the attention of restorative practitioners across England. Analysis of the data collated provided a renewed insight into the types of hate crimes/incidents that occur every day in Britain's multicultural communities, including information on the relationships that exist between offenders and victims. Unlike most other studies which have investigated the nature of hate crime, the study was not completely reliant on police records (see eg McDevitt et al 2002; Mason 2005). The problem with relying on 'official' records of hate crime is that those incidents that are never reported, or which are reported but never recorded, will be missed by the researchers. Although the current study's sample was not randomly selected from the entire pool of hate crimes that occur in England, the cases researched did come from a broader range of organizations. Some had reported the case to the police, others to housing associations, schools and colleges, and in several cases the victim had self-referred to a mediation centre. The large number of cases that were reviewed therefore reflected a broader range of incidents than those which are dealt with only by the police. This has allowed me to identify key characteristics that were common to several distinct types of hate crime/incident. Though by no means exhaustive, the most common types of incident that I came across were as follows:

(1) Incidents that occur within broader inter-personal conflicts

The most common type of hate incident identified across the datasets was incidents that occurred within acrimonious inter-personal conflicts, commonly involving neighbours and/or individuals known to each other. Cases involving warring neighbours were most representative of those that came to the attention of the HCP. However, such incidents were also evident in Devon and Cornwall and from the case examples given by various other restorative practitioners at interview. Thus although the sample of mediation cases may have skewed the overall number of 'inter-personal conflict' cases researched in this study, it was clear this type of hate crime/

---

[1] Several of the practitioner interviews were in relation to cases I had observed and victims I then went on to interview.

incident frequently came to the attention of other criminal justice and third sector practitioners.

Hate incidents that occur during inter-personal conflicts typically involve a variety of social factors and aggravating circumstances. For example, in most of the cases researched in Southwark, complaints (and counter-complaints) about noise pollution had led to a volatile altercation between the parties. These initial fracas sparked feuds between neighbours which then escalated over the course of weeks, months, and sometimes years. As frustrations and feelings of anger built, the (perceived) behaviour of one party finally led to the commission of an incident/s marked by the use of racist or homophobic (for example) language (ie the hate crime/incident).

Other causal factors identified were: screaming children and the playing of music too loudly (both of which are exacerbated by poor insulation between apartments); inconsiderate disposal of refuge; alcohol and drug misuse; smoking in communal hallways; and mental health issues (for both victims and offenders). These precipitating variables antagonize individuals who feel aggrieved by their neighbours' behaviours. As conflicts worsen, feelings of frustration and anger increase, at which point the parties become prone to 'lashing out' at each other. In cross-cultural conflicts, this gives rise to opportunities for one party to use the other's 'difference' as a means of most directly hurting them (Iganski 2008). Consequently, the vocalization of prejudice during *some* inter-personal conflicts is less an attempt to send a symbolic message of hatred to an entire community (though it is likely to have such an effect), and more likely to be a means of hurting the other party's feelings. In other words, it is a heat-of-the-moment outburst used as a way of 'getting back' at someone.[2]

While some hate incidents committed during neighbour disputes are done so largely out of spite, there were many other cases where incidents were more intricately infused with the perpetrator's perceptions as to the way certain 'Others' live their lives. Within the Southwark study, for instance, complaints about 'foreign smelly' foods, 'foreign music' and 'foreign voices' often suggested that the perpetrator's actions were motivated, at least in part, by the complainant victims' 'difference' (see also Sibbitt 1997). Offenders' beliefs are likely to be the result of superficially held prejudices that are directly linked to the negative stereotyping of minority identity

---

[2] See *DPP v Woods* [2002] EWHC Admin 85.

groups (Levin & McDevitt 1993; Chapter 1). We might conceptualize such incidents therefore as the projection of internalized frustration antagonized by social context and co-dependent with negative attitudes about identity 'difference'.

Fundamental to the conceptualization of intractable neighbour disputes is that, in some cases, both complainant victims and accused perpetrators will share at least *some* culpability for the broader conflict in which they have become embroiled. In fact, rarely is it the case that only one party is guilty of anti-social behaviour. Hence, the labelling of one person as an 'offender' and another as a 'victim' does not always truly represent both parties' culpability and/or responsibility for the broader conflict (see further 'What did hate crime tell us about the practice of restorative justice?'). To some extent the complexity of inter-personal conflicts creates an epistemological barrier to understanding hate-motivated incidents. Such cases do not fit within the traditional conceptions of hate crime or the stereotypical conception of what a domestic dispute entails. The myriad social factors, and their nexus with varying degrees of prejudice, make the conceptualization of hate incidents within inter-personal conflict difficult to outline. What is clearer, however, is that in such cases the exploration of both parties' actions will provide for a more holistic understanding of the causes and consequences of hate-based conflict and, as such, will provide greater scope for the resolution of such disputes.

(2) Persistent targeted abuse

The second most common type of hate crime identified within the study was incidents characterized by ongoing and persistent forms of victimization that were aimed at victims seen only for their 'otherness'. Such cases were reflective of 'the process' of hate that was analysed in Chapters 1 and 3, and which has been conceptualized by various other hate crime scholars (see, for example, Bowling 1998; Garland & Chakraborti 2006). It is common for 'low-level' incidents to gradually increase in severity, frequently resulting in the physical abuse of the victim (see Chapter 4, Case Study 1). Cases are also often marked by verbal outbursts by the offender and/or the commission of property damage, including racist/homophobic graffiti. As with messy neighbour disputes, targeted incidents are typically committed by people known to the victim, such as a neighbour. Offenders are likely to be vociferous in their disdain of the victim and others who display similar identity traits. Such cases are clearly motivated by animosity towards the victim's identity. These more deeply ingrained prejudices can be connected to one or more of several criminological explanations of hate crime (see Walters 2011). It is outside the scope of this book to examine these in any detail. I simply summarize here some of the main themes found within the literature.

Several criminologists have suggested that hate-motivated offenders will *fear* minority groups whom they see as posing a threat to society's dominant norms and cultural values (Perry 2001; see Chapters 1 and 3). Offenders use hate crime as a way of demonstrating power over already stigmatized individuals. Such acts prevent 'Others' from overstepping culturally prescribed boundaries while simultaneously ensuring that they remain marginalized within society. Other scholars have argued that hate crimes (especially racist or anti-immigrant) represent an expression of anger and frustration towards groups seen as taking away socio-economic resources from the dominant (white) group (Ray & Smith 2002). 'Others' are seen as having 'invaded' indigenous space, whereby they take local jobs and resources away from those seen as more deserving. Linked to concerns about local resources are offenders who are concerned about geographical ownership. These offenders target 'Others' in order to send a clear message to 'out-groups' that they are not welcome in the community (Green et al 1998; see also Levin & McDevitt's 1993, 2002 typology of offenders). Some criminologists have argued that these types of hate crime victimization are used as a way of projecting ontological insecurities onto those seen as causing society's economic woes (Ray & Smith 2002; Gadd et al 2005). Under this construction of hate crime, offenders' actions are conceived less in terms of ideological hatred and more as a reflection of the internalized feelings of socio-economic insecurity that are experienced by certain dominant (but simultaneously socio-economically marginalized) group members.

Restorative practitioners should be aware that these causal factors are likely to overlap and interconnect, most commonly through the emotion of fear. It will be the *fear* that 'Others' will change cultural norms, take away local jobs, and invade geographical space that motivates offenders to persistently target victims (Walters 2011). Many of these offenders are likely to have learnt their prejudices over many years. As a result, their fear of 'difference' will have become deeply ingrained into their consciousness (Levin & McDevitt 1993). This means that the offender's level of prejudice will be high (or at least of medium level), as too is its causal connection to the commission of the offence/s (see Jacobs & Potter 1998; Chapter 1, Table 9.1).

(3) 'One-off' attacks

The least common type of incident identified across the datasets was 'one-off' attacks committed by those previously unknown to the victim. A temporary relationship is commonly established between victim and offender via a preceding commercial transaction (see also Ray & Smith 2002; Gadd et al 2005). For example, incidents are frequently committed against takeaway restaurant employees, convenience shop staff, and taxi drivers. Most 'one-off' incidents amount to public order offences which involve the offender racially abusing the victim (commonly using anti-immigrant language such as 'go back to where you come from'). In some cases, offenders will go on to physically assault their victim where initial outbursts turn into aggressive altercations.

This type of hate crime/incident is usually triggered when an offender becomes incensed by the actions of the victim (the service/goods supplier). Grievances arise, for example, where the offender has been asked to extinguish a cigarette, or because the offender feels that the service provider has overcharged him or her. What would typically be an everyday interaction between customer and shop employee is viewed by the offender as an act of provocation, which in turn elicits a *partly* hate-motivated response from the offender (see also Ray & Smith 2002; Gadd et al 2005; Iganski 2008). This supports Paul Iganski's routine activity analysis of hate crime in which he argues that we need to examine the situational foreground of hate incidents in order to more fully understand the structural contexts that inform the actions of offenders (Iganski 2008). Iganski argues that most hate offences occur in the context of our everyday lives through the actions of everyday people. Many 'one-off' incidents therefore represent part of the everydayness of hate crime. They are the culmination of daily social interactions within multicultural communities which provide opportunities for simmering bigotries to boil over as perpetrators 'lash out' against 'difference'.

However, not all 'one-off' attacks will involve social interactions that have given rise to a sense of grievance. For example, attacks against gay and lesbian people often occur outside or near commercial premises, such as bars and/or shops that are frequently patronized by gay and lesbian people. Many of these homophobic

Table 9.1 Key types of hate crime/incidents

Type of hate crime/incident	Characterization	Common social factors	Victim/offender relationship	Level of prejudice/causal connection
Incident/s form part of an inter-personal conflict	Conflicts escalate over protracted periods of time culminating in the commission of an incident marked by the use of racist, homophobic, anti-religious, or disablist language.	Local authority housing, noise pollution, alcohol and drug abuse; mental health issues; multiple disputants.	Known, typically neighbours.	Low-medium/ Low-medium
Persistent targeted abuse	Persistent and ongoing targeted abuse of victims that occurs over prolonged periods of time (process-led).	Local authority housing, alcohol/drug abuse.	Known, neighbours or local community members.	Medium-high/High
'One-off' attacks	'One-off' incidents typically committed in public areas.	Offences frequently occur late at night during commercial transactions, such as at takeaway food establishments. Alcohol intoxication is common.	Previously unknown, commercial relationship based on goods/service provider and customer.	Medium-low/ Medium

incidents occur late at night and are committed by young men who are out on the town looking for trouble. Such incidents can be linked to Jack Levin and Jack McDevitt's now famous typology of hate crime offenders (1993, 2002). They found in their study that most offenders were 'thrill seekers' who actively targeted 'Others' in order to gain excitement (see also Byers et al 1999; Franklin 2000). Although the current study did not concur with Levin and McDevitt's finding that *most* hate offenders are of this type,[3] it did support the suggestion that *some* hate incidents were committed late at night by young offenders. However, differing from Levin and McDevitt's typology was the finding that most 'one-off' attacks were committed by people who had consumed large amounts of alcohol and who had stumbled across the victim by chance, rather than by purposively seeking them out.

The level of prejudice held by offenders who commit 'one-off' attacks is neither deeply seated nor superficial. By this I mean that is not the offender's sole purpose to specifically target certain minority individuals to victimize, nor is it his or her intention to simply hurt the victim's feelings out of spite. Instead, the offender's animosity towards certain identity groups, while genuinely held, will remain latent and only comes to the surface when the offender is confronted with a perceived grievance (see Iganski 2008). The offender's medium-level prejudice is the result of the same causal socio-cultural and socio-economic factors explained above for persistent offenders, ie those relating to the encroachment of cultural and socio-economic norms (see Perry 2001; Ray & Smith 2002). However, unlike persistent offenders, in the majority of 'one-off' attacks, offenders' hate-motivated actions are triggered *only* once the offender feels a sense grievance. The intoxication of aggressors serves only to lower the offender's level of self-control and in turn his or her tolerance of 'Others' (Walters 2011). For this reason, it is suggested that 'one-off' attacks are the result of medium–low-level[4] prejudices, which are of medium-level causation.

Demarcating the various types of hate crime/incidents which occur within our multicultural cities and towns helps us to understand the

---

[3] Levin and McDevitt's typology used police reports, meaning that only those offenders who had been arrested by the police came to the attention of the researchers.

[4] The reversal of low–medium to medium–low reflects the likelihood of prejudices being at the medium part of the scale.

varying levels of prejudice and their causal connection with the offence/incident committed. As we can see, most of these 'types' of hate crime are interlinked with each other. The same macro-level causal factors will be present for each type of hate crime (Walters 2011). Common to most incidents is that offenders' prejudices are unwittingly learnt over long periods of time. Biased beliefs are likely to be the result of pernicious stereotypes that have been propagated through society's communication networks, including the media (see Gordon 1994; Sibbitt 1997: 13–14). Negative messages about certain identity groups promote a culture of prejudice through which general beliefs about the worthiness of group members is cultivated. The varying degrees of prejudice which these sociological processes propagate must, however, be connected with various other social factors and conditions. Only when we view the situational contexts in which hate crimes occur can we begin to differentiate between types of hate offenders and the types of incidents committed.

It has been through the empirical examination of RJ within this book that a more nuanced picture of hate crime has emerged. Important to the restorative process in hate crime cases was that offenders were rarely labelled and punished as 'haters'. Instead, perpetrators were asked to explain their motivations before witnessing first hand the consequences of their actions. Unlike conventional criminal justice measures, restorative interventions explored the disparate causes and consequences of hate, and thus created the conditions through which a more informed response could be delivered. The complex array of social factors which are causal to many disputes were not set aside by adversarial processes of justice that focus on the opposing roles of 'victims' and 'offenders' (see further below). Rather, inclusive dialogue provided opportunities to explore the roles that each party had played within broader conflicts, and for the parties, collectively, to find suitable ways of resolving damaged relations. Such a process enabled the stakeholders to determine, together, the types of reparation that would most effectively challenge the varying levels of hatred attached to hate incidents (see eg Chapter 8, Case Study 2).

What Did Hate Crime Tell Us About the Practice of Restorative Justice?

The empirical study not only provided greater understanding of the nature of hate crime/incidents but also created further insight into the capabilities and limitations of restorative practices. Reiterated throughout this book has been the finding that restorative practices must be administered by dedicated practitioners who adhere rigorously to core restorative values when facilitating dialogue (see specifically Chapter 5). At this final stage of the book it is perhaps worth reflecting further upon the processes used at the HCP at Southwark Mediation and the implications that my findings here may have on the future use of restorative practice for hate crime.

As has been highlighted above, and in Chapter 4, many hate incidents occur within intractable inter-personal conflicts. Such disputes could not always be resolved by the police or other state agencies due to their acrimonious and multifarious nature. Furthermore, the labelling of one party as the 'victim' and the other 'offender' did not always truly represent the culpability and responsibility of both parties, despite the fact that a crime had been committed within the broader conflict. These complex cases clearly have repercussions for both conventional justice processes and the successful application of restorative practice. Labelling those involved in a hate incident as 'victim' and 'offender' assumes diametrically opposing roles for each party (Christie 1986). The pre-constructed role of victim means that interventions rarely allow for the sharing of culpability between those involved in a crime. As such, the labels imposed upon stakeholders of hate crime by the state do not always reflect the multitude of anti-social behaviours that have been committed by all of the parties.

Most restorative interventions employ the labels of victim and offender when resolving conflict. Practices start from the premise that the commission of a crime has caused harm to a victim who will clearly require support, as well as reparation, in order to put him or her back into the position that he or she was before the offence was committed. There has been very little within the broader RJ literature that has attempted to deconstruct this particular understanding of victim (Dignan 2005; Walklate 2008). Indeed, our understanding of victimhood within RJ is usually one that is assumed. Victims are seen as neutral players within a social context that has resulted in them becoming harmed by criminal activity. The 'ideal' offender, on the other hand, is a wrong-doing, harm-causing deviant, who must go on to repair the damage he or she has inflicted. Yet, in many of the messy neighbour disputes researched, these roles were frequently blurred. Although in most cases one party had complained of having been the victim of a hate incident, the overall conflicts in which the parties were embroiled were far from one sided. Such a finding therefore directly challenged the traditional notion of victimhood and the state's responses to, and perpetuation of, methods of social control. Sandra Walklate has similarly noted:

> Victims are, after all, complainants in a criminal justice system as offenders are defendants...[however] victims are not necessarily the 'good' in opposition to the offender's 'bad'...This position serves to remind us that whilst crime does impact upon people's lives, victims of crime are people too...They are people, and people need to feel OK about themselves and sometimes need some help and support to achieve that. And what makes people feel OK? Respect. Whether male or female, whether a member of an ethnic minority, whether old or young, the maintenance of respect and the avoidance of contempt sustains a sense of well-being and contributes to people feeling OK (2008: 283–4).

Respect, therefore, is the key to maintaining and healing damaged communities. But how do we acknowledge the fact that offenders and victims are both 'people' in need of respect and who want to feel OK? Short of reconstructing the entire process of criminalization, we must seek out alternatives to the criminal process that promote respect and wellbeing for all parties involved in conflict. The community mediation services which have proliferated throughout the Western world now provide one such measure by incorporating a flexible, non-labelling approach to conflict resolution. Such dialogue is receptive to the exploration of broader social contexts, including consideration of the various anti-social behaviours acted out by each of the parties. 'Party one' and 'party two', as they were referred to at the HCP, were both provided with an opportunity to discuss what had happened, how it had happened, and how it had affected them. Had community mediation labelled the parties as 'victims' and 'offenders', the process would have become skewed and the pre-defined roles of the parties, as outlined above, would not always have truly represented the actions committed and the harms caused. Instead, the responsibility and culpability of the parties would have become one-sided, inevitably generating a feeling of injustice on the part of one of the stakeholders.

The commonality of complex inter-personal conflicts that result in hate incidents may have repercussions for the successful application of other restorative practices, such as police-led restorative disposals. Practices that focus solely on the predefined roles of 'victims' and 'offenders' may inadvertently perpetuate the oversimplification of some crimes as being entirely one-sided events, therefore circumventing the complex array of social factors that lie behind many inter-personal conflicts. This finding does not refute the fact that in many cases the labels 'victim' and 'offender' will provide a fair reflection of the relationship that exists between the parties involved in a hate crime/incident. In fact, in a large proportion of the cases researched for this book, it was clear that one party had been harmed and that it was necessary for the other to help repair that harm. Rather, it has been by illuminating the dynamics of complex inter-personal disputes that I endeavour to suggest that the convoluted nature of *some* hate conflicts cannot be resolved by imposing dichotomous labels. In such cases restorative practices may be better served by implementing only *some* of the restorative principles that have been articulated within the literature. In particular, the focus given by some scholars to offenders taking responsibility *before* participating in restorative processes (Braithwaite 1989) and the intrinsic importance given to apologies and material reparation as being central to repairing the harms, articulated by others (Strang 2002), may actually work to inhibit conflict resolution. Without doubt, individuals who feel aggrieved by the actions of the other party are unlikely to respond positively to a one-way process that asks them to repair harm only.

Of course, the failure to carve out carefully defined roles for the stakeholders of crime risks confusing the dialogic process and frustrating the ultimate goal of reparation for those who have been harmed. Nevertheless, this book asserts that emotional recovery is not necessarily predicated on the attainment of direct reparation, such as an apology, but instead is based more on the participants' inclusion in a process that provides them with a voice. 'Storytelling' empowers all stakeholders, who find that they are finally being listened to. The most important form of reparation indicated by complainant victims throughout this study was the promise provided by accused perpetrators not to repeat their actions.[5] Hence, the effectiveness of community mediation was based not on the predefined roles of the parties or on the attainment of an apology, but on inclusive dialogue that focused on resolving conflicts and preventing

---

[5] In fact, apologies that were perceived as disingenuous acted only to antagonize victims.

re-victimization.[6] It is by illuminating the commonality of these highly complex inter-personal cases that I highlight the need for police and other state agencies to refer cases to practices which incorporate a restorative approach that explores the harm-causing *and* harm-repairing role of *all* parties involved in such conflicts.

Re-conceptualizing 'community' and the importance of preparation

The analysis of RJ for hate crime inevitably gave rise to a consideration of the role of 'community' in restorative practice. In Chapters 6 and 7, I noted that the notion of community has generally been conceptualized homogeneously within restorative theory and practice. Advocates of RJ have been particularly prone to overstating its constructive role within restorative encounters (Crawford 2002). However, as we have seen, 'community' can serve both as a harming and healing entity. This book has therefore approached its collective spirit as being capable of both supporting and reintegrating stakeholders, while at the same time potentially promoting structural hierarchies and cultures of prejudice that can actively re-victimize participants. Accordingly, I argued that if RJ is to consistently repair the harms caused by hate victimization, we must first recognize that one of the central notions within its philosophy can be both a benevolent and malevolent force.

In the vast majority of cases it will be relatively easy to ascertain which elements of the 'community' are supportive. For example, a victim's family (part of their 'community of care') will usually (but not always) provide essential emotional support during restorative meetings. It is also through this supporting aspect of 'community' that I argued for the inclusion of local state agencies within the restorative framework. As we saw in Chapter 6, practitioners who implement a multi-agency approach to RJ can secure additional emotional and social support for victims.

In other cases, the notion of 'community' may be viewed as causal to hate incidents. Communities fearful of certain 'Others' often develop mechanisms of control that are used to marginalize minority groups (Perry 2001). A culture of prejudice can be perpetuated

---

[6] This conclusion does not deny the benefits that can be gained from obtaining genuine apologies (Strang 2002). It simply suggests that apologies are not prerequisites for emotional recovery.

amongst dominant community members, effectively preventing certain identity groups from gaining social capital. Restorative practitioners must therefore be alive to the risks posed by certain aspects of communities which serve to dominate and subordinate minority group victims. Of gravest concern is that restorativists who continue to apply blindly the benevolent ideal of community may simply mask the social inequalities and structural hierarchies that give rise to minority group oppression. The risk, therefore, is that RJ could potentially perpetuate the 'process' of hate, rather than repairing its harms.

While these theoretical concerns must not be underplayed, neither must they prevent the utilization of RJ for hate crime. Restorative theorists and practitioners who understand both the harming and healing qualities of 'community' will be able to utilize the notion by focusing on those parts of it that are helpful, while guarding against those which may become victimizing. This proposition may sound as if it is fraught with uncertainties and potential complexities; however, as we have seen, avoiding domination and repeat victimization can be successfully and consistently achieved through the careful preparation of participants. Although I had understood the need for preparation at the beginning of this book I had thought little about its importance before undertaking the empirical study. This was partly due to the fact that 'preparation' and what it entails is largely absent from RJ literature. For example, in neither of the two main handbooks on RJ (Johnstone & Van Ness 2007b and Sullivan & Tifft 2008a) do any of the authors discuss in detail the intrinsic value of preparation and/or how this precursory process affects the success of restorative practice. Through researching the use of RJ for hate crime it became patently clear that preparation was the key to successfully aiding the reparation of hate harms. It allows facilitators to judge whether the parties are ready for direct dialogue, whether indirect dialogue is more appropriate, or whether any party is likely to re-victimize the other. It is also during preparation that practitioners can work with other stakeholders to determine who might best support each of the main parties during direct dialogue. Furthermore, preparation enables practitioners to ascertain the depth of prejudice that an offender holds and its level of causality with the offence. Such is the importance of preparation that it later helps practitioners to effectively facilitate discussion on the causes and consequences of prejudice, and facilitate appropriate reparation work that will help to aid the recovery of hate victims (see eg Chapter 8, Case Study 2). As such, the preparation stage of RJ must not be understated. Further exploration of its intrinsic importance to the application of RJ, including determinations about the various roles played by 'community', is required within the broader literature.

The future of restorative justice for hate crime: effective training

The current UK government has stated that it is committed to rolling out RJ across all parts of the criminal justice system (MoJ 2012). Furthermore, as part of the new Code of Practice for Victims of Crime, victims will be given the option to participate in RJ (MoJ 2013). The draft code states:

> Restorative justice can take place whilst criminal proceedings are ongoing or after the conclusion of criminal proceedings subject to availability. Where available, this will be led by a trained restorative justice facilitator who will take your needs into consideration.

The success of RJ across the criminal justice system may depend largely on whether restorative facilitators are employed from within or outside criminal justice agencies. Practitioners who are brought from outside pre-existing organizations will bring greater levels of independence and impartiality with them and, as such, will be more inclined to avoid the institutional prejudices which have permeated so much of the criminal justice system (Macpherson 1999; Bowling & Phillips 2002). Where agencies decide to train justice professionals from within the system (such as Devon and Cornwall Police), the organization's institutional values and practices will inevitably compete with those of RJ, ultimately undermining the integrity of restorative practice. If this is the case, and I expect it will be, it becomes imperative for practitioners to work exclusively on restorative facilitation. Only then will the values of conventional criminal justice become secondary to the work of restorative practitioners.

Furthermore, if RJ is to offer hope to hate crime victims and the communities they come from, practitioners will clearly need to undertake extensive training on the causes and consequences of hate in order to effectively negotiate the minefield of socio-cultural issues pertinent to such cases (McConnell & Swain 2000; see also Maxwell 2008). The HCP manager, having spent ten years mediating hate crime cases in one of London's most diverse boroughs, was discernibly well qualified and experienced in dealing with prejudice-motivated conflict. I spoke with two other practitioners who had undertaken training on the use of RJ specifically for hate crime. The vast experience that other practitioners had gained in dealing with conflicts in multicultural communities also meant that they had a broad knowledge base of the issues relevant to hate crime cases.

Nonetheless, in some cases, practitioners clearly failed to appreciate the complexities of hate-motivated offences. I have already noted some of the insensitivities expressed by agency employees in Chapters 5 and 6, which resulted in secondary victimization. Providers of RJ must therefore ensure that facilitators have a suitable comprehension of the issues relevant to hate crime in order that they carry out adequate preparation and effective facilitation of meetings. This will be RJ's greatest hurdle in effectively resolving hate crime cases. Other attempts to train criminal justice practitioners in community diversity have not always been a resounding success (see Rowe & Garland 2007). Resistance from within some institutions will inevitably prevent practitioners from fully benefiting from diversity training (Chan 1997; Reiner 2010); the old adage, you can take a horse to water but you cannot make it drink, springs to mind. Again, the use of practitioners from outside pre-existing institutions will reduce the likelihood of facilitators being influenced by institutional prejudices.

One way of protecting against bias within restorative practice is to ensure that administrators actively seek out facilitators from culturally diverse backgrounds. The practitioners I interviewed in London represented a broad range of cultural and ethnic identities. This was less evident outside of the metropolis, where practitioners tended to come from white, middle-class backgrounds. Though I would not go so far as to suggest that minority ethnic practitioners are better equipped to mediate cases involving minority ethnic participants, it is certainly the case that those who have themselves experienced socio-cultural marginalization will have a greater appreciation of the harms that discrimination and prejudice can cause. As Barbara Raye points out, '[p]ersonal experience of class, gender bias, culture, and race might inform us and cut short the barriers to understanding' (2004: 331). First-hand knowledge of 'difference', cultural diversity, and the socio-structural dynamics of hate crime will mean that facilitators are better able to understand pre-existing divisions and help encourage the emotional connections central to restorative dialogue (Raye 2004). Only when restorative practitioners represent the multicultural communities that they serve can restorative practices be truly inclusive of the differing cultures, ethnicities, and orientations of the people. If this can be achieved, restorative justice should be formally integrated into both state and community-based policies that aim to tackle the causes and consequences of hate crime victimization.

Appendix A
Interview Schedule: Victims and Complainant Victims

This interview makes up part of a research project being carried out by myself as part of my doctorate, at the Centre for Criminology, University of Oxford. The aim of the study is to explore how the restorative/mediation process affects people who have been involved in an incident or crime where an issue of race, religion, and/or sexual orientation has been raised. By taking part in this study you will be supporting research into the effectiveness of criminal justice initiatives aimed at helping to repair the harms caused by crime. The information you provide in this interview may be used in future publications, however this will not include any information which would identify your name or address. Please take time answering the questions and be as open and honest as you can.

Section 1: About You

1) What is your date of birth?
2) How would you describe your gender?
3) How would you describe your ethnicity?
4) What is your religion?
5) How would you describe your sexual orientation?
6) Do you consider yourself to be disabled?

Yes ☐ No ☐ I do not wish to disclose whether or not I have a disability ☐

If yes, would you mind telling me what disability you have?

Section 2: About the Incident

7) When did the incident/s (first) occur?

Within the past month	☐	1–2 years ago	☐
2–6 months ago	☐	2–5 years ago	☐
7–11 months ago	☐	More than 5 years ago	☐

8) Can you explain to me what happened?
Were the police involved? If so what action did they take?
Was the housing association involved? If so what action did they take?

9) Was there more than one perpetrator/other parties involved? If so how many people were involved?

One perpetrator	☐	More than three perpetrators	☐
Two perpetrators	☐	Not sure how many	☐
Three perpetrators	☐		

10) **How long did the incident/s last for?**

Just happened once ☐	1–3 months ☐	More than one year ☐
About one week ☐	4–6 months ☐	Still ongoing ☐
1–3 weeks ☐	7–12 months ☐	

11) **Do you believe the incident was motivated (or partly motivated) by prejudice against any of the following?** (You can tick more than one box if applicable).

Your race, ethnicity or nationality ☐

Your sexual orientation ☐

Your religious beliefs ☐

Your disability ☐

Don't know ☐

None of the above ☐

Other, please describe ☐

12) **Did you know of the other party(ies) involved in the incident before it happened?**

Yes ☐ No ☐

13) **If you did know the other party(ies) are they (tick as many boxes as apply):**

A neighbour ☐	A family member ☐	Other ☐
A friend ☐	A partner/spouse ☐	Did not know them ☐
An acquaintance ☐	Someone from work ☐	

14) **Did you sustain any physical injury resulting from the incident/dispute?**

Yes ☐   No ☐

If yes what was your injury (and please state if you required medical treatment)?

15) **Did you incur any financial costs associated with the incident/dispute?**

Yes ☐   No ☐

If yes what for?

16) Did the incident/dispute affect your emotional wellbeing?

Yes	☐	(If yes, go to question 17)
No	☐	(If no, go straight to question 18)
Rather not say	☐	(Go to question 17)

17) If so did you experience any of the following emotional or psychological impact/s because of the incident/dispute? (Tick as many boxes as you feel are applicable).

Feelings of anxiety	☐
Sleeplessness	☐
Nightmares	☐
Depression/feeling depressed	☐
Fear of being attacked/victimised again	☐
Feelings of self blame	☐
Loss of confidence	☐
Loss of self esteem	☐
Anger	☐
None	☐
Rather not say	☐
Other, please explain:	☐

18) Have you experienced any of the following since the incident/dispute occurred? (Tick as many boxes as you feel are applicable).

Avoid certain locations	☐	Housing difficulties	☐
More careful about what you say and do	☐	Employment difficulties	☐
Try to change your appearance/way you act	☐	Rather not say	☐

19) In your own words can you explain to me more generally how the incident has affected you and those around you?

Section 3: About the Restorative/Mediation Process

20) Do you feel that the mediator/facilitator provided you with adequate information about what would happen during the restorative justice (mediation) meeting?

Yes ☐   No ☐   Can't remember ☐

21) Were you told what the restorative (mediation) process aimed to achieve?

Yes ☐   No ☐   Can't remember ☐

22) Why did you agree to attend the restorative justice/disposal (mediation) meeting?

23) Did you take part in a face to face meeting with the other party or were your meetings with the facilitator only?

Face to face ☐   Indirect mediation ☐

24) Did you feel the mediator/facilitator acted fairly during the RJ (mediation) meeting/s?

Yes ☐   No ☐

Can you elaborate?

25) Did the facilitator provide you with an opportunity to explain how the incident had affected you?

Yes ☐   No ☐

Can you elaborate?

26) Did you feel that the facilitator tried to help you resolve the problems that the incident had caused?

Yes ☐   No ☐   To some extent ☐

Can you elaborate? Were any other agencies, organisations involved during your mediation meetings?

27) Did you ever feel at a disadvantage during the restorative (mediation) process due to any of the following? (Tick as many boxes as you feel are applicable).

Your age	☐
Your race, ethnicity or nationality	☐
Your religious beliefs	☐
Your sexual orientation	☐
Your gender	☐
Your disability	☐
Your language skills	☐
Other	☐
I did not feel at a disadvantage	☐

28) If you felt that you had been disadvantaged in any way can you explain how you were disadvantaged?

29) Did the offender/other party apologise to you during or after the meeting (or via a letter or message sent to you by the facilitator)?

Yes ☐   No ☐

How did it feel to hear the offender/other party apologise?/did you feel the apology was genuine?/do you feel the offender/other party should have apologised?

30) Overall do you feel that the restorative (mediation) process has improved your emotional wellbeing?

Yes ☐   No ☐   Not sure ☐

Can you explain how it has improved your emotional wellbeing/why it did not help?

31) Did you find any of the following parts of the restorative (mediation) process helpful to your emotional wellbeing?

Just having the opportunity to take part	☐
Explaining to the other party how you felt (sending a message to the other party about how you felt)	☐
Being able to explain how the incident had affected your life	☐
Meeting the other party involved in the incident	☐
Seeing the other party understand how the incident/dispute has made me feel	☐
Receiving an apology from the other party	☐
Obtaining assurances that the incident(s)/dispute would stop	☐
Don't know	☐
None of the above	☐
Other, please explain:	☐

Interview Schedule: Victims and Complainant Victims

32) From the following list which other factors have helped with your emotional wellbeing since the incident/dispute?

The passing of time	☐
Support from partner, friends and/or family	☐
Support from a housing officer	☐
Support from a non government/charity organisation	☐
None	☐
N/A	☐
Other, please explain:	☐

Please indicate how much you agree or disagree with the following statements.

33) You were fearful of the other party/ies (offender/s) directly *before* the restorative (mediation) process

Strongly Agree	Agree	Neither Agree Nor Disagree	Disagree	Strongly Disagree	N/A
☐	☐	☐	☐	☐	☐

34) You were fearful of the other party/ies (offender/s) directly *after* the (mediation) restorative process

Strongly Agree	Agree	Neither Agree Nor Disagree	Disagree	Strongly Disagree	N/A
☐	☐	☐	☐	☐	☐

35) After the restorative (mediation) process you felt that the other party/ies (offender/s) had a better understanding of how the incident had affected you?

Strongly Agree	Agree	Neither Agree Nor Disagree	Disagree	Strongly Disagree	N/A
☐	☐	☐	☐	☐	☐

36) Can you describe to me a little bit more about your feelings of fear towards the offender and how this has changed, if at all, since the restorative (mediation) process?

On a scale from 1 to 10, with 1 being 'very mild' and 10 being 'very severe':

37) On a scale of 1–10, 1 being very low and 10 being very high, please indicate the level of ANGER you were feeling towards the other party/ies (offender/s) directly *before* the restorative (mediation) process. (N/A if did not experience anger).

1	2	3	4	5	6	7	8	9	10	N/A
☐	☐	☐	☐	☐	☐	☐	☐	☐	☐	☐

Low level of anger   Medium level of anger   High level of anger

38) On a scale of 1–10, 1 being very low and 10 being very high, please indicate the level of ANGER you were feeling towards the other party/ies (offender/s) directly *after* the restorative (mediation) process. (N/A if did not experience anger).

1	2	3	4	5	6	7	8	9	10	N/A
☐	☐	☐	☐	☐	☐	☐	☐	☐	☐	☐

Low level of anger   Medium level of anger   High level of anger

39) On a scale of 1–10, 1 being very low and 10 being very high, please indicate the level of ANXIETY you were feeling about the incident/dispute directly *before* the restorative (mediation) process. (N/A if did not experience anxiety).

1	2	3	4	5	6	7	8	9	10	N/A
☐	☐	☐	☐	☐	☐	☐	☐	☐	☐	☐

Low level of anxiety　　Medium level of anxiety　　High level of anxiety

40) On a scale of 1–10, 1 being very low and 10 being very high, please indicate the level of ANXIETY you were feeling about the incident/dispute directly *after* the restorative (mediation) process. (N/A if did not experience anxiety).

1	2	3	4	5	6	7	8	9	10	N/A
☐	☐	☐	☐	☐	☐	☐	☐	☐	☐	☐

Low level of anxiety　　Medium level of anxiety　　High level of anxiety

41) Can you explain how your feelings of anxiety and anger have changed, if at all, since going through the restorative (mediation) process?

```



```

Section 4: Your Feelings Towards the Other Participants

42) Do you think the restorative (mediation) process had a positive or negative effect on your feelings towards the other party/ies (offender/s) involved in the incident?

Positive ☐　　Negative ☐　　Neither positive nor negative ☐

274   Appendix A

43) Can you explain how the restorative (mediation) process affected your feelings, if at all, towards the offender/other party/ies?

44) If your feelings towards the other party/ies (offender) changed, were any of the following factors relevant to that change (tick as many as apply)?

Just meeting the other party	☐
Hearing them tell me about why they acted as they did	☐
Obtaining assurances that they would not repeat their actions	☐
Listening to the facilitator	☐
Finding common goals	☐
Understanding where the other participant/s was/were coming from	☐
Knowing that they listened to me	☐
Knowing that they had taken on board what I had to say	☐
Understanding more about their cultural/identity background	☐
Other, please explain:	☐

Interview Schedule: Victims and Complainant Victims   275

45) Please indicate how much you agree or disagree with the following statement. (Tick just ONE box).

Going through the restorative (mediation) process enabled the other party to better understand my cultural and/or individual identity background.

Strongly Agree	Agree	Neither Agree Nor Disagree	Disagree	Strongly Disagree	N/A
☐	☐	☐	☐	☐	☐

Can you explain why you think this was/wasn't the case?

Section 5: The Overall Impact of the Restorative Process

46) Overall, did you find the restorative (mediation) process a positive or negative experience?

Very positive ☐   Positive ☐   Negative ☐   Very negative ☐   Not sure ☐

Appendix A

47) Please indicate how much you agree or disagree with the following statement. (Tick the relevant level of agreement)

Since the restorative (mediation) process you feel you can put the whole incident behind you?

Strongly Agree	Agree	Neither Agree Nor Disagree	Disagree	Strongly Disagree	N/A
☐	☐	☐	☐	☐	☐

48) Overall how satisfied were you with the restorative (mediation) process?

Very Satisfied ☐   Satisfied ☐   Dissatisfied ☐   Very Dissatisfied ☐

49) Would you recommend restorative justice (mediation) to others involved in a similar incident?

Yes ☐   No ☐   Not sure ☐

50) Do you have any further comments you would like to add about your experience of restorative justice (mediation)?

Thank you for taking part!

Appendix B
Interview Schedule: Restorative Justice Practitioners

Introduction

Before we begin could you tell me a little bit about what your experience as an RJ practitioner has been? What training did you receive?

Can you explain to me what you think the main components of the Restorative Disposal/conference/mediation process are?

1) Can you describe to me an RD/mediation meeting/conference that you have facilitated which involved a crime/incident which had been motivated (or partially motivated) by the victim's race, sexual orientation and/or religion?
2) Do you know why it was decided that this incident was appropriate for RJ/mediation/conference?
3) Did you explain to the parties involved what the restorative/mediation process was and what it aimed to achieve?
4) Can you describe to me what happened in the meeting/during the process?—was the victim & offender (both parties) and their supporters there?
5) Was the victim/complainant able to explain how the crime/incident had affected him/her?
6) Was the perpetrator/accused party able to explain why he/she committed the crime/incident?
7) Were issues around prejudice or hatred based on race, religion, sexual orientation or disability raised in the meeting? If so how did the victim/offender respond to these issues?
8) Did you feel that the different backgrounds of the participants inhibited the dialogue in any way? For example were there any language difficulties or differences in styles of communication that made it difficult for the participants to understand each other?
9) Do you think the meeting made any difference to the offender's understanding of the victim and the victim's cultural/identity background?
10) Was a reparation/mediation agreement made? If so what did it include?
11) Did the offender apologise?
12) Do you think that all the parties present were happy with the reparation agreement? Did the victim accept the apology and in your opinion did they perceive it as being genuine?

13) Do you feel that the meeting helped reduce any emotional harms that the victim/parties had experienced? If so how?
14) I want to ask you a few more general questions about RJ in hate crime cases but before I do, was there anything else about this case that you think would be helpful for me to know?

About RJ Conferencing in General

15) What issues specific to hate crime cases do you think need to be addressed during a RJ/mediation meeting?
16) Are there any types of hate crime that you feel would not be suitable for a face-to-face restorative mediation? Why?
17) How can RJ/mediation practitioners manage the risk of victims (participants) being re-victimised during meetings?
17a) How likely do you think it is that a victim would be re-victimised in hate crime cases?
18) Hypothetically, how would you react if one of the parties began to make any racist/homophobic/anti-religious comments during the conference/mediation?
19) Generally speaking, would you recommend RJ/mediation as an effective way of responding to hate crime?
20) Do you have any other comments you would like to make about RJ/mediation in hate crime cases

References

Abbas, T. (2007), 'Introduction: Islamic Political Radicalism in Western Europe', in T. Abbas (ed), *Islamic Political Radicalism: A European Perspective*, Edinburgh: Edinburgh University Press.
Ahn Lim, H. (2009), 'Beyond the Immediate Victim: Understanding Hate Crimes as Message Crimes', in P. Iganski (ed), *Hate Crimes*, Volume Two. London: Praeger.
Albrecht, B. (2010), 'Multicultural Challenges for Restorative Justice: Mediators' Experiences from Norway and Finland', *Journal of Scandinavian Studies in Criminology and Crime*, 11: 3–24.
Allport, G. (1954), *The Nature of Prejudice*, Cambridge, Mass: Addison-Wesley.
Amstutz, L. (2004), 'What Is the Relationship Between Victim Service Organizations and Restorative Justice?', in H. Zehr, and B. Toews (eds), *Critical Issues in Restorative Justice*, Cullompton, Devon: Willan Publishing.
Ashworth, A. (2002), 'Responsibilities, Rights and Restorative Justice', *British Journal of Criminology*, 42: 578–95.
Ashworth, A. (2003), 'Is Restorative Justice the Way Forward for Criminal Justice?', in E. McLaughlin, R. Fergusson, G. Hughes, and L. Westmarland (eds), *Restorative Justice: Critical Issues*, London: Sage.
Association of Chief Police Officers (ACPO) (2000), *ACPO Guide to Identifying and Combating Hate Crime*, London: ACPO.
Association of Police Chief Officers (ACPO) (2005), *Hate Crime: Delivering a Quality Service: Good Practice and Tactical Guidance*, London: ACPO.
Association of Police Chief Officers (ACPO) (2012), *Total of Recorded Hate Crime from Regional Forces in England, Wales and Northern Ireland During the Calendar Year 2011*, London: ACPO.
Attorneys General's Department (2003), *You Shouldn't Have to Hide to be Safe*, Sydney: Attorney's General's Department of New South Wales.
Ball, J (2012), 'Data Showing How Young Black Men Have Been Hit By Unemployment', *Guardian*, 9 March 2012.
Bard, M. and Sangrey, D. (1979), *The Crime Victim's Book*, Brunner: Mazel Publisher, cited in Garnets, L., Herek, G., and Levy, B. (1992), 'Violence and Victimization of Lesbians and Gay Men: Mental Health Consequences', in L. Garnets and D. Kimmel (eds), *Psychological Perspectives on Lesbian, Gay, and Bisexual Experiences*, Chichester: Columbia University Press.

Barnes, A. and Ephross, P. (1994), 'The Impact of Hate Violence on Victims: Emotional and Behavioural Responses to Attacks', *Social Work*, 39(3): 247–51. Barnett, R. (1977), 'Restitution: A New Paradigm of Criminal Justice', *Ethics*, 87: 279–301.

Becker, H. (1963), *Outsiders: Studies in the Sociology of Deviance*, London: Free Press.

Bell, J. (1997), 'Policing Hatred: Bias Units and the Construction of Hate Crime', *Michigan Journal of Race and Law*, 2: 421–60.

Bell, J. (2002), *Policing Hatred: Law Enforcement, Civil Rights, and Hate Crime*, New York: New York University Press.

Bibbings, L. (2004), 'Heterosexuality as Harm: Fitting In', in P. Hillyard, C. Pantazis, S. Tombs, and D. Gordon (eds), *Beyond Criminology: Taking Harm Seriously*, London: Pluto Press.

Bottoms, A. (1995), 'The Philosophy and Politics of Punishment and Sentencing', in C. Clarkson and R. Morgan (eds), *The Politics of Sentencing Reform*, Oxford: Clarendon Press.

Bowling, B. (1993), 'Racial Harassment and the Process of Victimization: Conceptual and Methodological Implications for the Local Crime Survey', *British Journal of Criminology*, 33(2): 231–50.

Bowling, B. (1994), 'Racial Harassment in East London', in M. Hamm (ed), *Hate Crime: International Perspectives on Causes and Control*, Cincinnati: Anderson Publishing.

Bowling, B. (1998), *Violent Racism: Victimization, Policing, and Social Context*, Oxford: Oxford University Press.

Bowling, B. and Phillips, C. (2002), *Racism, Crime and Justice*, Harlow: Longman.

Bowling, B. and Phillips, C. (2003), 'Racist Victimization in England and Wales', in D. Hawkins (ed), *Violent Crime, Assessing Race & Ethnic Differences*, Cambridge: Cambridge University Press.

Bowling, B. and Phillips, C. (2007), 'Disproportionate and Discriminatory: Reviewing the Evidence on Stop and Search', *Modern Law Review*, 70(6): 936–61.

Boyes-Watson, C. (2004), 'What Are the Implications of the Growing State Involvement in Restorative Justice?', in H. Zehr and B. Toews (eds), *Critical Issues in Restorative Justice*, Cullompton, Devon: Willan Publishing.

Braithwaite, J. (1989), *Crime, Shame, and Reintegration*, Cambridge: Cambridge University Press.

Braithwaite, J. (1999), 'Restorative Justice: Assessing Optimistic and Pessimistic Accounts', *Crime & Justice*, 25: 1–127.

Braithwaite, J. (2002), *Restorative Justice and Responsive Regulation*, New York: Oxford University Press.

Braithwaite, J. (2003), 'Restorative Justice and Social Justice', in E. McLaughlin, R. Fergusson, G. Hughes, and L. Westmarland (eds), *Restorative Justice: Critical Issues*, London: Sage.

Braithwaite, J. and Braithwaite, V. (2001), 'Part I. Shame, Shame Management and Regulation', in E. Ahmed, N. Harris, J. Braithwaite, and

V. Braithwaite (eds), *Shame Management Through Reintegration*, Melbourne: Cambridge University Press.

Bridges, L. (1999), 'The Lawrence Enquiry—Incompetence, Corruption and Institutional Racism', *Journal of Law and Society*, 26 (3): 298–322.

Bruce, M., Roscigno, V., and McCall, P. (1998), 'Structure, Context and Agency in the Reproduction of Black-on-Black Violence', *Theoretical Criminology*, 2(1): 29–55.

Burke, M. (1993), *Coming out of the Blue*, London: Cassell.

Burney, E. and Rose, G. (2002), *Racist Offences: How Is the Law Working?*, London: Home Office.

Busch, R. (2002), 'Domestic Violence and Restorative Justice Initiatives: Who Pays if We get it Wrong?', in H. Strang, and J. Braithwaite (eds), *Restorative Justice and Family Violence*, Cambridge: Cambridge University Press.

Byers, B., Crider, B., and Biggers, G. (1999), 'Bias Crime Motivation: A Study of Hate Crime and Offender Neutralization Techniques Used Against the Amish', *Journal of Contemporary Criminal Justice*, 15(1): 78–96.

Chahal, K. and Julienne, L. (1999), *We Can't All Be White!': Racist Victimisation in the UK*, York: Joseph Rowntree Foundation.

Chakraborti, N. and Garland, J. (2009), *Hate Crime: Impact, Causes and Reponses*, London: Sage.

Chakraborti, N. and Garland, J. (2012), 'Reconceptualising Hate Crime Victimization through the Lens of Vulnerability and "Difference"', *Theoretical Criminology*, 16(4): 499–514.

Chakraborti, N. and Zempi, I. (2013), 'Criminalising Oppression or Reinforcing Oppression? The Implications of Veil Ban Laws for Muslim Women in the West', *Northern Ireland Legal Quarterly*, 64(1): 63–74.

Chan, J. (1997), *Changing Police Culture: Policing in a Multicultural Society*, Cambridge: Cambridge University Press.

Cheng, W., Ickes, W., and Kenworthy, J. B. (2013), 'The Phenomenon of Hate Crimes in the United States', *Journal of Applied Social Psychology*, 43: 761–94.

Christie, N. (1977), 'Conflicts as Property', *British Journal of Criminology*, 17(1): 1–15.

Christie, N. (1986), 'The Ideal Victim', in E. Fattah (ed), *From Crime Policy to Victim Policy*, Basingstoke: Macmillan.

Coates, R. B., Umbreit, M. S., and Vos, B. (2013), 'Responding to Hate Crimes Through Restorative Justice Dialogue', in G. Johnstone (ed), *A Restorative Justice Reader*, Abingdon: Routledge.

Cohen, S. (1985), *Visions of Social Control: Crime, Punishment and Classification*, Cambridge: Polity Press.

Coker, D. (2002), 'Transformative Justice: Anti-Subordination Processes in Cases of Domestic Violence', in H. Strang and J. Braithwaite (eds),

Restorative Justice and Family Violence, Cambridge: Cambridge University Press.

Considine, J. (1995), *Restorative Justice: Healing the Effects of Crime*, New Zealand: Ploughshares Books.

Craig, K. (2002), 'Examining Hate-Motivated Aggression: A Review of the Social Psychological Literature on Hate Crimes as a Distinct Form of Aggression', *Aggression and Violent Behaviour*, 7(1): 85–101.

Crawford, A. (2002), 'The State, Community and Restorative Justice: Heresy, Nostalgia and Butterfly Collecting', in L. Walgrave (ed), *Restorative Justice and the Law*, Cullompton, Devon: Willan Publishing.

Crawford, A. and Newburn, T. (2003), *Youth Offending and Restorative Justice: Implementing Reform in Youth Justice*, Cullompton, Devon: Willan Publishing.

Criminal Justice Joint Inspection (CJJI) (2012), *Facing Up To Offending: Use of Restorative Justice in the Criminal Justice System*, London: HMIC, HMI Probation, HMI Prisons, HMCPSI.

Criminal Justice Joint Inspection (CJJI) (2013), *Living in a Different World: Joint Review of Disability Hate Crime*, London: HMCPSI, HMIC, HMI Probation.

Crown Prosecution Service (2010), *Disability Hate Crime—Guidance on the Distinction between Vulnerability and Hostility in the Context of Crimes Committed against Disabled People*, London: CPS.

Crown Prosecution Service (2012), *Hate Crime and Crimes Against Older People Report 2010–2011*, London: CPS.

Cunneen, C. (1997), 'Community Conferencing and the Fiction of Indigenous Control', *Australian and New Zealand Journal of Criminology*, 30: 1–20.

Cunneen, C. (2003), 'Thinking Critically about Restorative Justice', in E. McLaughlin, R. Fergusson, G. Hughes, and L. Westmarland (eds), *Restorative Justice: Critical Issues*, London: Sage.

Cunneen, C. and Hoyle, C. (2010), *Debating Restorative Justice*, Oxford: Hart Publishing.

Daly, K. (1999), 'Restorative Justice in Diverse and Unequal Societies', *Law in Context*, 17(1): 167–90.

Daly, K. (2001), *South Australia Juvenile Justice Research on Conferencing Technical Report No. 2. Research Instruments in Year 2 (1999) and Background Notes*, Brisbane, Queensland; School of Criminology and Criminal Justice, Griffith University, <http://www.aic.gov.au/criminal_justice_system/rjustice/sajj/~/media/aic/rjustice/sajj/tech-report-2.pdf> (accessed 11 September 2011).

Daly, K. (2002a), 'Mind the Gap: Restorative Justice in Theory and Practice', in A. von Hirsh, J. Roberts, A. Bottoms, K. Roach, and M. Schiff (eds), *Restorative Justice and Criminal Justice: Competing or Reconcilable Paradigms?*, Oxford: Hart Publishing.

Daly, K. (2002b), 'Restorative Justice: The Real Story', *Punishment & Society*, 4(1): 55–79.

Daly, K. (2002c), 'Sexual Assault and Restorative Justice', in H. Strang and J. Braithwaite (eds), *Restorative Justice and Family Violence*, Cambridge: Cambridge University Press.

Daly, K. (2006), 'Restorative Justice and Sexual Assault: An Archival Study of Court and Conference Cases', *British Journal of Criminology*, 46(2): 334–56.

Daly, K. (2008), 'The Limits of Restorative Justice', in D. Sullivan and L. Tifft (eds), *Handbook of Restorative Justice: A Global Perspective*, Abingdon: Routledge.

Daly, K. and Immarigeon, R. (1998), 'The Past, Present and Future of Restorative Justice: Some Critical Reflections', *Contemporary Justice Review*, 1: 21–45.

Davis, M. H. (1983), 'Measuring Individual Differences in Empathy: Evidence for a Multidimensional Approach', *Journal of Personality and Social Psychology*, 44: 113–26.

Dick, S. (2008), *Homophobic Hate Crime: The Gay British Crime Survey 2008*, London: Stonewall.

Dignan, J. (2005), *Understanding Victims & Restorative Justice*, Cullompton, Devon: Willan Publishing.

Dixon, B. and Gadd, D. (2006), 'Getting the Message? "New" Labour and the Criminalization of "Hate"', *Criminology and Criminal Justice*, 6(3): 309–28.

Dunbar, E. (2006), 'Race, Gender, and Sexual Orientation in Hate Crime Victimization: Identity Politics or Identity Risk?', *Violence and Victims*, 21: 323–37.

Dunn, P. (2009), 'Crime and Prejudice: Needs and Support of Hate Crime Victims', in P. Iganski (ed.), *Hate Crimes*, Volume Two. London: Praeger.

Dzur, A. (2003), 'Civic Implications of Restorative Justice Theory: Citizen Participation and Criminal Justice Policy', *Policy Sciences*, 36: 279–306.

Dzur, A. and Olson, S. (2004), 'The Value of Community Participation in Restorative Justice', *Journal of Social Philosophy*, 35(1): 91–107.

Eglash, A. (1977), 'Beyond Restitution: Creative Restitution', in J. Hudson and B. Galaway (eds), *Restitution in Criminal Justice*, Lexington, MA: D.C. Heath.

Ehrlich, H. J. (2009), *Hate Crimes and Ethnoviolence: The History, Current Affairs, and Future of Discrimination in America*, Boulder, Colorado: Westview Press.

Ehrlich, H. J., Larcom, B., and Purvis, D. (1994), *The Traumatic Effect of Ethnoviolence*, Towson, MD: Prejudice Institute, Center for the Applied Study of Ethnoviolence.

Enright, R. and North, J. (eds) (1998), *Exploring Forgiveness*, Wisconsin: University of Wisconsin Press.

Fattah, E. (2004), 'Gearing Justice Action to Victim Satisfaction: Contrasting Two Justice Philosophies: Retribution and Redress', in H. J. R. Kaptein and M. Malsch (eds), *Crimes, Victims and Justice: Essays on Principles and Practice*, Aldershot: Ashgate Publishing.

Fekete, L. (2009), *A Suitable Enemy: Racism, Migration and Islamophobia in Europe*, London: Pluto Press.

Franklin, K. (2000), 'Antigay Behaviors Among Young Adults: Prevalence, Patterns, and Motivators in a Noncriminal Population', *Journal of Interpersonal Violence*, 15(4): 339–62.

Fuller, A. and Davey, G. (2010), *Equality Groups and Apprenticeship, EHRC Triennial Review: Education (Lifelong Learning)*, Southampton: University of Southampton.

Gadd, D. (2009), 'Aggravating Racism and Elusive Motivation', *British Journal of Criminology*, 49(6): 755–71.

Gadd, D., Dixon, B., and Jefferson, T. (2005), *Why Do They Do It? Racial Harassment in North Staffordshire*, Keele: Centre for Criminological Research, Keele University.

Garland, J. (2013), 'Tragedy, Prejudice and Opportunism: How the Murder of a Soldier Revitalised the English Defence League', *International Network for Hate Studies*, [blog] 3 June 2013, available at: <http://www.internationalhatestudies.com/tragedy-prejudice-and-opportunism-how-the-murder-of-a-soldier-revitalised-the-english-defence-league-2/> (accessed 1 September 2013).

Garland, J. and Chakraborti, N. (2006), 'Recognising and Responding to Victims of Rural Racism', *International Review of Victimology*, 13(1): 49–69.

Garland, J. and Chakraborti, N. (2007), '"Protean Times?" Exploring the Relationships Between Policing, Community and "Race" in Rural England', *Criminology and Criminal Justice: An International Journal*, 7(4): 347–66.

Garland, J. and Chakraborti, N. (2012), 'Divided By a Common Concept? Assessing the Implications of Different Conceptualisations of Hate Crime in the European Union', *European Journal of Criminology*, 9 (1): 38–51.

Garland, J., Spalek, B., and Chakraborti, N. (2006), 'Hearing Lost Voices: Issues in Researching "Hidden" Minority Ethnic Communities', *British Journal of Criminology*, 46(3): 423–37.

Garnets, L., Herek, G., and Levey, B. (1992), 'Violence and Victimization of Lesbians and Gay Men: Mental Health Consequences', in G. Herek and K. Berrill (eds), *Hate Crimes: Confronting Violence Against Lesbians and Gay Men*, Newbury Park: Sage.

Garofalo, J. (1997), 'Hate Crime Victimization in the United States', in R. Davies, A. Lurigio, and W. Skogan (eds), *Victims of Crime*, Thousand Oaks, CA: Sage.

Gavrielides, T. (2007), *Restorative Justice Theory and Practice: Addressing the Discrepancy*, New York: Criminal Justice Press.

Gavrielides, T. (2012), 'Contextualising Restorative Justice for Hate Crime', *Journal of Interpersonal Violence*, 18(27): 3624–43.

Gavrielides, T., Parle, L., Salla, A., Liberatore, G., Mavadia, C., and Arjomand, G. (2008), *Restoring Relationships: Addressing Hate Crime Through Restorative Justice and Multi-agency Partnerships*, London: ROTA.
Gerstenfeld, P. (2004), *Hate Crimes Causes, Controls, and Controversies*, London: Sage.
Gordon, P. (1994), 'Racist Harassment and Violence', in E. Stanko (ed), *Perspectives on Violence*, Howard League: London.
Gordon, P., McFalls, L., and Smith J. (2001), 'Hate Crime: An Emergent Research Agenda', *Annual Review of Sociology*, 27: 479–504.
Gordon, P., Strolovitch, D., and Wong, S. (1998), 'Defended Neighbourhoods, Integration, and Racially Motivated Crime', *American Journal of Sociology*, 104(2): 372–403.
Green, S. (2007), 'The Victims' Movement and Restorative Justice', in G. Johnstone and D. Van Ness (eds), *Handbook of Restorative Justice*, Cullompton, Devon: Willan Publishing.
Hall, N. (2005), *Hate Crime*, Cullompton, Devon: Willan Publishing.
Hall, N. (2010), 'Law Enforcement and Hate Crime: Theoretical Perspectives on the Complexities of Policing Hatred' in N. Chakraborti (ed), *Hate Crime: Concepts, Policy, Future Directions*, Collumpton, Devon: Willan Publishing.
Hall, N. (2013), *Hate Crime*, London: Routledge.
Haney, C. (2005), *Death by Design: Capital Punishment as a Social Psychological System*, New York: Oxford University Press.
Hare, I. (1997), 'Legislating Against Hate: The Legal Response to Bias Crime', *Oxford Journal of Legal Studies*, 17(3): 415–39.
Harris, N. and Maruna, S. (2008), 'Shame, Shaming and Restorative Justice: A Critical Appraisal', in D. Sullivan, and L. Tifft (eds), *Handbook of Restorative Justice: A Global Perspective*, Abingdon: Routledge.
Harris, N. Walgrave, L., and Braithwaite, B. (2004), 'Emotional Dynamics of Restorative Conferences', *Theoretical Criminology*, 8(2): 191–210.
Hayden A. (2013), 'The Promises and Pitfalls of Restorative Justice for Intimate Partner Violence'. IJRJ, available at <http://www.rj4all.info/library/promises-and-pitfalls-restorative-justice-intimate-partner-violence>.
Herman, S. (2004), 'Is Restorative Justice Possible Without A Parallel System for Victims?', in H. Zehr and B. Toews (eds), *Critical Issues in Restorative Justice*. Cullompton, Devon: Willan Publishing.
Herek, G. M. (2004), 'Beyond "Homophobia": Thinking about Sexual Stigma and Prejudice in the Twenty-first Century', *Sexuality Research and Social Policy*, 1(2): 6–24.
Herek, G. M. and Berrill, K. (eds) (1992), *Hate Crimes: Confronting Violence Against Lesbians and Gay Men*, Thousand Oaks, CA: Sage.
Herek, G. M., Cogan, J., and Gillis, J. (1999), 'Psychological Sequelae of Hate-Crime Victimization Among Lesbian, Gay, and Bisexual Adults', *Journal of Consulting and Clinical Psychology*, 67(6): 945–51.

Herek, G. M., Cogan, J., and Gillis, J. (2002), 'Victim Experiences in Hate Crimes Based on Sexual Orientation', *Journal of Social Issues*, 58(2): 319–39.

Herek, G. M., Cogan, J., Gillis, J., and Glunt, E. (1997), 'Hate Crime Victimization Among Lesbian, Gay, and Bisexual Adults: Prevalence, Psychological Correlates, and Methodological Issues', *Journal of Interpersonal Violence*, 12(2): 195–215.

Hillyard, P., Pantazis, C., Tombs, S., and Gordon, D. (eds) (2004), *Beyond Criminology: Taking Harm Seriously*, London: Pluto Press.

Holland, B. (2011, June), *Making Restorative Approaches Inclusive for People with Special Needs*. Paper presented at Oxfordshire Restorative Justice Network, Worcester College, University of Oxford.

Holter, A., Martin, J., and Enright, D. (2007), 'Restoring Justice Through Forgiveness: The Case of Children in Northern Ireland', in G. Johnstone and D. Van Ness (eds), *Handbook of Restorative Justice*, Cullompton, Devon: Willan Publishing.

Home Office (1981), *Racial Attacks*, London: HMSO.

Home Office (2005a), *Improving Opportunity, Strengthening Society: The Government's Strategy to Increase Race Equality and Community Cohesion*, London: Home Office.

Home Office (2005b), *Race Equality in Public Services*, London: Home Office.

Home Office (2013), *Hate Crimes, England and Wales 2011–2012*, London: Home Office.

Home Office, Office for National Statistics and Ministry of Justice (2013), *An Overview of Hate Crime in England and Wales*, London: Home Office, Office for National Statistics and Ministry of Justice.

Hood, R. (1992), *Race and Sentencing*, Oxford: Oxford University Press.

House of Commons Home Affairs Committee (2009), *The Macpherson Report—Ten Years On*, Twelfth Report of Session 2008–09, London: House of Commons.

Hoyle, C. (2002), 'Securing Restorative Justice for the Non-Participating Victims', in C. Hoyle and R. Young (eds), *New Visions of Crime Victims*, Oxford: Hart Publishing.

Hoyle, C. (2007), 'Policing and Restorative Justice', in G. Johnstone, and D. Van Ness (eds), *Handbook of Restorative Justice*, Cullompton, Devon: Willan Publishing.

Hoyle, C. (2012), 'Victims, Victimisation and Restorative Justice' in M. Maguire, R. Morgan, and R. Reiner (eds), *The Oxford Handbook of Criminology*, (Oxford: Oxford University Press.

Hoyle, C. and Zedner, L. (2007), 'Victims, Victimization, and Criminal Justice', in M. Maguire, R. Morgan, and R. Reiner (eds), *Oxford Handbook of Criminology*, Oxford: Oxford University Press.

Hoyle, C., Young, R., and Hill, R. (2002), *Proceed with Caution: An Evaluation of the Thames Valley Police Initiative in Restorative Cautioning*, York: Joseph Rowntree Foundation.

Hudson, B. (1998), 'Restorative Justice: The Challenge of Sexual and Racial Violence', *Journal of Law and Society*, 25: 237–56.
Hudson, B. (2003), *Justice in the Risk Society*, London: Sage.
Hunter, C., Hodge, N., Nixon, J., Parr, S., and Willis, B. (2007), *Disabled People's Experiences of Anti-Social Behaviour and Harassment in Social Housing: A Critical Review*, London: Disability Rights Commission.
Hurd, H. (2001), 'Why Liberals Should Hate "Hate Crime Legislation"', *Law and Philosophy*, 20(2): 215–32.
Idriss Mazher, M. [2002], 'Religion and the Anti-Terrorism, Crime and Security Act 2001', *Criminal Law Review*, 890–911.
Iganski, P. (1999), 'Why Make Hate a Crime?', *Critical Social Policy*, 19(3): 386–95.
Iganski, P. (2001), 'Hate Crimes Hurt More', *American Behavioural Scientist*, 45(4): 626–38.
Iganski, P. (2002), 'Hate Crime Hurts More But Should They Be Punished More Harshly?', in P. Iganski (ed), *The Hate Debate*, London: Profile Books.
Iganski, P. (2008), *Hate Crime and the City*, Bristol: The Policy Press.
Jackson, A. L. (2009), 'The Impact of Restorative Justice on the Development of Guilt, Shame, and Empathy Among Participants in a Victim Impact Training Program', *Victims and Offenders*, 4(1): 1–24.
Jacobs, J. and Potter, K. (1998), *Hate Crimes*, New York: Oxford University Press.
James, Z. (2007), 'Policing Marginal Spaces: Controlling Gypsies and Travellers', *Criminology and Criminal Justice*, 7(4): 367–89.
Jantzi, V. (2004), 'What Is the Role of the State in Restorative Justice?', in H. Zehr and B. Toews (eds), *Critical Issues in Restorative Justice*. Cullompton, Devon: Willan Publishing.
Jenness, V. (2002), 'Contours of Hate Crime Politics and Law in the United States', in P. Iganski (ed), *The Hate Debate: Should Hate Be a Crime?* London: Jewish Policy Research.
Jenness, V. and Grattet, R. (2001), *Making Hate a Crime: From Social Movement to Law Enforcement*, New York: Russell Sage.
Jiwani, Y. (2005), 'Walking a Tightrope: The Many Faces of Violence in the Lives of Racialized Immigrant Girls and Young Women', *Violence Against Women, An International and Interdisciplinary Journal*, 11(7): 846–87.
Johnson, K., Faulkner, P., Jones, H., and Welsh, E. (2007), *Understanding Suicide and Promoting Survival in LGBT Communities*, Brighton: University of Brighton.
Johnstone, G. and Van Ness, D. (2007a), 'The Meaning of Restorative Justice', in G. Johnstone and D. Van Ness (eds), *Handbook of Restorative Justice*, Cullompton, Devon: Willan Publishing.
Johnstone, G. and Van Ness, D. (eds) (2007b), *Handbook of Restorative Justice*, Cullompton, Devon: Willan Publishing.

Kauffman, J. (2008), 'Restoration of the Assumptive World as an Act of Justice', in D. Sullivan and L. Tifft (eds), *Handbook of Restorative Justice: A Global Perspective*, Abingdon: Routledge.

Kay, J. W. (2008), 'Murder Victims' Families for Reconciliation: Storytelling for Healing, as Witness and in Public Policy', in D. Sullivan and L. Tifft (eds), *Handbook of Restorative Justice: A Global Perspective*, Abingdon: Routledge.

Kelly, T. L. (2002), 'Is Restorative Justice Appropriate in Cases of Hate Crime' (published in the Western Pacific Association of Criminal Justice Educators Conference Papers, Lake Tahoe: Nevada).

Kennedy, P. and Roudometof, V. (2004), 'Transformation in a Global Age', in P. Kennedy and V. Roudometof (eds), *Communities Across Borders: New Immigrants and Transnational Cultures*, London: Routledge.

Kenway, P. and Palmer, G. (2007), *Poverty Among Ethnic Groups: How and Why Does It Differ?*, London: New Policy Institute.

Kurki, L. (2000), 'Restorative and Community Justice in the United States', *Crime and Justice: A Review of Research*, 27: 235–303.

Lash, S. (1994), 'Reflexivity and its Doubles: Structure, Aesthetics, Community', in U. Beck, A. Giddens, and S. Lash (eds), *Reflexive Modernization: Politics, Tradition and Aesthetics in Modern Social Order*, Cambridge: Polity Press.

Latimer, J., Dowden, C., and Muise, D. (2005), 'The Effectiveness of Restorative Justice Practices: A Meta-Analysis', *The Prison Journal*, 85(2): 127–44.

Lawrence, F. (1999), *Punishing Hate: Bias Crimes under American Law*, London: Harvard University Press.

Lawrence, F. (2002), 'Racial Violence on a "Small Island": Bias Crime in a Multicultural Society', in P. Iganski (ed), *The Hate Debate*, London: Profile Books.

Levin, B. (1999), 'Hate Crime: Worse by Definition', *Journal of Contemporary Justice*, 15(1): 6–21.

Levin, J. (2002), 'Hatemongers, Dabblers, Sympathizers and Spectators: A Typology of Offenders', in P. Iganski (ed), *The Hate Debate*, London: Profile Books.

Levin, J. and McDevitt, J. (1993), *Hate Crimes: The Rising Tide of Bigotry & Bloodshed*, New York: Plenum.

Levin, J. and McDevitt, J. (2002), *Hate Crimes Revisited: America's War on Those Who Are Different*, New York: Basic Books.

Liebmann, M. (2000), 'History and Overview of Mediation in the UK', in M. Liebmann (ed), *Mediation in Context*, London: Jessica Kingsley Publishers.

Llewellyn, J. (2007), 'Truth Commissions and Restorative Justice', in G. Johnstone and D. Van Ness (eds), *Handbook of Restorative Justice*, Cullompton, Devon: Willan Publishing.

Lyons, T., Lurigio, A., Roque, L., and Rodriguez, P. (2013), 'Racial Disproportionality in the Criminal Justice System for Drug Offenses: A State Legislative Response to the Problem', *Race and Justice*, 3(1): 83–101.

Mackie, D. M. (1986), 'Social Identification Effects in Group Polarization', *Journal of Personality and Social Psychology*, 50(4): 720–8.

Macpherson, W. (1999), *The Stephen Lawrence Inquiry*, Cm 4262-I, London: The Stationery Office.

Malik, M. (1999), '"Racist Crime": Racially Aggravated Offences in the Crime and Disorder Act 1998 Part II', *Modern Law Review*, 62: 409–24.

Maroney, T. (1998), 'The Struggle against Hate Crime: Movement at a Crossroads', *New York University Law Review*, 73: 564–620.

Marshall, T. (1999), *Restorative Justice: An Overview*, Research Development and Statistics Directorate, London: Home Office.

Maruna, S., Wright, S., Brown, J., Van Marle, F., Devlin, R., and Liddle, M. (2007), *Youth Conferencing as Shame Management: Results of a Long-term Follow-Up Study*, Belfast: Youth Conferencing Service.

Mason, G. (2005), 'Hate Crime and the Image of the Stranger', *British Journal of Criminology*, 45(6): 837–59.

Mason-Bish, H. (2010), 'Future Challenges for Hate Crime Policy: Lessons From the Past', in N. Chakraborti (ed), *Hate Crime: Concepts, Policy, Future Directions*, Cullompton, Devon: Willan Publishing.

Matza, D. (1969), *Becoming Deviant*, Englewood Cliffs, NJ: Prentice-Hall.

Maxwell, G. (2008), 'Crossing Cultural Boundaries: Implementing Restorative Justice in International and Indigenous Contexts', *Sociology of Crime Law and Deviance*, 11: 81–95.

Maxwell, G. and Morris, A. (1993), *Families, Victims and Culture: Youth Justice in New Zealand*, Wellington: Institute of Criminology, Victoria University of Wellington and Social Policy Agency.

Maxwell, G. and Morris, A. (2002), 'The Role of Shame, Guilt, and Remorse in Restorative Justice Processes for Young People', in E. Weitekamp and H. Kerner (eds), *Restorative Justice: Theoretical Foundations*, Cullompton, Devon: Willan Publishing.

Maxwell, G. and Morris, A. (2006), 'Youth Justice in New Zealand: Restorative Justice in Practice?' *Journal of Social Issues*, 62(2): 239–79.

Maxwell, G. Robertson, J., Kingi, V., Morris, A., and Cunningham, C., with Lash, B. (2004), *Achieving Effective Outcomes in Youth Justice: The Full Report*, Wellington: Ministry of Social Development.

McCold, P. (1996), 'Restorative Justice and the Role of Community', in B. Galaway and J. Hudson (eds), *Restorative Justice: International Perspectives*, Monsey, NY: Criminal Justice Press.

McCold, P. (2000), 'Toward a Holistic Vision of Restorative Juvenile Justice: A Reply to the Maximalist Model', *Contemporary Justice Review*, 3: 357–414.

McCold, P. (2004), 'What Is The Role of Community In Restorative Justice Theory And Practice?', in H. Zehr and B. Toews (eds), *Critical Issues in Restorative Justice*, Cullompton, Devon: Willan Publishing.

McCold, P. and Wachtel, B. (1997), 'Community Is Not a Place: A New Look at Community Justice Initiatives', paper presented to the International Conference on Justice without Violence: Views from Peacemaking Criminology and Restorative Justice, Albany, New York, 5–7 June 1997.

McCold, P. and Wachtel, B. (1998), *The Bethlehem Pennsylvania Police Family Group Conferencing Project*, Pipersville: Community Service Foundation.

McConnell, S. and Swain, J. (2000), 'Victim–Offender Mediation with Adolescents Who Commit Hate Crimes' (paper presented at the Annual Conference of the American Psychological Association, Washington DC, 4–8 August).

McDevitt, J., Balboni, J., Garcia, L., and Gu, J. (2001), 'Consequences for Victims: A Comparison of Bias- and Non-bias-Motivated Assaults', *American Behavioral Scientist*, 45(4): 697–713.

McDevitt, J., Levin, J. and Bennett, S. (2002), 'Hate Crime Offenders: An Expanded Typology', *Journal of Social Issues*, 58(2): 303–17.

McGarrel, E., Olivares, K., Crawford, K., and Kroovand, N. (2000), *Returning Justice to the Community: The Indianapolis Restorative Justice Experiment*, Indianapolis: Hudson Institute.

McGhee, D. (2005), *Intolerant Britain?: Hate, Citizenship and Difference*, Maidenhead: Open University Press.

McGhee, D. (2008), *The End of Multiculturalism? Terrorism, Integration and Human Rights*, Maidenhead: Open University Press.

McGlynn, C., Westmarland, N., and Godden, N. (2012), '"I Just Wanted Him to Hear Me": Sexual Violence and the Possibilities of Restorative Justice', *Journal of Law and Society*, 39(2): 213–40.

McLagan, G. and Lowles, N. (2000), *Mr. Bad: The Secret Life of Racist Bomber and Killer David Copeland*, London: John Blake Publishing.

Merry, P. (2009), 'Youth Restorative Disposals in Norfolk' (paper given at the Association of Panel Members Annual Conference, 7 April).

Messner, S. F., Mchugh, S., and Felson, R. B. (2004), 'Distinctive Characteristics of Assaults Motivated by Bias', *Criminology*, 42: 585–618.

Miers, D., Maguire, M., Goldie, S., Sharpe, K., Hale, C., Netten, A., Uglow, S., Doolin, K., Hallam, A., Enterkin J., and Newburn, T. (2001), *Crime Reduction Research Series Paper 9: An Explanatory Evaluation of Restorative Justice Schemes*, London: Home Office.

Milmo, C. and Morris, N. (2013), 'Woolwich Backlash: Ten Attacks on Mosques Since Murder of Drummer Lee Rigby', *The Independent*, 28 May.

MIND (2007), *Another Assault*, London: MIND, available at <http://www.independent.co.uk/news/uk/crime/woolwich-backlash-ten-attacks-on-mosques-since-murder-of-drummer-lee-rigby-8633594.html>.

References

Ministry of Justice (2012), *Referral Order Guidance*, London: Ministry of Justice.

Ministry of Justice (2012), *Restorative Justice Action Plan for the Criminal Justice System*, London: Ministry of Justice.

Ministry of Justice (2013), *Draft Code of Practice for Victims of Crime*, London: Ministry of Justice.

Moore, D. B. and O'Connell, T. (1994), 'Family Conferencing in Wagga Wagga: A Communitarian Model of Justice', in C. Alder and J. Wundersitz (eds.), *Family Conferencing and Juvenile Justice: The Way Forward or Misplaced Optimism?* Canberra: Australian Institute of Criminology.

Moran, L. and Skeggs, B., with Tyrer, P., and Corteen, K. (2004a), *Sexuality and the Politics of Violence and Saftey*, London: Routledge Taylor & Francis Group.

Moran, L., Paterson, S., Tor Docherty, T. (2004b), *'Count me in!': A Report on the Bexley and Greenwich Homophobic Crime Survey*, London: Bexley and Greenwich Council.

Morris, A. and Young, W. (2000), 'Reforming Criminal Justice: The Potential of Restorative Justice', in H. Strang and J. Braithwaite (eds), *Restorative Justice: Philosophy to Practice*, Dartmouth: Ashgate Publishing.

Morrison, B. (2007), 'Schools and Restorative Justice', in G. Johnstone and D. Van Ness (eds), *Handbook of Restorative Justice*, Cullompton, Devon: Willan Publishing.

Morsch, J. (1991), 'Problem of Motive in Hate Crimes: The Argument against Presumptions of Racial Motivation', *Journal of Criminal Law & Criminology*, 82(3): 659–89.

Netto, G. and Abazie, H. (2012), 'Racial Harassment in Social Housing: the Case for Moving Beyond Action Against Individual Perpetrators', *Urban Studies*, 50(4): 1–17.

Newburn, T., Crawford, A., Earle, R., Goldie, S., Hale, C., Hallam, A., Masters, G., Netten, A., Saunders, R., Sharpe, K., and Uglow, S. (2002), *The Introduction of Referral Orders into the Youth Justice System: Final Report*, London: Home Office.

Newburn, T., Shiner, M., and Hayman, S. (2004), 'Race, Crime and Injustice?: Strip Search and the Treatment of Suspects in Custody', *British Journal of Criminology*, 44(5): 677–94.

Noakes, L. and Wincup, E. (2004), *Criminological Research: Understanding Qualitative Methods*, London: Sage.

Noelle, M. (2002), 'The Ripple Effect of the Matthew Shepard Murder: Impact on the Assumptive Worlds of Members of the Targeted Group', *American Behavioral Scientist*, 46: 27–50.

Noelle, M. (2009), 'The Psychological and Social Effects of Antibisexual, Antigay, and Antilesbian Violence and Harassment', in P. Iganski (ed), *Hate Crimes*, Volume Two. London: Praeger.

O'Brien, M. (2000), 'The Macpherson Report and Institutional Racism', in D. Green (ed), *Institutional Racism and the Police: Fact or Fiction?*, London: Institute for the Study of Civil Society.

References

Office for Democratic Institutions and Human Rights (ODIHR) (2013), *Hate Crimes in the OSCE Region—Incidents and Responses—Annual Report for 2012*, Warsaw: ODIHR, OSCE.

Olsen, W. (2004), 'Triangulation in Social Research: Qualitative and Quantitative Can Really be Mixed', in M. Holborn (ed), *Developments in Sociology*, Ormskirk: Causeway Press.

O'Mahony, D. and Deazley, R. (2000), *Juvenile Crime and Justice: Review of the Criminal Justice System in Northern Ireland*, London: HMSO.

O'Mahony, D. and Doak, J. (2004), 'Restorative Justice—Is More Better? The Experience of Police-led Restorative Cautioning Pilots in Northern Ireland', *Howard Journal of Criminal Justice*, 43(5): 484–505.

O'Mahony, D. and Doak, J. (2013), 'Restorative Justice and Police-Led Cautioning', in Johnstone, G. (ed), *A Restorative Justice Reader*. Abingdon, Routledge.

O'Mahony, D., Chapman, T., and Doak, J. (2002), *Restorative Cautioning: A Study of Police Based Restorative Cautioning Pilots in Northern Ireland*, Northern Ireland Office Research & Statistical Series: Report No. 4, Belfast: Northern Ireland Statistics & Research Agency.

Pavlich, G. (2004), 'What Are the Dangers as Well as the Promises of Community Involvement?', in H. Zehr and B. Toews (eds), *Critical Issues in Restorative Justice*, Cullompton, Devon: Willan Publishing.

Perry, B. (2001), *In the Name of Hate: Understanding Hate Crimes*, New York: Routledge.

Perry, B. (2003), 'Where Do We Go From Here? Researching Hate Crime'. *Internet Journal of Criminology*, 1–59.

Perry, B. and Alvi, S. (2012), '"We Are All Vulnerable": The In Terrorem Effects of Hate Crimes', *International Review of Victimology*, 18(1): 57–71.

Phillips, C., and Bowling, B. (2007), 'Racism, Ethnicity, Crime and Criminal Justice', in M. Maguire, R. Morgan, and R. Reiner (eds), *Oxford Handbook of Criminology*, Oxford: Oxford University Press.

Quarmby, K. (2008), *Getting Away With Murder: Disabled People's Experiences of Hate Crime in the UK*, London: SCOPE.

Raye, B. (2004), 'How Do Culture, Class and Gender Affect the Practice of Restorative Justice? (Part 2)' in H. Zehr and B. Toews, (eds), *Critical Issues in Restorative Justice*, Cullompton, Devon: Willan Publishing.

Raye, B. and Roberts, A. (2007), 'Restorative Processes', in G. Johnstone and D. Van Ness (eds), *Handbook of Restorative Justice*, Cullompton, Devon: Willan Publishing.

Ray, L. and Smith, D. (2002), 'Hate crime, violence and cultures of racism', in P. Iganski (ed), *The Hate Debate*, London: Profile Books.

Ray, L., Smith, D., and Wastell, L. (2004), 'Shame, Rage and Racist Violence', *British Journal of Criminology*, 44(3): 350–68.

Reiner, R. (2000), *The Politics of the Police*, Oxford: Oxford University Press.

Reiner, R. (2010), *The Politics of the Police*, Oxford: Oxford University Press.
Restorative Justice Council (2011), *RJC Code of Practice for Trainers and Training Organisations of Restorative Practice*, London: RJC, <http://www.restorativejustice.org.uk/resource/rjc_code_of_practice_for_trainers_and_training_organisations_of_restorative_practice__january_2011/> (accessed September 2011).
Retzinger, S. and Scheff, T. (1996), 'Strategy for Community Conferences: Emotions and Social Bonds', in B. Galaway and J. Hudson (eds), *Restorative Justice: International Perspectives*, Monsey, NY: Criminal Justice Press.
Rice, S. (2003), 'Restorative Justice: A Victim's Personal Exploration Towards Acceptance' (paper presented at the Sixth International Conference on Restorative Justice June 1–4). Full text accessed at: <http://www.sfu.ca/restorative_justice/cresources.html>.
Robinson, G. and Shapland, J. (2008), 'Reducing Recidivism: A Task for Restorative Justice?', *British Journal of Criminology*, 48(3): 337–58.
Roulstone, A., Thomas, P. and Balderson, S. (2011), 'Between Hate and Vulnerability: Unpacking the British Criminal Justice System's Construction of Disablist Hate Crime' *Disability and Society* 26(3): 351–64.
Rowe, M. (2004), *Policing, Race and Racism*, Cullompton, Devon: Willan Publishing.
Rowe, M. and Garland, J. (2007), 'Police Diversity Training: A Silver Bullet Tarnished?', in M. Rowe (ed), *Policing Beyond Macpherson*, Cullompton, Devon: Willan Publishing.
Sawin, J. and Zehr, H. (2007), 'The Ideas of Engagement and Empowerment', in G. Johnstone and D. Van Ness (eds), *Handbook of Restorative Justice*, Cullompton, Devon: Willan Publishing.
Scarman, Lord J. (1981), *The Brixton Disorders, 10–12th April (1981)*, London: HMSO.
Schiff, M. (2007), 'Satisfying the Needs and Interests of Stakeholders', in G. Johnstone and D. Van Ness (eds), *Handbook of Restorative Justice*, Cullompton, Devon: Willan Publishing.
Schweigert, F. J. (1999a), 'Learning the Common Good: Principles of Community-Based Moral Education in Restorative Justice', *Journal of Moral Education* 28(2): 163–83.
Schweigert, F. J. (1999b), 'Moral Education in Victim Offender Conferencing', *Criminal Justice Ethics* 18(2): 29–40.
Shapland, J., Atkinson, A., Atkinson, H., Chapman, B., Colledge, E., Dignan, J., Howes, M., Johnstone, J., Robinson, G., and Sorsby, A. (2006), *Restorative Justice in Practice: The Second Report from the Evaluation of Three Schemes*, Sheffield: The University of Sheffield Centre for Criminological Research.
Shapland, J., Atkinson, A., Atkinson, H., Chapman, B., Dignan, J., Howes, M., Johnstone, J., Robinson G., and Sorsby, A. (2007), *Restorative Justice:*

The Views of Victims and Offenders: The Third Report from the Evaluation of Three Schemes, London: Ministry of Justice Research.

Sharpe, S. (2007), 'The Idea of Reparation', in G. Johnstone and D. Van Ness (eds), *Handbook of Restorative Justice*, Cullompton, Devon: Willan Publishing.

Sheffield, C. (1995), 'Hate Violence', in P. Rothenberg (ed), *Race, Class and Gender in the United States*, New York: St. Martin's Press.

Shenk, A. (2001), 'Victim–Offender Mediation: The Road to Repairing Hate Crime Injustice', *Ohio State Journal on Dispute Resolution*, 17: 185–217.

Sherman, L. and Strang, H. (2007), *Restorative Justice: The Evidence*, London: The Smith Institute.

Sherman, L., Strang, H., Angel, C., Woods, D., Barnes, G., Bennet, S., and Inkpen, N. (2005), 'Effects of Face-to-Face Restorative Justice on Victims of Crime in Four Randomized Controlled Trials', *Journal of Experimental Criminology*, 1(3): 367–95.

Sherman, L., Strang, H., Barnes, G., Braithwaite, J., Inkpen, N., and Teh, M. (1998), *Experiments in Restorative Policing: A Progress Report on the Canberra Reintegrative Shaming Experiments (RISE)*, Australian Federal Police and Australian National University

Sherman, L., Strang, H., and Woods, J. (2000), *Recidivism Patterns in the Canberra Reintegrative Shaming Experiments (RISE)*, Canberra: Centre for Restorative Justice.

Sibbitt, R. (1997), *The Perpetrators of Racial Harassment and Racial Violence*, Home Office Research Study 176, London: Home Office.

Simester, A. P. and von Hirsch, A. (2011), *Crimes, Harms and Wrongs: On the Principles of Criminalisation*, Oxford: Hart Publishing.

Smith, K. (2006), 'Dissolving the Divide: Cross-Racial Communication in the Restorative Justice Process', *Dalhousie Journal of Legal Studies*, 15: 168–203.

Smith, K., Lader, D., Hoare, J., and Lau, I. (2012), *Hate Crime, Cyber Security and the Experience of Crime Among Children: Findings From the 2010/11 British Crime Survey: Supplementary Volume 3 to Crime in England and Wales 2010/11* (Home Office).

Snow, P. C., and Sanger, D. D. (2011), 'Restorative Justice Conferencing and the Youth Offender: Exploring the Role of Oral Language Competence', *International Journal of Language & Communication Disorders*, 46(3): 324–33.

Southwark Council, Southwark Probation, and Southwark Primary Care Trust (2005), *Southwark Supporting People five year strategy 2005–2010*, London: Southwark Council, Southwark Probation, and Southwark Primary Care Trust.

Spalek, B. (2006), *Crime Victims: Theory, Policy and Practice*, Hampshire: Palgrave Macmillan.

Spalek, B. (2008), *Communities, Identities and Crime*, Bristol: The Policy Press.

Spohn, C. and Holleran, D. (2000), 'The Imprisonment Penalty Paid by Young Unemployed Black and Hispanic Male Offenders', *Criminology*, 38(1): 281–306.

Stanko, E. (2001), 'Re-conceptualising the Policing of Hatred: Confessions and Worrying Dilemmas of a Consultant', *Law and Critique*, 12: 309–29.

Stanton-Ife, J. (2013), 'Criminalising Conduct with Special Reference to Potential Offences of Stirring Up Hatred Against Disabled or Transgender Persons', Law Commission.

Strang, H. (2002), *Repair or Revenge: Victims and Restorative Justice*, Oxford: Oxford University Press.

Strang, H. and Braithwaite, B. (2002), *Restorative Justice and Family Violence*, Cambridge: Cambridge University Press.

Strang, H. and Sherman, L. (2003), 'Repairing the Harm: Victims and Restorative Justice', *Utah Law Review*, 15(1): 15–42.

Strang, H. and Sherman, L. with Angel, C., Woods, D., Bennett, S., Newbury-Birch, D., and Inkpen, N. (2006), 'Victim Evaluations of Face-to-Face Restorative Justice Conferences: A Quasi-Experimental Analysis', *Journal of Social Issues*, 62: 281–306.

Strang, H., Sherman, L., Woods, D., and Barnes, G. (2011), *Experiments in Restorative Policing: Final Report. Canberra Reintegrative Shaming Experiments (RISE)*, Canberra: Regulatory Institutions Network, College of Asia and the Pacific, and Australian National University.

Stubbs, J. (2007), 'Beyond Apology? Domestic Violence and Critical Questions for Restorative Justice', *Criminology and Criminal Justice*, 7(2): 169–87.

Sullivan, A. (1999), 'What's So Bad About Hate: An Unsentimental Reflection on Schoolyard Shootings, Matthew Shepard, Genocide and the Easy Consensus on Hate Crimes', *New York Times*, 26 September, <http://www.nytimes.com/1999/09/26/magazine/what-s-so-bad-about-hate.html?pagewanted=8> (accessed 11 September 2013)

Sullivan, D. and Tifft, L. (2001), *Restorative Justice: Healing the Foundations of Our Everyday Lives*, Monsey: Willow Tree Press.

Sullivan, D. and Tifft, L. (eds) (2008a), *Handbook of Restorative Justice: A Global Perspective*, Abingdon: Routledge.

Sullivan, D. and Tifft, L. (2008b), 'Section III: The Needs of Victims and the Healing Process', in D. Sullivan and L. Tifft (eds), *Handbook of Restorative Justice: A Global Perspective*, Abingdon: Routledge.

Sykes, G. and Matza, D. (1957), 'Techniques of Neutralization: A Theory of Delinquency', *American Sociological Review*, 22: 664–70.

Talbot, J. (2010), *Seen and Heard: Supporting Vulnerable Children in the Youth Justice System*, London: Prison Reform Trust.

Tangney, J. P. (1991), 'Moral Affect: The Good, the Bad, and the Ugly', *Journal of Personality and Social Psychology*, 61: 598–607.

Tomsen, S. (2009), *Violence, Prejudice and Sexuality*, London & New York: Routledge.

Triggs, S. (2005), *New Zealand Court-Referred Restorative Justice Pilot: Evaluation*, Wellington: New Zealand Ministry of Justice.

Umbreit, M., and Coates, R. (1993),'Cross-Site Analysis of Victim–Offender Mediation in Four States', *Crime & Delinquency*, 39(4): 565–85.

Umbreit, M., and Coates, R. (2000), *Multicultural Implications of Restorative Justice: Potential Pitfalls and Dangers*, Center for Restorative Justice & Peacemaking, St. Paul, Minnesota: University of Minnesota.

Umbreit, M., Coates, R., and Roberts, A. (2000), 'The Impact of Victim–Offender Mediation: A Cross-National Perspective', *Mediation Quarterly*, 17(3): 215–29.

Umbreit, M., Coates, R., and Vos, B. (2001), *Juvenile Victim Offender Mediation in Six Oregon Counties: Final Report*, Oregon: Dispute Resolutions Commission.

Umbreit, M., Coates, R., and Vos, B. (2002), *Community Peacemaking Project: Responding to Hate Crimes, Hate Incidents, Intolerance, and Violence Through Restorative Justice Dialogue*, Minnesota: Center for Restorative Justice.

Van Camp, T. and Wemmers, J-A. (2013),'Victim Satisfaction with Restorative Justice', *International Review of Victimology*, 19(2): 117–43.

Van Stokkom, B. (2002), 'Moral Emotions in Restorative Justice Conferences: Managing Shame, Designing Empathy', *Theoretical Criminology* 6(3): 339–60.

Victim Support (2006), *Crime & Prejudice: The Support Needs of Victims of Hate Crime: A Research Report*, London: Victim Support.

Walgrave, L. (2002), 'From Community to Dominion: In Search of Social Values for Restorative Justice', in E. Weitekamp and H. Kerner (eds), *Restorative Justice: Theoretical Foundations*, Cullompton, Devon: Willan Publishing.

Walgrave, L. (2007),'Integrating Criminal Justice and Restorative Justice', in G. Johnstone and D. Van Ness (eds), *Handbook of Restorative Justice*, Cullompton, Devon: Willan Publishing.

Walklate, S. (2008), 'Changing Boundaries of the "Victim" in Restorative Justice: So Who Is the Victim Now?', in D. Sullivan, and L. Tifft (eds), *Handbook of Restorative Justice: A Global Perspective*, Abingdon: Routledge.

Walters, M. (2005), 'Hate Crimes in Australia: Introducing Punishment Enhancers', *Criminal Law Journal*, 29(4): 201–16.

Walters, M. (2011),'A General *Theories* of Hate Crime? Strain, Doing Difference and Self Control', *Critical Criminology*, 19(4): 331–50.

Walters, M. (2012),'Hate Crime in the UK: Promoting the Values of Dignity and Respect for Young Victims Through Restorative Justice', in

T. Gavrielides (ed) *Rights and Restoration Within Youth Justice*, Whitby, Ontario: de Sitter Publications.

Walters, M. (2013a), 'Conceptualising "Hostility" for Hate Crime Law: Minding "the Minutiae" when Interpreting Section 28(1)(a) of the Crime and Disorder Act 1998' *Oxford Journal of Legal Studies*, doi: 10.1093/ojls/gqt021.

Walters, M. (2013b), 'Why the Rochdale Gang Should Have Been Sentenced as "Hate Crime" Offenders', *Criminal Law Review* 2: 131–44.

Walters, M. (2014), 'Restorative Approaches to Working with Hate Crime Offenders', in N Chakraborti and J Garland, *Hate Crime: The Case for Connecting Policy and Research*, Bristol: Policy Press.

Walters, M. and Hoyle, C. (2010), 'Healing Harms and Engendering Tolerance: The Promise of Restorative Justice for Hate Crime', in N. Chakraborti (ed), *Hate Crime: Concepts, Policy, Future Directions*, Cullompton, Devon: Willan Publishing.

Walters, M. and Hoyle, C. (2012), 'Exploring the Everyday World of Hate Victimisation through Community Mediation', *International Review of Victimology*, 18(1): 7–24.

Weinstein, J. (1992), 'First Amendment Challenges to Hate Crime Legislation: Where's the Speech?', *Criminal Justice Ethics*, 11(2): 6–20.

Weisberg, R. (2003), 'Restorative Justice and the Danger of "Community"', *Utah Law Review*, 1: 343–74.

White, R. (1994), 'Shaming and Reintegrative Strategies: Individuals, State Power and Social Interests', in C. Alder and J. Wundersitz (eds), *Family Conferencing and Juvenile Justice: The Way Forward or Misplaced Optimism?*, Canberra: Australian Institute of Criminology.

Whitlock, K. (2001), *In a Time of Broken Bones: A Call to Dialogue on Hate Violence and the Limitations of Hate Crimes Legislation*, Philadelphia: The American Friends Service Committee, Community Relations Unit.

Wilcox, A., Hoyle, C., and Young, R. (2005), 'Are Randomised Controlled Trials Really the "Gold Standard" in Restorative Justice Research?', *British Journal of Community Justice*, 3(2): 39–49.

Williams of Mostyn, Lord (1997), *Second Reading Speech*, 16.12.97, HL Deb col.

Williams, M. L., and Robinson, A. L. (2004), 'Problems and Prospects with Policing the Lesbian, Gay and Bisexual Community in Wales', *Policing and Society*, 14(3): 213–32.

Witte, R. (1996), *Racist Violence and the State: A Comparative Analysis of Britain, France and the Netherlands*, London: Longman.

Wolfe, L. and Copeland, L. (1994), 'Violence Against Women as Bias-Motivated Hate Crime: Defining the Issues in the USA', in M. Davies (ed), *Women and Violence*, London: Zed Books.

Wundersitz, J. and Hetzel, S. (1996), 'Family Conferencing for Young Offenders: The South Australian Experience', in J. Hudson, A. Morris,

G. Maxwell, and B. Galaway (eds), *Family Group Conferences: Perspectives on Policy and Practice*, Sydney: Federation Press and Criminal Justice Press.

Zehr, H. (1990), *Changing Lenses: A New Focus for Crime and Justice*, Scottdale: Herald Press.

Zehr, H. and Mika, H. (1998), 'Fundamental Concepts of Restorative Justice', *Contemporary Justice Review*, 1: 47–55.

Index

agreements *see* mediation agreement
alcohol
    hate crime and 109, 121, 127, 250, 251
Allport, Gordon 7–8
Amstutz, Lorraine 170
anger 43, 52–3
    inter-group backlashes 86–7
    restorative disposal 133–4
anti-hate crime movements 2–3
anti-Semitic harassment case study 116–17, 230–2
anti-social behaviour xxvii, 21, 32, 35, 41–3, 59, 112, 150
    both parties 94–5, 105, 109, 120, 247, 253–4
    self-blame 71
    targeted 71
Anti-Social Behaviour Order 150
Anti-Social Behaviour Units 92, 169
anti-vilification laws 5
anxiety 62, 71, 78
    community mediation 98–9
    levels 133–4
    restorative disposal 133–4
    Wilcoxon Signed-ranks test 99
apologies 51, 228–9
    aim of restorative justice 34
    body language and gesture 51, 135
    cajoled 129, 138, 142, 239–40
    closure 51
    community mediation 42, 117–18
    disingenuous 51, 136–7, 157, 191
    emotional relief to victim 228–9
    forced acceptance 139–40, 197
    forgiveness 51
    remorse 35
    restorative disposal 126, 128–9, 135–40, 142, 197, 239–40
Association of Chief Police Officers (ACPO)
    hate crime definition 23–4, 92, 155
    hate incident definition xxvi, 23–4, 92, 155

Association of Panel Members (AOPM) xxvi
asylum seekers 66–7

Bard, Morton 71–2
behaviour
    anti-social *see* anti-social behaviour
    cognitive behavioural therapy 49
behaviour change
    by offender 57, 59, 220
    by victim 81, 85
    code switching 85
Bethlehem Police Family Group Conferencing Project (Pennsylvania) 124–5
bias crime *see* hate crime
blame
    assignment in multi-layered disputes 110
    self-blame 71, 74, 75
    shifting onto Other 60, 190
body language and gestures 213
    apologetic gestures 51, 135
    case study 217–18
    community mediation 42, 135
    contrition 92, 93, 103–4, 119, 135, 208
    defensive 195, 217–18
    eye contact 195, 217
    misunderstanding of 215–16, 243–4
    shaking hands 42, 93, 119, 135, 201
Bowling, Benjamin 2, 3, 4, 19–20, 23, 68–9, 73, 141, 149, 151, 155, 161, 171, 174, 258
Braithwaite, John xxiv, 32, 33, 34–6, 94, 101, 135, 167–9, 183, 187, 199, 201, 208–9, 211, 255
British Crime Survey 76–7
British National Party 87

causation
    prejudice and crime 9–10
cautions
    conditional 40, 126
    police 40, 126

cautions (*cont.*)
  restorative 33, 41, 43, 142
  Thames Valley Restorative Caution 125
censure xxi, 236
Centre for Restorative Justice (Australia) 124
Chakraborti, N 2, 4, 10, 15, 19, 21, 22, 75–6, 144–5, 149, 152, 153, 224, 237
Cheng, Wen 81
citizens advice bureaux 169
code switching 85
  see also behaviour change
cognitive behavioural therapy 49
Cohen, Stan 25
community/communities
  breaking down differences 184
  dominance over difference 63–4, 65, 76, 187–9
  dominant groups 188
  excluding Others 172
  harm causing aspects 171–4, 186–93, 243
    excluding Others 172
    imposition of dominant norms 172–3
  in-groups 188
  macro- 168, 170
  meaning of 166–9
  as metaphysical phenomenon 168–9
  micro- 168, 171
  minority group marginalization 18, 29, 185, 192, 202, 259
  perpetuation of norms 185
  power imbalances 191
  re-conceptualizing 256–7
  re-victimization and 193–204, 234, 243
  restorative goals through 169
  secondary victimization by 186–93
  social condemnation 59, 60, 176, 177, 184, 185, 187, 201, 226
    failure to elicit 60, 185, 210
    inadequate 201
  social distance between stakeholders 191
  sociological conceptualization 167
  state agencies as 166–7
  state-run agencies 167–9
  totalitarian effects 191
  uniting force of 185
  universal norms 230
  see also community stakeholders; community supporters
community of care 171
  offender's 185, 192
    hostility to victim 201, 202–3
    validation of negative views 190–1
  victim's 192
community mediation 42–3
  age-related stereotypes case study 110–13
  aims and objectives 42, 92–3
  anti-Semitic case study 116–17, 230–2
  anxiety 98–9
  apologies 42, 117–18
  body language and gesture 42
  contrition, non-verbal expressions of 103–4
  desistance, assurances of 93, 104–5, 233–4, 235
  dialogue 255–6
  difference, discussion of 102
  direct mediation 97
  direct meetings 42
  disablist violence case study 107–8
  emotional harms 98–100
  failure reasons 121
  fear 98, 99–100
  ground rules 93
  Hate Crime Project (HCP) xxv, 91–122, 174–6
  homophobic case study 107–8, 110–13
  housing officers 171
  identity issues 111, 116–17
  indirect mediation 42, 97
  mediation agreement 42, 93, 105
    multi-agency partnerships 175–6
    no legal enforcement 94
  mediator role 106–8
    post-mediation 106–7
  meetings before mediation 93
  multi-agency partnerships and 174–6
    disablist abuse case study 176–7
    group conferences 175
    mediation agreement 175–6
    schools 176–8
    unresolved cases 180–1
  multi-layered disputes 108–13

INDEX   301

assignment of blame 110
case studies 110–13
escalating incidents 109
neutral labelling 109
neighbours 120
neutral labelling 43, 94, 95, 109, 254–6
participation, willingness 93
practitioner experiences 115–19
  identity issues 116–17
  reparation 117–18, 119
  storytelling significance 116–18
preparation 199–200
  importance 93
  meetings before mediation 93
promises to desist 93, 104–5, 233–4, 235
re-victimization *see* re-victimization
referrals to 43
repairing harm 97–115
  assurance of desistance 93, 104–5, 233–4, 235
  healing emotional harms 98–100
  ineffective state intervention case study 178–80
  non-verbal contrition 103–4
  other support factors 113–14
  practitioner experiences 117–18, 119
  satisfaction 97–8
  talking about harm 101–2, 103
  victims not helped 113–14
restorative nature 93–5
satisfaction with 97, 101
seriousness of crimes/incidents 96
shuttle mediation 42, 97
social condemnation 176, 177
social contexts of crimes 94–5
socio-structural conditions and 121
stakeholder empowerment 97
storytelling 101–2, 108, 116–18
  learning impairment cases 103
types of crime 95–6
understanding of incidents 119–20
undertakings 93
see also multi-agency partnerships
Community Restorative Boards 39–40
  contracts 39–40
  reoffending 40
Community Safety Units 145, 155, 179
community stakeholders 141, 173, 183, 192

state agencies 160, 161–6
community supporters 149–50, 164
  appropriate pro-social 201–2
  exclusion of co-offenders 201
  state agencies as 164, 169–71
community-based policing initiatives 40–1
conditioning theory 49
contrition
  body language or gesture 92, 93, 103–4, 119, 135, 208
control groups
  methodology and 53–4, 76
conviction rates
  hate crimes 27–8
Copeland, David 4, 10
Crawford, Adam 187
Crime Survey for England and Wales 76–7
criminal censure xxi, 236
criminal justice agencies
  secondary victimization by 149
criminalization of hate crime 3–4
  causal relationship 9–10
  censure xxi, 236
  combating bigotry xxi
  declaration of wrongfulness xxi
  enhanced punishment xix, xx, 3, 14, 30, 236
  low-level or domestic disputes 237
  mens rea 8–12
  repairing harm xxii
  retributive approach xx, xxiii, 25–30, 236
  where no prosecution 237
  see also legislation
Cunneen, Chris 191, 192

Daly, Kathy 54–5, 194
denunciation xxi, 209, 210, 237
  see also social condemnation
depression xxi, 51, 62, 72, 74, 77, 78, 79, 90, 103, 109, 158
desistance, assurances of 93, 104–5, 233–4, 235
Devon and Cornwall Police Service xxv
  see also restorative disposal
dialogue 32, 35, 47, 193
  between community members 87
  body language *see* body language and gestures
  communicational barriers 213–15

dialogue (cont.)
  community mediation 255–6
  cross-cultural 203
  derogatory remarks 194
  empathic divide 216–19
  on identity 203
  language barriers 213–15
  paralanguage 215–16
  process 32
  restorative disposal 129, 138–40
  universal norms in 230
  victim–offender mediation 37–8
  see also storytelling
Dick, Sam 74, 85
difference
  community and 184
  dominance over 63–4, 65, 76, 187–9
  emotional connections 208
  empathic divide 216–19
  humanizing 184, 207–35
  offender's understanding of 59
  shame and guilt 209–11
  social harms of 65–7
  storytelling, importance of 219–34
  threat of 64
  to identity norm 188
  see also doing difference
Dignan, James 44
dignity xx, 230
disablist abuse xxviii, 2, 24
  community mediation case study 107–8
  conviction rate 27–8
  HCP 96
  hostility 75
  multi-agency partnership case study 176–7
  vulnerability 75
discriminatory selection model 12, 13
diversity training 144–5
doing difference 18, 63, 188
  offender's community of care 190
  subordination of outsiders 188–9
dominant groups 188
domination
  dominance over difference 63–4, 65, 76, 187–9
  and re-victimization 193–204, 234
  socio-structural 34, 36, 204, 234

economic competition 9
emotional harm xx, 193
  community mediation and 98–100
  empirical findings 76–80
  future victimization and 78
  indicators xxvi
  periods of trauma 77–8
  victims by intervention type 79
  see also individual emotions eg empathy; fear; shame
empathy 49–50, 57, 59
  direct mediation meetings 221
  empathic concern dimension 212
  empathic connection 216–19
  empathic divide 213
  encouraging remorse through 211–13
  fantasy dimension 212
  indirect (shuttle) mediation 221–2
  personal distress dimension 212
  perspective taking dimension 212, 213
  social diversity and distance 212–13
empirical study
  data sources xxv
  emotional harm of hate crime 76–80
  impact on minority communities 84–6
  mixed method approach xxvi–xxvii
  physical harm 81–2
  see also methodology
employment
  inequalities 69, 70
  unemployment 82–3
empowerment
  by storytelling 255
  community mediation 97
  restorative disposal 197
  of victims 47, 57, 58, 97, 197
encounter conception 33
English Defence League 87
enhanced punishments xix, xx, 3, 14, 30, 236
equality xxxi, 36, 163, 164, 192, 230
  legislation 70
ethnic prejudice 7
ethno-violence see hate crime

facilitators
  control of meeting 32, 33
  police as 140–3
  see also practitioners
family group conferences 38–9, 40
  collective responsibility 38

INDEX 303

New Zealand 38–9
   restorative policing 40–1
   state agencies and 39, 165
fear 62, 71
   anger and 43, 52
   community mediation 98, 99–100
   conditioning theory 49
   confrontation of 49
   deconditioning 49
   levels of 52
   likert-type questions 99–100
   of minority groups 248
   repeat victimization 50, 78, 80
   restorative disposal 133–4
   victim xxi
   victim's group xxi
forgiveness 35, 51, 55, 58
freedom of expression 25

Gadd, David 225
Garland, Jon 2, 4, 10, 15, 19, 21, 22, 75–6, 144–6, 149, 152, 153, 155, 156, 174, 224, 237
Gavrielides, T 34, 42, 57–8, 208, 227, 229
gays *see* sexual orientation abuse
gestures *see* body language and gestures
Goodall, Kay 26
Green, Donald, et al 8
grievance
   offender's perception of 27, 189, 223, 249, 251
group selection model 12, 13
guilt 207, 209–11, 216, 219, 234, 235
   adversarial system 11
   denial of 60, 190
   shame-guilt 209, 211, 212, 217, 219

Hall, Nathan 5, 12, 17, 18, 25, 64, 70
Hardwick, Francecca 20
harm 88–9
   anxiety *see* anxiety
   communities *see* community/communities, harm causing effects
   emotional *see* emotional harm
   exacerbation by criminal justice process 45–6
   fear *see* fear
   heightened for hate crime victims 76–8
   impact phase 72
   legalizing harm 67–8
   levels of xix, xx
   low-level ongoing acts 19–21
   physical 81–2
   psychological trauma xx
   recoil phase 72
   reorganizing phase 72
   repairing *see* reparation
   ripple effect 62
      see also community/communities, harm causing effects
   secondary victimization 46
      repairing harms 177–8
      state agencies 171–4
   socio-harm
      empirical results 82–4
      perspective of 70–1
   socio-political experiences 71
   state agencies 171–4
   storytelling as aid to healing 48–9
   see also individual harms eg anger; anxiety
Harris, Nathan 209
hate
   categories xxviii
   deep-seated 9, 227–9, 248–9
   prejudice as hate 7–8
   superficial 9, 223–7
   see also prejudice
hate crime 7–8
   ACPO definition 23–4, 92, 155
   conviction rates 27–8
   enhanced punishment xx, 3, 14, 30, 236
   harm *see* harm
   hostility 28
   labelling 10
   labelling *see* labelling
   legislation *see* legislation
   low-level ongoing acts xxvii–xxviii, 18–21, 23–5, 141, 222–3, 237
      see also hate incidents
   meaning 2–6
   mens rea 8–12
   motivation 16, 28
   nature of 244–52
   net-widening 25, 30, 141
   one-off acts 18, 249–52
   over-reporting 25–6
   over-policing 27
   proving motivation 28
   public policy xix, 3
   seriousness xix

hate crime *(cont.)*
　as social problem 2, 4
　socio-cultural underpinnings 17–18
　typology of 244–52
　victimization *see* victimization/victimization process
Hate Crime Project (HCP) *see* community mediation; multi-agency partnerships
hate incidents 11
　ACPO definition xxvi, 23–4, 92, 155
　escalating violence 20
　hate crime policy and 23–5
　lacking seriousness 28
　low-level ongoing acts xxvii–xxviii, 18–21, 23–5, 141, 222–3, 237
　harms caused 23
　persistent targeted abuse 247–9, 250
　retributive approach 25–30, 236
　within broader conflicts 245–7, 250
hate speech 15
　criminalization xix
　during commission of offence 15–16
hatred motivation model 12, 13
Herman, S 170
homophobia *see* sexual orientation abuse
hostility 14–15, 26, 28, 31, 75, 151, 223
　community of care as source 201, 202–3
　disablist abuse 75
　during commission of offence 4, 26
　legislation 5, 7, 12, 14–15, 75
　mens rea 31
　offender's community of care 201, 202–3
　proof 28, 31
　in restorative meetings 194
　towards presumed or actual identity xv, 5, 6, 11, 14–15, 23, 26–8, 95–6, 152–3, 227, 232
　vulnerability and 75
housing officers and associations
　anti-social behaviour orders 150–1
　community mediation 171
　as community supporters 169
　duty of care 154
　false complaints 83
　hostility towards presumed or actual identity 152–3

racial harassment 151–2
secondary victimization by 83–4, 150–9
support from 70
trivialization of complaints 152–4
warning letters 92, 105
see also multi-agency partnerships
Hoyle, Carolyn, et al 50
Hudson, Barbara 55
human rights abuses
　reparations for state-led 162–3

identity 62
　attacks based on 73–4
　collective 17
　community mediation 111, 116–17
　difference as threat to norm 188
　hostility to presumed or actual xix, 5, 6, 11, 14–15, 23, 26–8, 95–6, 152–3, 227, 232
　individual 224–5
　storytelling and 49, 116
　subjugation of, by victim 26
　transgender 24
identity groups
　harms ripple out to 62
Iganski, Paul xxi–xxii, xxiii, 2, 18, 19, 23, 57, 63, 73, 76–7, 80, 84, 88, 98, 174, 222–3, 224, 236, 246, 249, 251
immigrants 218
　British jobs 215, 228, 248
　pressure to fit in 66–7
　social harms of difference 66–7
　welfare benefits, perceived access to 8, 214–15, 248
incitement to racial hatred 4, 5
inclusivity 46–8
　procedural fairness 47
indirect mediation 37, 42, 45, 97
　empathy and 221–2
　repeat victimization prevention 228
inequalities
　education 69, 70
　housing 70
　income levels 69
　of power 166, 191
　socio-economic conditions 63, 65, 69–71, 257
　socio-structural xxix, 63–71, 121–2, 191, 220, 241, 257
　unemployment 69, 70

INDEX

infantilization 75
information provision
  participation and 46–8
  procedural fairness 47
  restorative disposal 127–8, 197
insecurity 53, 62, 71
inter-group conflict and backlash 86–7
  inclusive dialogue 87
interpreters 213–15, 217
  reasons for refusal of 214–15
Islamic clothing
  animosity to wearing of 67–8
Islamophobia 67–8

Jacobs, James 88
Johnstone, G 36
Joint Committee Against Racialism (JCAR) 4

Kay, Judith 49
Kennedy, Paul 167
Kitchener experiment 37
Kurki, Leena 93–4

labelling 10
  adversarial processes 252
  community mediation participants 43, 94–5, 254–6
  neutral labelling 43, 94, 95, 109, 254–6
  opposing roles 252, 253–4
  restorative disposal 135
  stigmatization of offenders 26–7, 28, 30, 32
  victim–offender mediation participants 94–5
language barriers 243–4
  dialogue and 213–15
  interpreters 213–15
  paralanguage 215–16
Lash, Scott 167
Lawrence, Stephen 4, 68, 154
legislation
  hostility 14–15
  ill will or malice 13
  racial or religious aggravation 13–14
  sentence enhancement xix, xx, 3, 14, 30, 236
  UK 13–14
  US 3, 12–13
Levin, Jack 251

McCold, Paul 50, 168, 170
McDevitt, Jack 251
MacPherson, Sir William 68
Macpherson Report 4, 68, 145, 149, 155
Maori Land Courts (New Zealand) 163
material reparation 34, 48
  see also reparation
Maxwell, Gabrielle 202, 211
mediation
  community *see* community mediation
  control groups 53–4, 76
  direct 97, 221
  ground rules 93, 195, 200–1
  indirect 37, 42, 45, 97, 221–2
  repeat victimization prevention 228
  labelling of participants *see* labelling
  paralanguage 243–4
  shuttle 37, 42, 45, 97, 221–2
  training *see* training of practitioners
  victim–offender *see* victim–offender mediation
mediation agreement
  community mediation 42, 93, 94, 105
  moral learning in 59, 230, 235
  multi-agency partnerships 175–6
  no legal enforcement 94
  undertakings 93
  victim–offender mediation 38
MENCAP 113
mens rea
  hostility 31
  mixed motivations 10–11
  prejudice as 8–12
Merry, Peter 44
Messner, Steven 81
methodology xxv–xviii
  closed questions xxvi
  connection of process variables xxvi
  control groups 53–4, 76
  interviews xxvi, 54
    practitioners 277–8
    schedules 261–76
    victims 261–76
  likert-type responses xxvi, 99–100
  limitations relating to 53–6
  mixed method approach xxvi–xxvii
  questionnaires 54

methodology *(cont.)*
  restorative disposal study 127–8
  Wilcoxon Signed-ranks test 99
Metropolitan Gay Policing Group 113
Metropolitan Police Services
  institutional racism 68–9, 149
minority communities
  inter-group backlashes 86–7
  negative impacts on 84–6
  vulnerability 84
minority groups
  escalation of violence 86–7
  hate crime legislation xxii
    encouraging victimization xxiii
    as support xxiii
  history of victimization 2
marginalization 18, 29, 185, 192, 202, 259
offender's fear of 248
social wellbeing xxii
socio-cultural structures 18, 29, 192, 259
socio-economic disadvantage 21
subjugated by hegemonic norms 204
welfare, perceived access to 8, 89, 189, 214–15, 248
  see also Others
mission offenders 10
mixed motivations 10–11
moral learning 59, 229–32, 235
  universal norms 230
Morris, Alison 211
multi-agency partnerships 242
  agency employees 163–5
  community of care 171, 173
  community mediation and 174–6
    disablist abuse case study 176–7
    group conferences 175
    mediation agreements 175–6
    schools 176–8
    social condemnation 176, 177
    unresolved cases 180–1
  community stakeholders 161–6
  community supporters 164, 169–71, 242
  community tool 171
  conflicts of interest 165
  financial provision 161–2
  impartiality 165, 177–8
  inclusivity principle 160
  listening project 170
  participants 160
  practitioner impartiality 165, 177–8
  Race-Hate Crimes Forum (London) 174
  secondary victimization
    reduction through 159–81
    repairing harms 177–8
  state agencies
    as community 166–7
    as community stakeholders 161–6
    as harmers 171–4
  storytelling 164, 165
  victims denied voice 174
multi-layered disputes
  assignment of blame 110
  case studies 110–13
  community mediation 108–13
  escalating incidents 109
  homophobic intimidation case study 110–13
  neutral labelling 109

National Front 3
neighbour disputes 11, 15, 20–2, 28, 73, 81, 83, 96, 107–14, 120–1, 152–8, 175–6, 179, 181, 190, 194, 217–19, 223–4, 245–7, 250, 253
  hate incidents during 245–7, 250
neighbourhood policing teams 169
net-widening 25, 30, 141
New Zealand
  family group conferences 38–9
  Maori Land Courts 163
noise disputes xxvii, 11, 96, 109, 121, 218, 222, 224, 246, 250

O'Connell, Terry 40–1
offenders
  acceptance of responsibility 220, 226
  admission 35
  alcohol and 109, 121, 127, 250, 251
  antagonistic effects of legislation 26–7
  apologies *see* apologies
  attitude change 36
  behavioural change 57, 59, 220
  blaming victim 190
  community of care
    hostile to victim 201, 202–3
    social condemnation 201
  consequences of actions 49–50
  contrition 136, 137, 211

INDEX

body language 92, 93, 103–4, 119, 135, 208
denial of prejudice/hate 194–5, 223–7
denial of seriousness of offence 189–90
desistance 93, 104–5, 233–4, 235
domination of proceedings 193–204, 234
empathy 49–50, 59
  remorse through 35, 211–13
explanation of motive 35
fear of minority groups 248
grievance
  perceived 27, 189, 223, 249, 251
  sense of 189–90
justification, sense of 60, 190
moral learning 59, 229–32, 235
neutralization techniques 189–90
over-criminalization 26–7
perceived grievance 27, 189, 223, 249, 251
perceived motivation and actual intention 25–6
post sentence meetings 41
promises made by 59
  to desist 93, 104–5, 233–4, 235
reintegrative shaming 209–10, 211
remorse 35, 51, 117, 136, 207–10, 216, 234
  recidivism reductions 211
  through empathy 35, 211–13
reoffending rates 48
reparation *see* **reparation**
repeat offending 221
responsibility for actions 37, 220, 226
returning to community 184
self 216
shame 35, 36, 209
see also **guilty**
social condemnation 176, 177, 184, 185, 187, 201, 226
social distance between victim and 59
stigma of labelling 26–7, 28, 30, 32
storytelling by 59
  empowerment 255
thrill seekers 251
understanding of hurt caused 35
victim–offender mediation 94
as victims 26–7

Others/Otherness
  blame shifting onto 60, 190
  community harmers excluding 172
  culture of prejudice 64
  deep-seated prejudice against 9, 227–9, 248–9
  fear of 248
  history of victimization 2
  Islamophobia 67–8
  marginalization *see* **minority groups, marginalization**
  normalization of 221
  not like us 188
  perceived threat from 227
  persistent targeted abuse xxviii, 247–9, 250
  process of Othering 63
  social mobility 64
  society pandering to needs of 27
  state discrimination against 189
  stigmatization of group 64
  as threat to dominant group 188–9
  welfare, perceived preferential access 8, 89, 189, 214–15, 248
  see also **minority groups**
Oxford Youth Offending Service xxv

paralanguage 215–16
participation
  animosities 220
  coercion 131–2
  indirect 45
  information provision 46–8, 127–8, 197
  neutral labelling of participants 94
  reluctance
    anger or fear 43
    repeat victimization 43
  statistics 44
  victim, importance of 43–5
  willingness 93
Pavlich, George 191, 192
Perry, Barbara
  doing difference 18, 63–71
  dominance over difference 187–9
  see also **doing difference**
physical harm
  empirical results 81–2
  hospitalization rates 81
  stress symptoms 82
Pilkington, Fiona 20–1, 23
Pilkington Case 180

308 INDEX

police
  cautions 40, 41
  community-based policing initiatives 40–1
  culture of prejudice 154–5
  institutional racism 68–9, 149
  secondary victimization by 149, 154–6, 159
  street-level RJ 41, 123, 126, 142
  victim liaison officers 41
  Wagga model of conferencing 40–1
  youth restorative disposal 41
  see also multi-agency partnerships; restorative disposal
Pollard, Charles 41
populist punitiveness xxiii
post-traumatic stress 72
Potter, Kimberly 88
practitioners xxvi
  empathic connection 216–17
  experiences of 115–19
    HCP 116–19
  gauging prejudice levels 228
  methodology
    interview schedule 277–8
    interviews xxvi
  storytelling significance 116–18
  training 93, 195, 200–1, 258–60
    cross-cultural dialogue 203–4
    diversity training 144–5
    multi-cultural training 259–60
    restorative disposal 143–6
  see also community mediation, practitioner experiences
prejudice
  culture nurtured within community 59
  deep-seated 9, 227–9, 248–9
  denial of 194–5, 223–7
  ethnic 7
  explored in safe environment 58
  gauging levels at preparatory meetings 228
  as hate 7–8
  learned 222
  low-level ongoing acts xxvii–xxviii, 18–21, 23–5, 141, 222–3, 237
  mens rea 8–12
  mission offenders 10
  moral learning 59, 229–32, 235
  storytelling shows impact 208
  superficial 9, 223–7

  underlying causes, punishment and xxii
  see also hate
prejudice motivated violence *see* hate crime
preparation
  acceptance of responsibility 199
  avoiding re-victimization by 198–200
  community mediation 199–200
    importance of 93
    meetings before mediation 93
  gauging prejudice levels 228
  hate-motivation identification 16
  importance of 93, 257–8
  mini-conferences 198
  offender's willingness to engage 199–200
  restorative disposal 240
procedural fairness
  inclusivity 47
  information provision 47
  restorative disposal 130–2
  restorative justice 46–8
promises made by offender 58–9
  to desist 93, 104–5, 233–4, 235
property
  reparation 34, 48
  see also reparation
proportionality
  retributive principle of xx
public order offences 19
public policy 3
punishment
  enhancement xix, xx, 3, 14, 30, 236
  populist punitiveness xxiii

Race Relations Acts 5
race riots 87
Race-Hate Crimes Forum (London) 174
racial abuse xx, xxviii, 2, 24
  criminal justice system 68–9
  harassment case study 157–8
  Hate Crime Project (HCP) 95
  institutional racism 68–71, 149
  legislation in UK 3, 4
  Metropolitan Police Services 68–9, 149
  proving 28
  remands 68–9
  repetitive nature 19–20
  restorative disposal case study 139–40

victim's emotional harm 76–7
racial animus model 12, 13
racial hatred, incitement to 4, 5
racism *see* racial abuse
Raye, Barbara 200, 259
re-victimization 193–204, 204
  avoidance 193–204
    ground rules 195, 200–1
    preparation 195, 198–200
  communities and 193–204, 234, 243
  community harming effects 243
  perceptions of disadvantage 196–8
  practitioner view of 205
referral orders 39–40, 231
reintegrative shaming 209–10, 211
Reintegrative Shaming Experiments 124, 125
religious beliefs abuse xxviii, 2, 24
  anti-Semitic community mediation case 116–17
  anti-Semitic harassment case study 230–2
  sexual orientation 24
  UK legislation 5
religious garments, bans on 67–8
remorse 35, 51, 117, 136, 207–10, 216, 234
  recidivism reductions 211
  through empathy 211–13
reoffending 33, 40, 48, 125, 141
reparation 32, 33, 57
  aim
    restorative justice 34
    victim–offender mediation 37
  apologies *see* apologies
  community mediation 97–115
    assurance of desistance 93, 104–5, 233–4, 235
    healing emotional harms 98–100
    ineffective state intervention case study 178–80
    non-verbal contrition 103–4
    other support factors 113–14
    practitioner experiences 117–18, 119
    satisfaction 97–8
    talking about harm 101–2, 103
    victims not helped 113–14
  empirical findings 238–41
  financial compensation 34
  incomplete 55

limitations of RJ 241–2
material 34, 48
mediation *see* mediation
moral learning 59, 229–32, 235
promises made by offenders 58–9, 93, 104–5, 233–4, 235
property 34, 48
punishment and xxii
restorative disposal 129–46, 130–2, 239–40
  anger levels 133, 134
  anxiety levels 133, 134
  emotional wellbeing 132–3
  fear levels 133–4
  procedural fairness 130–2
  satisfaction levels 129–30, 131
  support of facilitators 132–3
  support of others 134
satisfaction with RJ and 48
secondary victimization 177–8
  ineffective state intervention case study 178–80
structural harm 241–2
victim support xxiii, 169, 170
reparation agreement 38
  moral learning in 230, 235
resentment 51
  between identity groups 8, 136
  welfare, perceived bias 89
respect xx, 36, 47, 59, 124, 210, 230, 232, 240, 254
  denial of xx, 62, 68, 71, 84
  mutual 102, 135
restorative cautions 40, 41
restorative disposal 123–47, 157, 254–5
  apologies 126, 128, 135
    cajoled 129, 138, 142, 239–40
    disingenuous 136–7, 157
    forced acceptance 139–40, 197
  Devon and Cornwall Police Service xxv, 126–9
  dialogue 129, 138–40
  direct mediation not offered 221
  diversity training 144–5
  dominant cultural norms 141–2
  empowerment of victim 197
  information provision 127–8
    inadequate 197
  labelling of victim and offender 135
  low-level offences 141
  methodology 127–8

310 INDEX

restorative disposal (cont.)
  participation, pressurized 131–2, 142, 157, 162
  police control of 240
  police culture and 144–5
  police as facilitators 140–3
  policing 124–9
  preparation 129, 137, 240
  preparations 157
  procedural fairness 130–2
  racial abuse case study 139–40
  re-victimization see re-victimization
  repairing harm 129–46, 239–40
    anger levels 133, 134
    anxiety levels 133, 134
    emotional wellbeing 132–3
    fear levels 133–4
    procedural fairness 130–2
    satisfaction levels 129–30, 131
    support of facilitators 132–3
    support of others 134
  restorative nature 127–9
  satisfaction levels 129–30, 131
  secondary victimization 143
  street-level RJ 41, 123, 126, 142
  training of practitioners 143–6
  types of crime 126–7
  victim–offender mediation meetings 128
  young offenders 123
restorative justice
  agreement see mediation agreement
  aims 34–6 see also reparation
  apologies see apologies
  bringing stakeholders together 34
  capabilities and limitations of 252–6
  challenges and opportunities 56–60
  communities of care 192
  community in 167–9
  community mediation see community mediation
  community restorative boards see Community Restorative Boards
  community stakeholders 141, 160, 161–6, 173, 183, 192
  community supporters 149–50, 164, 169–71, 201–2
  community-based policing initiatives 40–1
  conceptual and practical difficulties 30
  conceptualizing for hate crime 32–61
  cultural differences 57
  dialogue see dialogue
  domestic abuse xxiv, 155, 190, 237
  domination of minority group 34, 35, 192, 193–204, 234
  empathy 49–50, 57, 59
    empathic divide 216–19
  empowerment 36, 255
    of victim 47, 57, 58, 97, 197, 255
  encounter conception 33, 34
  EU Directive 36
  failure to recognize individual and social needs 191
  family group conferences see family group conferences
  financial provision 161–2
  future of 258–60
  ground rules 93, 195, 200–1, 205
    practitioner training 203–4
  hate-motivation identification 16
  ideals and practice 54–6
  inclusiveness 32
  inequality 57
  information provision 46–7
  legislation for use 162
  meaning of 33–45
  mediation see victim–offender mediation
  methodology
    issues 53–6
    limitations of methodology 53–6
  participants 46–8
    animosities 220
    preparation 195, 198–200
    victim 43–5
  platform for storytelling 48–9
  police-led see restorative disposal; restorative policing
  power imbalances 191
  preparation 195, 198–200, 205
    importance of 257–8
  procedural fairness 46–8
  re-victimization
    perceptions of disadvantage 196–8
    see also re-victimization
  rebuilding relationship goal 93
  reforming effects 243–4
  reparation of harm 32, 33
  restorative process 36–7

INDEX

satisfaction levels 46–8
sexual offences xxiv
shame-guilt emotion 209, 211, 217, 219
social differences 59
social inequalities 57
state involvement 162–3
storytelling *see* dialogue; storytelling
street-level 41, 123, 126, 142
theoretical pitfalls 59–60
theoretical promises 58–9
training *see* training of practitioners
transformative conception 33, 34
UN Resolution 36
values *see* equality; respect
vulnerability of victims 73, 74–6, 190
Wagga model of conferencing 40–1
Youth Offender Panels 39–40
Restorative Justice Action Plan for the Criminal Justice System (Ministry of Justice 2012) 45
restorative policing 157
Bethlehem Police Family Group Conferencing Project (Pennsylvania) 124–5
Reintegrative Shaming Experiments 124, 125
Thames Valley Restorative Caution 125
see also restorative disposal
restorative practitioners *see* facilitators; practitioners; training of practitioners
retribution
criminalization of hate crime 25–30, 236
ideology xxiii
proportionality xx
retributive approach 25–30, 236
rioting 87
Roberts, Ann 200
Roche, Declan 165
Roudometof, Victor 167
Rowe, Michael 145–6

Sangrey, Dawn 72
schools
as community supporters 169
multi-agency partnerships 176–8
secondary victimization 46, 148–50
by community 186–93
by offender's community of care 185
by state agencies 106
hate crimes as domestic disputes 155
housing officers and associations 83–4, 150–9
multi-agency partnerships
repairing harms 177–8
see also multi-agency partnerships
police 154–6, 159
racial harassment case study 157–8
reparation, ineffective state intervention case study 178–80
restorative disposal 143
state agencies 241, 241–2, 242, 259
as community harmers 171–4
taking responsibility for harm 173
self xxiii
negation of 65, 66–7
offender's 209
renewed sense of 216
victims 62, 71, 74, 216
see also identity
self-blame 71, 74, 75
sexual orientation abuse xxviii, 2, 4
alteration of behaviour 85
community mediation case study 107–8
emotional harms 78
Hate Crime Project (HCP) 95
heterosexual norms and 65–6
homophobia 74, 249, 251
impact on minority community 85
UK legislation 5, 65–6
shame 35, 36
reintegrative shaming 209–10, 211
role of 209–11
stigmatic shaming 209–10
uncontrolled levels 210
see also social condemnation
shame-guilt emotion 209, 211, 212, 217, 219
Shapland, Joanna, et al 50
Shenk, Alyssa xxiv
Sherman, Lawrence, et al 49
shuttle mediation 37, 42, 45, 97, 221–2
see also indirect mediation
skinheads 3

social benefits *see* welfare benefits
social care units
  as community supporters 169
social condemnation 35, 59, 176, 177, 184, 185, 209, 210–11, 226
  community and 187
  community mediation 176, 177
  failure to elicit 60, 185, 210
  inadequate 201
  see also denunciation
social harms
  empirical results 82–4
socio-cultural factors 17–18
  collective identity 17
  limitations of RJ to repair 241–2
  marginalization 18, 29, 192, 259
socio-economic inequality 69–71
socio-structural domination 204, 234
South Australia Juvenile Justice Research project 55
Southwark Mediation Centre xxv, 91, 92, 165
  see also community mediation; Hate Crime Project (HCP)
stakeholders
  bringing together 34
  domination by 34, 36, 193–204, 234
  see also community stakeholders
state agencies 70
  as community harmers 171–4
  as community supporters 164, 169–71
  family group conferences 39, 165
  institutional culture 258–9
  secondary victimization 106, 241, 241–2, 259
state welfare *see* welfare benefits
state-run agencies
  as community 166–7
  see also housing officers and associations; police
stereotypes/stereotyping 9, 64
  dismantled 208
  fallacious 222
  negative 7
  preconceived ideas 220
  spurious fall away 221
storytelling 48–9, 58
  by offender 50, 59
  cognitive behavioural therapy 49
  community mediation 101–2, 103, 108, 116–18

  learning impairment cases 103
  practitioners' views 116–18
  empowerment by 255
  humanizing difference by 219–34
  identity and 49, 116
  impact of prejudice 208
  see also dialogue
Strang, Heather 44
stranger danger 18, 22

talking about harm *see* storytelling
targeted victimization
  legislative protection against xxii
targeted violence xix
  see also hate crime
terrorism
  Islamophobia since 9/11 67–8
Thames Valley Police Service
  restorative policing 41
Thames Valley Restorative Caution 125
training of practitioners 93, 195, 200–1, 258–60
  cross-cultural dialogue 203–4
  diversity training 144–5
  multi-cultural training 259–60
  restorative disposal 143–6
transgender identity 24
transphobic crime xxviii

unemployment
  inequalities 69, 70
  social harm 82–3
universal norms
  equality, dignity, and respect 230

Van Ness, D 36
Van Stokkom, Bas 209, 211
victim liaison officers 41
victim support xxiii, 169, 170
  as community supporters 169, 170
victim–offender mediation xxiv, 37–8
  aims 37
  classification of parties 94
  control groups 54
  dialogue 37–8
  indirect meetings 37, 45
  Kitchener experiment 37
  mediation agreement 38
  mediators 37
  offenders 94
  reparation agreement 38
  shuttle mediation 37, 45

INDEX

victims 94
victim–offender relationships 21–3
  customer-service transactions 21, 22, 127, 223, 233, 249, 250
  known to each other 21–3
  neighbours 22
  strangers 18, 22
victimization/victimization process 17–18, 63
  accumulation of social harms 20
  articulation of experiences 48–9
  commonalities in 72, 73–7
  deserving of 190
  direct impacts 71–89
  entire social group 62
  expectation of 36
  fears of repeated 50
  future, perception of 78
  historic processes xvii
  impact phase 72
  lack of role 29
  low-level ongoing acts xxvii–xxviii, 18–21, 23–5, 141, 222–3, 237
  minority communities 84–6
  no sense of justice 29
  normalization of acts 20
  re-victimization *see* re-victimization
  recoil phase 72
  reorganizational phase 72
  repeated attacks 73
    fear of 78, 80
  secondary *see* secondary victimization
  short- and long-term impacts 71–2
  socio-cultural marginalization 18, 29, 185, 259
  socio-structural processes 242
  studies 2
  vulnerability 73
  where no prosecution 237
victims
  anger 43, 52–3, 133–4
    backlash 86–7
  anxiety 62, 71, 78
    community mediation 98–9
    restorative disposal 133–4
  apologies to *see* apologies
  blamed by offenders 60, 190
  change in behaviours 81, 85
  deconditioning 49
  depression 72
  deserving of victimization 190

dialogic process, risks 185
emotional trauma *see* emotional harm; harm
employment difficulties 69, 70, 82–3
empowerment 47, 57, 58, 97, 197
  by storytelling 255
fear 52, 71
  community mediation 98, 99–100
  confrontation of fears 49
  restorative disposal 133–4
financial costs 83
hate crimes and other crimes 88–9
housing problems 83
identity *see* identity
infantilization 75
insecurity 53, 71
marginalization 18, 29, 185, 192, 202, 259
methodology, interview schedule 261–76
offenders as 26–7
participation in RJ 43–5
  coercion 131–2
  preparation and 44
  reluctance 43–4
  statistics 44
physical harm 81–2
post-traumatic stress 72
pressure to fit in 66–7, 74
self 62, 71, 74, 216
self-blame 71, 74, 75
social condemnation *see* social condemnation
social distance between offender and 59
social harms 82–4
storytelling *see* storytelling
subjugation of identity 26
victim–offender mediation 94
voicing experience of crime 57
vulnerability 73, 74–6, 190
vulnerability 73, 74–6
  disablist abuse 75
  dominance over difference 76
  hostility and 75
  minority communities 84
  victim 73, 74–6, 190

Wachtel, Ted 50
Wagga model of conferencing 40–1
Walklate, Sandra 254

welfare benefits
  perceived preferential access 8, 89, 189, 214–15, 248
Wilcoxon Signed-ranks test 99
xenophobia xx

Yantzi, Mark 37
Youth Offender Panels 39–40

Youth Offending Teams 39
youth restorative disposal 41

Zehr, Howard xxiv, 32, 33, 34, 39, 46, 48, 49, 50, 71, 97, 106, 130, 160, 161, 166, 187